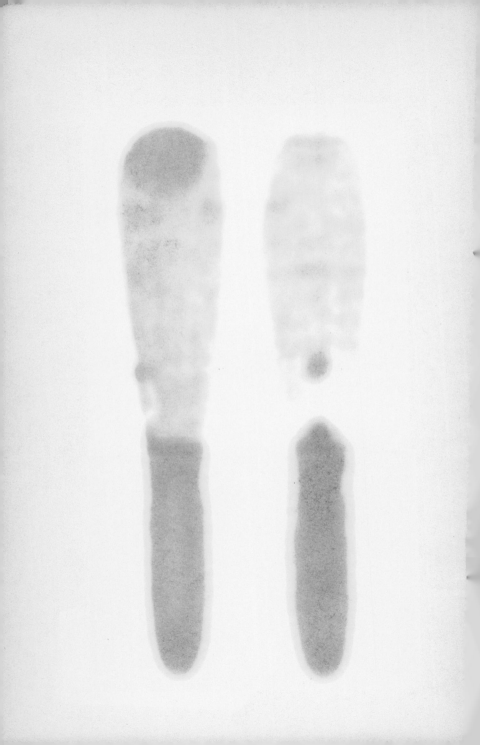

THEORETICAL ECONOMIC SYSTEMS

A COMPARATIVE ANALYSIS

WALTER S. BUCKINGHAM, JR.
PROFESSOR OF ECONOMICS
GEORGIA INSTITUTE OF TECHNOLOGY

THE RONALD PRESS COMPANY • NEW YORK

Those who give themselves to ready and rapid practice before they have learned the theory resemble sailors who go to sea in a vessel without a rudder.

——Leonardo Da Vinci

Preface

This book aspires to establish more of a balance between theory and description in the study of comparative economic systems. It presents, compares, and evaluates the leading theories advanced to explain the operation of the major types of economic systems, and offers tentative conclusions on the direction in which modern economies seem to be headed.

The book has a dual purpose. First, it is designed as a text for college and university courses on the assumption that there is an increasing need for an analysis of the theories underlying the operation and function of contemporary national economic systems. Second, the book attempts to provide the economist with a summary of the various concepts of economic systems which are nowhere compiled or evaluated in a single volume—or even easily discoverable from a search of the literature. It is hoped that the analysis and evaluation within these pages will prove useful to the large number of economists who devote their minds and energies to specific areas of economic theory and practice, and who are not primarily concerned with the over-all theories of economic systems.

The present volume attempts to isolate and analyze the pure theoretical types of economic systems. This is felt to be a reasonable and useful objective since it is on a foundation of theory that modern industrial economic systems are built. Purposely the book does not attempt to describe the economic institutions or experience of the United States, the United Kingdom, the Soviet Union, or other nations. Descriptive information, as such, is not stressed, although frequently reference is made to the facts to illustrate, to verify, or to refute theoretical conclusions. The emphasis is contemporary not historical.

The author has tried to be as objective in the compilation and analysis of economic ideas as any economist dares to be. Objectivity, of course, does not mean the complete avoidance of critical evaluations. It means only that personal biases be frankly recognized and that facts which do not conform to the writer's analysis be given reasonable respect. Thus, in drawing conclusions, the author's opinions no doubt will become obvious. No conscious attempt was made to disguise these opinions, and hence no apology can be offered for their occasional appearance.

Many people made invaluable contributions in the preparation of this book. Professor Arthur Schweitzer of Indiana University, probably unknowingly, inspired it; the University Center in Georgia helped underwrite the original research; and The Georgia Tech Foundation supported what must have seemed an almost endless typing operation. But Marie, my wife, and my three children made the greatest contribution. As the occasion demanded, they alternated between the roles of willing co-workers and widow and orphans. My most profound appreciation and deepest gratitude are extended to all of these who gave so willingly of time, advice, and resources.

Walter S. Buckingham, Jr.

Atlanta
    January, 1958

Contents

Part IV

TOWARD ONE ECONOMIC SYSTEM

Part I
INTRODUCTION

Methodology for
Studying Economic Systems

Study without thought is vain; thought without study is
perilous.——Confucius

The history of science demonstrates beyond a doubt that
the really significant advances come not from empiricism
but from new theories.——James B. Conant

FUNCTIONS OF AN ECONOMIC SYSTEM

Economic problems exist because people's material needs
and wants exceed their capacity to satisfy them. These
problems are related to the quantity and character of production and employment, to the allocation of productive
resources among alternative uses, to the distribution of income to the members of society, and to the causes of economic change and development. Every society faces these
problems. It must, therefore, have a system for determining its objectives and controlling its economic processes in
order to attain them.

GOALS OF ECONOMIC ACTIVITY. The principal goals of any
modern economic system must include, first, the fullest reasonable employment of all of its resources. Depressions
must be abolished. Second, the greatest practical degree of
stability in the employment of these resources must be maintained. Old-fashioned business cycles are out. Third, the

highest satisfaction of consumers' desires must be achieved. The pattern of resources and product allocation must be such as to satisfy people's needs in the order of their urgency. Fourth, production must be completely efficient. This means that physical output divided by costs in human effort, physical resources, and lost opportunities should be as high as possible. And the fifth goal is maximum progressiveness. Productivity must increase as rapidly as it can.

The first goal has only recently become widely accepted as both an economic and a political necessity. Since the Great Depression, there has been a growing realization that there is no automatic regulator that guarantees full employment. The enormous costs of unemployment of all resources—but particularly labor—have been well-documented. People are not like machines or ore deposits. Human resources normally depreciate with time rather than use; and, because of the decline of knowledge, skills, and morals, they wear out at an accelerated rate when they are unemployed. The main economic cost of unemployment is in production that is permanently lost. Yet the social costs of unemployment far exceed even the economic costs, since unemployment also contributes in large measure to crime, disease, family disintegration, race and religious prejudice, suicide, and war.

The second goal, stability, is also of recent acceptance. In the highly specialized, high-speed, and interdependent economy of today the costs of fluctuations are high. The industrialist must maintain expensive inventories and hedge against price changes, if possible, or else risk loss or bankruptcy. The consumer-saver risks inflation, which erodes away the real value of his wealth and income, or deflation, which cuts off his livelihood. The worker who lives from day to day usually suffers first and most acutely when his source of income is cut off by unemployment. It is now a clearly recognized responsibility of businessmen and the government, since they are the basic economic decision-makers in the country, to insure as high and stable a level of production and employment as possible.

In general there is no more reason to expect a recurrence of the wide cyclical fluctuations of the nineteenth and early twentieth centuries, or of the depression conditions of the 1930's, than there is reason to expect another epidemic of smallpox. For severe business cycles as for some diseases, the causes are well known, and the remedies are effective if they are properly applied. But the modern industrialized economic system has a tendency toward an ever greater oscillation. Large enterprises, high fixed costs, and the necessity for continuous operation of industry magnify the adverse consequences of shutdowns. Furthermore, prosperity itself is a potential threat to continued stability. The abundance of production which increases living standards also frees people from spending all their incomes unless they so desire. Whenever basic necessities can be secured by most people with only a part of their incomes, full employment and stability become precarious because prosperity is then sustained by that portion of total spending which is dependent on confidence rather than physical needs. A prosperous economy is always potentially unstable in the sense that small changes in expectations can have magnified effects. A wealthy economy like that of the United States must continue to be reasonably equalitarian because its prosperity depends on mass purchasing power.

The third goal is the traditional goal of classical economic theory, aggregate consumers' satisfaction. The successful economic system was thought to be the one which brought the greatest good to the greatest number of people through an optimum allocation of scarce resources among competing uses. This is still a major objective of any economic system and in its broadest sense is the only goal. But maximum economic welfare—called *utility* by economists—has been found to be much more complex and difficult to attain than was once thought. It has been necessary to add the other goals mentioned here to achieve maximum welfare in its fullest sense.

The fourth goal is a corollary of the third. If the most efficient use is not made of the available economic resources, then the resulting losses are ultimately borne by consumers, the people whose welfare the economic system seeks to maximize. All wasted human efforts, exhausted physical resources, and lost opportunities must be charged against the inefficient economic system.

The fifth goal, progressiveness, is a recognition of the dynamic element in modern economic systems. Classical economists looked on the economic system as a static mechanism in perfect equilibrium. But regardless of the virtues of this view as a methodology, it overlooked an essential characteristic which may even dominate the economic history of the second half of the twentieth century. Technological improvement and its consequent increased productivity are the order of the day.

Of course, these five goals cannot all be attained simultaneously. For example, maximizing short-run aggregate living standards requires a more or less equal distribution of income if it is assumed (and it cannot be proved otherwise) that different people have the same basic needs and the same capacities for enjoyment. But equal income distribution, and hence maximum human satisfaction, is partially inconsistent with progressiveness because some inequalities of income are necessary to provide the incentive to increase productivity and hence long-run living standards. Stability is partly inconsistent with both efficiency and progressiveness. Consequently, some optimum combination of these five goals, particularly some compromise between short- and long-run living standards, must be sought.

MEANS OF ATTAINMENT. Different types of economic systems exist in the world for attaining these five major objectives. An economic system is essentially a group of interdependent controls over all the resources of production. To be effective the system must operate consistently to encourage, direct, restrain, or prohibit human activity through rewards and penalties so that the processes will achieve the goals with the least waste of effort or materials. The control function may be exercised through free-market competition, labor and employer groups, tradition and custom, public opinion, or government influence, persuasion, or decree.

There are three main reasons why there can be essentially different economic systems in the world even if all people are assumed to be educated and rational. First, the social goals, as distinguished from the five economic goals set forth above, may diverge in different societies. In a belligerent dictatorship, military power could be a major objective. In an ecclesiastical society, either spiritual attainment or church dominion may supersede all other goals. In a democratic, materialistic nation, such as the classical economists assumed, the supreme social goal is the greatest material good to the greatest number of people. In any system, economists can inform policymakers of the most efficient way to attain their goals and of the consequences of their political actions without passing judgment on the social desirability of the goals themselves. Economists can demonstrate, for example, whether a certain course of action will accomplish its goals effectively, will be self-defeating, or will cost more than the results warrant.

In the second place, different kinds of economic systems may exist because there are different ways of doing the same thing. Steel production can be increased by subsidy, tax concessions, government regulation, nationalization, defense stockpiling, or changes in tariff policy. Whiskey consumption can be reduced by rationing, tax increases, price-fixing, or propaganda. National income can be redistributed by planning and direct physical controls or by the market system and indirect fiscal and monetary controls. The prevailing attitudes of the people are the major limiting factors determining which methods are most effective. Rationing and direct controls may work in war but not in peace. Nationalization may work well in Great Britain but not in America. Democracy itself works better where people are educated and mature.

In the third place, the people of different cultures or environments may place different priorities on the economic goals themselves. An economy with a large laboring class would probably desire full employment above efficiency and progressiveness, whereas an economy with a prosperous middle class of small business and professional men might place efficiency and progressiveness above full employment. If consumers should ever organize and become articulate, consumers' welfare might attain the status in reality that it has long had in theory.

Both businessmen and workers could be equally devoted to the concept of individual freedom, but freedom could have a different meaning to most of the people in each group. Abraham Lincoln is supposed to have said that freedom seldom means the same thing to a wolf that it means to a lamb. If you build a shelter to protect the lambs, then wolves will howl that the lambs have lost their freedom. Social services and union protection undoubtedly do restrict some kinds of freedom (such as the "right to work" without joining a union or a group pension plan), but they may safeguard or even create other kinds of freedom (such as freedom from arbitrary dismissal). Unemployment, insecurity, and poverty can destroy the freedom to choose or change occupations and locations or to secure needed education more effectively than can laws and regulations. The freedom to change jobs, for example, requires that there be other jobs to change to. The freedom to make a living, even to pursue happiness itself, requires full employment and some degree of individual job security in a modern, highly industrialized economy.

To the worker, then, freedom often means the opportunity to change jobs easily, to advance in pay or grade rapidly, or to know that he will not have to take certain risks such as unemployment, sickness, or industrial accidents. Confiscation of inheritance will not alarm workers who have received no legacy and who see no hope of accumulating an estate. The worker may care no more for freedom from government interference with business than the businessman cares for the worker's freedom from the capriciousness of foremen. Where this attitude predominates, planning schemes and even direct controls may be readily accepted, and tax laws may discriminate against "unearned" income like rents and dividends.

On the other hand, the businessman may think of freedom as permission to invest money in an enterprise without having to share the profits with the government. Or freedom may mean the ability to hire workers individually without having to bargain with representatives of the group. Businessmen with secure positions and savings may care little about layoffs and the effects of insecurity on workers. Where such attitudes prevail, laws may be passed restricting union activity and granting favorable tax benefits to corporations and stockholders even though such laws may cause wages to be low and working conditions bad.

Thus, while the problems of all modern economies are similar and cannot be escaped, the exact type of economic system employed to cope with these problems may vary from place to place and from time to time. Not only is the American economic system different from the British but the American economic system of today is different from the American economic system of 1860, 1910, or 1932.

A study which deals with contemporary economic systems must start with the assumption that there can be distinctly different kinds of economic systems in industrialized countries, not just different degrees of the same system. This assumption may seem so obvious that an explicit statement of it is unnecessary. However, it should be remembered that the classical tradition in economics, which began with Adam Smith in the late eighteenth century and prevails in varying degrees of dilution today, admitted of no such thing. Of course, the fact of the evolution from the feudalism of the Middle Ages through the mercantilist and the controlled capitalism of the sixteenth and seventeenth centuries to the laissez faire capitalism of the Victorian era was accepted by the early classical economists. But the classicists viewed the economic systems which preceded laissez faire capitalism as being merely the gropings of prescientific societies which had not yet learned to throw off the yoke of political subjection. The economic problems of all industrialized nations were thought to be the same, regardless of time, place, or traditions. The particular type of capitalism which David Ricardo so rigorously analyzed in the early nineteenth century was believed to be universally applicable both as a theoretical explanation and a policy guide for all rational businessmen and statesmen. Furthermore, the system was believed to have no goals other than to permit members of societies to pursue their own individual aims with the most opportunity and least resistance.

Of course some of the economic principles enunciated by the classical economists more than 125 years ago are basic to all modern economies. For example, the laws of diminishing returns and division or specialization of labor are universally recognized as valid for explaining some of our modern industrial phenomena. However, the existence of radically different economic systems in industrial nations today is evidence that other economic laws may well be relative both to time and circumstances. The problems which all economies face are concerned with the allocation of scarce resources among competing ends in such a way as to maximize human wants with the least sacrifice of opportunities. Yet the methods or systems which are employed to solve these problems are by no means uniform, and this study takes the hypothesis that these systems may differ in kind as well as degree.

The world is not as simple and well ordered as it was before World War I when all industrial economies could be reasonably classified as capitalist. Today there are several distinct types of economic systems in operation. Noncapitalist industrial systems have persisted long enough to prove their economic practicability. There is no longer any need to wait for them to collapse. Furthermore, such great changes have occurred in capitalist systems that both the present status and future prospects of capitalism are subject to considerable speculation.

THEORETICAL APPROACH TO UNDERSTANDING

There is something of a tradition in the United States that abstract theory is to be viewed with suspicion if not alarm. Many Americans are suspicious of intellectual activity, especially when it is in the fields of economics, psychology, and the other social sciences. Most of these practical-minded folk are willing to accept the benefits of scientific progress; yet many of them are quick to attack scholarly research and its logical conclusions. It is fashionable in some quarters to praise anti-intellectualism as being the healthy reaction of a frontier-type American pragmatism to the plotting of government planners or, at best, the sterile web-spinning of obscure wizards.

CULT OF IRRATIONALITY. Those who oppose intellectuality or theory overlook two important facts. First, cults of the irrational are as old as time and usually have been on the side of destroying the hard-won values of civilization and democracy. Seldom have irrational sects, with their distrust of logic and organization, succeeded in creating any new or lasting values. Characteristically they display a reliance on superstition for their philosophy, emotionalism for their vehicle, and mysticism for obscuring their goals. They often begin by demanding anarchy in order to liberate the free wills which have presumably been imprisoned by ordered society or some other "collectivism" or "bureaucracy." But those who have attained political power almost always have tried to suppress free thought and expression and have sought to require conformity of opinion.

Second, practical common sense, even when free of its mystical and irrational trappings, is often not the contempt for reason and theory that it pretends to be. Frequently what passes for common sense is little more than the refinement of the abstractions of an earlier generation, hallowed by antiquity and familiarity, but possibly less practical than when first advanced. The eighteenth-century originators of such modern common-sense principles as competition and laissez faire were called "philosophical radicals" because their ideas were considered so revolutionary and impractical. Adam Smith's theories were denounced by government and press as dangerously radical. Within present memory the income tax, collective bargaining, and minimum-wage laws all have been attacked as theoretically unsound and entirely unworkable in practice.

Yet some distrust of reason is understandable. In the social sciences, abstract theories which deal effectively with modern economic and political problems have been notably absent since the world upheavals triggered by World War I. Statesmen and scholars have had to proceed empirically during the last forty years as gigantic economic and political problems multiplied with fantastic rapidity. The institutional changes of recent years have been carefully described and documented, but still no comprehensive theory of capitalism in the modern world has appeared.

Furthermore, pragmatism and a certain distrust of theory are well grounded in American tradition. The long period of the open frontier in America and the equalitarian democracy which is so admired, in principle at least, have contributed to a suspicion of the kind of theorizing which is necessary if modern political, economic, and social problems are ever to be solved.

Still it is from the areas in which much empirical work is going on that theoretical systems are most likely to appear. Although Americans have been more inclined toward accumulating knowledge than to developing hypotheses, and although they seem suspicious of abstract reasoning, it is not improbable that theoretical conclusions of great value may emanate from the same places in which abstract theory is most distrusted. Facts often suggest hypotheses even to the unwary.

NECESSITY FOR ABSTRACTION. In economics, as in any other quantitative discipline, scientific conclusions can be reached only from hypotheses based on observation and intuition and carried forward by logical steps. In order to explain any complicated set of circumstances, models must be constructed using the process of abstraction. This merely means that the object of analysis is simplified by making certain assumptions about it. These assumptions strip the object of analysis of its individual characteristics, leaving a mental construction of the original which retains only those attributes that are to be examined. The remaining properties of the object can then be combined in several different ways, and by means of logical reasoning various resulting events or conditions can be established or predicted.

The use of abstraction is necessary for the economist since only by stripping a complex problem to its barest essentials can causal relationships be determined. If the relationships among two or more elements are to be understood, it is necessary to study them apart from other elements. The frequent use of *certeris paribus* assumptions ("other things being equal") by the economist permits him to come to grips with manageable problems even though he may have to sacrifice realism in his conclusions. In like manner, physicists frequently assume the absence of gravity or the existence of an absolute vacuum in their theoretical models in order to study the behavior of objects in motion. Assuming ideal conditions can be of great use in promoting understanding when what is omitted is outweighed by the value of the systematic explanation which emerges only from the simplifying of complex problems.

Conclusions drawn from abstractions are of little value unless based on and verified by observation. They are of even greater value when they can be confirmed by carefully controlled experiments. Economics, since it deals with collective human behavior, does not lend itself easily to controlled experiments. There are too many variables which cannot be held constant. But limited experiments can be made. Predictions can be made in terms of probabilities and expressed statistically. Economic theory is thus not inferior to the theories of the physical sciences. After all, some physical sciences, such as astronomy, must rely entirely on hypothesis and observation without experiment being possible.

The one thing common to all scientific analysis is abstraction. Without it nothing new is ever learned. Observation may furnish millions of real facts, but only reason can offer a guide to the relevant ones. Unless there is an original hypothesis concerning the relationships among the phenomena to be studied, there is no basis for selecting the data to be observed, classifying them and relating them so that meaningful conclusions can be drawn. There cannot even be any such thing as a fact unless there is a theory to relate it to other phenomena. Without some kind of theory there can only be meaningless observations. Of course the process of selection, classification, and evaluation may lead to the necessity of modifying or even discarding the original hypothesis in the interests of consistency. Indeed, objectivity demands that unproved hypotheses be replaced. However, even a wrong hypothesis is better than none at all because at least it organizes observation and thought so as to expose itself as inadequate or erroneous if such it should be.

Having selected a hypothesis, the economic theorist proceeds to build his model. It may be a limited model of a single firm under a set of particular circumstances such as a 10 per cent increase in output. Many economics textbooks are focused on models of this type, and most classical economists were concerned exclusively with them.

On the other hand, the theoretical model may be a more general one such as an entire industry faced with a tax increase. There is a growing interest in models of this type which are concerned with groups such as cartels, labor unions, "communities of interest," and economic organizations in general which are seeking wealth, security, or an enhanced status for members of a group. Modern monopoly and oligopoly theories and new developments in collective bargaining and industrial management areas are concerned with analysis at this level.

The model chosen by the economist may be a really ambitious one of an entire economic system faced with the problems of maximizing the welfare of its citizens, defending itself against its enemies, and making the most efficient use of its resources. This is essentially the modern orthodox model of the capitalist economic system in general equilibrium. A dynamic or historical model of the economic system could also be devised which is concerned with explaining the causes of economic growth or development and changing institutions over a period of time. The German historical models and the Marxian model tried, without much success, to do this for capitalism. The future will probably bring more model building at this level.

Theories, actually, are models of some aspect of the world which try to explain the interrelationships of certain variables such as taxes, employment, technological growth, and the value of goods and services produced. The more limited the theory, the fewer variables there are to consider and the more accurate are likely to be the predictions which can be advanced from the principles developed. The greater its scope, the less accurate will be the quantitative predictions. However, the conclusions will be more general and relevant for national economic policies. There is much more controversy over the relative merits of alternative economic systems than there is over the different possible ways of increasing the output of the copper mining industry or raising the funds to build a highway system. These more specific problems can be solved and the consequences of different policies predicted with sufficient accuracy to convince most reasonable people to accept the policy which offers obvious advantages. But when an issue arises involving entire economic systems, there are so many variable factors and value judgments concerning their relative importance that the words used to refer to the systems become charged with feeling. The argument becomes one of semantics, which cannot be resolved as long as words like "capitalism," "socialism," "welfare state," and "planning" mean different things to different people. Generalized epithets obscure the real issues, and the practical problems remain untouched.

Of course, abstraction can be carried too far. This is true especially when hypotheses do not start out from facts, and if deductions are not compared regularly with general experience, or if the hypotheses or even the assumptions are not modified when the results do not conform to observed reality. But merely to complain because there is no resemblance to the original object is to misunderstand the nature of scientific method. If the results obtained from manipulating the few remaining variables in a highly abstract model yield new knowledge which explains actual behavior, then the critic has no basis for objecting to the abstraction. If changes made in the model increase its realism and its complexity but result in reducing its accuracy for prediction, then the realism must be sacrificed. After all, abstraction and logical deduction can produce knowledge which all the observation in the world could never uncover. It is only through reasoning from abstract models that underlying causes and reasons can be determined.

Actually models are not used by theoreticians exclusively. Everyone who thinks or talks uses models of varying degrees of abstraction. A road map is an abstract model. Reading a calendar or telling time requires a modest ability to think in abstract terms. To classify things, or to speak of qualities or types of things, involves a considerable degree of simplification. Once a category of objects or events is established, then the items placed in that category become simplified models of the original, stripped of some of their primary characteristics.

LIMITS OF ACCURACY. Beyond the difficulties inherent in the prudent use of logical method in economics, there are still limitations to scientific accuracy in economic theory. First, economics, like many other disciplines, attracts a large number of laymen who have neither professional standing nor economic training. This situation is understandable. Everyone is engaged in finding solutions for the specific economic problems which face him. Nearly everyone has to try to maximize his satisfactions by allocating his limited income among his many competing needs and wants. However, the limited familiarity with a minute sector of the economy one person may acquire through long but specialized experience is not sufficient to make him an authority on economics in general.

The second limitation involves semantic difficulties. When an economist wants to discuss a particular concept, he all too often gives it a name which is already in general use and has many different colloquial meanings. Such economic terms as monopoly, capital, demand, competition, and investment are given special meanings different from those in everyday usage. The future of economics as a science lies in its ability to develop a substantial body of premises which the majority of professionals can accept and which, because they are more or less subject to verification through experiment, can be accepted by the lay public. As long as there are widely publicized disagreements over economic matters, economics will lack the prestige of a science even though the disagreements are caused primarily by pseudo-economists or by language difficulties within the profession.

Another limitation to theory is one that is often not recognized. Contrary to some modern "functional" or "operational" philosophies of science, a theory is not necessarily true merely because it works. Kicking a television set may cause it to function again, but the real trouble cannot be deduced from this remedy. Freudian psychotherapy cured insanity in a remarkable number of instances, but other diametrically opposed theories worked equally well on people with the same symptoms. In economics, cures based on several contradictory theories all may work. Inflation may be arrested by policies based on several theories of the business cycle. The reason for this is that in economics, as in other sciences, events are not the result of any single, specific cause but are the result of many interacting processes. For the most part it is useless in studying economic systems to look for scapegoats to blame for particular occurrences. The problems are far too complex for this.

On the other hand, the economist has two trump cards not available to physical scientists which he can use when rigorously scientific conditions cannot be achieved. First, economists and other social scientists can be certain that they are dealing with the basic, irreducible particles of society since their studies are concerned with the activities of human individuals. The economist may be further from an objective analysis of human behavior than the physicist is from a predictable knowledge of his atom, but the physicist can never be sure that he has dug down to the unbreakable foundation of his subject. In fact the atom itself has now been split into several components. Now both mass and energy have been equated at a level of abstraction which is subject to mathematical expression but not to empirical description. Conversely, the economist or social scientist need never fear that upon analysis his basic unit, the human being, will vanish into a cloud of mathematical symbols leaving nothing but the vast emptiness which confronts the physicist as he probes deeper into the secrets of nature.

Second, an advantage to the social scientist is that he can make use of a method which is not available to the physical scientist. He can rely on his experience and knowledge to gain insight into the motives and movements of others. The physicist cannot put himself in the place of a molecule and say, "What would I do if I were in this situation?" Molecules have no historical development, no cultural setting, no memory, no hopes, no fears, no will, and no responsibilities for their actions. But the social scientist is trained to observe human behavior (except his own, of course) and the circumstances which control it so that he can often predict with surprising accuracy what effect some change in the physical environment will have on the actions of people.

Jacob Marschak calls this method "imagined introspection" and says it is the main advantage which social scientists have over natural scientists.[1] When we study people, he suggests, we can put ourselves in their situation, imagine their thought processes, and speculate as to their reactions.

[1] "A Discussion on Methods in Economics," *Journal of Political Economy*, (1941).

Those who study genes and electrons, not themselves being genes or electrons, cannot do this.

In addition, because much of the data of the economist is reducible to quantitative form and subject to statistical expression, economics does have a distinct advantage over the other social sciences. Furthermore, developments in electronics and communications in recent years offer the hope that electronic computers may make economic theory, prediction, and control subject to greater practical verification and implementation.

Of course, it should not be claimed that the speculative method is as useful as the established scientific procedures, but it does enable a social investigator to check his results periodically with what seems to him to be reasonable. This study abounds with suggestions and speculations as indeed any study of this type necessarily must. Capitalism and socialism are fit subjects for speculations, and professional economists are no less inclined to go off on flights of intellectual fancy than anyone else. They may even be more so. But to aspire to scientific authenticity, the economist must retain a healthy regard for observed facts. Even this will not insure immunity from sharp controversy when the subject matter is economic systems, but it will certainly dispel much of the cloud of semantic confusion and restrict the debate to relevant facts and issues. The present study aspires to no more than this.

HYPOTHESES AND DEFINITIONS

It is sometimes said that an idea "is all right in theory but won't work in practice." Such a statement is not very meaningful. If a thing "won't work in practice"—that is, if practical application cannot be made of the conclusions resulting from theorizing because the conclusions are obviously inconsistent with statistical or observed phenomena—then the theory is certainly not "all right." The principal purpose of developing a theory is to arrange facts into a pattern which will permit greater understanding of the relationships among them.

There has long been disagreement over whether knowledge and understanding can best be furthered by formulating a generalization and then trying to apply the conclusions resulting from it to individual situations in order to predict the occurrence of actual data—*deduction*—or whether it is better to observe particular cases of actual phenomena and then, by reasoning from these, develop general principles applicable to other situations—*induction*. Experience has proved that both methods are necessary and that they supplement each other.

The method attempted in this book is to start with a few simple generalizations based on observation. Then the principal theoretical economic systems are examined in light of these generalizations and in an order or organization which seems logical in view of the hypotheses. Finally, some major conclusions are drawn which in fact limit somewhat, but do not destroy, the original premises.

It is assumed here that the process of economic development conditions most people who live in industrialized economies to think in terms of economic values. This means that success comes to be evaluated in material or economic terms and that most people, most of the time, strive to attain their own economic self-interest. Also, rationalism, or reliance on reason as against tradition, custom, or authority, is relied on to solve most problems. It is presupposed further that the principles of specialization of labor and machinery are well known and accepted. A fairly high degree of technology, literacy, and political realism must also necessarily be assumed. This book also takes, as a hypothesis, the fact that contemporary industrial economic systems may reasonably be classified, for procedural purposes, into two basic types—capitalistic and socialistic. The present study, therefore, must start with its own definitions and proceed from there toward conclusions regarding the significance of the various elements of the systems and any trends in the evolution of actual working systems.

analysis of these pure or theoretical systems which have
been developed as explanations of existing economies is
undertaken.

This book attempts to classify the major theories of capitalism and socialism and to examine, compare, and evaluate
them. A careful classification itself should provide more
than a mere tidy arrangement of previously known facts.
It should give some insight into positive, new knowledge.
Classification must be preceded by a reasonable hypothesis,
however, and combined with statistics. Every social re-
searcher should have a keen awareness and healthy regard
for facts. The theoretical systems of capitalism considered
here include the purely competitive system of the British
classicists, the German and American evolutionary systems,
the socialist doctrines of capitalism, the implications of the
Keynesian economics for capitalism, the theories of monopoly capitalism, and, finally, oligopoly capitalism, or the
theories of modern big business. Theoretical socialist systems are considered in three categories: historical development of socialist economics, the theory of liberal socialism,
and the theory of central planning.

It would be a mistake to jump to the conclusion, from this
classification, that this book intends to discuss the popular
concepts of "capitalism vs. socialism." Most of the common
stereotypes of socialism, communism, liberalism, conservatism, anticommunism, and so on disappear when the theories
are examined at all carefully. Nor can it be easily assumed
that one or more of the theoretical economic systems discussed here can be applied without much modification to
the United States, Great Britain, the Soviet Union, or any
other nation. The chapter on classical competitive capitalism is not intended to picture contemporary America;
the chapter on liberal socialism is not necessarily British
laborism; the chapter on central planning is not an examination of the economics of the Soviet Union. It is true that
much American thinking about capitalism harks back to the
English classicists, that liberal socialism was defined by
British laborites, and that the theory of central planning was

inspired partly by Marxism. But the coincidence ends here. The relationships between theory and operation are not nearly as simple as these neat classifications suggest.

The line between classical capitalism and socialism is often hard to find. Great classical economists, such as John Stuart Mill and the contemporary A. C. Pigou of Cambridge, who is widely regarded as one of the last exponents of classical orthodoxy, have found socialism and capitalism to be very similar at the level of pure theory. To add to the difficulty, those who are called liberals today often defend government control and oppose laissez faire although traditionally it was the liberals, following Adam Smith, who attacked the controls of mercantilism and defended freedom of economic decisions. This is not the place to attempt to resolve these confusions. This is reserved for later chapters, but these considerations are raised here to aid the reader in clearing out any preconceived notions which he might be harboring. There is no field of knowledge which cries out more for open-minded study than contemporary capitalism and socialism.

The controversy of capitalism versus socialism is sometimes held to be obsolete, and to some extent this is true at the levels of applied economics and practical politics.[2] But the economic systems in operation today are actually more similar than the theoretical bases which underlie them because in practice systems tend to become mixed as they face common political and military realities. Economic theorists must inevitably yield to the expedients of political feasibility. Thus economic systems in theory may differ more widely than economic systems in fact. Indeed a major conclusion of this study is that practical, working economic systems are becoming more alike than different. Nevertheless, the attempt is made here to examine the theoretical underpinnings which do come from widely different sources and even today orient the several major national economies in various directions. The analysis of economic systems under-

[2] R. A. Dahl and C. E. Lindblom, *Politics and Economic Welfare* (New York: Harper and Brothers, 1953).

taken in this book is based on the assumption that there are two major *theoretical* types, capitalism and socialism, which can be distinguished as applicable to modern, industrial economies. Fascism is considered as a special form of capitalism and communism as a special form of socialism. Actually, all so-called capitalistic systems contain large elements of "socialism," and all so-called socialistic systems, even professed communist systems, contain recognizable capitalistic institutions.

In spite of the recent integration of these different systems of thought, it seems fruitful to consider them separately at first and then point out the results of the consolidation. For one thing, the theories of capitalism were actually developed by people who for the most part were specifically concerned with capitalism in a rather pure form. This was particularly true of Marx, the German historical school, the Fabian socialists, the American institutionalists, and Keynes. The classical school did not analyze capitalism as such but assumed that all industrial economies would be capitalist in form. Others abstracted models which were intended both to describe and to explain the purely capitalistic elements of an economic system in which it was assumed that these elements dominated and subjected all other types of economic behavior to their sovereignty.

The theories of socialism, likewise, were developed by people who believed that an economic system which was radically different from capitalism in its major elements was theoretically possible and politically practicable. The proponents of theories of capitalism and socialism still hold these views, and governmental policies are being based on them. Thus, the differences may be more apparent than real.

It is hoped that a study of this kind will provide some insights into contemporary economic systems which comparative descriptions do not ordinarily permit. And it is hoped also that a step or two has been made toward understanding this vast and complex world in which all of us must make our living.

Part II

THEORIES OF CAPITALISM

2

Competitive Capitalism:
The English Classical and
Neoclassical Theories

> What Astronomy does for the phenomena of the heavenly
> bodies; what Dynamics does for the phenomena of motion;
> what Chemistry does for the phenomena of chemical com-
> bination; what Physiology does for the phenomena of the
> functions of organic life; that Political Economy does for
> the phenomena of wealth; it expounds the laws according
> to which those phenomena co-exist with or succeed each
> other . . . the science is neutral between social themes
> . . . as Chemistry stands neutral between competing plans
> of sanitary improvement.——J. E. Cairnes

> The besetting sin of the (classical) economists was their
> preference for argument over observation.——F. S. Oliver

INTRODUCTION

The study of modern capitalism began in England with
the classical school of economics which received its original
impetus in 1776 from the publication of Adam Smith's
famous book, the *Wealth of Nations*. This new theory of
economic "liberalism" spread quickly to parts of Europe and
the United States and persisted for about a century as the
only orthodox and respectable economic philosophy.[1] The

---

[1] The classical school consisted of a large number of economists of whom
Adam Smith (1723–1790), T. R. Malthus (1776–1834), David Ricardo
(1772–1823), and John Stuart Mill (1806–1873) are the best known

classicists never developed a specific theory of capitalism, nor did they even attempt to analyze economic phenomena from the standpoint of particular economic systems. Except for John Stuart Mill, they assumed that economic principles had universal application and hence that the similarities among national economies were more significant than their differences.

Adam Smith, the canny Scottish philosopher and moralist, did devote considerable space to a discussion and criticism of mercantilism which was the politico-economic system of England and France (and of several other countries to a lesser extent) from the fifteenth to the eighteenth centuries. This was not inconsistent with the assumption of universality of economic laws, however, because mercantilism was a system having distinct national characteristics, varying by countries, which obviously came from the close relationship between the business community and the government. Economics and politics had been so closely wedded that the economic institutions and their operations displayed characteristics which were strongly influenced by the political, religious, and social systems of the individual countries in which they existed. Smith and the other classical economists believed that a genuine economic system had not existed prior to the advent of free enterprise capitalism. The coming of laissez faire and economic regulation by free markets rather than governments was thought to lead to a universal economic system which was largely free of the influences of both historical tradition and contemporary environment.

---

today. Others who were well known in their day were James Mill (1773–1836), the father of John Stuart Mill, J. R. McCullouch (1789–1864), Nassau Senior (1790–1864), Thomas De Quincy (1785–1859), J. E. Cairnes (1823–1875), and J. B. Say (1767–1832). All were British except Say, who was French. Several recent authoritative studies indicate that the classical philosophy apparently did not penetrate the United States very deeply until well after 1860. The merchantilist doctrine of state regulation seems to have been accepted in the United States in theory and practice until fairly recent times. See, for example, M. S. Heath, *Constructive Liberalism* (Cambridge: Harvard University Press, 1954), or the present author's review in *Economica*, August, 1955.

MEDIEVAL AND MERCANTILE BACKGROUND

The Middle Ages had been a period of strict control over economic life. True, there were few strong national states in Europe before the fifteenth century. Political power was typically local in scope, and land ownership, from which nearly all economic power arose, was vested mostly in petty feudal lords and in the Church. Medieval society was also built around the social power of status, duty, and custom. These noneconomic controls were not as immediately obvious as the formal directives of an all-powerful central state, but still they existed in abundance. In spite of the extreme decentralization of authority, however, both the serfs and town citizens were shackled by invisible chains. Today, with the trend toward strong, centralized governments and the enforcement of regulations by rapid and efficient transportation, communication, and electronic control systems, it is easy to forget that the highly decentralized, personal, informal controls of the Middle Ages achieved a tyranny over men's minds and activities which has not since been equaled.

Through an odd mixture of economic and theological ideas, the Church subtly dictated both the material and spiritual requirements of society. The Church sanctioned a social caste system and insisted that it be perpetuated by economic conduct. The test of justice was applied to all economic activity, and justice was defined as a set of conditions which would continue the established social stratification. The doctrines of just price and fair wages enforced a code of economic behavior which would keep everyone living appropriately in the status quo. Hence property, slavery, and guild organization were sanctioned although lending money at interest was condemned.

In addition to ecclesiastical authority, local governments controlled trading in the markets and enforced property rights. The guilds exercised the most detailed control over wages, hours, quality of product, entrance into trades, and other matters affecting production. Serfs, of course, were tied to the land they could never hope to own by the most exacting and confining status relationships. The strongest of all controls, however, was that of custom, which was perpetuated by the Church almost without change for over ten centuries. Manners, dress, and virtually all human activities were carefully scrutinized. Independent thought and expression, except occasionally in the arts, were all but nonexistent. Technological change was equivalent to treason.

The first outside force to threaten this apparently stable and perpetual equilibrium of poverty and stagnation was the Black Death of the fourteenth century. A general labor shortage resulting from the plague gave rise to demands for higher wages. These demands had to be suppressed in England by the Conspiracy Acts. The Acts outlawed concerted efforts to improve wages and made it a serious offense to entice away another's workman by offering him more pay. Land tenure reforms began to be demanded, and soon the peasantry experienced the first major changes in established relations in a thousand years.

The Reformation and the Renaissance added impetus to the movements for change. Finally, by the early sixteenth century, the feudal system had been largely replaced by a new commercialism which developed under the protection and control of new monarchies that were rapidly absorbing the petty lords and principalities of the Middle Ages. The informal controls of the Church, guild, landlords, and custom, which declined with the rise of commerce and industry, were replaced with direct and formal systems of rights and order by the newly centralized national states of England, France, and Germany.

The growth of individualism and materialism, and the exploits of science and technology of the Renaissance, led inevitably to a demand for freedom. Once free inquiry developed in the natural sciences, it tended to expand through the social sciences, commerce, and politics. The businessmen who had achieved economic power through state encouragement and control began to demand freedom to pursue an unlimited self-interest. The scientific discoveries of Copernicus, Galileo, and Newton seemed to demonstrate the existence of a state of nature governed by definite, immutable laws.

Inevitably, philosophers such as John Locke, David Hume, and Francis Hutchison applied these concepts to human affairs. It was soon being argued that the world was governed by "self-evident" natural laws. The popular Deist philosophers Adam Smith and Thomas Jefferson rejected the doctrine of "revealed religion" and argued that God had created man, put him in a world of nature, and left him to work out his material and spiritual salvation without any further divine intervention. A group of humanist philosophers went even further, rejecting the doctrine of specific creation altogether and maintaining that man was a product of his natural environment and subject to the objective laws of universal nature. To both groups, whose influence on the French and American revolutions is well known, it was futile to attempt to circumvent natural laws.

The concept of natural law held up none too well under careful examination. It soon became apparent that natural laws could never be scientifically verified, and so the whole idea was soon rejected by most philosophers. Nevertheless, many people continue to this day to act as though there are immutable laws in the universe which will frustrate any attempts to improve economic or social conditions.

From the original idea of the perfect and unchangeable state of nature developed the doctrine of individualism with its policy implications of self-interest and laissez faire. Much later the doctrine of individualism was to be put on a sounder philosophical basis than natural law, but in the late eighteenth century it seemed to fit the needs of businessmen who had tasted the fruits of technological improvement and were beginning to chafe under the artificial and formal regulations of the day. The concept of individualism, meaning the inherent worth of the individual as contrasted with some abstraction like the state or some interest group or religious community, is a very old one. The Greek philosophers expounded it for certain classes of free citizens. Early

Christianity was based to some extent on individual values although Christianity moved away from individualism in medieval times and oriented itself more in terms of the communal salvation. This idea of cooperative values still exists today in the Roman Catholic church as well as in some Protestant denominations, although the general Protestant view tends toward individualism, at least spiritually.

In the eighteenth century, economic and political conditions were ripe for an expansion of individualism as they had never been before. Many startling inventions sprang up, including the steam engine, cotton gin, blast furnace, and spinning machines. These required a great specialization of labor and provided an economic basis for the kind of individualistic philosophy which soon led to a rapid and gigantic growth of private capital. Thus individualism reproduced itself, once it got started, by stimulating invention and technological changes which in turn paved the way for a further individualism.

The mercantilist economic system which emerged from feudalism in the sixteenth to eighteenth centuries had many of the elements of capitalism. Its institutions included private property, a modified use of the profit motive, credit, banking, currency, and a growing rationalistic philosophy. But the state played such an important role in granting monopoly rights and subsidies and regulating wages, employment, production, foreign trade, interest rates, and prices that markets were not really free or competitive. Yet it was the immediate ancestor of the free-market capitalism of the nineteenth century.

At best the enforcement of laws in the mercantilist period was difficult. There were no efficient transportation, communication, or record-keeping systems. By the eighteenth century, businessmen had secured positions of economic power which even the kings were forced to respect, although the kings had permitted and even encouraged this growth of power. Consequently, it became progressively easier for the regulations of the mercantilist governments to be sabotaged. Adam Smith recalled, for example, that the principal business in his native town of Kirkaldy, Scotland, had been smuggling, and there is no doubt that this expression of a pent-up desire for commercial freedom left a lasting impression on Smith and the classical economists.

CLASSICAL ECONOMIC SYSTEM

The classical system of Adam Smith laid the theoretical foundations for capitalism as it is known today. No one had ever before tried to explore the complete system of processes which combine to make up the economic order. Before discussing how Smith's economic system operated, however, the assumptions underlying it need to be set forth in some detail since, with some modification, they are applicable to the orthodox concept of competitive capitalism as it exists today. Out of these assumptions a definition of modern capitalism can be derived.

ASSUMPTIONS. First, as already mentioned, Smith assumed that there was a natural order in the universe and that all economic processes sought to conform to it. This order was in a state of static equilibrium, and if artificial restrictions, such as tariffs, monopolies, and wage controls, were removed, labor, capital, and natural resources would all seek the most profitable and efficient employment.

The concept of an economic equilibrium was weak when based on an apparently unprovable natural order, but it was strengthened by the social philosopher Jeremy Bentham. Bentham rejected intuitive concepts of natural law and laid the basis for economics as a science of subjective feelings by contending that economic institutions could be justified rationally. A century later Alfred Marshall was to show that the total welfare of the community could be maximized by policies based on the assumption that such a natural law existed even though no such law could even be proved. The same equilibrium could be reached even without assuming a natural order behind it. But in its original form the assumption of a natural order gave the classical system a philosophy of universality of economic laws which was not limited by time, place, or institutional surroundings.

Unfortunately, the nature philosophy also deluded the classicists into the belief that they had fashioned a system which, being natural and eternal, was therefore perfect. Hence, there was no need to reflect on the historical or evolutionary development of their science nor was there any room for improvement. The result was that there was an increasing concentration on perfecting the details of the system and a lack of attention to verifying its theoretical conclusions with the facts of the real world.

Second, the classical economists assumed the existence of the fabled "economic man." This assumption implied that man is rational and hence constantly tries to pursue his economic self-interest, as distinguished from esthetic or other "self-interests" which might conflict with it. Behind the concept of the economic man was the "hedonistic" or "pleasure-seeking" psychology of Bentham. Maximum happiness was conceived as the algebraic sum on a scale of pleasure and pain. Each person was assumed to be able to calculate, and evaluate carefully, the quantitative advantages and disadvantages of every action or decision he makes. It logically followed that each individual would be the best judge of his own pleasures and pains and hence could best attain this psychic equilibrium under conditions of individualism and laissez faire. To Bentham, total human happiness could be measured as the simple sum of every individual's happiness, the pleasures of each person being assumed to be comparable and measurable. In this system of social mechanics every individual counted as one.

Hedonistic psychology can be stated in modern economic terminology. Businessmen try to maximize their profits and minimize their costs; workers try to improve their wages and working conditions and minimize their efforts; consumers try to purchase at the lowest possible price the maximum quantities and qualities of goods in such combinations as most nearly satisfy their individual needs and wants. It

follows from this that businessmen will manage their businesses efficiently, will be constantly aware of the market
for their products, and will take those risks which are necessary to promote economic progress. Workers will freely
move to better employment, and consumers will relentlessly
seek the "best buys."

Of course, all motives are not economic motives. If such
were the case, there probably would not be much religion,
education, culture, or public service in connection with capitalism. The economic system would become a perfectly
working commercial machine without feelings or emotions,
without beauty or esthetics, and without any values which
could not be determined by capitalizing incomes into fixed
sums of money. The classical economists were not ignorant
of the noneconomic motives, which make life worth living
after the living has been made. But they chose to ignore
noneconomic motives because they believed that economic,
or selfish, motives were the basic, natural urges of men and
dominated all others. The rationality of the capitalistic economic system comes from the alleged coordination of the
countless rational economic decisions taken by individuals
in response to the automatic price changes of the free
market.

The postulate of pecuniary rationality is one of the truly
powerful tools of contemporary economic analysis. If any
firm, person, or household can be assumed to act rationally,
its decisions can be predicted in any given situation by use
of the rules of logic. Without the assumption of rationality,
detailed studies of the patterns of decisions of the unit
would have to be made and all uniformities noted before
any predictions could be ventured.

The assumption of economic rationality and the consequences of it imply that producers and consumers know
what alternatives are available to them in terms of prices,
quantities, and qualities of productive resources, final products, consumers' wants, and profit and employment possibilities. Furthermore, once this information is known, capital and labor must be free to move in the direction of their

best economic interest, and consumers must be able to buy what they need.

Mobility of economic resources means not only freedom to move but the inclination to move. The lethargy of tradition and emotional or sentimental ties must be shaken off. Businessmen must seek to transfer their talents and capital into new and untried ventures which offer economic reward rather than trying to gain governmental or monopolistic protection for their declining enterprises. Workers must be eager to follow higher wages, even if this means breaking family and community ties, rather than asking that industry be brought to them.

Implicit in the concept of economic man were additional assumptions which were necessary if the pursuit of self-interest was to have any meaning. Among these were assumptions that individuals are free to own property and use it as they see fit. A necessary condition of classical capitalism is that firms and individuals be given the authority to control their own economic actions, and this requires, among other things, the right of private property. Producers must be able to decide what to produce, how it shall be produced, and, in fact, whether to produce or not. Consumers must be able to do as they please with their incomes within the limits imposed by the protection of public health, safety, and morals. Otherwise, consumer purchases will not reflect genuine demands. People must be free to hoard, squander, accumulate capital through investment, consume, forego any income at all by remaining idle, or otherwise follow their individual whims.

There must also be a division of labor in society to permit maximum use of technology. Furthermore, there must be a system of exchange so that highly specialized labor can be traded for a variety of goods and services. Individuals must be protected by laws enforcing contracts, and forms of business organization compatible with an enterprise system must be available for use. Assuming further that no large organizations arise which can control prices or supplies of productive resources, then a free market will exist which will evaluate resources, goods, and services objectively according to the demand for them and the cost of making them available.

A third major assumption of classical economics can be called a harmony of interests. This took several forms. First, there was thought to be a harmony between producers and consumers. Producers depend on consumers' demand for their existence, and consumers depend on producers for their livelihood. Production generates purchasing power which in turn is used to buy the goods produced. As expressed by J. B. Say, the French classical economist, "Supply creates its own demand." This led to the conclusion that there could be no general unemployment or overproduction except from the malallocation of resources caused by government, business, or labor interference with the operation of the free-market economy.

Second, there was a harmony of interests between short-term and long-term considerations. The classical economists would not have accepted the argument, for example, that oil conservation laws are necessary to prevent a rapid and inefficient exploitation of oil lands following a sudden rise in the price of oil even though such opportunism might lead to a loss of some oil altogether and to a dangerous shortage in the future.

Third, and most important, the harmony of interests equated the sum of every individual interest with the general public interest. Thus, individuals following their own selfish aims could not help but benefit society.

From these assumptions it logically followed that there should be a policy of laissez faire. Unless the government played a very limited role in the economy, the forces of the market could not work themselves out so as to allocate resources efficiently, and individuals could not effectively pursue their economic self-interests. To Adam Smith, the government should restrict itself to (1) the promotion of national defense, (2) the preservation of law and order, including the enforcement of property and contract rights, and the establishment of uniform standards for business activity, such as weights and measures, and (3) the provision for certain public works. This latter function included providing for needs, such as hospitals, cemeteries, or harbors, which are needed by the community but are not suited to development by private enterprise because of their inherent unprofitableness. It also included functions such as fire fighting, which endanger public safety if service is curtailed, and lighthouses or defense, of which the product or service is indivisible, making payment according to use impossible. This public works function would seem to open the door for any or all enterprises to be undertaken by the government if a good argument for the failure of private enterprise could be made. Such arguments have been successfully used to justify government operation of schools, roads, low cost housing construction, home and farm financing, electric power production, and many other government undertakings.

There can be little doubt that Smith was led astray into an adulation of laissez faire by the low standards of government in his time. He lived after the destruction of the fairly decent government of the Cromwellian period and before the reforms of the Chartist era. The Hanoverian kings who reigned during Smith's adult life have been immortalized in poetry as being the worst of a bad lot. Smith failed to see that cooperation among men through government could be as simple and natural as the competitiveness and acquisitiveness which he seemed to believe in so strongly. The invisible hand which he saw pointing to personal economic gain was not so easily seen by most people of his time. To many of those who saw it at all, it pointed the other way, toward unselfish, righteous living, as it had for at least the preceding twelve hundred years. The avarice which seemed to the thrifty Scot to be natural behavior had to be patiently learned by the generation which was growing up in the Industrial Revolution.

It is true that Smith advocated numerous government regulations, such as the liquor tax, which were designed to control specific industries. One study revealed twenty-six exceptions to laissez faire advocated by Smith to protect the public interest.[2] These arguments are widely scattered through the *Wealth of Nations*, but when they are collected they appear to refute the general case for economic freedom. However, the *Wealth of Nations* was not a closely reasoned book, and Smith did not base his conclusions on the aggregate of his specific arguments. His over-all conclusion concerning the role of government fell short even of a social security system.[3]

Smith was aware of the natural growth of monopolistic organizations. He observed that businessmen seldom get together even socially without the conversation drifting around to the subject of fixing prices. Not foreseeing the nineteenth- and twentieth-century technological requirements of economies of scale, Smith advocated the use of the partnership over the then incipient "limited-liability company" (corporation) as a business organizational device. The partnership form of enterprise limits the size of any undertaking to the capital which a few trusting and congenial people can raise among themselves. Since every member of a general partnership is responsible for all debts of the firm, obviously each would insist on having a voice in the management. By preventing delegation of managerial functions, this would also seriously limit the effectiveness of all but the smallest organizations.

Laissez faire, to Adam Smith, meant freedom from laws or agreements regulating trade, prices, wages, working conditions, and output. Accordingly, there could be no monopolies, business cartels, or labor unions. No organization could be large enough, or influential enough, to control prices, wages, or employment to the extent that consumers, producers, or workers would have no reasonable alternatives from which to choose.

OPERATION OF THE CLASSICAL ECONOMIC SYSTEM. What is the motivating force behind economic activity? From

[2] Jacob Viner, "Adam Smith and Laissez Faire," *Journal of Political Economy*, April, 1927.
[3] *Wealth of Nations* (London: C. Black, Ltd., 1863), Book V, chaps. i and ii.

whence does the "wealth of nations" come? Adam Smith was the first to analyze production and break it into the components of land, labor, and capital. (A fourth factor, management, was added by later classicists.) From classical economics it is possible to argue for any of these factors exclusively. Current disagreements over the relative shares of the national output which should go to property owners, workers, money lenders, or managements are based on this early analysis. Landowners have claimed that there is a sacred right of private property and that without the hope of accumulating property there would be no incentive for effort and hence no production. Others have argued, more recently, that most, if not all, production is due to capital equipment, the accumulation of which is due to the fact that someone, somewhere, refrained from consumption, thereby saving his income and making it available for capital accumulation. Of course, there could be no output at all without labor since this is the only physically active component of production. So labor could claim the total product. Management likewise has claimed that without planning, organization, and supervision the other factors of production could not be combined to produce anything. The fact is that the contribution of each of the four factors is important although they are inseparable.

Smith rejected the contemporary French Physiocratic doctrine that land was the sole cause of wealth. It might be surprising to some of his present-day disciples that he also rejected the argument that management was responsible for the creation of values. He gave capital some credit by showing that specialization in production permitted the use of machinery which would greatly increase total output. But the origin of wealth itself was to be found in labor. In this he meant manual or "productive" labor, not what would today be called personal or other services. Smith called these "unproductive."

Adam Smith doubted whether business profits were in the social interest and argued strongly that the rents charged by landlords were monopoly returns due to the relative scarcity of land and not rewards for any productive activity of landlords. Smith and the other classicists hated the landlords. To these theorists of the new commercial and manufacturing system, landlords represented the decaying feudal aristocracy which opposed progress and industry. During the early nineteenth century the clash between the landed classes and the newly arising capitalists was as fundamental as later labor-management disputes were to become. It was not until 1846, with the repeal of the Corn Laws, that liberal capitalism won a clear-cut victory over the landowners. From then on, corn could be freely imported. This had the expected results of (1) lowering food prices, which lessened the pressure for higher wages, and (2) providing foreigners with currency with which to buy British manufactured goods. The goal of British capitalists—to make Britain the workshop of the world—was finally in sight.

But even seventy-five years earlier than this victory for laissez faire and free trade, Smith was not disposed to interfere with the "parasitic" landlords and remove their "economically unjustified" rents because he believed that a laissez-faire policy would accomplish this objective more effectively through competition. Besides, interfering with the system would have disadvantages outweighing the advantages since private property and self-interest would be thwarted. To Smith, the major motivating force—the prime mover of the economic system—was self-interest. It was expressed in prices and wages in a free market and molded into an organizing force for cohesion, rather than chaos, by the power of competition. With remarkable consistency, Smith advocated freedom for those he considered unproductive as well as for the productive.

In the opening sentence of the *Wealth of Nations*, Adam Smith stated that the purpose of all production was consumption. Although he then devoted his entire study to production and never got back to mentioning consumption again, the classical system of capitalism did put the consumer in the driver's seat for the first time in history. Producers were to be guided by the desires of consumers as expressed by the prices which they were willing to pay. High demand for a certain item was to be translated into rising prices and profits. Producers would shift resources from the production of loss-producing or low-profit goods to high-profit goods so production would follow the changing patterns of consumers' wants and needs. Thus consumers would ultimately control the prices and output of the goods and services furnished by producers. In an attempt to improve their economic position, consumers would seek out the best bargains—in terms of both price and quality— and producers who failed to meet consumers' demands or were inefficient to the extent that other producers undersold them would face bankruptcy. Producers, in striving to increase their sales and reduce their costs, served society as well as themselves.

The classical system of capitalism operated through the "invisible hand" of competition. Individual producers, in trying to increase their profits, would seek out and purchase the lowest priced resources and combine them in the most efficient way to increase the output obtainable thereby. As long as no suppliers, whether farmers, workers, or producers of semifinished products, could control the prices at which their goods or services were sold, then the buyers would have sufficient alternatives so that they could secure the best possible bargain. An inefficient supplier would be forced to become more efficient or face economic extinction.

Profit is the goal of the businessman, and its justification is in the risks he takes by being daring, imaginative, and energetic. Profit is more than the wages of management. Executive salaries are costs and not profits at all if they are in the form of fixed compensation paid for the competent performance of established routine management tasks. True profits come from uncertain and dynamic elements in the economy, and, since classical analysis was in a static equilibrium framework, some of the classical economists were led to the conclusion that profits would tend to disappear in the long run. If competition prevailed, the long-run gross revenue for any business would be just high enough to cover the competitive costs of labor, materials, and other production requirements, to pay enough interest and dividends on capital to retain the use of it, to induce the businessman to remain in business a little longer, and no more. There would be no provision for growth, development, experimentation, or research. Of course, it was generally recognized that profits could come from monopoly, but monopoly was not expected to prevail in the long run.

Smith observed that in civilized countries there is a tendency for people to specialize and do the things they like to do or can do best. Then they exchange their labor or their goods for a variety of the products of others. Labor can thus become more skilled, time can be saved, and there can be a concentration on particularized tasks which leads to the development of machinery to perform them. Vastly increased production comes from this division of labor, but the degree of specialization depends on the extent of the market. The larger the market area, the more a particular person or nation can specialize and the greater the total value that can be produced. Logically, the maximum production attainable with existing resources and technology would be achieved if goods could be exchanged freely anywhere in the world. Since a laissez-faire policy followed from the classical assumptions, the removal of restraints on trade, especially international tariff barriers, became a matter of immediate concern.

Domestic monopolies posed no immediate threat, labor unions were illegal for most purposes and were to remain so for another century, and domestic mercantilist regulations were becoming increasingly difficult to enforce. But there were high tariffs everywhere, and free international trade offered a real opportunity for experiment. The classical theory of international trade, which was put into practice by England shortly thereafter, was destined to transform that nation into the greatest commercial power in the world within a quarter of a century.

The classical theory of free trade was based on two arguments. One relied on the quantity theory of money, which

had been first advanced in the sixteenth century by David
Hume, the philosopher and teacher of Adam Smith. Stated
simply, the quantity theory of money held that prices would
be proportional to the amount of money in existence. Hume
had contended that a long-run excess of exports over imports, even for a particular country, would be impossible
because exports would cause an increase of gold in a country. This would cause prices to rise relative to other countries, and hence exports would fall below imports. Conversely, as gold flowed out of a nation which had an excess
of imports, prices would fall, foreigners would then buy
more goods, and a long-run balance of trade would inevitably be restored.

Modern experience has shown prices to be based more
on the level of total expenditures than on the quantity of
money. Since prices are not proportional to total spending
except under conditions of full employment, and since even
under full employment spending may not be proportional
to the quantity of money in circulation (because of pessimism or optimism of consumers and investors), the quantity theory of money has been replaced by a new theory
discussed in Chapter 6.

A sounder argument for free trade was physical rather
than monetary. The classicists rightly declared that with
free trade each nation would concentrate on producing
those goods in which it had the greatest comparative advantage. Not only would each nation specialize in producing what could be made cheaper than in other countries, but if it could produce two products cheaper than
another country and produce one of these products cheaper
than the other one, it would concentrate on producing the
lowest-cost product and import the other. England, for example, might be able to produce both shoes and hats more
efficiently than Germany but could produce shoes even
more efficiently than hats. It would pay the English to specialize completely in shoes and import hats from Germany,
even though England could produce hats more efficiently
than Germany, because more value in exchange could be

produced in shoes alone than by dividing the same resources between shoes and hats. England, in this case, might be able to produce enough shoes with a given amount of resources to trade for more hats than could be produced at home with the same resources, even though she could produce hats more efficiently than anyone else. By specialization and trade, England would have more total goods for a given amount of effort and resources, and so would Germany.

The essence of this "law of comparative advantage" is that by specializing each nation can gain. What one nation gains is not lost by another. An extreme example would be a case where, because of resource advantages, one nation could produce tractors but no gasoline, and another could produce gasoline but no tractors. Obviously a trade of just one tractor for a drum of gasoline would benefit both. Or suppose one country could produce only left shoes and another only right!

Free trade philosophy had a great appeal in England in the early nineteenth century and became a major political issue. It not only promised profits for manufacturers but was consistent with the rationalism and humanitarianism of the time. All nations could gain if trade barriers were removed and each nation specialized in producing those goods for which it was best suited and traded with other nations for those which could be produced more efficiently elsewhere. This was merely an extension to the whole world of the factory system which had already proved itself domestically. Moreover, there were political benefits beyond the obvious economic ones. Since all nations would become mutually interdependent, there would be greater international understanding and less danger of war. If goods could freely cross international boundaries, it would not be necessary for armies to do so.

Population and Labor. The ever increasing division and specialization of labor posed a serious problem for workers in Adam Smith's time. Having been deprived by the Enclosure Acts of the security which accompanies a rural existence, they were forced into the teeming slums of the new cities. A great public outcry based on moral indignation arose at the deteriorating plight of the growing industrial working class, whose living standards fell as their numbers kept increasing.

The explanation of the role of the workers was supplied by the classical economists David Ricardo and Thomas Malthus. Employing a quantity theory of labor, as contrasted with Smith's more vague labor-purchase theory, Ricardo argued that there was a functional relationship between the amount of physical labor expended on a commodity and the value of the commodity. He then reasoned that the natural price of a commodity tended to approximate the value of the labor in it and that market prices were merely reflections of natural prices. Labor itself was a commodity, and wages, which were its price, were based on the supply of labor relative to the need.

Malthus added his famous population theory to this system with the result that the outlook for labor became pessimistic indeed. Malthus argued, rigorously at first although in later editions of his book he accepted many modifications, that population tended to increase in geometric ratio (1,2, 4,8,16,32, etc.) whereas the means of subsistence tended to increase in arithmetic ratio (1,2,3,4,5,6, etc.). Thus the population would tend to double while the means of subsistence increased by an amount equal to the increase in the previous period. If each period is taken to be twenty-five years, roughly a generation, in one hundred years a given population would increase eight times while the means of subsistence increased only four. Unless voluntary population controls were practiced, in Malthus' time meaning late marriages and "moral restraint," the limits on population would be the starvation, disease, and wars which inevitably follow conditions of extreme poverty.

Ricardo agreed that the only check on population was the level of subsistence. The worker's subsistence could be received only through wages since any agricultural pursuits were impossible under crowded urban and industrial circumstances. If "real" wages (the purchasing power of money wages) fell, the population would decline through lower birth rates and higher death rates, thus causing a relative shortage of labor. Competition for workers would then cause real wages to rise again. Likewise, an increase in real wages, regardless of the reason, would only multiply the population. With a larger working force, there would be greater competition among workers for the existing jobs. Wages would be forced back down, and the equilibrium of wages at subsistence level would return.

Since population was based on subsistence and wages were based on population, the natural wage rate would be that rate which would perpetuate the labor force at the subsistence level without any increase in population. Adam Smith had optimistically hoped that what was accepted as subsistence by the workers would gradually rise. He observed that subsistence was more a state of mind than a physical condition. The Irish, he noted, would live, work, and reproduce their kind if given a mud hut and a potato. He questioned whether the English worker would submit to this standard of living. Smith trusted that as time went on the accepted subsistence level would rise and population would be constant, even with rising living standards.

Ricardo and Malthus were pessimistic, however. Their conclusions were that labor was hopelessly bound by the "Iron Law of Wages," according to which it would be useless for workers to organize or for the government to interfere by imposing minimum wage and hour laws, child labor laws, or even granting relief for the poor. Nor could employers fairly be held responsible for the problems caused by the rapid increase in the laboring population. Maintaining a scientific attitude throughout, Ricardo dispensed with all ethical and moral responsibility for the consequences of his reduction of economic theory to a system of iron-clad laws of wages, population, supply, demand, international trade, and rent. No wonder economics became known as the "dismal science." It was left for Karl Marx to exploit the apparent conclusion that the only hope for the working man was to be found in abolishing the capitalistic economic system entirely.

A more refined theory was worked out by James Mill, father of John Stuart Mill, to rationalize the existing plight of labor. This famous "wages fund" theory held that there was a definite but limited amount of money available for wages. If the number of workers increased, or if existing workers received wage increases, the increase of wages would necessarily be at the expense of profits. Like the "iron law," any improvement in wages would be self-defeating. This kind of thinking was not disagreeable to businessmen, for it justified the great inequalities of wealth which existed at the time. This theory became widely accepted even though it failed completely to explain why the highest wages and highest profits usually existed simultaneously in the same industries. It was for an American, Francis Walker, to show later that rising productivity from machinery could increase both profits and wages, and that there was no necessary conflict between management and labor for any fixed and predetermined sum of money.

The working out of these economic "laws" requires that there be a free-market mechanism and a monetary system so that prices reflect rational individual valuations of buyers. In this way, the goods buyers want will be produced in the quantities and varieties they want. Furthermore, goods will have to be produced in the most efficient way known. The greatest happiness will be secured by the greatest number of people, and all this is to be accomplished quite automatically through the market.

Competition in a free market consequently tends to reduce costs and profits, to increase efficiency, to stimulate technological progress, to insure payments to everyone in proportion to contribution, and to increase the quality, quantity, and variety of goods produced in accordance with consumers' desires.[4] These conclusions can be derived from

[4] These functions of competition are summarized briefly and clearly by the National Association of Manufacturers, Economic Principles Commission in *The American Individual Enterprise System* (New York: McGraw-Hill Book Co., Inc., 1946), pp. 58-59.

an analysis of classical competition, and modern theory goes back to Adam Smith's optimism rather than Ricardo's gloomy science. Unfortunately, classical economics was remembered for a long time more for Ricardo's systemization than for Smith's original gropings. Unlike the original and creative Adam Smith, Ricardo was a rigorous thinker and profound logician. He had a large following among intellectuals, who admired his abstract models and deductive reasoning. It was Ricardo who molded the classical doctrine into a system of abstract, inexorable economic laws quite as rigid as their counterparts in physics yet far more devoid of reality.

MILL'S RESTATEMENT. John Stuart Mill, the last of the great classical economists and one of the truly great thinkers of all time, further refined and systematized the classical theory but with some important modifications which permitted the peaceful evolution of theoretical classical capitalism into a more acceptable form. To Mill, production followed the unchanging, fundamental laws stated by Smith and refined by Ricardo, but to him distribution of the income generated by production was governed by human or man-made principles. Free competition was an abstract ideal which could never occur in the real world. It was useful for logical analysis and as a guide for policy only. Mill admitted that supply and demand determine prices, but he recognized that they also guide production and hence react on themselves in later time periods. In other words, supply and demand affect prices, prices affect production, and production affects supply and demand.

Mill seems here to have caught a glimpse of one of the basic difficulties of competitive market analysis which have plagued orthodox economists more recently. Under some conditions, competitive markets tend toward supply and demand equilibriums, and prices tend to reflect relative wants and costs. Under other circumstances, there seems to be circularity of cause and effect resulting in cumulative upward or downward spirals. For example, the labor market seems to be self-regulating when supply of labor and wages is moving in the same direction. Higher wages call forth a greater supply of labor which in turn provides a check on rising wages. Falling wages, in a particular industry at least, tend to reduce the supply of labor as workers seek better jobs elsewhere. This movement tends to check the wage decline. Below a certain minimum wage, however, falling wages will increase the supply of labor because women, children, and other dependents will be forced into the labor market to supplement the inadequate income of the breadwinner. Unless checked by outside regulation of some kind, a vicious downward spiral of wages will begin.

Another example comes from agriculture. It is well known that falling farm prices in a free market tend to cause increased production and a wasteful depletion of natural resources as farmers try to compensate for their reduced incomes by increased plantings. There are many other circumstances, such as industries with large fixed investments, where short-term adjustments to changed market conditions are either impossible or so slow that self-adjustment is not forthcoming and cumulative spirals get under way. Mill, of course, did not propose ways out of these difficulties, nor are the problems yet solved, but he did recognize that the competitive market did not always work to the maximum benefit of all concerned, and he did propose interfering with it when necessary.

Mill recommended promoting competition and letting the market do the regulating in the area of production because he believed, with the other classical economists, that natural laws governed this sector of the economic system. However, in the distribution of returns to the factors of production—wages to labor, profits to the businessman, rent to the landowner, and interest to capital—he believed that human endeavor could improve existing inequities. Cooperative efforts through labor unions, profit-sharing plans, voluntary associations, and government legislation could all be used.

Mill also believed that a better organization of property laws would remove the more intolerable aspects of private ownership. Although strongly favoring private property, he condemned those aspects of it which tended to deny to some people the fruits of their own labor. He favored the inheritance tax as a means of collecting the social increment or surplus which accrues to land as the population increases.

Thus, in advocating collective action in distribution and modification of property relationships, Mill stood between the rigorous tradition of Ricardo and the ethical and emotional appeals of the socialists who by this time (the mid-nineteenth century) were making deep inroads into the dominance of orthodox economic thought. However, Mill was a strong advocate of laissez faire on political, psychological, administrative, and economic grounds. Yet he admitted that in every age there would be some activities which the government should undertake because they were urgently needed and private individuals could not or would not perform them. In his later years Mill gradually relaxed his limits to government activity until the Fabians claimed that he died a socialist. This is disputed, but there is no doubt that the Fabian socialists do trace their own philosophy back to the classical theory through some of the later writings of John Stuart Mill.

MARGINAL UTILITY SCHOOL

By the mid-nineteenth century, classical economic theory was in a bad state of affairs. Although the Industrial Revolution had been in full swing for well over half a century, Ricardo, Mill, and the other classicists seemed to be unaware of it. The new technology was rapidly increasing the degree of economic interdependence. Government regulation to provide a minimum of security and protection for the weak was becoming imperative. Yet the economists continued to praise individualism and to oppose interference with even the most outrageous exploitation. Those who were aware of the hideous poverty and unspeakable abuses which were part of the daily lives of at least three-fourths of the population seemed mystified that such conditions could exist.

The classicists ignored the Industrial Revolution partly because they did not like it. John Stuart Mill, for example, wrote that "it is questionable if all the mechanical inventions yet made have lightened the day's toil of any human being." Furthermore, Mill might well have been satisfied to see technological improvements stop because the resulting "stationary state" which was the basis of his theorizing would have become a reality, and the facts of life would then have conformed more closely to the constructions of his theory.

Another difficulty with the classical theory lay in the fact that the contradictions provided by the labor theory of value had given Marxism all it needed to win the support of radicals and liberals alike. And to make matters worse a group of highly conservative and respectable Austrian economists were challenging the classicists successfully in the better social circles. The Austrians, with their characteristic interest in psychology, were saying that neither labor costs nor any other costs determine value in a capitalist economy. Rather, they insisted, value is determined by what consumers are willing to pay, and this willingness is based on what consumers *think* goods are worth to them. Not cost but utility, usefulness, the capacity to satisfy desires—these are the causes of value. What, they might have asked, is a mouse trap worth which costs a million man-hours of labor if no one knows of its existence, or it will not work, or there are no mice that need catching? In all these cases the mouse trap has no value.

Three anticipators of what is now generally called the Austrian school were Hermann Gossen (a German), Stanley Jevons (an Englishman), and Leon Walras (a Frenchman). Gossen first enunciated what are now the accepted laws of demand saying (1) that people have diminishing desires for goods as they acquire successive units and (2) that the consumers will attain maximum welfare when the satisfaction of the last units of all goods and services purchased are proportional to their respective prices. Given a certain income and a choice of goods to buy at given prices, consumers will purchase those goods which give them most satisfaction. As the satisfaction of the successive units of goods falls, consumers will shift to other goods. Finally, they will maximize their individual satisfactions when the last unit of every good purchased gives a quantitatively measurable amount of satisfaction (marginal utility) which is equal to the utility of the money paid to acquire the last unit (the price). This amount of utility will also be equal to the utility of the last unit of every other good the consumer has acquired. Thus, according to Gossen, marginal utility determines prices (since in a competitive system prices will adjust to reflect collective marginal utilities). Prices will reflect desires and hence are the measure of value. Jevons and Walras came to similar conclusions independently, Walras suggesting also that value was a function of scarcity.

The three principal Austrian marginal utility economists, Karl Menger, Friedrich von Wieser, and Eugen von Bohm Bawerk, all refined marginal utility theory into laws of demand. Emphasis was placed on the subjective nature of value and on the marginal calculus as the device for determining prices and outputs in a free market. With the systemization of demand theory by the Austrians, economics was put on a more scientific basis. Ever since this time new theories have been based on older ones. There has been a continuity of economic thought going back to the Austrian school, and economists have concentrated on building on established foundations rather than creating entirely self-sufficient systems as Smith and Mill had done.

NEOCLASSICAL CAPITALISM

It was for Alfred Marshall, an English genius of the first order, to resolve the conflict between the classical and Austrian value theories, shore up the philosophical underpinnings of classical capitalism and take the initiative away from the Marxists. Marshall's restatement of classical economics, which is still the basis of most price-output-distribution analysis, was sophisticated and (within its assumptions) complete. Assuming that in the market were many buyers and sellers having full knowledge of alternatives, acting independently, and dealing in identical goods, Marshall discarded natural law and made the Austrian utility theory the basis of economics. The goals of the economic system became the maximization of efficiency and total satisfaction. These could be achieved automatically through pure competition and laissez faire. The pleasure-pain psychology of Bentham was replaced by a more tangible concept of utilities and costs. Of course, utilities or satisfactions are not quantitatively measurable, but the prices people are willing to pay, or have to pay, can be used to compare them relatively and qualitatively.

Marshall settled the cost versus demand conflict in value theory by use of his famous scissors thesis saying, by analogy, that both blades are needed to cut. In the short run, demand (utility) determines prices and sales or outputs; in the long run, costs are determining. If prices in the long run do not cover total costs, the supply will decline through contraction of output or bankruptcies, and prices will rise. If prices exceed total costs in the long run, supply will rise and prices fall as new firms enter the industry or existing firms expand output up to the point where they maximize their aggregate profits.

The concept of the function of a purely competitive market has not been notably advanced since Marshall's first statement of it. Consumers' preferences are expressed as demand for goods and services. People will buy more at lower prices than higher prices because the utility of the last unit purchased (marginal utility) is less than the utility of the next to last unit purchased. Marginal utility declines, as does the price which consumers will pay, as output rises because the satisfaction given by a unit of output is an inverse function of the number of units which the consumer already possesses or has recently consumed.

If the supply of goods declines relative to demand, the price will rise because consumers will bid against each other by offering higher prices. However, since the intensity of different peoples' desires or needs varies, the goods and services will tend to go to those who want them most as evidenced by these peoples' readiness to pay more and hence sacrifice something else to get them. If the supply increases, the prices will fall because sellers will compete by offering lower and lower prices. Thus price measures preference. The desires people have will be measured by the prices they are willing to pay. Of course, this would only be strictly true if incomes were equal. Otherwise, the whims of the rich could be satisfied before the urgent needs of the poor.

Prices in the Marshallian system tend to stabilize where demand equals supply. If the price is above this point, sellers compete, and prices fall. If the price is below this point, buyers vie with each other, and prices rise. If a high price arises because tastes change or income or population grows, new suppliers will enter business, or existing firms will increase their output or capacity. Since the law of diminishing returns causes average costs of production to rise eventually, an equilibrium point will be reached at which the price consumers are willing to pay just equals the cost of producing the last unit of output to meet this demand. Thus prices not only reflect the relative intensities of human wants, plus ability to pay, but they are also the automatic governors of an economic system that distributes goods and services according to demands of consumers and costs of production.

The last great theorist of the classical school is the British economist A. C. Pigou, who succeeded to Marshall's chair at Cambridge. It is interesting to note that in his well-known book *Socialism versus Capitalism* he follows Marshallian logic to what appears to be an inevitable socialist conclusion. If the goal of the competitive economic system is to maximize material human welfare, and laissez-faire capitalism with free competition is the device through which this goal is achieved, then it follows that income equality is necessary to secure the goal. Only with income equality will the high-priority demands some people have for necessities be satisfied before the lower-priority demands of others for luxuries. Of course, equal incomes would reduce progressiveness by destroying incentives, but then classical economics was essentially static and looked toward achieving an equilibrium of satisfactions and costs, not an optimum rate of growth through time.

The collapse of the market system in 1929 and the large and durable unemployment which followed for a decade dealt a severe blow to the classical theory. It finally laid to rest the accepted, classical conclusion that the production of a supply of goods creates an effective demand which automatically clears the market, thus making general overproduction or unemployment impossible. In the early 1930's, however, many economists sought an explanation for the Great Depression in what was obviously a disappearance of those features of the market system which were assumed to be necessary if pure competition was to prevail.

Particularly, the latter-day classicists argued that general unemployment was due to monopolies and inflexibilities in the capitalistic economies of the world. The basic arguments were, in general, well taken. It was obvious that output and employment had fallen far more than prices in the manufacturing sector where production was controlled by a few firms. In agriculture, where no such concentration existed, output had remained relatively constant or increased while the price structure had completely collapsed. However, the practical difficulties involved in restoring competition in industry were enormous. Furthermore, the political sympathies of some classicists were with the business community. It seemed to them to be unfair to blame businessmen for the depression especially since the degree of business concentration could well be due mostly to technical economies of scale. Some classicists, therefore, sought an explanation for the depression in labor activity. The refusal of workers—both organized and unorganized—to accept pay cuts, they said, prevented labor costs from falling and hence caused business losses when demand fell.

This reasoning failed to recognize what was becoming an obvious relationship between wages and demand. As a consequence, professional acceptance was not enthusiastic. Since the unemployment was general throughout most of the industrialized world and not restricted to a single firm or industry, since industry generally depended on mass consumption, and since workers and their families comprise most of the population, wage cuts would surely have reduced demand still further and intensified the cumulative downward spiral of production and employment.

A practical difficulty arose as well. The changed political climate of the 1930's shifted power toward labor, and it became as unpopular and impractical to advocate wage reductions and union-busting as it had been to advocate price reductions and trust-busting in the 1920's. Thus, no serious attempt was made to reform the economy along the lines of the assumptions of the theoretical classical or neoclassical models.

In 1933, almost simultaneously and apparently coincidentally, two strikingly similar theoretical studies appeared. These studies attempted to analyze the capitalist market system in terms of monopolistic practices which had grown, or been grafted, onto otherwise competitive situations. The new approach, called monopolistic or imperfect competition, was nicknamed the "Cambridge Theory" for its two creators, Joan Robinson and Edward H. Chamberlain, who worked independently—the former at Cambridge, England, and the latter at Harvard in Cambridge, Massachusetts.

The general framework of the Cambridge Theory was not essentially different from the orthodox system of neoclassical economics developed by Marshall. Economic models were still abstracted from reality by assuming a static set of conditions in which institutions are permanent, the historical context was ignored, and the rationality of households, workers, and entrepreneurs still instituted the forces which determine prices and production. However, some of the neoclassical assumptions concerning the factors which influence the operation of markets were abandoned for a more realistic set of conditions relative to numbers of firms and consumers, differentiation of products, elasticity of supply and demand, consumers' sovereignty, and, in general, non-price competition. Robinson and Chamberlain were most interested in market situations in which there were many small sellers, each selling a product differentiated by design or advertising to the extent that buyers expressed effective preferences, but where prices and outputs of the firms were relatively independent of each other.

Some significant new conclusions were reached by these economists. Advertising and product differentiation, which produce consumer preferences for products, cause demand to be less elastic. This permits price increases to be profitable, although the monopoly profits from limited control over prices tend to be absorbed by the selling costs rather than accrue to the seller. Thus high monopolistic prices and restricted production might be accompanied by normal, competitive profits. Nevertheless, imperfect competition theory has remained inadequate as anything more than a partial explanation of market behavior in a few selected situations which are limited largely to the retail markets for consumers' goods.

The neoclassical theory in general has not been outstandingly successful in dealing with the economic system as a whole. Its usefulness has been limited to providing sound guides for governmental policies toward competition in the market. Modern capitalism in America and abroad no longer conforms to the limiting neoclassical assumptions of pure competition among small, independent, rational producers. Yet the methodology is, so far, the best available for analyzing many of the particular phenomena of prices, production, and the distribution of income payments for the use of labor, capital, natural resources, and management. Furthermore, the neoclassical concept of the rational market economy, in which all resources are put to their most profitable and productive uses and in which human welfare is maximized with the least cost, has become the cornerstone of all economic systems. All other models of the economic system must demonstrate that the advantages they claim for increased realism and relevance are not more than offset by the loss of objectivity and quantitative expression of which only the neoclassical model of competitive capitalism can boast.

3

Evolutionary Capitalism:
German Historical Theory

He who would divine the future must study the past.
——Plutarch

By the science of National or Political Economy, we understand the science which has to do with the laws of the development of economy of a nation, or with its economic national life.——Wilhelm Roscher

ATTACK OF THE GERMAN HISTORICAL SCHOOL

An economic doctrine as abstract and rigid as the classical theory of Adam Smith and Ricardo was destined to produce strong repercussions. One of the most penetrating and durable of such reactions was found in the rise of the German historical school. While the classical school held sway in England and France during the 1840's and before John Stuart Mill had tempered the more rigid features of it, a reaction began in Germany with the writings of Wilhelm Roscher, Bruno Hildebrand, Karl Knies, and, somewhat later, Gustav Schmoller.

BACKGROUND. These economists were strongly influenced by the German philosopher Georg Hegel and the legal theorist F. K. von Savigny. Hegel had stressed the importance of the state as an institution and the necessity for studying history in order to interpret the present. Savigny had explained the legal institutions of Germany in terms of a long evolutionary development. In general, Germany had long been governed by a powerful political bureaucracy, and consequently there had been great stress on the study of public administration. Government control was so pervasive that Germans characteristically looked on it as an integral part of their lives. This was in sharp contrast to England where the classical school grew up in an atmosphere of impersonal social organization with great emphasis on the importance of the individual. Classical economics hardly referred to the state at all except for some superficial allusions to taxation.

The early English classicists and J. B. Say in France had reduced economics to a system of refined theoretical propositions concerning rent, profits, wages, and exchange which could be expressed with mathematical precision. Although use of scientific methods had separated economics as a discipline from philosophy and history and thus significantly raised its stature in a world dominated by growing rationalism, the new theoretical economic system nevertheless consisted in essence of a few obvious truths having only a remote connection with the real world.

First reactions are often the most violent, and many of the opponents of classical political economy were tempted to abandon all abstract theory and confine economics to mere description of economic institutions and events. While classical economics was in its ascendency in the first decades of the nineteenth century, socialists were already criticizing it for its excessive reliance on untested theories and for its unrealistic conclusions. But the socialists employed history only for illustration, and it was not until the German historical school arose that any attempt was made to reconstruct economics as a science through a combination of theoretical analysis and observation of economic phenomena.

Early in the nineteenth century some criticism of the English classicists had come from the German romanticist economists Adam Mueller and Friedrich List. Mueller (1779-1829) is generally considered the founder of the romantic school of economic thought. Following the social philosophies of Rousseau and Hegel, Mueller thought of the economy as a spiritual being which was more than the sum of its individual components. It was assumed to be a continuing entity which governments should nourish by creating national feeling and consciousness. To Mueller this was a religious necessity because he believed that salvation came not through rationalistic individualism, which he felt promoted personal greed, but through occupational organizations, which alone could promote humility, charity, and the proper respect for order and status. Mueller was critical of the Industrial Revolution, the English classicists, individualism, rationalism, and personal freedom. He especially deplored classical individualism, preferring a return to the static system of medieval times. To him, the Middle Ages represented the highest achievement of order, security, and spiritual life. He advocated the establishment of a national economic order because he believed the state to be a spiritual entity responsible for protecting economic institutions.

Friedrich List (1789-1846) went on to argue that the welfare of the nation rather than that of individuals was most significant and that to increase this national welfare required measures which varied with differing circumstances. Economic laws were thus assumed to be relative to their environment. List became the leading spokesman for a distinctly national economy. Particularly, he was concerned with trade. He believed that a nation passed through stages of economic development and that the policies appropriate for one stage were not appropriate for another. Free trade might be the best policy for England at the time but unsuitable for Germany and America since the latter nations had not yet established themselves in the commercial and industrial world. Accordingly, he advocated extreme protectionist and nationalist policies for Germany in the 1840's.

It was later in the nineteenth century, however, that the historical economists first came to grips with the classicists on basic issues. On the descriptive side, the historical economists amassed mountains of relevant and irrelevant factual information. On the practical side, they put their theory into practice by producing volumes of economic, sociological, and historical studies which greatly influenced legislation in Germany and throughout the world. On the critical side, they analyzed the classical system of political economy and pointed to some of its theoretical weaknesses. On the positive theoretical side, they attempted, for the first time, to formulate an explicit theory of capitalism. Although all of these aspects of historical economics were important, emphasis in this chapter is on the theory of capitalism as developed by later historical economists. Of course, some preliminary references to the concrete criticisms of classical economics is necessary in order to put the positive theory of capitalism in proper perspective. In spite of its weaknesses, the theory of capitalism was the first analytical model of an economic system. It formed the foundation for the theorizing of more recent economists who have constructed useful models using the framework first suggested by the historical school.

The earlier historical economists, especially Wilhelm Roscher (1817-1894), Bruno Hildebrand (1812-1878), and Karl Knies (1821-1898), attacked the classical economics of Smith and Ricardo on three major points. First, they deplored the alleged classical claim for universality of economic laws. Roscher, who was the first German historical economist, did not actually deny that abstract theory had any value, but he nevertheless insisted that investigation and description were more important and that the study of history would ultimately round out existing theories. Hildebrand, who was in some respects the most extreme and intolerant critic of classical economics, also believed that the historical method would recast economics along more scientific lines.

Knies, the most persistent and thorough of the early historical economists, distinguished between natural and economic laws and accused the classicists of claiming absolutism for economic laws which were in fact only relative tendencies. The implication was that whereas there might be universal laws in natural science, there would not be any in economics. Hildebrand did not go as far as this but did charge the classicists with claiming that certain basic economic principles underlay all economies at all times. The historical economists generally believed that such claims were untenable in view of the widely varying social, legal, and religious institutions in different countries.

In answer to this criticism, it should be pointed out that, in general, the classical economists made no such extravagant claims. Smith spoke almost entirely in terms of tendencies, and, although Ricardo formulated rigorous laws, most of the historical economists leveled their attacks on the classical school after John Stuart Mill's *Principles* had been published in 1848 and in which the strictness of Ricardian doctrine was tempered considerably. Knies' classification of natural and economic laws seems particularly ill-founded (in retrospect) since the more recent acceptance of the idea that all laws are relative to given factual situations. Physical scientists themselves today hold that their laws are only generalizations from their hypotheses and experiments. New facts or new hypotheses are constantly modifying scientific laws. Nevertheless, the historical critics performed a needed service in reminding those classicists who were prone to forget that claims for universal application of principles are out of place anywhere and particularly in the social sciences.

The second major point on which the historical economists attacked the classicists involved the latters' excessive use of deduction, or reasoning from general premises to particular cases. It is all too true that classical economists often started with inadequate premises and gave insufficient attention to observation which would have tested their conclusions. Ricardo, particularly, engaged in long chains of deductive reasoning which led to the most unrealistic conclusions. His logic could not be contested, but the excessive use of it—to the exclusion of empirical verifications which would have easily demonstrated the fallacies in his assumptions—can hardly be defended.

The German historical economists performed a service here also, but some of them went too far and attacked abstraction itself. They argued that new knowledge would come only through the accumulation of descriptive and statistical material, not through reasoning from old, abstract propositions. Probably the inductive method of generalizing, or reasoning from particular instances to general conclusions, is more useful in economics than deduction. But the classical overemphasis on deduction hardly invited an attack on abstract reasoning itself or even deduction. For how else are we to learn anything new? In a field as complex and as subject to complicating outside influences as economics, deductive analysis is often the only way of reaching any higher level of knowledge. Of course, if the assumptions are unrealistic, the analysis will not be very useful. But when the assumptions embody some force which, among other forces, predominates, then the analysis will lead to conclusions of great value.

The third attack of the historical economists was on the psychological assumptions of the classicists. Smith and Ricardo had assumed that man was dominated entirely by the pursuit of personal gain. The Germans reminded them that other motives ranging from vanity to altruism exist and that habits, customs, or the dominance of environment may replace personal motives altogether.

Here the same answer can be made as that to the attack on abstract reasoning. If self-interest is the major influence on human behavior, then an analysis based on it has more value than a mere description of a host of motives. The later classicists, from John Stuart Mill on, treated self-interest as the most constant and permanent motive in collective human behavior, and it is with this aggregate human activity that economics is concerned, not the random actions of individuals. The later classicists did not deny the existence of noneconomic motives but merely considered them, en masse, less important than self-interest. Nevertheless, the Germans did force the classicists to be more precise in stating their premises and distinctions.

HISTORICAL ECONOMIC THEORY. From a positive theoretical standpoint, the early German historical economists contributed an entirely new concept of the scope and method of economics. The later writers of this school tried to explain economic phenomena by constructing a theoretical model of capitalism and analyzing its development and operation. This was the first systematic attempt to study economics in terms of an entire national system.

Early Historical School. The early historical concept of the scope and method of economics was largely implicit in the criticism of classical economics. No economist, it was said, should be content to try to explain economic phenomena entirely in terms of mechanical principles without reference to history. The present could have no meaning without reference to the historical context in which current affairs exist. The purely mechanical concepts of changes in prices, wages, rent, interest, and profits may well be adaptable to the application of scientific and engineering principles, but a whole host of important economic phenomena was being ignored if economics confined itself to this. The differences between nations, or between different areas or groups within the economy, had not been explained, nor had the conditions leading to long-run changes in economic institutions, such as commercial policies, monetary systems, industrial relations, etc. If all of the different aspects of economic life were to be explained, economic activity would have to be studied in relation to its cultural environment because man's economic action constantly interacts with his physical, social, and political surroundings.

The social environment was considered by the historical economists to be evolving rather than fixed, as the classicists had assumed. Since institutions are developing through time, explanation requires a resort to history. Thus the historical economists tried to explain economic phenomena in terms of changing historical conditions. Here they had a clue to the view which modern economists hold toward history. History, according to Hildebrand, should be used to reformulate economic theory. Economics was to become a science of growth and national development. In spite of their rejection of the natural economic laws of the classicists, some of the historical economists tried to formulate new laws of economic development. Roscher, for example, noted that different nations pass through similar phases in the course of their economic development. He maintained that there were economic laws at work here and by studying the history of existing civilizations in view of these laws it would be possible to predict the course of their future development.

Unfortunately, the historical economists did not succeed in finding any economic laws or founding any economic science based on historical development. History can help in clarifying and testing basic assumptions of economic theory, but the use of historical data does not easily lead to scientific prediction because true science requires generalizations history can never provide. For one thing, the right kind of historical records are seldom available. Often when they are, they usually record only what happened but not why it happened. Even the opinions of trained observers on the scene are often unreliable because there are many causes of every historical event and some of the main ones may not become obvious until much later. It has been said that history only repeats itself for those who refuse to learn its lessons. Actually, history never repeats itself exactly. Even when the same event occurs again, it cannot be said to have been repeated for exactly the same reasons if only because the later event has more history behind it. The economic historian must pick out what seem to him to be the most important causes, and this always involves subjective opinions and feelings based on his personal experiences. Thus the German historical school increased the world's store of descriptive facts but could not raise the level of its knowledge. This can come only through abstract reasoning toward logical conclusions. This reasoning may partially explain an event which occurred in a particular set of circumstances if both the event and the circumstances are relatively simple and isolated from other events and circumstances. But the major events of history still do not yield to scientific analysis upon which generalizations can be based because no simple, logical succession of events, such as animal reproduction or water vaporization, can be assumed to occur in history.

Later Historical School. The later historical school was represented by Gustav Schmoller, who wrote mostly in the 1870's, and by Max Weber and Werner Sombart, who wrote in the early twentieth century. Schmoller's contribution to economics consisted mostly of his collection of large amounts of empirical data. Although he tried to combine theory and institutions, his writing is almost completely descriptive. In fact, he did not believe that anything new could be learned from deductive reasoning but that the only progress would have to come from collecting current and historical statistics over a long period of time and then making some observations from this data. Schmoller doubted whether enough data could be collected in one or even two or three generations to permit any valid generalizations. His writings, consequently, contain very little of anything that could be called theory. He represents the ultimate reaction against the pure deduction of Ricardo. His four-volume study of economic principles deals almost entirely with economic conditions and institutions such as property, population, technology, business enterprises, banks, and unemployment insurance. Nevertheless, they are authoritative, penetrating, and mature.

In a manner characteristic of the Germans under the Bismarck regime, Schmoller was engrossed in the study of countless practical problems and did little generalizing from his data. Hence, his contribution to theory was meager, and this was to be his greatest weakness. No amount of description, no matter how accurate, can be anything more than the first step toward new knowledge. A science must be explanatory, not merely descriptive, and explanation requires reasoning from the facts. As Raymond Poincaré has said,

"An accumulation of facts is no more a science than a heap of stones is a house." Still, Schmoller made a contribution by placing economic problems in a more proper political context. He was a strong advocate of conservative German nationalism and constantly recommended policies to be pursued in order to achieve his objectives. In this way, he showed that economics could be closely allied with political policies.

Of far greater significance to economic theory were the sociological-historical-economic works of Max Weber, Werner Sombart, and the celebrated British Christian socialist R. H. Tawney. Although these writers were concerned with institutions, as were the other historical economists of their day, they all wrote in the early twentieth century when the inductive method of Schmoller's day was beginning to fall into disrepute. Interest in Germany was turning once again to theory although enriched by the broad political and institutional studies of the earlier historical school.

The great contributions of Sombart, Weber, and Tawney were in their studies of the rise, growth, and characteristics of the capitalistic economic system. Although Weber and Sombart were to some extent influenced by another German economist, Karl Marx, they went considerably beyond Marx in studying the relation between economic, social, and religious institutions. Sombart went even further than Tawney in trying to build a theoretical model of the capitalist system. Earlier, Marx had developed a new economic methodology and had analyzed the capitalist process from a historical point of view, but his assumptions were highly classical in some respects, and his approach was so revolutionary that he was immediately in a class by himself. He was never accepted as a member of the German historical school. Furthermore, the historical school lost ground in the twentieth century for its failure to produce any worthwhile theory and collapsed almost altogether after the defeat of Germany in World War I. However, Marxist economics grew steadily in influence in the early twentieth century, particularly in continental Europe. For these reasons, the Marxist theory of capitalism and its later revisions are reserved for a separate chapter.

THEORIES OF THE RISE OF CAPITALISM

Werner Sombart tried to trace the rise of capitalism to certain qualities of the Jews who began to become important in Northern Europe in the late Middle Ages. To Sombart, the Jewish religion was a construction of the intellect designed to control nature and create a worldly empire in her stead. The Jew combined the qualities of a perfect capitalist. He was held, by Sombart, to be intelligent, rational, thrifty, humorless, and devoted to the single purpose of making money. Sombart's obsession with the Jewish mentality led him to some fantastic conclusions and caused him to ignore the fact that Judaism ranks priests, scholars, and soldiers over merchants. Sombart also overlooked the fact that in the early capitalist social order Jews were usually excluded. Furthermore, capitalism sprang up in places like Spain and Scotland where Jews were notably absent. Sombart argued suggestively rather than scientifically, and there has never been any validation of his argument associating Jews with the rise of capitalism. Unfortunately, although he was not anti-Semitic himself he unwittingly played into the hands of the Nazi racists.

In his philosophy and method of studying economic phenomena, Sombart was influenced by both Schmoller and Marx but managed to combine some of the stronger elements of both and reject the weaker. Following the tradition of the earlier historical school, Sombart believed that there were no absolute, universal economic laws and that consequently economic institutions were relative both in space and time. However, he rejected the extreme empiricism of Schmoller and tried to engage in constructive logical analysis which could lead to generalizations. Sombart considered Schmoller a "mere historian," capable of description only, and not an economist capable of analysis. Yet at the same time Sombart avoided, without specifically rejecting, the refined, abstract, deductive types of analysis which Marx used and which were so typical of the early classical school —particularly Ricardo and Nassau Senior. Instead, Sombart introduced a speculative type of analysis which suggests possible solutions without reducing the variables to mathematical precision. In this respect, the flavor of Sombart's writing is reminiscent of the old German Romantic novels.

An example of this speculative, romantic analysis is Sombart's study of culture. Culture, he believed, is a projection of the mind and consequently does not exist in concrete reality as does nature. Economics, law, religion, and art are all cultural systems which derive their existence from human minds and not from any supernatural source as perhaps natural systems, as chemistry, do. People, then, may understand and appreciate a cultural system by going through the same experiences and thought processes together but not by weighing empirical evidence objectively.

Sombart, Weber, and Tawney used essentially this kind of analysis to trace the growth and development of capitalism although they came to somewhat different conclusions. Of the three, Sombart made the greatest contribution to the theory of capitalism, but Weber and Tawney were far more accurate in analyzing the development of the system. It was the Weber-Tawney theory of the rise of capitalism which became the generally accepted one.

Weber and Tawney both argued that Protestantism created the moral and political conditions in which capitalism could grow.[1] Capitalism was impossible before the Reformation because of the prevailing religious philosophy, which emphasized respect for authority and tradition, suppression of worldly desires, and striving for spiritual salvation in the next world. Tawney, especially, tried to show that the au-

---

[1] Max Weber, *The Protestant Ethic and the Theory of Capitalism* (London, 1930). R. H. Tawney, *Religion and the Rise of Capitalism* (New York: Harcourt Brace & Co., Inc., 1926). See also Tawney's *The Acquisitive Society* and *Equality* which analyze the social framework of capitalism.

thoritative domination of the Roman Catholic church deterred the evolution of the underlying fundamentals leading toward economic liberalism and capitalism.

In the Middle Ages, all thought led to religion, and religion guided all thought. Economics was a part of ethics which was, in turn, a part of religion. According to Tawney, the best and most typical of medieval thought did not scorn or ignore economics as something pertaining only to this world. Rather, economic activity, like all human activities, was controlled and guided by the concept of a Christian society so that it would not interfere with, but rather would contribute to, man's spiritual life. Trade and manufacture were regarded as means, not ends. Interest was roundly denounced because it was a species of the deadly sin of avarice. Thomas Aquinas, for example, had argued that interest was a payment for time, that time belonged to God, and hence man should not be paid for that which was God's. Exceptions nevertheless were made to allow the great banking houses to charge for the use of funds. The exceptions were allowed partly because of the pressure of commercial interests on the Church and partly because the Church realized that the loans made by the banks were not for the purpose of consumption but to increase production—an important distinction. Then as now, it was the small loan shark whose evil practices were subject to attack, not the great commercial banks.[2]

The Church itself indulged in certain of the practices which it condemned. Priests indulged in trade and usury, and cathedrals lent money at high interest rates. In fact, the Papacy is said to have been the greatest single financial institution of the late Middle Ages.

The early Protestant reformers accepted the medieval Catholic view of business practices. Luther and other Protestant leaders felt that the truly Christian society had been

[2] The author is indebted to a former graduate student at Georgia Institute of Technology, Mr. Porter Dobbins, who first expressed some of the ideas discussed in an unpublished review of Tawney, *Religion and the Rise of Capitalism*.

betrayed by the Catholic church in the Renaissance by just such practices as described above. Calvin's Geneva was as anti-individualistic and antimaterialistic as the sternest ascetic could wish. Yet trouble soon developed as prosperous businessmen began to resent the clerical control of their activity which often appeared in the name of furthering and maintaining the Christian community. Nor was the resentment limited to Geneva. In England the commercial possessors of former church property were tasting the pleasures of high profits and were not disposed to listen to the clergymen who told them their business activities should be operated with the good of society in view. Business ethics were being separated from religion. The old unity of outlook was dissolving. Life, instead of being thought of as an organic whole, culminating and controlled by religion, was becoming a tightly compartmentalized affair where religion on the one hand and economics and life in general on the other were carefully and happily isolated from each other.

The first Protestant reformers did not advocate individualistic capitalism. The religious revolt coincided with vast economic changes brought about by new geographic discoveries and changes in trade routes. The rising middle classes were quick to realize that since the uniformity of Christian economic thought was already broken, the new and pliant Protestant thought could be reconciled to defend the new economics. Thus economic forces were at work molding religious beliefs.

The new commercial classes, who everywhere were challenging the monarchs and the landed aristocracy, found themselves also challenging the established churches, whether Catholic or Protestant, because the churches and monarchs were in close alliance. Thus the new capitalists revolted against the Anglican church in England, the Lutheran church in Scandinavia, and the Catholic church in Italy. Even where the churches survived these attacks, they became increasingly secularized until religion became largely a matter for Sunday observance. The basic incompatibility between classical capitalism, with its mechanistic, individualistic philosophy, and Christianity was forgotten, and a dualism arose which uncertainly embraced both. The churches accepted capitalism in principle very easily and confined their criticism not to private property and the profit motive but to the commercializing of human values. Thus capitalism emerged as political victor over the monarchs and philosophical victor over the churches, both Protestant and Catholic. A possible exception is the Spanish peninsula where it is said that there has been every kind of revolution except the Industrial Revolution.

Under Calvin and Luther, material success became evidence of spiritual salvation if tempered with worldly asceticism. The goal of material success created a capitalistic spirit. Man had a moral duty to make the best use of his talents and produce as much as possible. He also had a duty to restrain his consumption. Thus the admonition to maintain the homey virtues of thrift and modesty, while producing vigorously, logically led to the large savings necessary for the accumulation of capital goods upon which capitalism has to be based. But diligence in production and restraint in consumption, while inevitably producing savings, would still not necessarily lead to the creation of capital. However, a third distinctive feature of the new Protestant theology was that the surplus should be productively invested. Other philosophies have required other uses for any economic surplus. In ancient Egypt it went for pyramids, in India for palaces and hosts of servants, in medieval Europe for cathedrals and charity. Some other philosophies have required productive investment too, but in the Protestant theology of this period is found a unique combination of the hard, consecrated effort, the thrift, and the productive investment that leads to capitalism.

Two concepts were summoned to justify the new capitalist movement. One was Calvin's doctrine of the calling. Just as a man had a spiritual calling so did he have a temporal one. Success in his temporal calling showed his hard work and proved that God had personally favored him. The doctrine of the calling was an attempt to link religion and economics, but unlike medieval thought the new philosophy subordinated ethics to economics. Thrift was considered a virtue. Charity, high wages, or shorter working hours were considered means of ruining the characters of workers who tended naturally to loaf or live riotously.

The other device used to justify the new capitalistic system was the law of nature. The advancement of private interests was thought to be to the advantage of the public. Pursuit of self-interest was considered the law of nature, which itself was the Law of God. Soon John Locke was to assert the sanctity of private property, and Adam Smith the beneficence of competition. Certainly Darwin's theories, as much later applied (or prostituted) by Herbert Spencer to economic life, strengthened the idea that capitalism was a reflection of the law of nature. The biological concept of survival of the fittest became with Spencer the economic basis for laissez faire. In a jungle of uncontrolled competition, the strong would devour the weak and the race of capitalists would improve.

Avarice, denounced in the Middle Ages as a deadly sin, was now, under other names, the goal of life, and material success the standard by which men were to be measured. As J. M. Keynes expressed it, "Modern capitalism is absolutely irreligious, without internal union, without much public spirit, often, though not always, a mere congeries of possessors and pursuers."

Max Weber also studied social organization extensively and concluded that the most significant feature of advanced capitalism was bureaucracy. This was the inevitable product of the division of labor. Particularly, he argued that the goals of the capitalistic system modify and ultimately control people's lives, turning them into functional offices rather than rounded individuals.

In his last major study, which was on comparative religion, Weber took a broader view. He concluded that the Christian religion in general was favorable to capitalism— that differences between Christianity and other religions were greater in economic significance than the differences between Catholicism and Protestantism. The Chinese who was not satisfied with the world tried to adapt to it; the Hindu tried to withdraw from it; whereas the Christian's solution to this problem was to change the world to suit his needs or desires. To Weber, only the Christian view was compatible with the growth of a materialistic, progressive, scientific, and capitalistic spirit. True, the dominant Catholic attitude in medieval times resembled more the Hindu in that tacit acceptance of the status quo was advocated, but this view rapidly broke down with the Renaissance and even in medieval times trade and commerce flourished in nominally Catholic cities such as Genoa and Florence.

Thus, with some exceptions, the Weber-Tawney theory of the rise of capitalism as a product of the Protestant Reformation seems valid. Medieval Christianity did deter the capitalistic spirit and capital investment. Early Protestantism, while not advocating individualism as such, did encourage initiative, thrift, restraint in consumption, and productive investment. Where these conditions had existed in medieval times, it was because church authority was weak and its rules were not enforced. It may have been the fact of the Reformation itself, which permitted experiment and change, as much as Protestant philosophy, which led to capitalism, but capitalism did follow Protestantism everywhere it broke out. Capitalism of a sort did flare up briefly in Catholic northern Italy, but only from Protestant-dominated areas did it grow and spread to other areas to become a predominant and lasting economic system.

SOMBART'S THEORY OF CAPITALISM

Werner Sombart's greatest achievement was in his gigantic three-volume *Der Moderne Kapitalismus,* which examined and analyzed the evolution of capitalism from the beginning of the Renaissance down to the present time.[3] He classified

[3] *Der Moderne Kapitalismus* (Munich, 1921–1927). The following pages are based on Sombart's celebrated article, "Capitalism," in *Encyclopedia of the Social Sciences,* rather than his original monumental study because in the shorter article the system is most aptly and concisely summarized.

capitalist development in three periods. The first, called early capitalism, began about the year 1200 and lasted until about 1750. This period was characterized by small scale, nonmechanized home industry. The economic environment was dominated by feudal attitudes, particularly traditionalism. Factory production was slight and carried out by guild craftsmen using nonscientific, rule-of-thumb methods. Informal, personal elements played a major role in commercial trade, industrial relations, and the operation of such other organized economic processes as existed at the time.

The second period, called full capitalism, began about 1750 (roughly with the Industrial Revolution) and ended with World War I. This was the most important stage in the evolution of capitalism because it was here that the form and characteristics of the system became established. The Reformation and Renaissance had so weakened the feudal stranglehold on Europe that by the middle of the eighteenth century a new scientific outlook was in vogue. This attitude ultimately gave rise to a series of startling new inventions (such as the steam engine) which made technological progress possible.

The scope of economic activity grew as new inventions and techniques caused production, business units, and markets to expand. The development of scientific technology, motivated by the pursuit of profit and facilitated by a growing rationalism, led to a widespread institutionalization of human relationships. For example, prices, credit relations, and wages became determined by fixed norms rather than on the basis of friendships and personal acquaintances. Economic life became intensely commercialized through rigid application of principles of mechanization and standardization to economic relations, particularly to the credit system with its negotiable securities, speculative markets, futures dealing, and so on. Ownership became divorced from management, and labor and capital became highly specialized. Even within management itself, all sorts of specialists arose such as the production and labor expert, the market specialist, and the financier.

In this period of full capitalism, the dominant spirit, according to Sombart, is based on three concepts. First, acquisition, particularly of money, becomes the motivating purpose of economic activity. This is in sharp contrast to precapitalist societies where making a living involved producing goods for human needs based on long-accepted standards of justice. In full capitalism, acquisition tends to center about an abstraction, the stock of material goods, and is carried out through many abstract, impersonal devices such as the corporation, the holding company, lease, and trust. Acquisition tends to become unconditional and absolute so that it dominates not only the economic realm but spills over into other cultural areas and tends to reduce all values to commercial ones.

The attitudes of acquisition lead to the second concept comprising the capitalistic spirit—competition. In the struggle to acquire material wealth (or money which is merely a claim to material wealth) moral and personal inhibitions are abandoned. The test of behavior becomes its functional suitability for acquisition and nothing more. Thus competition tends to become keen or even ruthless.

Sombart's third concept, on which the capitalistic spirit is based, is rationality. In order to compete for the stock of goods there is an increasing tendency for the perfection of commercial enterprises and institutions to become an end rather than a means. Long-range planning executed through exact calculation is one expression of the acquisition drive. Management, marketing, and industrial relations become increasingly scientific in the sense of the application of exact, quantitative procedures. However, as the enterprise becomes more rational the system as a whole remains irrational, according to Sombart, because unlimited acquisitiveness leaves the regulation of the over-all economic process uncontrolled. Thus many strains and contradictions in capitalism arise.

Individual freedom and private property are important institutions of capitalism. The legal framework protects these institutions so that the private entrepreneur is free to pursue his self-interest within broad limits. This activity is the mainspring of the economic machine. However, an aristocratic social structure is maintained through the high standards of technical knowledge and organizational skill required of the entrepreneural class. This structure prevents the large majority of people from gaining control of the means of production.

The high degree of labor specialization and the well-developed system of exchange based on definite contract rights require that the capitalistic system maintain a high rate of production. Otherwise, the functional separation of management and technical operation breaks down. Hence there is a constant striving for technical improvements because they lead to temporary profit differentials which accrue to the entrepreneur until the improvements become generally used.

The capitalist enterprise is the vehicle for economic activity. The enterprise, or corporation, is an entity in its own right. According to Sombart, it has life, goals, rationality, and even virtues (thrift and stability) which are separate from, and transcend, those of any human individuals. The enterprise infuses human beings with its spirit. The individuals in the management become conditioned to a certain pace and intensiveness of activity which carries over to other activities and thus propagates the capitalist spirit and spreads uniformity of goals and procedures.

The capitalist entrepreneur, says Sombart, is an innovator, conquerer, organizer, and merchant par excellence. More than a mere adventurer, he combines the instincts of the professional trader with the shrewd calculation of the skilled negotiator. Thus, although the capitalist enterprise molds the personalities of the entrepreneurs and submerges the personalities of employees, the individuality of the top leaders remains significantly outstanding. While standardization and specialization have produced a world of almost monotonously uniform productive units, the individual industrial leader is more important than ever. As the capitalist enterprise becomes larger and more complicated, there is a growing need for the humans to tend it. As in governmental or military bureaucracies, the leader becomes ever more indispensable. The Communists in Russia, according to Sombart, failed to see this and almost wrecked their economic system by banishing the entrepreneur. On the other hand, Americans tend to glorify the individual personality over the enterprise, group, or capital as the primary motivating force. More credit goes to individual business leaders, he suggests, than they probably deserve.

Late capitalism, Sombart's third period of capitalist development, began with World War I and is continuing today. In this period industrialization spreads throughout the world and the institutional gap between industrial and agricultural countries closes. The purely capitalistic elements of the economy become blurred as public, cooperative, and mixed enterprises rise up to meet the needs of disadvantaged groups. The ever-growing size of the business enterprise brings a decline in risk, and the entrepreneur finds planning based on systematic calculation increasingly fruitful. As speculation and intuition give way to careful budgeting of production, finances, and sales, the private business organization begins to resemble more a public agency than a capitalist enterprise. The quest for profit may even decline, as evidenced by the tendency for fixed dividend rates, planned reinvestment of surplus, specialized risk-taking, and the creation of reserves. Eventually, concentration and cartels lead to a general decay of the capitalist spirit.

Meanwhile, controls grow. Some come from within, such as bureaucracy, cartels, and, in general, monopolistic organization. Other controls come from organized labor, and still others come from the government in the form of social legislation and direct price or production regulations. Industrial relations become a matter of public concern. Minimum and even guaranteed wages, pensions, workmen's compensation, and unemployment benefits turn labor into a fixed cost to either the entrepreneur or the community. The general drive for stability and security by business, labor, and government cause rigidities to form in the economy. Sombart did not expect capitalism to disappear, but he did anticipate growing state regulation, comprehensive national economic planning, and an increase in cooperative and mixed enterprises. However, a large private sector of the economy, especially in agriculture and small business, was expected to endure indefinitely.

Sombart's evolutionary concept of capitalism was a notable advance, particularly in its classification of the periods of development and the forms and functions of capitalist enterprise. Its description penetrates beyond that of previous writers. However, the lack of empirical data and the statistical techniques to treat them leaves his theory largely in the speculative category. When the data becomes available in the proper form, it is possible that Sombart's general methodology and frame of reference may be used to determine the direction of capitalist evolution.

RECENT HISTORICAL THEORIES OF CAPITALISM

A recent article by Arthur Schweitzer of Indiana University has made a notable contribution to the theory of capitalism by reviewing, comparing, and criticizing the work of the historical economists Karl Polanyi and Bruno Seidel.[4] Polanyi traced the development of capitalism through stages of mercantilism, laissez faire, and social protection. He saw commercialism as separating man from nature and destroying, particularly for farmers and laborers but also for landlords, colonials, and business organizations, the stability and safety man derives from nature. The market system, he felt, created economic disadvantages which would lead to the destruction of both human and natural resources unless prevented by systems of social protection. The concept of

[4] This section is based on Arthur Schweitzer, "Theories of Controlled Capitalism," *Kyklos*, November, 1956, pp. 492-507. Reference is made to Polanyi, *The Great Transformation*, (New York, 1944), and Seidel, *Industrialismus und Kapitalismus* (Meisenheim/Glan: Verlag Anton Hain, 1955).

social protection was defined to include all deviations from the market system including social security, cartels, protective tariffs, and imperialism.

Schweitzer contends that the continuity of Polanyi's social protection concept is overstated. He correctly points out that, in the United States at least, history does not uphold the theory. Except for the farmer-labor movement, social reform movements have typically been directed against specific defects in the market system, not against the system itself. The weakness of Polanyi's theory is seen to be in its failure to define the automatic market system precisely enough. Hence the market system is concluded to be indivisible, universal, and interdependent although there is no proof of how these are deduced. Nor, says Schweitzer, is the theory of economic disadvantage specific enough to support the conclusion that social protection will arise. He gives three reasons. First, there is no theory of markets that exhibit any persistent tendencies toward disequilibrium. Second, Polanyi does not separate inherent market defects from cyclical or monetary disturbances. Third, there is no distinction made between genuine reform movements and mere attempts at monopolistic protection.

Seidel, like other economists in the historical tradition, traces the development of economic systems but makes an important distinction between capitalism and industrialism. His book traces their evolution, interaction, and ultimate conflict. According to Seidel's definitions, industrialism consists of large scale enterprises, mechanization, and an increasing specialization of functions and consequent interdependence. Capitalism is composed of private ownership of productive resources and a market system and is characterized by cyclical fluctuations which are regarded as inevitable consequences of capitalist institutions.

Unlike some other historical theorists, Seidel makes capitalism a prerequisite to industrialism although they reinforce each other. Specifically, the market mechanism of capitalism permits industrial methods to penetrate the most remote sectors of the economic system. After this has occurred, industrialism becomes independent of capitalism. This occurs because Seidel, like Marx, contends that the mode of production is more fundamental than property and income structures. Thus industrialism, especially in its more advanced stages, becomes independent of capitalism and continues to grow unchecked after capitalism—particularly the market system—becomes tamed or controlled.

The essence of industrial technology is in the saving of labor time—an objective which can hardly be opposed. Yet while industrialism has increased living standards enormously it has left man dependent on the total economy. Technology requires extreme specialization, large markets, uniformities of taste, and receptivity to mass advertising. By separating work from living, Seidel sees the door opened to family disintegration, demands for mass entertainment and sports, political demagoguery, and fascism. But, as Schweitzer correctly observes, the conflict between economic and sociological consequences of industrialism and especially the concept of the mass man is long on deductions and short on evidence.

As a remedy, Seidel proposes industrial and residential decentralization. The intervention which has occurred so far has consisted of offsetting workers' economic disadvantages, humanizing of work, and the substitution of group for individual competition. The result: planned capitalism.

Schweitzer clearly analyzes this theory and points up its deficiencies. First, he says, industrialism is not independent of capitalism. He recommends that future research follow the tradition of Sombart and Joseph Schumpeter (see Chapter 7) who, like Marx, include technology in their concept of capitalism. Second, he criticizes Seidel for overemphasizing the impact of technology on society. Third, he rightly objects to a theory of intervention which is so broad as to include the control of many dissimilar groups with different goals and resources.

Schweitzer concludes with his own hypothesis that concentrated property causes technological growth and that both property monopoly and rising living standards have put off any serious movements to control this growth. He recommends further study to develop new theories of (1) property monopoly and its effects on both technology and the market system, (2) deficient and controlled markets, (3) social protection and economic reform under capitalism, and (4) the public sector of the economy. There should be widespread agreement that Arthur Schweitzer's penetrating analysis in this and numerous other articles has contributed greatly to understanding the evolution of capitalism.

CONCLUSION

Underlying the study of all economic systems is the assumption that an economic system has distinguishing characteristics which require special treatment and analysis before an adequate understanding of it can be secured. By implication, the study of economic systems assumes that economic principles are to some extent relative to both time and place. In the classical scheme of things, the study of economic systems would have been largely irrelevant because of the assumption of universal economic laws. It was the German historical school, with its attack on universality of economic laws and its emphasis on evolutionary development and economic relativism, that made the study of economic systems possible. Of course, it is now generally agreed that the early historical economists went too far toward empiricism and disregard for pure theory. The judgment of history has been visited on the historical school itself. Its demise is evidence that an attitude that tends to glorify the past at the expense of failing to apply rigorous thinking to contemporary problems will lose its hold on reality and its appeal to scholars. The modern pragmatic philosophy, which owes so much to the historical school, invokes history only in so far as it aids in the solution of contemporary problems and has much more appeal than the German historical view of attempting to explain all economic problems by reference to their past development. Nevertheless, the contribution of the original historical school was significant for it opened the door to the study of specific economic systems and paved the way for more fruitful analyses which were to follow.

4

Evolutionary Capitalism:
American Institutionalist Theory

> A merchant's desire is not of glory, but of gain; not of public wealth but of private emolument; he is, therefore, rarely to be consulted on questions of war or peace, or any designs of wide extent and distant consequence.——Ben Jonson

> Cumulatively, therefore, habit creates usages, customs, conventions, preconceptions, composite principles of conduct that run back only indirectly to the native predispositions of the race . . . Each new situation is a variation of what has gone before it and embodies as causal factors all that has been effected by what went before——Thorstein Veblen

BACKGROUND OF AMERICAN INSTITUTIONALISM

America has produced numerous outstanding economists, such as Henry Davenport, John Bates Clark, Frank Knight, Alvin Hansen, and many others, who have stood out as brilliant individual lights in the early dawn of American intellectual development. However, most of these particular economists were strongly influenced by more truly original thinkers in England. (One exception was Henry George who has had more influence abroad than in his native America.) Thus Clark represents the best American elaboration and refinement of Alfred Marshall's neoclassical economics while Hansen owes his inspiration to John Maynard

Keynes. While probably the greatest individual economists in America have been identified with the neoclassical and Keynesian schools, there has been only one completely native *school* of economics in America. This is institutionalism. Like the Granger and Populist movements and the early New Deal which were its political counterparts, the institutional school represents a radical, pragmatic, but thoroughly home-grown reaction to complacent American and English orthodoxy.

The institutional school centered around the writings of Richard T. Ely, Thorstein Veblen, John R. Commons, and, in later years, J. M. Clark, Wesley Mitchell, and others. A partial list of the major institutionalists would have to include, in addition to those already mentoned, Adolf Berle, Gardiner Means, Rexford Tugwell, Walton Hamilton, Clarence Ayres, Robert F. Hoxie, M. A. Copeland, and Sumner Slichter.[1] Most of the purely institutionalist writing was done during the first three decades of this century. Although it had a great impact, institutionalism did not develop into a well-ordered movement to the extent that Marxism or English classicism did. Since the 1930's, institutionalism has lost its existence as a separate school in economics and has gradually spread out to affect nearly all contemporary economists. This, if anything, has enhanced its influence.

An institution is a system of norms, rules of conduct, or established ways of thinking. Every economic system operates within a framework of institutions which govern property and income relationships, the division of labor, the methods of distribution, and so on. These institutions influence individual and group economic status, the occupational pattern, control over the means and purposes of production, and the distribution of economic benefits. Institutions had

---

[1] In his exhaustive and authoritative *Modern Economic Thought* (Englewood Cliffs, N. J.: Prentice-Hall, Inc., 1947), Allan Gruchy examines in detail the theories of Veblen, Commons, Mitchell, J. M. Clark, Tugwell, and Means. This is undoubtedly the best restatement of institutional economics in existence although Gruchy imparts more coherence and organization to the institutional school than the present author is prepared to admit.

largely been taken for granted by the classical economists. There had been a tendency on the part of some to ignore institutions altogether while others assumed that they were identical for different societies or that they remained unchanged through time. The rise of institutional economics was largely in response to this obvious inadequacy of the classical system. In this sense it resembled the German historical school.

Economic "laws," like all other "laws," are universal only in abstraction and will operate only within the limiting conditions on which they are based. The institutional economists recognized this and attempted to reconstruct economic theory so that it would conform more closely to the modern world of organized interest groups and rapid change. Institutional economics made its major task the synthesis of economics with other social sciences so that the assumptions of economic theory would be realistic, and hence the conclusions more valid, for a highly industrialized capitalist economic system.

Institutional economics essentially began with the publication of Thorstein Veblen's *Theory of the Leisure Class* in 1899. The institutional approach was conceived in this volume and grew to maturity in the ten other books which Veblen wrote during his life and in the writings of many other economists who caught some of Veblen's spirit and allowed it to inspire them in their own specialized fields. Veblen (1857-1929), an economist and anthropologist of Norwegian parents, was one of America's most brilliant and severe critics. He made a lasting impression on economic and social thought by challenging the basic assumptions of classical theory. Particularly he analyzed and criticized such institutions as private property, profits, absentee ownership, and leisure as being the most influential in determining human behavior.

As Solomon observed, there is nothing completely new under the sun, and, of course, the institutionalists did not spring out of nowhere. Not a few of the leading American social scientists of the late nineteenth and early twentieth centuries studied in Germany, and this influence did not escape the institutionalists although hardly any of them actually studied in Germany themselves. There seems to have been, in fact, three major European influences on the institutionalists. Chronologically, the first was the evolutionary philosophy of the German philosopher Georg Hegel which is in evidence in institutional economics along with some of Marx's modifications of it. The institutionalists were by no means Marxists (Veblen himself was as critical of Marx as of the English classicists), but Hegel's concept of a changing rather than static universe and Marx's economic theory of historical development and emphasis on the changing nature of economic institutions helped to orient the institutionalists' thinking.

A second major influence came from England. Charles Darwin's *Origin of Species* put the Hegelian evolutionary philosophy on sound scientific ground, and the biological theory of evolution, as applied to social phenomenon by the English philosopher, Herbert Spencer, became one of the bases of institutional philosophy. This "Social Darwinism" looked on the economic system as an organism, greater than the sum of its parts, which was in a state of "emergent evolution." Spencer used this evolutionary concept, together with the theories of natural selection and "survival of the fittest," to support the contention that economic processes were deterministic, and hence laissez faire should be the proper attitude of government even though it followed from the theory that monopolization of industry was inevitable because monopoly was "naturally" more efficient than competition. If social evolution was natural, then the relative disadvantage of certain economic groups, or individuals, was natural also, and conscious social action by the government would be useless. The institutionalists rejected this conclusion but accepted the evolutionary assumptions, using them as a basis for collective social controls.

The third and most important heritage of the institutionalists came from Germany again—the influence of the historical school. The historical economists had placed great emphasis on facts rather than abstract ideas and had stressed the relativity of empirical data to particular stages of economic development. Although the early historical economists did not get far beyond the fact-gathering stage, the later writers, such as Sombart and Weber, attempted to theorize from the statistics. They were severely hampered, however, by a lack of refined statistical techniques and, hence, did not get far toward recasting economic theory. Where theoretical deductions were advanced they did not depend on or refer much to the mountains of evidence which they and their forerunners had accumulated. Consequently their theories often did not follow directly from their facts. The American institutionalists owe their greatest debt to the historical economists whose emphasis on gathering facts and studying them in relation to their historical significance rather than as isolated, objective data in a static, timeless model formed the basis for the institutionalist type of thinking.

HISTORICAL–INSTITUTIONAL TRANSITION

The transition from the German historical school to the American institutionalist school is best typified by Simon N. Patten (1852-1922) who has been called the most original and suggestive economist that America has yet produced. Although he studied in Germany and was greatly influenced by the historical economists' attacks on traditional beliefs, Patten cannot easily be classified either as a historical economist or an institutionalist. Like his German teachers, Patten rejected equilibrium theory and static economic models as being devoid of realism. He believed, with the American pragmatic philosophers William James and John Dewey, that social change was the order of the day and that change could not be studied in a static model. Patten revolted against the orthodox economics of his time. He attacked Malthusian population theory and Ricardan rent theory, denied the law of diminishing returns, claimed that monopoly, not competition, was the normal state of affairs, and advocated economic planning by the government. In spite of all this rebelliousness, however, Patten was a great disciple of John Stuart Mill. He accepted Mill's utilitarianism but believed that after a person makes the same "rational" choice time and again, he develops a habit which causes him to continue to make the same choices of goods in the future regardless of the utility received from them. Here Patten was bridging the gap between the classical utilitarian philosophy and the institutionalists' reliance on custom and habit as the motivating forces in consumers' demand.

Patten was the first leading American to recognize the importance of consumption. While the classicists were writing books on the production and distribution of wealth, Patten wrote a book on consumption in 1889. He believed that progress came through habits of consumption if the readily consumable goods were available. Patten also disputed the classical notion that profits tend to fall to a minimum or equilibrium level. Monopoly and the constant growth of technology prevented this, he argued. A perpetual optimist, Patten believed in an economy of abundance. He foresaw continually increasing labor productivity through improvements in capital equipment and development of natural resources. In these areas of thinking he was far ahead of his time.[2]

Patten deplored free competition, believing that it could lead only to a tragic survival of the unfit. Low standard groups would undermine high standard groups until nothing but low standard groups, or at best, mediocrity, would remain. This led to conclusions favoring immigration restrictions, protective tariffs, and strict regulation of private industry. Unfortunately Patten did not resort sufficiently to empirical data to verify his theories, and consequently he was often proved wrong. As in his arguments for tariffs based on his theory of free competition, he used the same abstract, deductive reasoning for which he criticized the classicists. He failed to marshal ordered facts to support his contentions

[2] See Patten, *The New Basis of Civilization* (New York: The Macmillan Co., 1912).

except for carefully selected illustrations which often turned out to be exceptions rather than the general rule. This led him to some ridiculous conclusions. For example, he maintained that low-interest rates were due to past extravagances, and at another time he argued that Americans should be required to eat corn bread rather than wheat bread because the nation was better adapted to growing corn than wheat. Often he was forced to change his position although when shown to be wrong he was always willing to admit his errors frankly. On balance Simon Patten was probably right more often than wrong on many of the subjects, such as labor unionism, pragmatic teaching methods, feminism, and industrial control, for which, among other things, he was an ardent campaigner.

Patten made several definite contributions to economic theory. First, he provided an effective criticism of the classical "economics of scarcity" by showing that in many instances there were increasing rather than diminishing returns to be secured from more intensive and extensive use of resources. Second, he focused thought on technological development and the possibilities of exploiting it. Third, he recognized some basic changes which were occurring in our economy, such as the vanishing of small-scale competitive industry and the rise of modern power relationships. In addition, he enjoyed a boundless optimism that the economic system can be made to serve the best interests of all.

Not only did Patten believe in the effectiveness of economic planning and control but also he discounted the popular opinions of his day (1890-1920) which were solidly against his ideas. Patten noticed that mental attitudes change more slowly than economic conditions but that reality must eventually be faced. He observed further than those ideas which are in the most precarious positions, or are actually in the process of crumbling, often appear to flourish most vigorously just before their collapse. The loudest arguments for some outmoded institution usually appear after there is no longer any economic justification for it. When the economic basis for an institution is gone, the mind must be most ingenious in its defense. In Patten's age, gross income inequality was fighting its fiercest battle against the rise of welfare legislation, and the domination of culture by military and landowning aristocracies was making its last ditch stand against the relentless rise of the industrial state.

BASIS OF INSTITUTIONALISM

INTRODUCTION. Like the sophists of ancient Greece, the institutionalists began with a rejection of all orthodox philosophy as conceived at the time and then proceeded to the arduous task of rebuilding where all the remnants of the past had been swept away. Their skill and brilliance shook the halls of smug complacency and slew many of the giants who had been misleading the classical intellectuals.

Like the historical school, the institutionalists are better known for their cogent and often stinging criticism than for positive, constructive contributions to economic theory. To a large extent this recognition is justified since it is always easier to see clearly certain things that are wrong than to suggest with any degree of precision what might be right. Furthermore, the classical orthodoxy had become so entrenched that the wrecking process itself would have required more than one generation of economists' endeavors before the ground could be cleared and plans for the new foundation put into effect. But the institutionalists did make substantial positive contributions for which proper credit is seldom given. This was because the institutionalists joined in unison in their criticisms (and were jointly recognized) yet did their positive work as individuals in their own specialized fields. Thus the institutional school is usually given credit for the decline of laissez-faire philosophy before Keynes, but the development of collective bargaining theory in America is usually attributed to John R. Commons and Robert Hoxie as individuals. The credit for the most penetrating analysis of corporate relationships and the evolution of concepts of property goes to Adolf Berle and Gardiner Means rather than to the institutional school. Another famous institutionalist, J. M. Clark, is often referred to today as the "dean of American economists" with no reference at all to his institutionalist philosophy.

In general the institutionalists and other dissenters had less faith in human nature than the classicists, who had lived in the "age of enlightenment." They doubted the existence of any harmony of interests, equilibrium, or mechanism whereby first things are automatically and necessarily done first. They looked on economics not as a physical science so much as a biological science in which evolution, change, and growth all play a part.

SOCIAL BEHAVIOR OF INDIVIDUALS. The basic assumptions of the institutionalists were mostly rejections of neoclassical economics. From their first basic assumption institutionalists argued that economics is essentially a cultural and not a formal science. Man, they claimed, is a creature of his cultural environment and cannot be studied apart from it as though he were the Robinson Crusoe who was the popular classical depiction of an "economic man." Man's behavior is social, they said, not individual, and there are no static, immutable laws which govern it. Human behavior is dominated by instincts, habits, and customs. Consequently, the study of collective human behavior is more relevant to economics than individual rationality.

The sociologist Charles H. Cooley had shown in the late nineteenth century that the market mechanism was not the ethically neutral device for recording individual preferences that the classical economists had thought it was. Instead it was a social institution with its own biases and, hence, did not record objectively the actual values of society at all. Individual rationality in the sense that the Austrians and some English neoclassicals thought of it—the product of a human reasoning machine—was therefore rejected.

The hedonistic psychology of Bentham, which had assumed that all of man's actions are an attempt to maximize pleasure or minimize pain, was singled out for special attack by the institutionalists. Veblen succinctly pointed this out in a widely-quoted passage.

The hedonistic conception of man is that of a lightening calculator of pleasures and pains, who oscillates like a homogeneous globule of desire of happiness under the impulse of stimuli that shift him about the area, but leave him intact. He has neither antecedent nor consequent. He is an isolated, definitive human datum, in stable equilibrium except for the buffets of the impinging forces that displace him in one direction or another. Self-imposed in elemental space, he spins symmetrically about his own spiritual axis until the parallelogram of forces bears down upon him, whereas he follows the line of the resultant. When the force of the impact is spent, he comes to rest, a self-contained globule of desire as before.[3]

Although the institutionalists contested the classical concept of human rationality, they certainly did not reject rationality itself. It requires a reasoning mind to question abstract rationality, as Veblen did. The essence of their argument was that rationality is relative to institutions and circumstances. Following the German Gestalt psychology, the institutionalists believed that logical, individual action, economic action, and social action move together like three billiard balls in a bowl. A movement of any one causes movements of the others. The same forces which cause an economy to be coercive, pecuniary, and mechanical also determine consumption habits, social attitudes, manners, and religion. These, in turn, affect economic motives.

A partial exception to this rather behavioristic psychology is found in Veblen's own writings although it was not accepted by all other institutionalists. Veblen distinguished between commercial managers and production managers in his concept of the business enterprise. The commercial or business managers were motivated by a desire for profits regardless of the social costs although their actions were explainable in view of the customs of their class rather than in terms of innate rationality. However, the production managers, the real producers according to Veblen, included the engineers, scientists, and technicians. This group was motivated by an "instinct of workmanship" which led them to seek greater production efficiency as an end in itself.

[3] Thorstein Veblen, *The Place of Science in Modern Civilization* (New York: The Viking Press, Inc., 1919), pp. 73-74.

These production managers, all called "engineers" by Veblen, were constantly being frustrated by the businessmen and financiers of the other group who were just as likely to seek profits through restriction of output or through securities manipulation as through cost reductions or technological innovations. A great social movement called Technocracy was later based on Veblen's assumption of the instinctual behavior of producers and the principles of scientific management developed by the industrial engineer, Frederick Taylor. The later eclipse of this movement demonstrated the inadequacy of both Veblen's and Taylor's hypotheses. Taylor's assumption that men could be treated like machines was as far-fetched as Veblen's belief that production managers behaved instinctually like bees producing honey.

There is certainly some truth, and much usefulness, in the institutionalists' concept of man as being dominated in large part by his society. However, the recognition and assumption of the extremely complex set of social and cultural variables which comprise our society is hardly a fruitful starting point for scientific analysis regardless of how realistic the assumption may be. No human mind can possibly hope to hold at once all the possible, or even principal, factors that determine human economic activity. Nevertheless, the institutionalists preferred to look directly at the sun, even though some might be blinded by its intense light, rather than trying to grope in an abstract world of simple shadows and deduce, by logic, the nature of reality.

The institutionalists were strongly impressed by the works of sociologists, particularly Charles H. Cooley, James Baldwin, and G. Stanley Hall, and anthropologists like William G. Sumner who were arguing around the turn of the century that man's ideas and behavior were largely determined by his social or cultural environment and that culture itself was an evolving process rather than a static condition to be taken as "given." Hence, a proper study of man's economic behavior had to be preceded by a study of his institutional surroundings. However, if the environment itself is undergoing a development of some kind, then the conditions which determine this process itself must be examined. This leads to a second basic assumption of institutionalism— the interrelation of the various parts of the social and economic organism.

"HOLISTIC" NATURE OF ECONOMICS.[4] The institutionalists took a broad or "holistic" view of economics compared with the narrower, more formal view held by the classicists. The word "holistic" was first used by Jan Christian Smuts, the famous South African scholar and statesman, to describe the collective or Gestalt approach to knowledge which seems to be required to explain social phenomena now that the spectacular conclusions of Darwin in biology and Einstein in physics have become generally accepted. This type of thought emphasizes the total over the individual, the evolutionary over the mechanistic, and the dynamic over the static nature of reality. The institutionalists held that the economic system is closely related to the culture in which it is immersed and that this entire milieu is an evolving and growing organism which is greater in scope and significance than the sum of its parts. In short, economics was defined as a study of the economic aspects of human culture.

Accordingly, the institutionalists had to face the problem of developing a methodology of their own which could be used to analyze this complex and evolving social process. The concepts and analytical methods of classical economics were inadequate since the orthodox orientation assumed that the economic system could be divorced, for analytical purposes, from its institutional setting and reduced to a highly refined system of general relationships which constantly sought a state of static equilibrium. The classical economists had developed their concepts and methodology from Sir Isaac Newton, who had advanced the theory of a closed, static universe whose operations were derived from unchanging laws. Later classical and Austrian economists had followed the physicists and tried to reduce the relationships

[4] Portions of the following paragraphs are based on Gruchy, op. cit., pp. 550-81.

in their system to a set of mathematical formulas. The classicists had taken the restricted view that economics is an abstract study of the disposition of scarce resources among given ends. Furthermore, some of them had permitted the formal methodology to become a ritual and hence a goal in itself. Thus, the real purpose of economic analysis, that of discovering the basic causal relationships of the system, was often lost. Too much of the effort and time of orthodox economists had been employed in further and further refinement of the tools of analysis. Many classicists never got beyond this point and, in fact, often maintained that their methodology could be used for analyzing any kind of economic system at any time. Hence, there was no need to study the system itself since it was merely the result of the several major economic forces and, in fact, would always be there later. It is as though a race of hunters spent most or all of their time over several generations in sharpening their arrowheads in the belief that the animals would always be there for hunting, but meanwhile agriculture and then industrial cities arose which made the profession of hunting largely irrelevant and certainly relatively unfruitful as an occupation.

It should be emphasized that the institutionalists did not reject the highly refined price theory of the orthodox neoclassicists as regards the pure mechanics of price determination and resource allocation. But they did question the relevancy of the assumptions which underlie the theory. An analysis of the economic system based on human behavior which is culturally determined requires more than logic and mathematics. In assuming that the entire economic and social system had to be studied as an organic unit, the institutionalists, then, rejected a large portion of the methodology of orthodox economics, particularly the device of studying one small aspect of the system at a time and then "aggregating" the results into a picture of total reality. The marginal approach to economic thinking came under particular attack since it was based on the hedonistic "pleasure-pain" psychology which had long since been rejected by psychologists themselves.

Even the more recent modification of hedonism, called utilitarianism, was rejected by the institutionalists. The utilitarian philosophers, following John Stuart Mill, had watered down hedonism to saying that man merely tried to maximize "utility," which is no more than that he tries always to better his economic position. Pleasure became utility or satisfaction for the consumer and "revenue" for the producer. Pain was transposed into "effort" for the consumer and "cost" for the producer. Hence, utilitarian psychology was less mechanistic than the old hedonism of the early nineteenth century yet still provided a basis for analyzing the actions of consumers and producers. Consumers were assumed to maximize their utility and minimize their efforts while producers were assumed to be maximizing profits by increasing revenue and reducing costs. The incremental, or marginal, methodology which studies and aggregates the minute changes in utility, effort, revenue, and cost which result from the rational decisions of consumers and producers is particularly well adapted to the utilitarian psychology.

The institutionalists said they could not accept the utilitarian psychology because if utility was defined narrowly enough to be a useful basis for the marginal analysis it would be nothing more than hedonism restated, while if it were defined broadly enough to be consistent with the more modern and enlightened notions of psychology, it would have no meaning at all. Thus, if utility is no more than something that a person maximizes, then utilitarianism becomes the meaningless truism that "man is trying to maximize whatever it is he is maximizing."

In addition to the psychological and philosophical assumptions of orthodox theory, the institutionalists criticized some of the procedural methodology. Pure competition, for example, was attacked as being too abstract, even for a simplifying first approximation. The institutionalists believed that the stage of competition in the economy had passed in the ninteenth century if, in fact, it had ever existed. They did not question the analysis of price and distribution but believed it to be irrelevant in today's world of giant corporations, labor unions, and strong central government. They were only willing to accept the orthodox theory of the individual firm as being relevant for analyzing economic behavior in those segments of the economy which were still competitive in the traditional sense.

The institutionalists were eloquent in their criticism, but they never accomplished the more difficult task of developing a constructive substitute for the old methodology. However, some progress was made, and this leads to the third assumption, the dynamic or evolving nature of the economic system.

ECONOMIC SYSTEM AS AN EVOLVING PROCESS. Hegel's concept of a constantly changing universe was the original point of departure from the essentially static concepts which started with Newton and were adapted by orthodox economists. If it is true that the predominant characteristic of the universe, including economic phenomena, is process or change, then radically new analytical tools may be necessary to explain the economic system. Although comparative statistics has been tried as a device for analyzing relationships involving the "fourth dimension" of time, it is still inadequate for explaining how or why conditions change from one time period to another. The theory of dynamics has been developed to analyze conditions of change but so far has not been very successfully applied to economic phenomena.

Change was of course possible in the mechanistic system of Newton, but it was of a type not particularly applicable to the processes which occur in biological, economic, or social phenomena. Change itself, as it occurs in physical data, is like the waves of the ocean, without cause, effect, or purpose. Mechanical changes, acting under the laws of probability, tend toward an equilibrium, and, hence, the underlying nature of the Newtonian physical system and classical economic system was static.

It was Darwin who showed that change could be more than merely endless and meaningless variation in data. It could contain qualities or forces which give it a determination and a rational significance. In his theory of biological evolution, Darwin demonstrated that one change might contain the seeds of another and that the entire process could be intelligently analyzed. This is not unlike the Hegelian concept of change in which every idea naturally gave rise to its opposite and out of a fusion of the two grew a new idea which was followed by the rise of another opposing idea and so on. This was the theory of change which provides the basis of the Marxian interpretation of history.

The institutionalists tried to apply the concepts of biological evolution to economics and in so doing discovered still another type of change which involved not a random variation tending toward equilibrium as in mechanics, not an evolutionary process based on natural selection as in biology, not an automatic progression as in Hegelian philosophy, but a social development motivated by a voluntary element attributable to the existence of human purpose. The cultural anthropologists who followed Darwin extended the concept of biological evolution to social phenomena. A culture or society, they said, can be considered like an organism which exhibits properties of activity resulting from the interaction of mutually interdependent parts.

John R. Commons (1862-1945) differentiated cultural evolution from biological evolution by claiming that biological evolution was still a mechanical system because its action arose from accidental or unintended changes whereas cultural or economic evolution contains purposeful or intended changes due to the voluntary nature of human decisions.[5] There is a partial inconsistency here with the first assumption of institutionalism—that human conduct is socially or culturally determined. The institutionalists tried to avoid this possible conflict by assuming that arbitrary human will and cultural determinants interact on each other so that individual free will contributes to the cultural environment and is, in turn, molded by the environment. On balance the institutionalists seemed to believe that custom and habits

---

[5] John R. Commons, *Institutional Economics* (New York: The Macmillan Co., 1934), pp. 732 ff.

were more important than reason in determining human be-havior. Commons, in analyzing change, differentiated the concepts of mechanism (physical), organism (biological), and going-concern (social and economic) and proposed special statistical treatment for the latter because of the unique nature of its voluntary content.

AUXILIARY ASSUMPTIONS OF THE INSTITUTIONALISTS. In addition to the three primary bases of institutionalism (social behavior of individuals, "holistic" nature of economics, and evolving characteristics of the economic system) there were several auxiliary assumptions which fall into two categories. The first includes those which follow from the primary assumptions and might be called conclusions except that they form the basis for subsequent arguments. The second set contains those assumptions accepted by some institutional economists but not by others.

An example of an assumption from the first group is the belief that there is no pre-existing harmony of economic interests underlying the system. If the primary assumption of evolution is accepted, then there is no reason to expect conflicts to resolve themselves automatically toward an equilibrium. Conflicts may lead to still other, more serious, conflicts, and this process may continue or even become a cumulative force leading to permanent disequilibrium. This is not to say that the developing of the economic system is haphazard or random. The institutionalists said that the process or emergence of an economic system was controlled by a "logic of events." This concept, never adequately defined, apparently meant that although the final outcome of an economic process was not predetermined, the state of technology exercised a selective function and, together with the voluntary elements in human conduct, reduced the number of possible choices to a relatively few. For example, condition A might lead to one of three results, B, C, or D. Whichever should occur (say C), this would lead to three further possibilities, etc. Although the end result of such a selective process might be an enormous number of possible solutions, it can hardly be said to be accidental, haphazard, or random. Nor can it be said to contain any underlying harmony or equilibrium.

Another assumption following from the concept of process is that the rate of technological change is greater than the rate of psychological adjustment to it. This is an observed fact in this era when medieval superstitions and nineteenth-century concepts of social control are frequently called on to cope with the problems of an atomic age. Those whose minds have not been deadened by the political and commercial propaganda of radio, television, and newspapers are likely to be appalled at the primitive messages which are often carried over these modern communicative devices. To the institutionalists one of the main economic problems was the lag in psychological adjustment to technological change.

The second set of secondary assumptions are those which result from the diversity of opinion among institutionalists. Not all the assumptions of one institutional economist were, or are, acceptable to all others. For example, Veblen's pessimism was not shared by his followers. Veblen was doubtful of the likelihood for continual adjustment and improvement. To him evolution did not necessarily mean growth; there was no "ameliorative trend." Things did not seem to be getting better. They did not tend toward anything. But to most of the other institutionalists, except possibly Gardiner Means, there was a sort of faith that there would be an improvement in economic and social conditions although this did not imply that there was any underlying harmony of interest as the classical economists had assumed.

Most institutionalists also disagreed with Veblen on human nature, holding that man is essentially a cooperative being. Veblen did not hold the opposite view, shared by the orthodox economists, that man was by nature competitive and profit-seeking. He accepted the selfish, acquisitive nature of man but believed that it was the result of the conditioning of a society which discourages ethics and altruism and which measures success in terms of money. To Veblen, man could be conditioned to be nearly anything. Most of the other institutionalists agreed with Veblen that man's observed acquisitiveness was a result of his institutional environment, but they believed further that there was a "natural" state in which men were inherently good and cooperative. All institutionalists agreed that the economic system could be controlled and made to function for the good of all. All believed in the need for some kind of over-all collective planning although the reasons for their beliefs and the kinds of planning favored varied among individuals.

INSTITUTIONAL THEORY OF AMERICAN CAPITALISM

The institutionalists were the first American economists to concern themselves with the question of defining and analyzing capitalism as an economic system. But because of their belief in the importance of institutions in determining the nature of an economic system they contented themselves to analyze American capitalism only. They believed that there could be no universal economic system as long as customs varied so widely throughout the world. Nor was there any point, at this stage of world history, in hunting for universal economic laws. Economic systems were thought to be the product of institutions. Since institutions were not universal, then economic laws and systems could not be universal either.

In setting out specifically to study American capitalism the institutionalists learned more about the system than previous economists ever had. Classicists had concentrated on further refinement of price and distribution theory and had considered their principles as having universal application. The institutionalists' principles were admittedly valid only in a particular cultural setting and for a given stage of economic development, but their end product was an analysis of the total relationships of an entire economic system.

The principal analytical tool employed was the inductive method of the old German historical school, but it was not carried to such extremes of empiricism as to make theoretical generalizations impossible. The Germans had made the error of accumulating mountains of facts which were not very useful because they never had any very clear notions of what to look for in their statistical studies. The institutionalists partly avoided this difficulty by developing a general notion or hypothesis of the nature of the American economic order thus enabling them to employ a selective process in their empirical studies. Their hypotheses were limited by the lack of a specific theory of capitalism, but the development of generalizations gave institutional economics more of a theoretical content than the largely descriptive historical school was ever able to attain. Of course, institutional theory is by no means as refined and exact as orthodox theory, but it is not so abstract and lacking in empirical content either.

The generalizations about American capitalism start with the assumptions outlined above. Many conclusions were logically drawn from these, but the institutionalists were careful to refer to the statistics and modify those results which they could not clearly prove. Their conclusions were not intended to be eternal economic principles but only to be applicable to the economy of the United States during the first half of the twentieth century. It was recognized that as the economy changes and expands, some underlying principles become obsolete and must be replaced by new ones. Theories applicable to a rural, agricultural economy must be replaced as the economy passes into a competitive, commercial stage and on into urban, industrialized and, later perhaps, monopolized stages.

Since institutionalist theory started out from facts it is not surprising that the theory of the economic order did not begin with the assumption of pure competition. Rather it pictured the market system as a whirlpool of economic activity with a center composed of monopolistic industries such as steel, chemicals, transportation and utilities, banks and insurance companies, government enterprises, trade associations, and national labor unions.

Outside this central core was a region of semimonopolistic enterprises operating in markets where there were often limited numbers of firms selling differentiated products and engaging in vast advertising programs in order to maintain their relative positions in these markets. In this region would be found the food, drug, and beverage manufacturers, wholesaling, retailing, dealership outlets for basic manufactured goods produced in the monopolistic core, and independent or unaffiliated labor organizations.

The outer region of the whirlpool contained what was left of the traditionally competitive economy. Here were the service industries and trades, such as restaurants, laundries and garages, small retailing, some manufacturing, such as cotton textiles, bituminous coal mining, and such agriculture as is without the protection of government programs or cooperative marketing agreements.

It did not matter to the institutionalists whether or not effective competition was ever the dominant form of market structure because economic conditions were seen to be rapidly changing and the era of free competition, if it ever existed, was one having a different institutional setting. The nineteenth century was a period of expanding physical frontiers, a lower level of technology, and crude transportation, communications, and public informational media. Of course, to understand the dynamics of market development resort must be made to the past, but the institutionalists doubted whether the institutions of the nineeenth century were sufficiently similar to those of their day to make any reasonable comparison possible. Here they differed with the historical school.

Four characteristics of business organization become apparent when viewed as a whirlpool with a monopolistic core and a competitive periphery. First, the degree of technology is highest in the center and decreases toward the circumference. Productivity per worker, the ratio of invested capital to labor, the ratio of fixed investment to gross income, the extent of mass production and division of labor, and many other measures of the state of capital development all indicate that the highest degree of mechanization and technology exists at the nucleus.

Second, the industries that comprise the core of the economic system have the greatest strategic importance to the economy. The basic capital goods producers and the lifelines of transportation, communication, and finance are located here. These industries are the most vital to modern warfare and are the most sensitive to changes in consumer demand, business confidence, legislation, and foreign developments. Here the nerve and production center of the economy is poised on a razor's edge of mass psychology, supersensitive to the slightest disturbance. A flood of momentous decisions which affect the economic lives of virtually every citizen may descend from this peak of business activity at the slightest provocation.

Third, there is a high degree of organization, both formal and informal, in this central core. Holding companies, interlocking directorates, patent pools, proxy machinery, and a host of informal conventions, such as price leadership, gentlemen's agreements, market allocations, preferred banking connections, and so on, are characteristic of the industries which comprise this central group. This high degree of organization has resulted in collective business action in the form of legislative lobbying and mass public relations and advertising campaigns by the dominant business group. According to the institutionalists, this interconnection of business interests has a tendency to centralize decision-making but decentralize risk since many of the usual business hazards disappear when there is an organization large enough to absorb them. Witness, for example, the tendency in large enterprises toward self-insurance, diversification of output for protection against market vagaries, and vertical integration to insure adequate supplies.

Fourth, the institutionalists believed that there was a strong centripetal force drawing more and more economic activity into the central core of monopoly. There were two reasons for this tendency toward centralization. The first was technological. The modern factory system of highly specialized mass production requires an immense capitalization, and this can be secured only through giant enterprises with specialized managements and limited liability. Furthermore, a high rate of technological innovation is required by modern production methods, and only large scale, centralized enterprises can provide the facilities for this. Conversely, the large enterprise stimulates further technological development, and thus an interacting process occurs whereby industrialization encourages an increase in the rate of technological growth and a state of advanced technology encourages an increase in the rate of industrialization. Those industries which are to survive the struggle for markets are consequently drawn into the highly centralized monopolistic core of the economy.

A second explanation for increasing centralization and monopoly was that the institutions of the maturing capitalistic system created a mental attitude in businessmen that is receptive to centralized power. Industrial and financial magnates vie with each other in building empires because financial manipulations are among the principal means for acquiring control and prestige. Thus, conscious human conduct plays a part in drawing firms into the whirlpool of monopolistic venture.

Veblen pursued this kind of argument even further than his followers by differentiating between pecuniary and industrial motives. He maintained that the businessman's desire for money led him to create artificial scarcities of goods, increase prices rather than output, produce goods of poor quality in order to insure profitable replacement business, and, in general, to sabotage the proper working of the economic system by engaging in many wasteful and extravagant practices. He saw the interests of the businessmen as opposed to those of the engineers or technicians who were the real producers in the economy and whose interests more nearly coincided with those of the general public.

Most other institutional economists were not willing to go along with Veblen's bitter attack on the pecuniary motives of businessmen which resembles somewhat the attack of Marxists on the "finance capitalists." However, throughout all institutional writing there is a strong feeling that the capitalistic system tends to misemploy the factors of production by allocating resources poorly and producing the wrong kinds and qualities of goods. Most institutionalists did not condemn the businessman but felt that the institutional arrangements within which he operates often lead him to anti-social ends. With this the most staunchly orthodox economists could hardly disagree since the traditional opponents of monopoly were in the classical school. However, orthodox economists did not accept the institutionalist view that monopoly is typical of the business world, that it is increasing in scope, or that it is an inevitable consequence of the capitalist system of production.

Veblen's most well-known and striking contribution to the theory of American capitalism is associated with his concept of the leisure class. Capitalism, with its unearned incomes and great inequality of wealth and opportunity, had, according to Veblen, created a minority upper class of people who do not need to work for a living. Capitalist institutions have so glorified material success that being a member of this class carries with it the greatest prestige. Members of the leisure class engage in "conspicuous consumption" and "conspicuous waste" in order to demonstrate publicly their social status. This often requires the leisure class to purchase things specifically because they are useless. The acquisition and display of such goods is evidence of leisure status and economic surplus. For example, white gloves, top hat, and tails have no usefulness whatever because one cannot do any work or even touch anything in this garb, yet it is the badge of socialites. Likewise, jewels or furs for "parasitic" women, the mastery of archaic languages for the academicians, insignias for the military men, and even sexual perversion for certain "artistically inclined" groups are all demanded because they are wasteful of resources and useless for human needs. According to Veblen, the most honorable employments, by capitalistic values, were the largest and the most useless. Jewelers, florists, and bankers were higher on his scale of assumed reputability than grocers or machinists.

The effect of conspicuous leisure is magnified when most consumers "emulate" the leisure class and, as far as possible, demand higher priced goods because they are fancy, luxurious in appearance, or simply nationally advertised. The industrious classes, seeking to identify themselves with the leisure class, try to be seen consuming those goods which advertisements picture as the daily fare of this week's "Man of Distinction." The effect of this kind of demand is to cause luxury goods to be produced rather than more practical and useful goods and could even cause prices of utility or standard quality goods to be higher because of the relatively small demand for them.

When the institutionalists examined the price system, they concluded that it did not (1) allocate resources efficiently, (2) adjust prices to reflect actual cost changes, (3) insure that the goods and services produced were of the qualities demanded by consumers, or (4) guarantee a full level of employment. This was particularly true in the more monopolistic sector, and it was here that the institutionalists centered their attention. It was soon recognized, however, that in markets dominated by a few large producers and characterized by formal or tacit collusion, price and output policies are largely indeterminate. Theorizing about these markets could not stray far from actual cases so the institutionalists could not make many useful generalizations concerning the price, output, or distribution decisions of large firms. Neoclassical price and production theory offered no dependable guides for prediction in cases where giant corporations dominate the market. Since the institutionalists, for the most part, were suspicious of uncontrolled big business, cynical about laissez faire, and often naively attracted by the possibilities of collective planning, they anticipated or advocated some form of over-all government control of the economy as an answer to capitalism's dilemmas.

If a freely working price mechanism does not provide a reliable guarantee of proper resource allocation, rational pricing, maximum consumer satisfaction, or full employment, something must be offered to replace it. Here the institutionalists parted company with each other. Most of them were in general agreement in their conception of the theoretical and institutional framework of American capitalism and in their analysis of the capitalist system even though the various economists chose to specialize in analyzing different aspects of the system. But when it came to recommendations they did not have so much in common. This may offer a clue to the reason why they showed strong cohesive tendencies between 1910 and 1933 while engaged in critical analysis of the economic system but tended to fall apart as a group or school when the New Deal gave the younger institutionalists an opportunity to make a positive, practical contribution toward rebuilding an economy which had broken down.

CONCEPTS OF SOCIAL CONTROL

Veblen was almost purely a critic, offering only fragments of a positive theory of capitalism and almost no practical policy proposals. But the institutionalists who followed him did provide some useful principles to guide the planning which would be needed as competition "declined." For example, John R. Commons, who was probably America's greatest labor economist, concentrated his studies on the role of labor organizations, collective bargaining, and workers' economic welfare. He is well known for his collective bargaining theory and for his contribution to the establishment of exemplary systems of public utility regulation and social security in Wisconsin.

Commons believed that conflict was inevitable in a private-property, free-enterprise economy. However, this conflict was not like the Marxist concept of a two-class division of society with a struggle between the capitalists and workers. Commons saw many groups all in conflict with each other. Within capitalist groups were big against small businesses, landlords against lessee manufacturers, debtors against creditors, financiers against industrialists. There were conflicts within labor such as conservative business unionism *versus* radical or socialist unionism. Then there were other conflicts such as those between rural and urban dwellers and agricultural, business, and labor interests.

Unlike Marx, Commons believed that these conflicts were resolved by compromise through bargaining rather than by the ultimate defeat of one side. However, he did not envisage any self-regulating forces which insured an equality of bargaining power. One side might be permanently superior to another through inherent economic power or even legal authority. Therefore, the government was seen as having to act as arbitrator of disputes and, when necessary, use its power to improve the bargaining strength of the weaker groups. Since most of the groups depend on each other for a livelihood, the government, acting through commissions, must ensure an equality of bargaining power.

Commons went from the study of bargaining to means of social control and finally to a theory of capitalism. He divided the evolution of the system into three stages: (1) merchant capitalism, (2) employer capitalism, and (3) banker capitalism. The first period consisted of the seventeenth and eighteenth centuries, an era of extensive trade and small scale production. The second period consisted of the late eighteenth and early nineteenth centuries, an era of growing industrialization. The third period began with the emergence of giant corporations and collective business controls in the late nineteenth century and continued into the 1930's.

In this last stage the investment banker emerged as the dominant force. Control of money and credit were the keys to power, and these were held by bankers who were concerned with the stabilization of their own profits. Their policies of restriction of credit and manipulation of security values often brought them into conflict with industrialists and almost inevitably thwarted labor's attempts to stabilize real wages. Commons was not pessimistic, however. He believed that the bankers might eventually come to place the public interest above their own private interests and thus make capitalism more "reasonable." The government, through administrative commissions, would formalize this self-regulation in the public interest.

Fortunately we do not need to rely on any growth of enlightenment among bankers. As Chapter 12 shows, capitalism is tending to rely more on "internal" financing from corporate profits for its capital investment and less and less on both bankers and the securities market. Thus, Commons' predictions about banker capitalism have not been borne out. Commons did not fear the encroachment of the government on individual liberties through these commissions. Like the economic system itself, he felt that the government has evolved from earlier and cruder forms and today has been broadened to include representation from many and diverse groups. This multiplicity of groups in government provides checks on the unrestrained power of any one group and insures a reasonable degree of democracy.[6]

Another leading institutional economist, Gardiner Means (1896-　　) is best known for his penetrating analysis of the role of the giant enterprise in the industrial economy. Modern capitalism, to Means, was a product of the "corporate revolution" in which the giant corporation has come to play such a dominant role that it has drastically altered its institutional environment and made entirely new assumptions appropriate for studying the economic system. Means and Adolf Berle, using elaborate statistics and closely reasoned analysis, dramatically brought nationwide attention, for the first time, to the fact that ownership of the means of production has become divorced from management, risk-taking has become divorced from wealth, and control over the nation's resources has become vested in less than 1 per cent of all corporations. These corporations, in turn, were, by 1932,

---

[6] J. R. Commons, *Institutional Economics* (New York: The Macmillan Co., 1924), *Industrial Goodwill* (New York: The McGraw-Hill Book Co., Inc., 1919), and *Legal Foundations of Capitalism* (New York: The Macmillan Co., 1924).

controlled by less than 2,000 individuals through interlocking directorates, proxy machinery, and communities of interest.[7]

Prices and distribution in the economy were "administered" by these giant enterprises, not automatically controlled by competition. In fact, the resulting inflexibilities actually prevent normal economic adjustments. Means did not condemn these inflexibilities in themselves even though they made depressions more prolonged and severe and placed the burden of economic adjustments on the more competitive areas of labor, agriculture, and small business. Administered prices, advertising, centralized control, and economic rigidities were the price which had to be paid for modern science and technology. But some method of raising the public interest above private interests had to be found. Means doubted that individuals acting independently could ever succeed in coordinating the economy or insuring its effective functioning.

To Means, the corporate revolution with its restrictions and inflexibilities had put capitalism out of balance and to restore this balance he advanced his theory of a managed equilibrium. The norm which was to be achieved was far less definite than the equilibrium of neoclassical economics since it varied region by region, industry by industry, and over periods of time. Nevertheless, Means believed that an equilibrium of full employment, maximum efficiency, progress, and an optimum distribution of resources and finished goods based on maximizing "real national income" could be approximated through economic planning. He observed that in depression times there was a tendency toward oversaving and a reluctance of businessmen to expand. These, he felt, could be offset by government borrowing for public capital expenditures. He spoke vaguely of a wide variety of finan-

[7] A. A. Berle and Gardiner Means, *The Modern Corporation and Private Property* (New York: The Macmillan Co., 1933), and *The Structure of the American Economy*, National Resources Committee, Washington (1939).

cial controls to balance savings with investment although in typically vague institutionalist style he avoided precise definitions of terms or quantitatively accurate proposals.

A third institutionalist, and a man who has perhaps been America's best-known economist for over thirty years, is John Maurice Clark (1884-   ). The son of John Bates Clark, America's leading exponent of classical economics, J. M. Clark taught at Chicago and later at Columbia where he holds the chair formerly held by his father. He enjoys the best of worldwide reputations, and is loved and respected by countless younger economists, including the present author, who have come under his influence.

In the 1920's Clark analyzed the role of the capital costs of giant enterprises in causing instability, unemployment, and monopoly. Then in later books and articles he developed a theory of social organization and proposed a system of "social-liberal" planning based on indirect government controls. Clark studied the giant corporation from a cost standpoint rather than the property and control standpoint of Berle and Means. He noted that one of the characteristics of modern capitalism is a high degree of capital immobility and specialization which leads to conditions of high fixed costs. To Clark, labor also is an overhead cost which needs to be properly maintained, whether producing or not, just like capital goods. Otherwise the cost of poorly treated, underpaid, or unemployed labor is a fixed cost to the community. The fact that businessmen consider labor a variable cost merely results in their shifting the burden of responsibility for some of capitalism's social costs, such as unemployment, old age, and insecurity, to the worker who in turn must pass it on to the community because of his inability to bear it all himself.

The same analysis of overhead costs can be applied to farmers and others who supply business with materials but who require public assistance to protect them from depressions brought on by business. This is not to imply that businessmen generate depressions on purpose. But when each firm tries to seek its own self-interest by following a policy of maintaining prices and reducing output, then when demand declines for some outside reason, there is a cumulative downward effect. Unemployment leads to reduced demand, and this in turn leads to more unemployment.[8]

A big problem, as Clark saw it, was to get business to bear all of the costs of its production. Capitalism had made labor and other groups dependent almost entirely on large business corporations for their existence. Many individuals had been required to live in crowded cities where they devoted their lives to learning and performing highly specialized tasks. Under these circumstances they could not easily earn a livelihood except from industrial employment. Often they were dependent on one or, at most, a few possible sources of employment for the money income upon which their livelihood was based. They were at the mercy of the corporation's employment-output policies and of business cycles generally. In short, capitalism had deprived them of their craftsmanship, property, and the relative security of a rural-agricultural society. Consequently, the business corporation should be made to bear the cost of maintaining these people in decent and secure conditions.

To solve this problem Clark proposed a comprehensive planning system which was not highly collectivist and did not involve either public ownership of industries or even direct controls. A purely advisory planning board would study the social needs of the community and, through fiscal policy and voluntary cooperation, try to achieve these social goals. Clark believed that the present economic system could be preserved and made to operate in the public interest because the facts of twentieth-century capitalism would become apparent and business, as well as other groups, would develop a spirit of responsibility for each other and for the community in general.

No discussion of institutional economics can omit reference to Wesley C. Mitchell (1874-1949) although for all his

[8] J. M. Clark, *Studies in the Economics of Overhead Costs* (Chicago: The University of Chicago Press, 1923), and *Social Control of Business* (2d ed.; New York: The McGraw-Hill Book Co., Inc., 1939).

influence Mitchell contributed little to the institutional theory of capitalism or to the concept of economic planning. He was the most pragmatic and least theoretical of the group, and his wide influence stems partly from this fact. Businessmen and statesmen seem more willing to follow arguments based on facts than on logic or philosophy, and it was to the accumulation of statistics that Mitchell devoted his many years as Director of the National Bureau of Economic Research.

Like Veblen, Mitchell rejected the classical concepts of human rationality, the effectiveness of competition, and the permanence of institutions and culture. A strong pragmatist, he emphasized the role of habits and instincts in human behavior. His greatest contribution was in his exhaustive empirical study of business cycles. He resembled the German historical economists more than other American institutionalists in that he concentrated on quantitive analysis of statistics and never developed any unified economic theory.

Mitchell exerted great influence on the other institutionalists by providing them with refined statistical techniques without which they would have suffered from much the same fate which befell the historical economists who were never able to utilize effectively much of the data which they accumulated. For example, when the institutionalists attacked the neoclassical economic "laws" and substituted "tendencies" for them, Mitchell provided the techniques for accurately measuring and proving the existence of "tendencies" or trends. He did not theorize much about capitalism beyond arguing that business cycles are a phase of an advanced and mature economic system.

Mitchell recognized that the nature of business cycles is far more complex than was previously imagined. Money, for example, had been considered as being a unit of calculation and a medium of exchange. Mitchell recognized it as more than this. It was a store of value and, in addition, a determinant of economic activity. Mitchell was cautious in recommending monetary controls, but he anticipated that some kind of over-all, comprehensive, financial planning of the economy would be required when more facts were known about money and business cycles.

A considerable number of institutionalist economists and administrators were associated with the planning aspects of the New Deal. Rexford Tugwell (1891-   ) is perhaps representative of this group which also included such men as Mordecai Ezekiel, Leon Henderson, and Chester Bowles. Tugwell was a student and disciple of Simon N. Patten but concentrated most of his efforts in the field of planning. He was a strong believer in cooperation over competition as a regulator of economic life and in the abundance of nature. When he was Assistant Secretary of Agriculture under Henry Wallace and later Governor of Puerto Rico, he recommended vast planning programs in order to realize what he believed were enormous production potentialities. He was an experimentalist with an insatiable curiosity which led him into many bold and imaginative schemes.

Tugwell observed that the evolution of capitalism had replaced individualist production methods with collective ones but had not produced collectivist distribution and consumption methods. This lag in distribution and consumption manifested itself in a "cultural disequilibrium" which upset the market system. Prices no longer responded to cost changes, incomes did not respond to productivity changes, inefficiency did not tend to disappear, and there seemed to be no assurance of full employment. To remedy this situation Tugwell proposed a planning board to plan for resource development.[9] Unused or exploited private land resources would be purchased for public preserves, the government would direct new investment, and taxes and subsidies would be used to raise living standards.

Tugwell was not fearful that planning would lead to undue regimentation. We have already submitted willingly (and rightly) to the regimentation of machine technology and urban civilization in order to enjoy the high living stand-

[9] R. G. Tugwell, "Experimental Economics," in *The Trend of Economics* (New York: Alfred A. Knopf, Inc., 1924), and *The Battle for Democracy* (New York: Columbia University Press, 1935).

ards produced by industry. Why should the regimentation of economic planning be any worse if it insures full employment and economic security?

CONCLUSION

At first glance it appears paradoxical that America, the last citadel of political conservatism in the world, should have produced and nourished as its most completely native contribution to economic thought a heresy which is less orthodox in its philosophy, in many respects, than Marxism itself. Institutionalism is a more complete rejection of economic orthodoxy than Marxism, because while Marxism attacked the established institutions of capitalism and predicted their downfall, institutionalism rejected the basic psychology, philosophy, and methodology of classical and neoclassical economics, something that Marxism never did entirely. Marxism was based on the labor and rent theories of the classicists and received its subversive reputation from the militancy of its disciples and the actual physical threat which they posed to existing institutions. Institutionalism was far more thorough in its criticism of the existing order but less specific in proposing positive remedies and more inclined to appeal to middle-class intellectuals than to oppressed working classes. Furthermore, institutionalism was never closely enough formulated to be acceptable as an ideology or a doctrine. None of the institutionalists succeeded in developing a complete theory of capitalism. The whole school died out before it ever got to this stage.

Of course, institutionalism disappeared by permeating other schools of thought and thus losing its separate identity, much like the old Socialist party did, but after all, this may be as good a way as any to spread a gospel to the normally conservative masses of people who may be reluctant to accept new ideas, particularly when they are aware of their intellectual origin. Probably because they never got far enough to agree among themselves on the essentials of public policy, the institutionalists perpetuated their philosophy not by enlisting followers as the Marxists have done but by propagating ideas which could unobtrusively infiltrate other philosophies. In this sense institutionalism has been enormously successful although there is hardly a first rate economist today who will admit he is an institutionalist. However, there are few indeed who do not owe a debt to these early heretics who battered at the foundations of the established order.

As a consequence of their lack of specific proposals for reform, their differences of opinion among themselves, and their emphasis on stimulating thought rather than enlisting blind adherents, institutionalists were ordinarily highly regarded by society, even by those groups, such as bankers, who came in for the most vitriolic attacks. On the other hand, the less subtle, less sophisticated Marxists were, and always have been, in disrepute nearly everywhere.

In spite of its radicalism, institutionalism is in the best American tradition. The Jeffersonian and Jacksonian ideals of human freedom and dignity, free expression of opinion, and social progress, together with an acute awareness of human suffering and sympathy for the oppressed, are nowhere better expressed than in the writings and devoted lives of the institutional economists. Nevertheless, institutionalism, in spite of its broadening influence on American economic thought, failed to establish a new theory of capitalism which was able to replace the orthodox one. In spite of the irrefutable arguments and solid facts which may be hurled against any established theoretical system, the enlightened human mind tends to cling to the old until a new, positive, and workable concept arises to replace it. From a theoretical point of view, the fundamentals of neoclassical economics survived the institutionalist onslaught, although not without the loss of many of its more unrealistic assumptions.

Finally, institutionalism was too closely associated with the conditions and institutions of pre-World War II America to be relevant to the rapidly expanding postwar era. The institutionalist study of capitalism pictured a passing era of business dominance, and the reform proposals were more relevant to depression than to economic expansion and inflation. Much of the institutionalist argument has since been rendered redundant or obsolete by newer theories.

5

Socialist Theories of Capitalism

The history of all hitherto existing society is the history of class struggles.——Marx and Engels

Capitalism did not arise because capitalists stole the land or the workmen's tools, but because it was more efficient than feudalism. It will perish because it is not merely less efficient than socialism, but actually self-destructive. ——J. B. S. Haldane

"SCIENTIFIC SOCIALIST" THEORY OF KARL MARX

One of the principal reasons why capitalism has been on the defensive in the intellectual cold war of the last fifty years has been that its critics submitted their case before the capitalist economists even realized that there was a controversy. Capitalism was first defined by its enemies. Their theoretical analysis of capitalism was also an attack on it. Only recently, and belatedly, has there been any respectable defense against it. The first comprehensive statement of the pure theory of capitalism as a unique economic system was the devastating attack led by Karl Marx whose genius proved to be the spark plug of a worldwide revolution. Ironically, the same genius and persuasiveness which gave Marxism its initial triumph also inspired a devotion and adherence among its disciples which has calcified the original theory into a fantastically rigid theology. New developments in both theory and fact are constantly revealing its inconsistency and irrelevance more clearly. Nevertheless, at first,

Marxism looked as though it might become a dynamically new theoretical approach to the analysis of economic systems.

Marx was a classical economist to the extent of understanding and accepting most of the basic Ricardan economic analysis, particularly the labor theory of value. However, he fitted the classical economics into a broad, historical framework which showed classical capitalism to be but one stage of a process of economic development.

ECONOMIC INTERPRETATION OF HISTORY. From early times, man has tried to discover the cause of historical change.[1] Historical events have been variously explained as the result of divine will, the exploits of great heros, the impact of ideas, and other causes. All these theories of history suffered from one deficiency, however: they did not lend themselves to any kind of quantitative expression. The divine-providence theory was indefinable because of the variety of subjective religious interpretations and conceptions. Carlyle wrote that "the history of the world is but the biography of great men." But this hero theory was deficient in two respects: it lacked a precise definition of greatness, thus making it subjective and variable, and it did not account for the continuity of history during the times when great men were not around. The idealistic theory was only partly valid and ignored the role of circumstances and their impact on ideas themselves. But Marx, with his determinant, quantitative, economic interpretation, provided a useful key to the study of history.

Stated simply, the Marxian interpretation of history held that the "mode of production" is what determines the social, legal, religious, and political institutions in any society. The "mode of production" was defined to include the resources, organization, and technology being used to create economic values. From this Marx argued that it was the economic fac-

---

[1] The following passages are based, in part, on *Capital*, Vol. I, and some critics, particularly G. D. H. Cole, *What Marx Really Meant* (London, 1934), and Paul Sweezy, *The Theory of Capitalist Production* (New York: International Publishers Co., Inc., 1942).

tor, the means of making a living, that determined the course of historical events.

The mode of production was not the only factor influencing history. Marx recognized that personalities and intellectual achievements influence the course of history but maintained that these were conditioned by economic circumstances. The fact that revolutions are necessary in Marxian theory in order to force the aristocracy out of its entrenched position after its economic justification has been undermined is evidence that social institutions are not affected positively and directly by economic changes. If Marx had believed that events are entirely determined by economic causes, there would obviously be no need for organized political action. If such action were taken, it would be futile unless economic forces had already made it unnecessary. However, Marx believed that all ideas were directly or indirectly derived from the economic organization of society and that eventually all thought and human actions would have to yield to economic domination.

The economic interpretation of history is thus a materialistic, rather than an idealistic, philosophy. In an agricultural economy, landowners would ultimately control the state and the social system. In an industrial economy, the owners or controllers of capital goods would determine the ideology of the society. The economic or materialistic basis for society would always determine who would be the ruling class. Marx said, "The hand mill gives you society with the feudal lord; the steam mill, society with the industrial capitalist." [2] In regard to material causes as the basis of all activity he probably would have said, contrary to modern biological theory, that a horse chews because he has teeth; he would likely not have maintained that he has teeth because of a need, desire, or obsession for chewing.

Since Marx's time three other types of economic determinism have been isolated and examined. One, which has its roots in the classical economics, is based on the assump-

[2] *The Poverty of Philosophy* (New York, no date), p. 92.

tion that materialistic motives dominate individual human activity. The accumulating evidence of sociologists and anthropologists has modified this theory by showing that motives and values vary extensively among different cultures.

Another type of economic theory of history interprets social change as a consequence of expanding technology. It is argued that technology is an independent variable and that culture patterns yield to it. For example, studies have shown how recreational and courtship customs have been modified by the perfection of automobiles. Of course, there are material causes of innovation. But there may be social causes of material consequences. For example, changes in goods, as from peace to war, may directly change the development of technology. Nevertheless, there is considerable usefulness in this theory under certain circumstances.

Still another type of economic determinism has been the theory that economic change is due to the independent innovations of entrepreneurs, or risk-taking business managers. The fourth factor of production—management—has been added to land, labor, and capital in recognition of this function which has been developed by Joseph Schumpeter and is considered in some detail in Chapter 7.

DIALECTIC MATERIALISM. The theory that the character of economic organization determines the shape of the social order was applied by Marx to the philosophical system which Georg Hegel had recently been expounding in the German universities. Hegel, who was an idealist, held that reality was only a manifestation of thought. Only ideas had real existence. The physical world was merely derived from thought. Without brains to think, the world of ideas would still remain. Hegel also believed that the world was in a state of endless change and development which took the form of a struggle between opposing ideas. This process, called the dialectic, was a method of dialogue or contradiction much like the process of debating in which a group of people, talking back and forth, or one person talking to himself, eventually reaches a predestined conclusion. To Hegel, an original idea, called a thesis, inevitably gave rise to its opposite, called an antithesis, and the ensuing struggle produced a third form, called a synthesis, which was a higher form of idea than either of the first two. The synthesis became a new thesis, and the process continued toward ultimate Truth.

Marx adopted the dialectic method but gave it a strictly materialistic application. To Marx, ideas were only reflections of the real world. Ideas exist because there are brains made of matter to think them. But the dialectic provided a vehicle for carrying out the economic theory of history. Existing economic institutions, while generating the social and cultural systems which overlay them, also generated their own opposites or contradictions. Historically the struggle between thesis and antithesis took the form of class conflicts. In the feudalistic system, original economic power was held by the landlord (thesis), but the institution of serfdom (antithesis) was generated and nourished until a stuggle ensued which led to a higher form of economic system, capitalism (synthesis). Under capitalism, the domination of the capitalist class was thought to lead to a struggle with a propertyless proletarian class out of which a higher form of system, communism, would evolve.

Here a contradiction appeared in Marxism itself because history must stop unless communism is to become the thesis for a still further struggle. Yet Marx envisioned communism as involving simultaneously the resolution of all conflicts and the beginning of a new era of history in which men, for the first time, would be able to realize all of their potentialities.

Regardless of this inconsistency, the method of dialectic materialism focused attention on changing relationships in the economic system rather than on permanent institutions and events as the classical theory had done. The Marxist economic system could be viewed as an interrelated series of events and processes which were changing through conflict, rather than consisting of separate operations which worked in harmonious equilibrium through the functioning of a neutral, changeless price mechanism.

THEORY OF CAPITALIST PRODUCTION. Using this ingenious methodology, Marx formulated a theory of capitalist production based on "surplus value." According to Engels, these two "great discoveries," the materialist concept of history and the theory of capitalist production through surplus value, made possible a precise, quantitative statement of economic relationships for the first time. The accuracy of prediction, using these discoveries, made Marxist economics a "true science" in the view of its followers.

Marx paid his respects to capitalism by admitting that it was a system far superior to feudalism and that it had achieved a remarkable increase in productivity, in capital accumulation, and in the output of material goods. But the basis of capitalist production, to Marx, was exploitation. According to Marx, this exploitation prevented the masses of the people from enjoying the fruits of their labors and launched the forces which would destroy capitalism itself. The proof of exploitation was to be found in the concept of surplus value.

Essential to the entire Marxian theory of capitalism was Marx's labor theory of value which was similar to the value theory of Ricardo except that it was even more detailed and abstract. To Marx, the value of goods was the labor which had been expended to wrest these goods from their free, natural state. This labor was conceived to be an abstract entity which was actually embodied in the goods and all value was attributable to it. Capital was merely stored-up labor. Marx reasoned that the value of the labor which can be extracted from a worker would always be more than the value poured into him. Unlike machines, the human organism could be made to produce an output which exceeded its input.

The only element common to all goods was labor value. This labor value was thought to be definitely quantitative and measurable in terms of duration of time expended at an average degree of skill or some multiple of this average for higher skills. But obviously anyone who would build a ship in the middle of the desert and transport it overland to the sea should not be compensated for the extra work which such inefficiency entails. A concept of "socially useful" labor was needed. In order to eliminate the possibility of idleness or wastefulness entering into value, Marx qualified the "duration of labor time" concept of the creation of value. He added that only that amount of labor which was "socially necessary" to produce the goods under normal conditions could be included in the value of the goods. Socially necessary labor would be the labor-time required for workers of average skill, working under normal conditions and at the current level of technology, to produce the article plus the labor value of the raw materials and the capital consumed in the process.

Whereas the classicists had concluded that goods would exchange in the market for other goods in proportion to their usefulness (exchange value would tend to approximate use value) Marx recognized no such fortuitous relationship. Yet he did argue that goods would exchange for other goods in proportion to the socially necessary labor that was in them. So, like the classical concept, this theory of value also ignores the role of demand and relative scarcity of supply in determining actual market prices. Natural resources command market prices as well as do many other commodities which have had little or no labor expended on them. To Marx, these could have no value although it is obvious that they exchange for other goods which do. However, in defense of Marx it is only fair to remember that his entire labor theory of value was based on that of the classical economists, particularly Adam Smith and David Ricardo, and this theory had already been rather uncritically accepted in respectable circles at the time. It is not mere coincidence that it so well supports the Marxian theory of exploitation. Marx borrowed the basis of it almost intact.

Labor power was itself a commodity, and its value in exchange was determined by the labor needed to produce those goods which would maintain the worker and his family at the subsistence level. This is consistent with classical economics in its results, but Marx parted with the classicists in his explanation of why wages tend toward subsistence. The classical explanation was based on Malthusian population theory which, in turn, rested on the so-called natural laws of reproduction and production of the means of subsistence. Marx had to reject the Malthusian population theory because it would have worked with equal effectiveness under socialism or communism. Instead he argued that capitalism creates a large army of unemployed workers which constantly depresses wages to the subsistence level.

The labor theory of value and the subsistence theory of wages provided the explanation for exploitation. The worker sells his labor power to the capitalist for a wage which is equivalent to the labor time required to provide the worker's subsistence. This might be, say, six hours a day. But the capitalist commands the worker's full labor power and can require him to work, say, twelve hours a day. The value of the goods produced by the worker during the last six hours, which is over and above the worker's subsistence, is retained by the capitalist and is called surplus value. It is the evidence of exploitation. Increases in the intensity of work, in the productivity of labor, and in the employment of women and children, unless prohibited by law, also create surplus value. It is not hard to see, from this reasoning, why Marx should argue that capitalism, particularly the use of machinery and labor specialization, degraded the worker from a well-rounded, skilled craftsman into little more than a beast.

The surplus value appropriated by the capitalist is translated into capital except for that portion which he consumes himself. Marx distinguished two types of capital—constant and variable. Constant capital consisted of the value of machinery and raw materials used up in production. Variable capital consisted of the value of labor used in production. Expenditures on constant capital produced final value because capital was thought to be merely stored-up labor. However, expenditures on variable capital produced surplus value, and it is the ratio of surplus value produced to total capital which is defined as the rate of profit.

It would appear that the capitalist would try to increase his ratio of variable capital to constant capital by substituting labor for machinery because only in this way could he increase the surplus value accruing to him and hence his rate of profit. However, competition forces him to use the most socially useful labor, and this means that he must employ labor at the highest known level of technology. Hence, the capitalist increases the ratio of constant capital to variable capital by substituting machinery for labor, thereby creating unemployment and depressing wage levels still further. The increase in the ratio of constant capital to total capital causes the rate of surplus value and, thus, profits to decline.

As in Smith's *Wealth of Nations,* Marx's arguments in *Capital* are not fully consistent. The increase in constant capital may cause the rate of surplus value accumulation to fall, but, in fact, it may just as easily cause it to increase since fewer workers are employed to create the same surplus value. Nor is the concept of constant capital itself entirely clear because if capital is stored-up labor, it should be equally possible to extract a surplus value from it. By using more machinery, the worker could produce his own subsistence in a shorter time, and this would automatically increase the surplus value he produced.

A further confusion arises because Marx assumed that the ratio of increase in constant capital is the same in all industries, which it obviously is not. He concluded that the rate of profit was the same in all industries because competition forced it to be so. If this argument is to be accepted, then the labor theory of value, upon which the whole theory of capitalism is based, must be abandoned because the labor theory requires that prices be based on labor costs only and not subject to change because of competition among firms.

These contradictions are further evidence that Marx began his analysis only after he had drawn up his conclusions in detail. No matter what the trend of capital accumulation, the result comes out to be increasing exploitation of the workers. Whether profit rates rise or fall, whether more or less machinery is used, the answer is always the same—increasing misery for the working class.

DOCTRINE OF INCREASING MISERY. The doctrine of the increasing misery of the proletariat, which is caused by the capitalists' frenzied efforts to wring as much surplus value as possible out of the workers, fits into the final stages of the theory of the class struggle. Marx assumed that there was a horizontal division of society and that there was an inherent conflict between the two groups, the bourgeois (capitalist) class and the proletarian (worker) class.

The capitalist class grows smaller as wealth becomes more centralized. The working class grows larger as the middle class of small merchants, professional people, white collar workers, and farmers are either squeezed out of their businesses and driven into the labor force or else see their opportunities for rising into the capitalist class disappearing and, hence, identify themselves psychologically with the proletariat.

The increasing inequality of income and wealth leads to a great surplus for the capitalists who invest it in more capital assets. The increasing abundance of capital causes a decline in the *rate* of profit, as discussed above. To offset this decline, capitalists would seek to make industry more efficient. The drive for efficiency would eliminate smaller, high-cost enterprises and lead to a concentration of economic power in a relatively few large-scale firms. According to Marx, this concentration of capitalist enterprise in large units inevitably creates a class-conscious, propertyless proletariat. The increased poverty and degradation of the proletariat creates a sense of solidarity and class consciousness. The antagonism between the two classes increases as the contrast between the economic circumstances becomes more pronounced.

Marxism was originally international and cosmopolitan because it was assumed that the economic basis for society was more important than the political or cultural institutions. Workers in America, for example, would have more in common with the workers in Russia than with their own employers. That modern Marxists have abandoned this position is evidenced by the strong nationalistic attitude of the Soviet government since World War II.

The increasing misery of the proletariat, due to falling wages, unemployment, and destruction of the capitalist middle class, which becomes merged with the working class, points dramatically to the "contradictions" of capitalism. The continued existence of capitalism depends on profits, and a declining profit rate appears inevitable in the Marxian logic for several reasons. The increase in constant capital, due to competition, leads to an oversupply of capital and hence lower profits. A decline in the consumption of the masses due to income inequality and unemployment also makes for a falling profit rate. To counteract the declining profit rate, capitalists seek to increase their capital investment which ultimately pushes profit rates even lower by adding to the supply of capital.

The increase in mechanization temporarily increases employment and wages which, in turn, reduce profits and capital values so that the movement for greater capital accumulation is reversed. Thus, capitalism produces business cycles or crises which occur every ten or fifteen years. These periodic depressions would become increasingly severe, according to Marxian theory.

CRISES OF CAPITALISM. The "contradictions" of capitalism inevitably bring about its downfall in the Marxian model. Capitalism is destroyed by its own success. These periodic and inevitable crises of capitalism, which eventually lead to the breakdown of the system altogether, are evidence of the dynamic elements in Marxian theory. The recurring crises become more severe, and emergence from them becomes increasingly difficult. This is because the destruction of capital in depression permits a further accumulation in the future, and since all capital is not destroyed, the accumulation which begins after the recovery commences at a higher absolute level than before. Finally, a crisis becomes too intense, a revolution occurs, and capitalism collapses altogether.

The explanation of these crises would complete the theoretical connection between the contradictions of capitalism and the collapse in revolution were it not for the fact that no single, clear explanation of the Marxian crisis can be found. Marx's own explanation is evidence both of his genius and his dogmatism. He anticipated nearly every business-cycle theory developed since his time, and some of his arguments are unique, original, and ingenious. The fact that they are all used to prove the same point even though they are inconsistent with each other serves to show, also, that Marx was more interested in proving his case than in seeking the truth.

In a few places, Marx uses a traditional socialist-underconsumptionist type of reasoning. Monopoly reduces total purchasing power by transferring incomes from the poor, who spend all their incomes, to the rich, who do not. This is accomplished by firms raising their selling prices while forcing down the prices of the resources which they purchase, particularly agricultural products and labor. Thus, consumers are exploited by high prices while small farmers and workers are exploited by the low prices paid by the business firm for their services. Monopoly also curtails production so as not to produce more than can be sold at the fixed high prices. In doing this, employment is curtailed, and, hence, wages and purchasing power are reduced still further. But this argument is directly repudiated by Marx in many other places. More often he argued that crises cannot be solved by wage increases nor can capitalism be saved by rearranging the distribution of income. Both of these are the goals of traditional socialists and other underconsumptionists. Thus it cannot be argued that Marx was basically either a traditional socialist or an underconsumptionist.

The crisis argument which Marx seemed most attached to, and which Lenin and others developed more fully, can more properly be called an overinvestment theory. Capitalism, being dependent on profits, must have an increasing rate of new capital investment because each new increment of capital adds to the base from which the rate of profit is calculated. Unless the rate of new capital investment is rising, the rate of profit under these circumstances will fall. Furthermore, new capital competes with existing capital so that the return on new capital will tend also to fall.

One consequence of this is a distortion in the allocation of resources. There is a continuing overproduction of capital goods until finally the rate of profit on new capital is reduced to nothing. Shortly before this point is reached, real wages will rise because in the race for more capital accumulation the rate of production will temporarily outrun the rate of population growth. This rise in real wages due to the relative labor shortage reduces the surplus value derived from employing labor. This is equivalent to a reduction in the rate of profit and hastens the crisis which will occur when profits disappear and production ceases. Here is further proof that Marx was not essentially an underconsumptionist because the final cause of the crisis is overproduction of capital under conditions that permit an *increase* in consumption—higher real wages and fuller employment.

In the resulting crisis, capital values are destroyed through physical destruction, deterioration from idleness, lack of repair, and, of course, a zero profit rate which, in a strictly commercial sense, means that capital has no value at all under the circumstances. Prices fall more rapidly than wages, so business losses will mount. If the working class is psychologically prepared to seize power at this time, the revolution will occur. If not, there are self-correcting forces at work, which will eventually restore capitalism to prosperity and give it another chance, but with poorer odds this time. Falling prices will sooner or later be reflected in lower costs to the business firm. Wages, also, will fall, and both of these tend to restore profit margins. The destruction of capital reduces its supply and, thus, increases its potential value. Further concentration of capital and increased mechanization also tend to restore aggregate profits, and a wave of new investment will get under way to start the cycle over again. It should be noted that this argument not only ignores the underconsumption or purchasing power effects but also assumes competition rather than monopoly to be the dominant market force.

Despite the logic of this overinvestment argument it is contradicted in nearly every detail by actual depression experience. The rates of financial concentration and industrial mechanization do not increase in depression because business consolidations depend on rising stock prices upon which new securities issues can be capitalized. Furthermore, mechanization requires increasing profits, full production, and a labor shortage, none of which exists in depression. Prices do not ordinarily fall faster than wages in a recession, and even if they did, pessimism about job security and expectations of lower prices would reduce both consumption and profits. Probably Marx's theory of the crisis would have been more realistic had he stuck to his few speculations on underconsumption.

IMPERIALISM. In an attempt to offset the falling profit rate, capitalists, according to Marx, resort to imperialism. By investing their surplus capital in backward countries where the rate of profit is still high because of the capital scarcity, they could postpone the inevitable financial crisis. Furthermore, the rising political threat brought about by the increasing misery of the proletariat might even temporarily be forestalled as domestic workers shared in the prosperity brought about by colonial exploitation. However, capital would ultimately become abundant in the colonies, a mature proletariat would arise, and capitalism would face collapse once again.

The competition of capitalist nations for colonies to exploit was also considered to be the principal cause of wars so that the actual collapse of capitalism might take any one of several forms. One would be a war with other capitalist nations. However, the proletariat classes in all nations would soon realize that no one but the capitalists themselves could possibly benefit from wars, and thus the masses would turn on their exploiters or at least refuse to fight for them. Marxism influenced the non-Marxian socialists with this argument, and the result was a strong movement for pacifism which continued in strength until World War I and lingered in some areas until 1939. Probably the greatest single blow to socialist prestige—both Marxist and non-Marxist—was the political naïveté of twentieth-century pacifism which divided most socialist movements down the middle. The dilemma of the pacifists was apparent when the German Kaiser forced Britain and France into war. The German socialists could not, or at least did not, resist the Kaiser but allowed themselves to be pressed into his service. Socialists in other countries had the choice of fighting, which would save their capitalist nations, or refusing to fight and thereby insuring a totalitarian victory which would engulf the world. Nationalism won, the workers fought for capitalism and the socialist movement was a long time in recovering from the schism which the pacifist doctrine opened up.

Marx thought that the most likely form that the revolution would take would be an armed revolt at home or in the colonies or both. Even though the capitalist countries had democratic governments, Marx believed that a violent overthrow would be necessary. The mere fact that workers were in a majority in a democratic country did not convince him that the workers could use democratic means for ameliorating their conditions. He was so blinded by his economic determinism that he believed economic inequality bred political inequality of the same degree. The capitalist control of the nation's wealth meant to Marx the control of employment and elections as well. With their superior financial resources, and the reserve army of unemployed as a threat to every job, the capitalists could intimidate their employees to vote against reforms and could use their advertising power and their control over the means of mass communication to sway the rest of the populace by propaganda.

Although there is more than a suggestion of truth in these arguments, Marx vastly underestimated the possibilities of democratic reform under capitalism. He did not foresee the rise of powerful democratic trade unions, the growing control of business managements by government and public opinion, or the spreading ownership of industry among large numbers of people through shareholdings.

Marx accurately foresaw the growth of large corporate combinations but incorrectly attributed this movement to a relentless capitalist drive for profits. He failed to see that technological progress and the resulting economies of large-scale organization—both technical and administrative—and the advantages of controlling the destructive competition which is likely to occur among big firms were also important motives behind corporate combinations.

MARXISM VERSUS SOCIAL REFORM. Marx is reported on several occasions in his later life to have admitted the possibility that in England and Holland a peaceful, parliamentary evolution from capitalism might be likely to occur instead of a violent overthrow of the government. However, these statements clearly contradict all his writings, and it is the formal theory, with its violent emotional appeal, which has inspired his followers. More important, the over-all logic of Marxian theory precludes any peaceful adjustment of the contradictions of capitalism. There is no place for economic or social reform in the Marxian version of capitalism.

Reforms actually postpone or even prevent the revolution because they destroy the basis for a radical upheaval and set the stage for the rejection of the fanatical dictatorship which Lenin taught must follow the collapse of capitalism. But Marx did not seem to be particularly worried about the possibility of democratic reforms. In his day, working class conditions were deplorable, and if they had worsened, as he thought they would, a revolution would probably have followed pretty much according to the logic of his analysis. Marx himself recognized that peaceful reform would threaten the revolution, and he actually preached that the working class should avoid reforms and short-term palliatives and strive for total abolition of the system.

Both Marx and his followers have been bitter in their denunciation of non-Marxian socialism and other democratic reform movements like the American New Deal. Modern Marxists seem to despise the British socialists and American New Dealers more than capitalists anywhere, possibly because they fear that social reform bumps their revolution off the track. Engels, in many passages published from his correspondence, expressed fear that returning prosperity would postpone the revolution.[3] For example, he wrote in 1857,

"It would be desirable for this 'improvement' to have merged into the chronic crises before a second and decisive blow falls. Chronic pressure is necessary for a while in order to warm up the populations. The proletariat will then strike better, with better consciousness of its cause and more unity."

In 1858, after the crisis was over and recovery was under way, he wrote,

"The only thing that would help here would be a few thoroughly bad years, and since the gold discoveries these no longer seem so easy to come by."

Marx and Engels felt that English prosperity was being prolonged because of imperialist exploitation of the colonies in which the English working class was benefiting by sharing the capitalists' profits. They welcomed American competition for British markets because they thought they would break the economic ties between the British capitalist and working classes and permit the resumption of the trend toward increasing misery for the proletariat. Engels wrote,

"This link was their common working of a national monopoly. That monopoly once destroyed, the British working class will be compelled to take in hand its own interests, its own salvation, and to make an end of the wages system."

This attitude indicates a belief that the revolution can be postponed although neither Marx nor Engels believed that it could be prevented altogether. Engels on occasion expressed doubts, but Marx does not seem to have been seri-

[3] The following three quotations are from Dona Torr, *The Selected Correspondence of Karl Marx and Frederick Engels* (New York: International Publishers Co., Inc., 1942).

ously disturbed about the possibility that effective reforms would be undertaken within the capitalist economic system. It is ironical that the very reforms which did occur and which may well have prevented revolution were widely condemned as "socialist" and "communist" by the more conservative businessmen who would have lost the most by a revolution.

Why, then, do Marxists often support reforms such as social security, wage increases, and better working conditions if the adoption of such reforms prevents the working out of the Marxian logic? Why do they support programs which they realize threaten their goals, or, at the very least, are useless? One possible answer was vividly illustrated by the late United States Congressman Vito Marcantonio of the pro-Marxist, and now defunct, American Labor-Party. Marcantonio once threatened to insure the defeat of a Democratic opponent by publicly supporting him and his program. If Marcantonio had really believed that his cause would best be served by blocking social reforms and, hence, furthering the misery of the workers and hastening the revolution, he was shrewd enough to have capitalized on the current unpopularity of Marxism by openly supporting the measures which he wanted defeated. However, most Marxists are too dogmatically sure of their beliefs to be as tactful and politically astute as was Marcantonio.

A much better answer has been authoritatively supplied by Gerald Runkle who carefully analyzed a great volume of Marxian literature and concluded that there are four factors motivating Marxists to work for reforms even though the adoption of them would postpone the accomplishment of Marxist goals.[4] First, Marxism must be sold to the working classes, and this can only be accomplished if Marxists can secure the friendship and confidence of those who really want reforms. To do otherwise would be to forfeit the support of the people who must revolt against capitalism. Runkle says, "The Communist[s] must always weigh the harm they

[4] Gerald Runkle, "Communism and Social Reform," *Atlanta Economic Review*, November–December, 1954, pp. 1-5, 10-11.

do in getting a reform against the friendship they win in working for it." [5]

This would explain why the British Communist leader Arthur Horner was able to defy the Party line with impunity in 1950 by refusing to call for a strike of the coal miners' union, of which he was Executive Secretary at that time. To have followed Moscow's orders would have been disastrous for British workers and would have cost Horner his position.

Second, the workers have to be indoctrinated into Marxian economics. Marxists believe that workers need to be taught that no concrete improvements can come to them except by a revolution which destroys all private ownership of the means of production and abolishes the wages system, thereby ending the accumulation of surplus value once and for all. The result of this kind of propaganda has been to retard the real economic and social gains of the working class by sabotaging their genuine efforts for improvement and destroying faith in democratic procedures.

Third, Marxists support reforms in order to make propaganda capital out of social and economic injustices. They seek not to eliminate the evils of capitalism but to exploit them. While genuine social reformers are trying to correct injustices, the Marxists are loudly going on record as being sympathetic to the oppressed, but for propaganda purposes only. The Marxists' real aim is revolution, and they do not hesitate to sacrifice the workers' own cause if it furthers their revolutionary goals.

Fourth, the modern Marxists who follow Lenin and the directions of the Soviet government will support reforms when ordered to do so to further the political interests of the U.S.S.R. Thus, Marxists in all four of these cases will favor social reforms only when, and as long as, their action seems to serve the ends of a violent revolution.

In general, the Marxian theory of capitalist production is so subtle and intricate, so deviously logical, so devastatingly complete, and so highly unrealistic that it is difficult to escape the impression that the conclusions were drawn up first

[5] *Ibid.*, p. 10.

and the theory worked out later to fit them. Of course, a working hypothesis is necessary to begin with, but Marx seems to have begun not by trying to test some suspected relationships but by trying to prove that capitalism exploited labor. This is a big order, and although a good case for capitalist exploitation can be made under some circumstances, Marx's case is too complete. Every minute detail, every remote connection, is strained to the logical breaking point to prove his case. Marx's followers often go beyond all credulity arguing, for example, that Biblical taboos against pork derive from the mode of production, that the reduced calorie content of the modern worker's diet is proof of increasing misery (despite rising real wages), or that the events in China in the past fifteen years prove anything at all about the Marxist theory of capitalist collapse and revolution.

Modern Marxists are not economic scientists. They are disciplined soldiers of an illogical faith who enjoy the security of fanatical devotion to a pseudoeconomic theology. Their system of thought provides ready-made answers to all questions, predigested opinions on all subjects, the promise of sweet revenge for all real and fancied wrongs, and even the soul-purifying fire of persecution or martyrdom for the most faithful.

REVISIONISM

The basic contradiction between the Marxian goal of revolution and more urgent immediate goals of economic reform eventually led to internal dispute among Marxists. A revolt against the rigorous Marxian orthodoxy, called revisionism, was led by a nineteenth-century German socialist economist, Edward Bernstein, who questioned the whole revolutionary basis of Marxism. He denied the doctrines of increasing misery and capitalist concentration and argued that capitalism would evolve peacefully into socialism if the necessary reforms could be instituted. Socialism was a movement, to Bernstein, not a distant goal to be achieved suddenly through a revolution. "The movement," he said, "is everything, the end is nothing."

Bernstein, although basing his analysis on Marxian reasoning and Marxian terminology, nevertheless criticized the Marxian theory on several grounds. Most important, he objected to the attitude of many Marxists that the Hegelian philosophy and the Marxian theory were in any sense sacred or immune from attack. In this vein he attacked Marx for speaking of deterministic laws and scientific, quantitative relationships as though they were physical laws of nature. At best, he said, Marx was describing general tendencies, and the claim of scientific infallability was certainly unjustified.

Bernstein concluded that the entire Marxian analysis was an oversimplification. The class struggle, for example, had not sharpened to the degree Marx had predicted. New capitalists entered to take the place of those who were eliminated, concentration and profit rates varied greatly among industries, and the middle class was showing little inclination toward disappearing. Conflicts and struggles existed, to be sure, and capitalists were pitted against workers, but they were also often pitted against each other.

In the same vein, Bernstein seriously questioned the economic interpretation of history. He argued that social and religious factors could also influence the course of history. He said that although the economic factor might be important, to assign to it the exclusive role of controlling civilization was again an oversimplification.

Bernstein accepted in principle the labor theory of value and the theory of surplus value but considered them merely eloquent abstractions, of little practical value. Marx, he said, was merely belaboring the obvious in his lengthy and involved explanations of these concepts. To Bernstein, they were true, but irrelevant, since the evolution of capitalism was to be based on practical, short-run reforms.

The general criticism of Marxian absolutism led Bernstein to question the accuracy of the Marxian predictions. The collapse of the capitalistic system, for example, was not held to be imminent as Marx had thought. Neither did the misery of the working class seem to be increasing nor were crises becoming more frequent or intense. Bernstein felt that experience had demonstrated the possibility that the capitalist state, with the addition of a fully democratic franchise, could be used to secure reforms and also transform the economy into a fully socialist system without revolution. Consequently, he urged that socialists cooperate with liberal groups for attaining social reforms and support parliamentary democracy at all times.

It is not surprising that orthodox Marxists bitterly denounced Bernstein because the principle of the class struggle and the appeal to class prejudice owe their continued existence to an ideal of economic determinism. When doubts about the inevitability of a revolution are introduced a good portion of the theory of class struggle is threatened. It is always easier to secure support for the inevitable, even if the inevitable requires this support, than to compete for popular support with a theory which is to be fulfilled through immediate working class benefits and reforms. Thus, revisionism flourished in practice, even though rejected and condemned by the official Marxian organizations. In Germany, Karl Kautsky led the defense of orthodox Marxism, and the revisionists were voted down. However, revisionist views were more in keeping with the trends in Europe and Great Britain at the beginning of the twentieth century so that the heresy continued to flourish. Even in Germany, where the socialist movement carried the official approval of orthodox Marxism, revisionism came to be accepted more and more in practice until today West German socialism is little more than a liberal or reformist movement.

THEORY OF FINANCE CAPITALISM

Following shortly after the introduction of revisionism at the turn of the present century, an Austrian socialist, Rudolph Hilferding, made a significant contribution to the theory of capitalism. Hilferding was the leading theorist of German socialism of the 1920's and Minister of Finance for the Weimar Republic. Later he was imprisoned by the Nazis and was killed by them in 1940.

Although basically a Marxist, Hilferding believed capitalism was evolving toward state socialism through the growth of trusts, cartels, and other collectivist organizations. His theory of finance capitalism used an approach which contained elements of both Marxism and institutionalism.[6] Like Veblen he was concerned with the giant business enterprise and its role in the maturing capitalist economic system. Like Marx, he used value theory as the basis for his analysis and was concerned both with the dynamic elements in the capitalist system, which cause its evolution, and with the ever-changing conditions in the world markets. Particularly, Hilferding was interested in imperialism which, of course, is an international matter and, hence, had been beyond the scope of the German historical and American institutional models of the economic system. Nevertheless, his study of the large capitalist enterprise parallels that of Veblen, Berle, and Means.

Hilferding's first hypothesis concerned a basic difference between small and large corporations. The establishment of a market for the stocks and bonds of the large corporations makes it possible for profits to be made by trading in securities as well as in producing goods and services. Like Veblen's distinction between the pecuniary and industrial motives and the financial and production capitalists, Hilferding distinguished the promoter from other businessmen.

The promoter deals in intangible values. He buys stock for capital gain, or sells short in order to profit from a firm's adversity or from the declining prices which follow an over-inflated or overoptimistic market. By arranging mergers or forming holding companies, trusts, or cartels during periods of rising prices and optimism, he may be able to sell far more securities than the business can ever reasonably support. The promoter, typically an investment banker in the United States and a commercial banker in Europe, may make large profits from overcapitalizing business firms.

[6] *Das Finanzkapital* (Vienna, 1918).

These profits take the form of capital gains on stock purchased and sold, commissions, stock payments, and bonuses.

An interesting example in which a producer rather than a financier made the initial profit from the promotion of such a financial enterprise comes from an American experience. J. P. Morgan formed a holding company, the United States Steel Corporation, in 1903 after being forced to pay Andrew Carnegie over $1,200 million for steel works having a book value reputed to be only about $400 million. Carnegie was able to secure such a price because his enterprise was essential to the success of the venture. Had he remained outside the umbrella of United States Steel control, he could have wrecked the entire venture by reducing his prices. The United States Steel Company did not secure control of the entire industry, only about 60 per cent, but Carnegie was strong enough by himself to have kept Morgan from gaining a monopoly. Furthermore, Carnegie was the kind of person who might have wrecked the whole scheme, and Morgan knew it. Carnegie was paid off only after United States Steel had sold more than enough stock to cover the difference between the book value and purchase price of his works. Thus, United States Steel began its life highly overcapitalized, and although subsequent profits enabled the "water" to be "squeezed out" of the stock and the venture to be ultimately justified, in terms of profits, secret price-fixing and stock-purchase agreements kept the stockholders from finding out what had happened until a more solid commercial foundation was completed several years later.

Hilferding argued that the existence of opportunities, like this, to make huge profits through the medium of the national securities markets and without regard for actual productive possibilities leads to a cumulative trend toward larger enterprises, concentration of investment capital, and control over production by financiers. The chief concern of the financiers is for maximizing speculative profits and safeguarding their investments. Typically, these financiers are on the boards of directors of many business corporations and banks so that they can know very little about the problems of production in any particular firm. Hilferding believed that there was a tendency in this stage of capitalist development for a small group of these finance-capitalists to effectuate an increasingly centralized control over the nation's productive assets. The diffusion of stock ownership permitting proxy control and the widespread use of bonds and nonvoting stock for raising capital could allow a small concentrated investment to control a large industrial empire.

Widely owned companies are, in fact, easily controlled by minorities. Often 5 to 10 per cent of the voting stock held by the management is ample to secure proxies from the rest. When holding companies are used to own controlling interests in other corporations, the control of financiers can be pyramided. A small investment in a holding company may control it and, in turn, control other holding companies and operating companies. In this way Samuel Insull was able, in the 1920's, to control $20,000 worth of operating assets for every $1 invested in the top holding company of his thirteen-story Associated Gas and Electric Company structure.

By the use of interlocking directorates, pools, trade associations, cartels, and communities of interest, it is possible for the few large financiers in each industry to join hands informally with those in others to secure coordinated national control. Prices can be fixed and administered as European experience testifies. Output can be restricted to keep supply in line with demand at the prices which maximize profits. Hilferding carefully analyzed the trends in capitalist countries at the beginning of the twentieth century and concluded that there was a tendency for informal controls to become formal and organic. Thus, a gentlemen's agreement might lead to a trade association, then to a cartel, then to a holding company, and finally to a consolidation in which all individual units would become merged into a single, organic enterprise. As this process goes on, the vast majority of shareholders and other investors become almost completely stripped of all control over the corporations which they legally own.

According to Hilferding, after finance capitalists have secured effective economic control over the capitalist nation's productive assets, they then extend their control over international borders. Following Marxian economic determinism, the government cannot help but be greatly influenced, if not completely controlled, by the economic oligarchy of finance capitalists. It will thus raise tariff walls high enough to keep foreigners out of the domestic market altogether. International cartels will be formed which keep world prices high and consequently must restrict production. The excess capacity which develops puts great pressure on capitalists, particularly those with high fixed costs and high break-even outputs, to seek new markets. Since new home markets cannot be opened up without reducing prices and since cartels and tariffs prevent trade with other capitalist countries, the pressure of excess capacity is released in exports of capital to underdeveloped countries which cannot retaliate. This capital is used to create surplus value and bolster the falling profit rate. Even these outlets are temporary, however, and soon capitalist nations will be dumping their surpluses in each others' markets in violation of their own cartel agreements and competing vigorously for the acquisition of more colonies to exploit.

Hilferding's theory of finance capitalism is one of the truly important contributions to the modern concept of capitalism. His conclusions have been borne out to a surprisingly high degree, and his theory of imperialism is, together with a somewhat earlier study by John A. Hobson, the standard work in its field.[7]

Hilferding's analysis represents a considerable advance over that of Marx, partly because it was more realistic in its approach and partly because it was written at a later date and could take into account developments which could not have been predicted in Marx's time. Likewise, a prin-

[7] *Imperialism* (London, 1902).

cipal weakness in the study lay in its failure to foresee the growth of powerful forces, such as organized labor, public responsibility, and administrative regulation from government, which were to divert the trends to complete finance domination which seemed inexorable and uncontrollable in the early twentieth century. The theory of finance capitalism was no doubt relevant in its day, but this day has long since passed.

FABIAN CAPITALISM

The movement toward more "liberalism" in the socialist analysis of capitalism seem to have culminated in the thinking of the Fabian socialists in Great Britain. However, unlike Bernstein's revisionism and Hilferding's finance capitalism, both of which are properly classified as right-wing deviations from Marxism, the British Fabian socialists have a concept of capitalism which is based on values inherited from the classical economists, with some influence from pre-Marxian socialists like Robert Owen.

The Fabians were the first cohesive group of socialists to be concerned about socialism itself, and their contributions to the theory of socialism are considered in Chapter 10. Nevertheless, Fabian contribution to the economics of capitalism has been significant in itself in that it partly closes the gap between the socialist and classical theories of capitalism. Because the Fabian Society was founded to advocate the transformation of capitalism into socialism, its members, of necessity, had to acquaint themselves with both systems. Since the Society embraces many of Britain's keenest minds, it is not surprising that they have made original contributions of lasting value. The Fabian philosophy is pragmatic, and there is no official Fabian doctrine. Each individual speaks for himself only. Yet, there is enough agreement on basic principles to permit a discussion of the Fabian position in general.

Most Fabians reject the dialectic basis of Marxian analysis. They do not believe that capitalism must inevitably destroy

itself or that it has no other possible successor than socialism. They argue that there is no automatic progress in society but only a nearly automatic accumulation of knowledge
and power which can be used equally for destruction or
emancipation.

The Fabians analyze capitalism empirically much like
Sombart, Hilferding, and the American institutionalists.
They have sought out trends in the evolution of capitalist
institutions and concluded that while capitalism is indeed
undergoing a metamorphosis into a different system, the
form of their new system is not predetermined at all. Capitalism in its more or less pure form is certainly doomed,
say the Fabians, but they are not unmindful of the possibility that something worse may replace it.[8] Whether or
not socialism is established depends on the development of
human will and conscience, and, of course, on the definition
of socialism which is used.

This conclusion is due to serious doubts which the
Fabians have concerning the Marxian economic interpretation of history. Being as interested in politics as in economics, the Fabians have observed that human freedom is
not automatically secured when economic justice is achieved.
As empirical economists, they have become aware that
control over the means of production is more significant than
ownership. As political scientists, they have seen that control over the means of mass communications and political
influence (the press, party machinery, schools, radio and
television, etc.) can concentrate more power than control or
ownership of the means of production. Thus, the Fabians
have been able to avoid many of the pitfalls of Marxism
which failed utterly to solve, or even recognize, the problems of power relationships in a modern, industrial economy.

When Marxists were preaching to the workers that there
was no hope for them except by a revolution, Fabians were
saying that if this were true, then there was no hope for
them at all. Salvation from poverty and insecurity would
have to be sought peacefully through democratic means or
[8] *New Fabian Essays* (London: Turnstile Press, Ltd., 1952), pp. 45-73.

it would never be achieved. Peace, they insist, is not achieved by the sword alone nor can democracy be installed by anti-democratic means. While Marx objected to the logic of capitalism the Fabians object only to its injustices. The success of the Labor Party's post-war program in Great Britain can be traced, in part, to the political realism of the Fabians. Rather than offering a pattern into which society was to be remolded the Fabian-dominated Labor Party took over the function of liberalism and proposed a program of practical social and economic reform.

The Marxian labor and surplus value theories were never accepted by the Fabians who trace their intellectual heritage to the neoclassical school and who draw their inspiration from the liberal movements of the nineteenth century. The Marxian surplus value concept leads to the notion of a simple horizontal division of capitalist society into a lower and upper class which struggle toward the inevitable revolution. Most Fabians reject this concept entirely. Like the institutionalists, they recognize the existence of many power groups within the economy and see that there is no predictable outcome of their struggles. Nor do they consider capitalists to be so irrational as to endure severe losses during depression, as Marx assumed, rather than accept reforms. There is a whole new generation of businessmen who prefer high profits even if this requires the acceptance of collective bargaining or some governmental controls. These new-type capitalists no longer oppose every encroachment on their prerogatives or status if to oppose means to forfeit profits. Furthermore, the obvious failures of capitalism which led to the Great Depression are now accepted by most businessmen who fear that another such economic collapse will bring total and permanent government control. Thus, they are actively interested in preserving full and stable employment, and while they are suspicious of reforms, as such, and cautious in promoting social change, the important fact is that the old feeling of certainty about capitalism's success and the absolute faith in business judgment is pretty much gone.

Finally, the dilution of the function of the pure capitalist entrepreneur through corporate rather than individual control over production and the widening separation of property ownership and industrial management have caused power to pass into the hands of professional managers who are more responsive to public pressure and to the demands of technological change.

Fabians recognize a substantial improvement in the political freedom and economic status of all classes of people in the Western capitalist democracies since World War I. Even in the Great Depression there was no evidence of an increasing misery of the proletariat. British national income rose 20 per cent from 1929 to 1938, real wages rose 20 per cent from 1913 to 1938, and income per person rose 21 per cent during this same period. Of course, there is no doubt of the great social injustices and unemployment of the depression, but Fabians have been realistic enough to see that much of the depression conditions were due to complex international relationships rather than purely to the contradictions of capitalism.

What some Fabians call the "post-capitalist society" looks very much like the American "mixed economy" of social services, government support of labor and agriculture, dilution of absolute property rights, and a fiscal policy dedicated to continuing prosperity. Like the American New Deal-Fair Deal philosophy, Fabianism seems to seek a distribution of responsibility through diversification of ownership, an enlargement of freedom of choice by revitalizing the market, and an equality of opportunity.

In only one major respect does Fabianism seem to go beyond the New Deal-Fair Deal philosophy, and this is in the area of social, rather than the economic, reform. Fabians seek a greater equality of *status* and favor some rather radical educational and labor-management changes to secure it. This is easily explainable since, except for the Negro situation in the United States, there is greater status inequality in Britain than in the United States. Hence, the Fabian arguments for workers' control or participation in industry and the further dilution of aristocratic prerogatives and property rights seem redundant in the United States. Otherwise, there is little difference between what many Americans call the free, competitive enterprise system and what many Britons call socialism.

In the final section of this book, where a synthesis of modern theories of capitalism is attempted, it will be shown that those who fear socialism may rest more easily. The Marxist version is now so completely unrealistic that it no longer remains a serious intellectual threat to modern capitalism, while the non-Marxist version closely resembles programs which have long since been adopted in all capitalist systems. What the Fabian type of thinking has achieved in the way of practical, capitalistic reforms has contributed immeasurably to the final discrediting of the Marxist theory of capitalism.

6

Guided Capitalism:
Keynesian Theory

Plenty of Money never fails to make Trade flourish, because where Money is plentiful, the People in general are
thereby enabled, and will not fail to be as much greater
Consumers of every Thing, as such plenty of Money can
make them.———Jacob Vanderlint

Money is like muck, not good except it be spread.———
Francis Bacon

INTRODUCTION

The neoclassical economics withstood the head-on attacks
of the institutionalists and socialists with the same remarkable resiliency that the old classical school had shown in
surviving the assault of the German historical economists.
The institutional school has now virtually disappeared although it has had a lasting effect on established theory.
Marxism is finally being successfully challenged intellectually, but the battle is by no means won since Marxism
has a tremendous emotional appeal. Yet the rigid Marxist
dogma itself now shows signs of yielding to twentieth-century demands. However, classical economics survived not
because of any special attraction which the traditional approach had for competent theorists but because of theoretical weaknesses in its challengers. The historical and institutional schools tried to deal simultaneously with too many

variables and, having sacrificed scientific accuracy for realism, failed to develop more than a few fragments of positive theory. Marxism also tried to embrace all of the social sciences at once, and although it did produce some constructive theory, it vastly oversimplified the complexities of reality and went on to develop a complete theology with all of the answers to everything. This kind of dogma, with its inevitabilities, certainties, and infallibilities, was too much for most modern scientific minds to take seriously. After a brief eclipse, orthodox economics emerged again.

The neoclassical economics did not fare so well when John Maynard Keynes, using the very tools of orthodox analysis, exposed capitalism's diseased flank of unemployment and proposed a positive general theory to explain it.[1] Keynes (1883-1946) was not only the most celebrated British economist of recent times but a noted statesman as well. His theory of employment has influenced economic policies of all major governments as probably no other economic theories have done. Although he was primarily concerned with the causes of unemployment a theory of capitalism can be rather easily inferred from his analysis and conclusions.

Essentially what Keynes said about capitalism was that it was not self-regulating. Accordingly it would be necessary for some kind of authority to direct it or it might destroy itself. Keynes did not deny the classical theory at all but merely consigned it to the realm of a special case—that of full employment—among many other equally possible employment levels. In this sense, the Keynesian theory is a general one. The classical system of economics was molded after the Newtonian system of physics, with its mechanistic, internally-consistent, self-regulating forces. Like Newton's universal law of gravitation, the classical law of markets had been accepted as ultimate truth. But just as there had later developed some phenomena which the Newtonian theory did not explain, so unemployment and instability plagued the classicists whose theory did not allow for them.

[1] J. M. Keynes, *The General Theory of Employment, Interest and Money* (New York: Harcourt, Brace & Co., Inc., 1936).

Just as Einstein's more general theory of relativity explained why very small objects traveling at high speeds through vast distances did not follow Newton's laws, so did Keynes' theory explain why business activity sometimes did not seek a full-employment equilibrium. To carry the analogy further, just as experiment later proved Einstein right, fiscal policy experience later upheld Keynes, in part at least. Actually, there is no "right" or "wrong" as between Newton and Einstein or between the classicists and Keynes. Each theory is relevant in its own area.

BACKGROUND IN MERCANTILISM

Keynes' "General Theory," although widely heralded as the "new economics," is in some respects not new at all but had its roots in the preclassical economic system of mercantilism which existed in Europe, and particularly England, in the seventeenth and eighteenth centuries. Mercantilism was in some respects a politico-economic extension of a philosophy which had existed and remained largely unchallenged from ancient times down to the successful revolt of the philosophical radicals and the classical school of economists in the late eighteenth century. One of the basic assumptions of mercantilist thought which had its roots in antiquity was the idea that it was a normal function of government to intervene in economic, social, religious, and cultural affairs. Until the Industrial Revolution broke the age-old grip of landlords and made possible some degree of personal improvement through talent and effort, rather than through inherited status as it had nearly always been before, there had never been any serious suggestions that the government ought to keep hands off the economic system. In fact in most countries, rulers were conceded a semidivine status as was the existing social structure itself.

When commercial capitalism first began to arise in the late fifteenth and sixteenth centuries, it was accompanied by a shift in the source of governmental power. The medieval lords and nobles were losing control to newly-formed monarchies everywhere in Western Europe. Capitalism required this growth of national states because trade and commerce had been harassed by such devices as tolls on rivers and highways which were imposed by independent petty rulers and landowners under feudalism. Capitalism, with royal aid, tended to unify the various provinces and facilitate trade among them. The new national governments not only removed the restrictions on the flow of trade within their borders but undertook the construction of highways, canals, and harbors.

The newly-formed national monarchies also promoted uniformity through laws and regulations. Standardized systems of coinage, tariffs, weights and measures, and rules governing business transactions were established. State aid for science, invention, and education was given to promote technology. A high birth rate was encouraged to provide an ample supply of laborers. Foreigners with industrial secrets were lured into the country with prizes. Consumption of foreign goods was discouraged by governmental promotional efforts. For example, an attempt was made to build up the fishing trade in England by encouraging people to eat fish on Wednesdays, Fridays, and certain holidays in order to increase the consumption of fish.

Even greater stimulus for local industry came from high tariffs, subsidies, monopoly franchises, patents, and direct grants of money from the government. For example, the British East India Company and the Mississippi Company in France got their start as legal monopolies. Colbert, the infamous French Finance Minister, granted tax exemptions, interest free loans, and military deferments to businessmen. Patents were granted for window glass, salt and sugar refining, starch, paper, thread, cutlery, and other manufacturing processes.

Government encouragement of industry and commerce was accompanied by government regulation of nearly every aspect of economic life. Specifications concerning such things as quality and methods of manufacture went into almost unbelievable detail. For example, shoemakers at one time were required to comply with a directive regulating the number of stitches in the sole of a shoe. All monetary and credit transactions were closely regulated and prices were controlled.

A national system of labor legislation was introduced in England in the form of the Statute of Artificers (1562) which placed limitations on the choice of employment so as to favor the rural districts at the expense of the market towns. All able-bodied men who had no trade could be compelled to serve as agricultural workers. Severe penalties were provided for leaving the farms. In an attempt to stabilize employment, workers were required to have testimonials from their last employers whenever they left their parish or they could not obtain another job. The apprenticeship of all artificers was to be for at least seven years. Justices of the Peace were given authority to regulate wages although there were apparently no principles established on which the Justices might proceed. One means of regulation which was widespread was the taxation of wages. There was little uniformity in the use of these taxes except that summer wages were always taxed higher than winter because of the higher living costs in the wintertime.

The first Poor Law was passed in 1601. Under this law relief of the poor became the responsibility of the local governments since the Reformation had stripped the ecclesiastical authorities of so much wealth and power that they were no longer able to carry out this function. Overseers were appointed to collect taxes, distribute relief, and punish all able-bodied people who refused to work.

In spite of the high degree of regulation of commerce, capitalism prospered. Gradually capitalists made good their bid for power and supplanted the monarchs as chief economic policymakers. However, labor did not succeed in emancipating itself from government control. While monarchs replaced lords and capitalists replaced monarchs in the struggle for control over the economic system, labor was to remain in subjection both economically and socially for several centuries to come. Thus, capitalism under the mercantilist philosophy grew with the new national states and under the protection and control of royal authority.

Two ideas dominated this era. The first was the ancient recognition that economic and social policies were proper areas for government guidance. The second was the newer belief that national states were the basic economic entities rather than the multitude of tiny feudal domains which had been characteristic of the Middle Ages. Taken together these two concepts provided the basis for the philosophy of state guidance and regulation to increase national welfare which dominated the mercantilistic era.

Since the growth of national states was accompanied by long and expensive wars, the financial requirements of the monarchs grew steadily. Consequently, the means of achieving the national goals of prosperity and enhancement of royal power centered about the monetary system. Banking and credit were not well established at the time so most transactions of government and private business had to be carried out in gold. England, France, and the other new nations had no gold mines so the immediate means of increasing the national wealth became the accumulation of bullion through foreign trade. Consequently, tariffs on imports were raised, and exports were encouraged. With an excess of exports over imports, the balance due would be demanded in gold.

Of course, the mercantilists were not so naive as to believe that all nations could simultaneously increase exports over imports, but obviously some nations could do so if there were important importing nations, like Spain, who had access to gold with which to pay. Nor did the mercantilists confuse gold with wealth itself although a minority of extremists, called bullionists, apparently fell into this trap. Most mercantilists considered gold as merely one of the most convenient forms of wealth. Gold was desired because it could be traded in the Orient for spices which, in turn, could be sold in Europe for twice as much gold as the spices had cost.

Besides attempts to achieve a favorable balance of trade, other measures were imposed to increase the volume of pre-

cious metals within the country. The use of gold for orna-
ments and utensils was discouraged, and the export of
precious metals was carefully regulated. A corollary of the
principle of the accumulation of gold, or other precious
metals, was that of rapid circulation. Since gold was universally acceptable, it provided a means whereby profits
could more easily be secured in the form of other commodities. Thus, a high rate of gold circulation could multiply the profits obtainable. To achieve an increasing velocity of money circulation, ceilings on interest rates were
set by law to discourage savings and encourage spending.
The economic argument for low interest rates was consistent with the moral spirit of the time, which condemned
usury, so interest rates remained relatively low from the
sixteenth to the eighteenth centuries.

Coincident with the low interest policy was the beginning of a full employment policy through government expenditures. Spending, even foolishly, was lauded by Mandeville
in his famous *Fable of the Bees* because it created employment. Tariffs and subsidies to home industry were advocated
not only because they increased gold but because they created domestic employment and promoted national defense
and self-sufficiency. Some of the mercantilists began to
develop a novel view of the national debt. Sir James Steuart,
one of the last of the mercantilists, argued in 1767 that the
public debt ought to be expanded in times of unemployment
as this would increase the volume of money in the country,
thereby creating a greater demand for goods and an increase in employment. He was not overly worried about
the national debt. As long as it was internally held and not
excessively high, so as to impose a burden in paying the
interest, it was thought to be both a good investment for
the government's creditors and the basis for a monetary
system. The problems of taxation and the national debt
were to be considered as subsidiary to the aim of a high
level of employment.

Keynes may not have been fully aware of this mercantilistic background when he wrote his General Theory in

1936. This is not to imply that his great work lacked originality. None of the mercantilists, not even Steuart, conceived of anything approaching the completeness or the closely-reasoned analysis of the Keynesian system. They had a few glimmerings of insight into the fiscal problems of their times, but they did not attempt an over-all analysis of the economic system or even a systematic approach to any particular aspect of economic phenomena.

GENERAL THEORY

CRITICISM OF CLASSICAL THEORY. The classical and neoclassical theories had not provided adequate answers to the problems of inflation, deflation, and unemployment. In the classical and neoclassical systems there were built-in, natural regulators which automatically tended to stabilize the capitalist economy at full employment. With these regulators it was possible to assume that the economy would tend to balance, as on a razor's edge, between inflation and deflation. The neoclassicists devoted their efforts to an analysis of the prices and patterns of distribution of resources which would occur under varying circumstances of demand, supply, and market organizations.

With some minor reservations the neoclassicists followed Say's law which says, "Supply creates its own demand," meaning that every act of production generates, through the payment of wages, rent, interest, and profits, enough purchasing power to buy back its product. General unemployment could not occur in competitive capitalism because an excess supply of labor over the demand for it at current wage rates would cause wages to fall until employers would be able to hire all available workers. There might be unemployment and business losses in particular industries where producers had misjudged consumers' wants, but this would be offset by great profits and labor shortages in other places. Labor mobility would soon rectify this imbalance.

The price mechanism, also, operated to bring about a falling profit rate when industrial expansion slowed down.

When profits fell, savings would likewise fall, and consumption would rise because income was being transferred from high income groups, who save, to low income groups, who consume. Businessmen, whose income comes from profits, would save less as their incomes fell, and workers would spend more as lower prices transferred purchasing power to them. Thus, in the neoclassical system declining demand led to falling profits which in turn led to lower prices, greater aggregate spending, and, hence, an increase in demand.

If general unemployment did exist, it was due to the restrictions on competitive wage adjustments which were imposed (1.) by the government, through minimum wage laws, for example, (2) by unions which would strike rather than accept wage cuts, (3) by individual workers, who preferred unemployment to lower wages, or (4) by monopolistic businesses which raised prices or restricted output and employment.

In both the professional and popular thinking of the classical era, savings and investment amounted to the same thing. Businesses were typically small, and economic expansion was rapid, so the average person who had savings either acquired or expanded some small business enterprise or else lent his savings to someone who would. There was no way for businessmen to invest except by acquiring other people's savings or saving themselves so that all savings got invested. Thus, to alleviate unemployment, or increase investment, it was popular to advocate greater personal saving and reduced government spending. This would permit lower taxes and, hence, make even greater saving possible. Since it was assumed that all savings would be invested in productive capital, the greater total savings in a competitive money market would lead to lower interest rates and, hence, an accelerated rate of investment and employment. Reduced government spending and falling wages and other costs would also encourage businessmen to increase their output and eventually expand their productive facilities as well.

Thus, an additional remedy for unemployment was a vigorous campaign against business monopolies, labor unions, and social legislation because all these were thought to reduce the flexibility of price and wage adjustments and retard the mobility of resources.

Money was neutral to the neoclassicists. It was merely a means of exchange. Saving was thought of in terms of abstinence from consumption and was rewarded by interest. The rate of interest to be paid was determined by the money supply available from consumers' savings and this money's demand for investment by businessmen. Thus, the rate of interest was the price at which all the people's savings would equal businessmen's needs for capital investment. Through the money market, with its interest rate, all savings found their way into productive capital equipment, the exploitation of natural resources, or commercial opportunities. Since the neoclassical economists placed the blame for depressions on rigidities and frictions in the capitalist system, their program for combatting depression involved a highly dubious, and unpopular, attempt to change the economy to make it conform to their theory.

Keynes objected to the neoclassical analysis both on the theoretical grounds that it failed to consider the role of aggregate demand (purchasing power) and on the practical grounds that the policies which followed from it would not likely be accepted in an enlightened and democratic society. The neoclassical economics, according to Keynes, was devoted to analyzing the operation of a capitalist economy under assumed conditions of a full employment equilibrium when actually this was only a special, and rather unlikely, case among a whole range of possible employment equilibriums. Thus, he called his theory a general theory because it explained the operation of the economy at any level of employment. Actually, he did not object to the neoclassical analysis of prices and distribution at full employment. He merely believed that varying degrees of unemployment were theoretically possible, that full employment would be unlikely to persist in a capitalist system, and that the government would have to adopt a positive fiscal program to maintain full employment if capitalism was to be retained.

Keynes denied Say's law, arguing, in effect, that the total supply of goods produced could exceed the total demand because demand consists not only of money but also the desire to spend it. He saw no relation between the rate of profit and the businessman's attitudes toward saving and consumption that would automatically correct maladjustments in the market. If demand falls, consumers will reduce their spending because they anticipate lower prices and fear either lower wages for themselves or unemployment. This element of business and consumer pessimism had a highly depressing effect on the spending of money. The later neoclassicists failed to see that savings are no longer automatically spent for investment. Savings and investment are now undertaken by different people with different motives. Increased savings may be purely unintentional—a by-product of the decision of consumers to reduce their spending. Investment is defined as actual money spent on new plants and machinery not merely the purchase of securities, which is only a form of saving. Investment is normally undertaken by businessmen who borrow or otherwise acquire other people's money and hope to employ it in some profitable venture. The same conditions of pessimism because of declining demand, profits, and output can cause savings to rise and investment to fall simultaneously. Consumers may, for many reasons, desire to buy less than has been produced and by saving their money reduce the total demand for goods. No mechanism has been observed that would accelerate the growth of consumption at the expense of saving, thus taking up the slack created by a decline in the rate of investment. The benefits of industrialization may tend to be dissipated in unemployment rather than enjoyed in an automatically increasing consumption.

Keynes also plowed up the field of interest. Early classicists had considered interest as being a payment for enduring the pain of abstinence. It was a reward for practicing the difficult virtue of thrift. But this theory had been ridiculed by critics who pointed out that most saving was done by the very rich whose interest incomes could hardly be called a compensation for suffering the pains of abstinence. So this theory was replaced by a more defensible theory of time preference. Present consumption is worth more than future consumption. Thus, interest rewards those who serve by waiting.

Keynes approached interest from the point of view that it was a premium which must be offered to people to induce them to part with their hoarded wealth. In a world of uncertainty, cash is the most desirable form of assets since cash permits its owners to take advantage of sudden opportunities and gives them extraordinary market power to secure advantageous prices in a world in which most incomes are committed to credit purchases before they are earned. Thus, to Keynes, interest was a payment necessary to get people to give up this valuable "liquidity."

Rather than regarding money as a neutral means of exchange, Keynes believed people had a desire to hold money itself (called liquidity preference) because it is (1) needed for transactions, (2) useful for speculation, and (3) provides a hedge against the uncertainty which had become only too prevalent in the twentieth century. He defined interest not as the reward paid to savers for their pains in abstaining from consumption but the price which would induce people to part with their cash and hold less liquid assets instead.

THEORY OF FULL EMPLOYMENT. To Keynes the principal problem of economics was the determination of the level of employment. This focused attention on a set of aggregate concepts, such as expenditures, income, consumption, saving, and investment, and away from the orthodox individual concepts, such as consumers' utility, demands facing a firm, or the supply of particular goods which are forthcoming under certain conditions of individual profit motivation. Keynes did not deny the importance of these individual concepts which are associated with price-output theory. In fact, he accepted the neoclassical analysis of these relationships, but he maintained that they were relevant only in a full employment economy.

The level of employment, according to Keynes, is determined by aggregate expenditures (or incomes, as one is necessarily equal to the other). Expenditures are due to the total demand for goods and services. Goods and services are demanded by consumers, businessmen, and government, and the motivating circumstances surrounding the demand for each are different.

The level of consumption is that portion of the national income that is spent for consumers' goods. The relationship between the size of the national income and the amount spent by the public for consumption is called the propensity to consume. Keynes assumed that this relationship was relatively stable in the short run but tended to decline in the long run as income rose. This notion was based on the common observation that people with high incomes spend a smaller portion of their earnings than those in low-income groups. The higher the income, the more that is saved; the lower the income, the less that is saved until subsistence is reached at which, and below which, all income is spent on consumption. In aggregate, as national income rises, consumption rises, but less than income. Conversely, as national income falls, consumption falls, but less than income.

As national income rises, and the proportion spent for consumption falls, the difference (savings) necessarily rises. Unless the demand for goods by businessmen or government increases to fill this gap, surplus production will flood the market, output will soon be curtailed as a result, and employment and purchasing power will decline. Thus, in order to have enough total demand to permit an increase in employment, private investment or government spending must rise.

In the Keynesian system, investment plays a most crucial role. Whereas in classical economics investment and employment were uniquely correlated through the interest rate, in Keynesian economics investment is largely autonomous.

In a capitalist economy, the purchase of new capital goods is carried out for the most part by private businessmen. These investment decisions are determined by the opportunity to make a profit (called the marginal efficiency of capital) and the rate of interest. If the return on new investment exceeds the cost of the funds required to make it, businessmen will invest. But profit potentiality is an independent variable, subject to extreme fluctuations, and is determined by such things as technological innovations, population growth, tax rates, expected demand, quantity of similar capital goods in existence, and inventory changes. The interest rate is, thus, not a primary cause of investment but merely a negative deterrent. If interest rates are too high, this may prevent investment, but low interest rates will not necessarily stimulate investment because the total return on new investment may be even lower than the rate of interest. In depression this "marginal efficiency of capital" is frequently zero.

Keynes believed the interest rate to be determined by the supply of money—which the monetary authority can control—and the desire of individuals to hold cash—which, like the marginal efficiency of capital, is largely autonomous. He believed that the marginal efficiency of capital was highly unstable and that it had a long-run tendency to decline because expenditures on investment were not liquidated but remained in the form of fixed equipment to compete with all other fixed equipment. There was a long-run tendency for profitmaking opportunities to decline because the stock of capital goods continued to grow. Thus, Keynes' theory is better classified as an underinvestment theory than an underconsumption theory. Of course, insufficient consumption plays an important role, and Keynes favored highly progressive income taxes as well as social services to help increase purchasing power and consumer spending, but the dynamic independent variable is investment. This is the key to maintaining full employment. Socialist theories are usually purely underconsumptionist, but Keynes' underinvestment conclusions led him not to socialism but to a search for increasing investment opportunities within the capitalistic economy.

Direct government spending for public works seemed to be the most likely solution as long as private investment was not thereby discouraged. This might lead to a "socialization of investment," which involved not only large permanent outlays for public works but also controls and special inducements for private investment within a national investment plan which coordinated all investment expenditures without, however, interfering directly with private property.

New investment would not only create new employment but would also actually have a multiplied effect on employment. New money injected into the system is spent and respent. Every respending of the same money creates new employment and may even increase business confidence so as to call forth further spending for increased inventories and plant expansion. Allowing for leakages from saving and other losses, it was estimated at the time that a dollar of new expenditures would, after allowing time for circulation, create about three dollars worth of total expenditure and a proportional amount of employment.

Actually the "Keynesian Revolution" was largely a reorientation of economic thinking with respect to the classical view of employment. It was presented in a most orthodox, respectable manner and in the most conservative tradition. The fact that it assumed the proportions of a vast social reformation is due less to its radical nature than to its most opportune appearance and its logical, obvious, and readily acceptable solution to the most vexing economic problem of the times—unemployment.

DERIVED KEYNESIAN CONCEPT OF CAPITALISM

IMPLIED PRINCIPLES. Although Keynes was concerned with certain aspects of capitalism, as an economic system, he had no comprehensive or consistent theory of capitalism as did Marx, Sombart, or Schumpeter. This is probably due to his background in neoclassical economics with its emphasis on universal economic laws, short-run interests, and static analysis. Keynes had been brought up in the neoclassical tradition, having studied under Alfred Marshall at Cambridge. But shortly after World War I his orthodoxy began to waver, especially in his attitude toward money. Particularly, he urged abandonment of the gold standard and the adoption of a program of public works and government loans as a remedy for Britain's unemployment of the 1920's.

In an early book, Keynes had noted that although India was one of the world's leading gold-consuming nations, the demand for liquid assets was so high in that country that no capital growth or technological progress had occurred.[2] The international gold standard had operated successfully in the past, according to Keynes, largely because India had consumed enough gold to keep it in short supply in Europe, and this had led to high interest rates, which deter investment.

More significant was a later small book, *The End of Laissez Faire,* in which Keynes pointed persuasively to the evolutionary character of philosophy and economics and the growing obsolescence of individualism. Here he rejected the naturalistic basis of laissez faire by saying, "It is not true that individuals possess a prescriptive 'natural liberty' in their economic activities. There is no 'compact' conferring perpetual rights on those who Have or on those who Acquire. The world is not so governed from above that private and social interests always coincide." Not only did Keynes deny the unseen hand which the classicists had said channels individual self-interest into the general stream of public good but argued that it may be in the private interest of individuals to aggravate antisocial forces.

Keynes was equally critical of Marxism, saying it "must always remain a portent to the historians of Opinion—how a doctrine so illogical and so dull can have exercised so powerful and enduring an influence over the minds of men, and, through them, the events of history." Later he came to the conclusion that it was the religious-like fervor that Marx-

[2] *Indian Currency and Finance* (London: Macmillan & Co., Ltd., 1913).

ism stimulated in its followers, which compensated for its intellectual bankruptcy and caused it to be a serious competitor for capitalist philosophy in the minds of men. Capitalism, he maintained, had logic on its side but not any of the qualities which appeal to the emotions.

Keynes was also critical of socialist policies advocating nationalization of industry, saying, "There is, for instance, no so-called important political question so really unimportant, so irrelevant to the reorganization of economic life of Great Britain as the nationalization of the Railways."[3] This cynical attitude toward socialism together with a confidence in big business which was not shared by either neoclassical or socialist economists was due to his belief in two counteracting or compensating forces. One was a belief that the giant enterprise tends to socialize itself as it grows even larger. The second was a belief that there would be a natural growth of semiautonomous, semipublic bodies within the state. Nor did Keynes leave vague the exact meaning of the semiautonomous bodies. He referred specifically to public corporations like the Port of London Authority, independent agencies like the universities, and self-socialized private corporations like the railroad companies. It was Keynes' contention that large corporations were socializing themselves because of (1) the weakening of the profit motive which accompanies the bureaucracy of large-scale enterprise and (2) an increasing need to stay in favor of the already prejudiced public eye. Both of these factors stemmed both from large size and from the separation of ownership and control in large corporations.

Nevertheless, Keynes was a strong supporter of the profit motive. He believed that his proposals for abandoning laissez faire were not inconsistent with the essential features of capitalism, namely, the money-making and money-loving instincts of individuals. To Keynes, a capitalist society was one in which production was directed toward obtaining money. Capitalism was operated through a monetary system,

[3] Quotes from *The End of Laissez Faire* (London: Hogarth Press, Ltd., 1926), pp. 39-40, p. 34, and p. 44 respectively.

and the motivating force was profit. For the profit motive to be meaningful he recognized that there must be a legal and institutional framework which permits and protects substantial accumulations of private property in both consumers' and producers' goods. Freedom of contract and freedom from arbitrary governmental interference with the price mechanism must be protected, and markets must be relatively free from private or governmental restraints.

The instability of employment under capitalism, however, tended to weaken the more strictly capitalistic elements of the system, particularly the profit motive, because social controls would be demanded by the workers especially during periods of unemployment. Keynes observed that stronger movements toward controlled economies arise in depression periods, such as England between the wars and America in the 1930's. But he believed that government action would most likely be required to prevent depression and that only through such fiscal actions as government investment on a large scale would capitalism be preserved. Such government action he deemed desirable because of his belief that capitalism assured the most efficient and progressive system of production and distribution. Keynes disagreed with those socialists who claimed that full employment could be maintained only through public ownership of industries and a more direct system of economic planning. To Keynes, the question of public ownership was irrelevant to maintaining full employment. An economic system could be controlled so as to regulate employment just as well, or better, through fiscal policies of the government than through nationalization of private industries.

This is not to say that Keynes wholeheartedly endorsed all phases of contemporary capitalism. Like Veblen, he distinguished between the industrial and financial aspects of the system although the distinction was more implied than expressed. For example, Keynes opposed the gold standard because it depressed home industry with its restriction of credit although it unquestionably increased Britain's international banking business. Keynes never tired of attacking financial and speculative abuses but, nevertheless, was always a defender of private, capitalist enterprise.

Keynes' proposals for government policy fall into three general categories: first, direct government investment through public works and control over private investment in order to keep investment levels rising; second, strong central control over the monetary system in order to regulate the supply of money and, hence, interest rates; third, highly progressive taxation and social services to reduce the saving of the wealthy and increase the consumption of the poor. These three policies would counteract the normal capitalistic tendencies toward greatly fluctuating investment and chronic underemployment due to declining consumption.

In the Keynesian system, the role of government is that of a huge business enterprise with an impartial attitude toward its own surpluses or deficits. When the economy had inflationary tendencies, the government would make it a policy to have a surplus and, thus, deflate the economy by acting in direct competition with private business which makes large profits during inflation. This competition by government would not be in the form of producing goods to be sold to the public but would be by raising taxes on both business and consumers and reducing government spending. Both of these actions reduce purchasing power. This would, in turn, reduce prices, thus increasing the value of money and having the effect of decreasing revenues and profits to business without actually flooding the market by producing goods, which might be considered an alternative if unused productive facilities were available.

On the other hand, in periods of deflation government policies would change to those of a rich consumer with a desire to spend his money. By lowering taxes and increasing government expenditures (hence running a budgetary deficit) new money is pumped into the economy from the banks who buy government bonds both as a riskless investment and for their reserves. These bonds, representing additions to the national debt, are paid for with new checking accounts made available to government agencies. This new money put into circulation increases purchasing power and, thus, reduces the competitive pressure which businesses exert on each other in periods of stable demand.

Keynes did not attempt to promote or reject competition within the market organization. He largely ignored traditional problems of business monopoly although his proposals had the effect of regulating competition by the use of fiscal policy. The government would act to compensate the private economy, increasing or decreasing its competition with the business world as needed. If depression threatened because businessmen and consumers did not spend enough to keep aggregate demand at the full employment level, the government would employ people, invest through deficit spending for public works, and encourage consumption through lower taxes, social services, and consumer subsidies. These policies cheapen money, increase demand, and reduce the government's own competition by buying goods, a sort of negative competitive policy. Thus, competition everywhere would be reduced to the point where the outlook for business is again profitable and expansion begins. If the economy tended toward inflation because businessmen and consumers wanted to buy more goods than could be produced at full employment, the "big firm" government would reduce its expenditures and go through a neutral position, allowing competition to increase by virtue of keeping the money supply constant. If inflationary tendencies persisted, the government would take positive action through taxation to reduce the money supply, making money harder to get and, thus, going into direct competition with all forms of business for the consumer's dollar.

This compensatory fiscal policy which Keynesian economics implies suggests a second way in which the government can act as an offsetting or compensating mechanism to maintain stability and full employment. Many government agencies are primarily engaged in welfare activities, and none (it is hoped) are engaged directly in profit-making ventures. The primary criterion of their services is need rather than profitability. Government services tend to be (and certainly should be) supplied on the basis of need without regard for ability to pay for them although they should be financed through federal taxation which is based largely on ability to pay. This is a contrast with private business firms which tend to supply goods and services in proportion to their profitability, irrespective of actual needs, which may correspond to profitability or may not. In planning its expenditures the government agency first determines what services are most urgently needed, then estimates their cost, and finally, tries to secure funds through appropriations which are ultimately financed through taxation or borrowing. Even if the expenditures are financed through government borrowing, taxpayers ultimately pay the interest and principal through taxation which is based largely on ability to pay. This procedure is precisely inverse to that of the private firm which usually estimates sales first and then decides how much money should be released into circulation through expenditures for labor and raw materials.

Under capitalism most public needs, and virtually all public whims, are met by private business firms. However, the most urgent public needs are sometimes never met by private firms because of their inherent unprofitably (i.e., low cost housing, education), impracticability of collecting for the service (i.e., lighthouses, roads), or possible antisocial consequences of private enterprise (i.e., firefighting, disease innoculation). Functions falling in these categories are traditionally undertaken by the government, and as society becomes increasingly complex and urbanized these functions may be expected to increase.

Thus, the government also compensates the unbalancing activities of private firms in the provision of goods and services as well as in terms of total expenditures. Since government can then regulate both the quantity of total expenditures and the qualities of goods and services supplied to the community, a theoretical equilibrium at full employment and maximum total utility could be obtained. Contrary to a popular notion that the government is nothing more nor less than a business or household to be operated according to time-honored rules of individual accounting, Keynesian fiscal policy implications provide for a government which is precisely the opposite. Using different principles entirely, the government would balance incomes with expenditures, utilities with social costs, inflation with deflation, and social needs with political expediency.

Although such a theory of government operation in the capitalist economy has never been precisely stated, an important approach to it has been made by Abba Lerner.[4] Lerner approaches only the fiscal side of the role of government but demonstrates that the government can, and ought to, balance inflationary and deflationary forces generated by the private sector of the economy and that balancing the budget should be considered as secondary to maintaining full employment. Canada and many Western European governments have adopted policies of balancing their budgets over a period of years, the duration of which is thought to coincide with cyclical fluctuations. Following this rule, Britain and Canada piled up substantial budgetary surpluses as an anti-inflationary measure in the decade following World War II. Unfortunately neither Democratic nor Republican administrations in the postwar United States succeeded too well in following such sound fiscal practices.

Keynes seemingly neglected the problems of monopoly and big business. This may have been due in part to the general orientation of his economics which was primarily concerned with aggregate concepts such as employment, income, investment, saving, and so on. It may also have been due to the belief that large corporations "socialize" themselves and, thus, become more like the Keynesian government, with more important movitations than the drive for profit. If General Motors, for example, launches a billion dollar expansion program when unemployment threatens (as it did in 1953), there is that much less slack for the

[4] *Economics of Employment* (New York: The McGraw-Hill Book Co., Inc., 1951).

government to have to take up. Keynes' concept of the role of government explains his lack of interest in nationalizing industries; through control of money the government already has all industries "socialized" in that the consequences of business action, or inaction, can either be channeled into the public interest or offset by counterfiscal actions of the government.

Keynes elevated the consumer into an important position by making prosperity dependent upon him. Recognizing that the present structure of the capitalistic economy has evolved slowly over a long period of time, he did not intend to force society to back-track toward a nineteenth-century kind of capitalism. But he did not intend to impede further change. Keynes rejected what he believed at the time to be the socialists' attempt to force economic and social trends into an ideological plan that would be unnatural and strained. Instead, he recognized the changing nature of the economy and advocated a control system in the form of a big government which, being as flexible as the people who are elected to constitute it, could also change with the economic situation, becoming aggressive or passive, larger or smaller, as required. This is not to imply that government knows best what is good for the public, but rather that the population itself would force required changes through their democratic institutions. Businessmen were assumed to seek and settle on the most efficient technical and organizational means of production. The profit motive was absolutely essential for this as well as for increasing efficiency and technological progress. All this is evidenced by Keynes' lack of concern for the atomistic elements of the capitalist society. Keynesian policy allows for any and all forms of organization to exist and develop. Keynes realized that the short-run decisions of businessmen are often incompatible with their own long-run pecuniary motives. They generally take the alternative that appears to give them the most profit or the least loss, until they reach such size as to become subject to pressures from government and public opinion. The positive role of government lies in the maintenance of income at a level which will be favorable to the businessman's expectations of expansion. Under these conditions businessmen will accomplish by themselves what other economic systems try to achieve through direct controls or public ownership.

POLICY IMPLICATIONS. The implications of Keynesian fiscal policy proposals, although not socialistic, do pose serious problems for the long-run maintenance of some capitalistic institutions. If the outlook for capitalism is an insufficiency of investment and a lagging consumption, then the policy measures to remedy these and maintain full employment could threaten some of the features of capitalism because a slow, long-run inflation is almost sure to follow. Full employment itself has inflationary potentialities because of the upward pressure on wages which exists under these conditions. In a modern, complex economy it is difficult to achieve full employment in depressed sectors without causing an excess of demand, and, hence, inflationary conditions, in others. For example, a government spending policy which favored a depressed New England area could cause inflation in the South and West where there was already full employment because it would not be possible to confine the respending to the needy depressed area. Furthermore, to maintain full employment there must be a surplus of jobs over workers because the labor market adjusts sluggishly from lack of knowledge, occupational and geographical immobilities, and other frictions. This also puts an upward pressure on wages.

Keynes never advocated inflation itself, but it is clear that he was less worried about it than he was about deflation. Inflation would undoubtedly lead to a gradual elimination of those classes of people who live on interest and other fixed incomes, but Keynes believed it would be better to see these classes forced into more productive employment than to have the country suffer the real waste of unemployed resources or risk the danger of social revolution which depression engenders. Like the socialists, he doubted that interest income was really "earned." As for pensioners, inflation requires social security with increasing benefits if they are to be protected.

Assuming that the only alternative to a mild inflation is a mild deflation, the reasons for favoring a modest inflation are obvious. The unemployment of machines and natural resources represents only a temporary loss of production to the economy, it is true, but the unemployment of men is a threefold absolute loss. First, depreciation of human beings is more a function of time than use. The loss of production through idle human time can never be recovered later by extending the life of the unemployed person. Second, skills and talents deteriorate during unemployment requiring extensive retraining to restore them if it is possible at all. Third, the psychological effects of unemployment lead to low morale, despondency, and often a shorter, less productive life because of enforced idleness. Suicide, murder, racial violence, and armed revolt are not unknown as consequences of unemployment.

Depression experience has shown that deflation puts a burden on workers whose wages fall faster than the prices of most of the things which they must buy. Deflation strengthens the "dead hand of the past." This would include those property owners who came to their positions through status, monopoly, or inherited wealth. Thus, Keynes envisaged the "financial" capitalist (promoter or manipulator) as declining in importance in the long run but the "industrial" capitalist (producer) as gaining in significance.

As for lagging consumption, Keynes believed social services and progressive taxation would not weaken any important aspects of capitalism but indeed would strengthen them. True, great inequality of incomes had led to capital accumulation in the first place. Capitalism could never have survived if equalitarianism had existed in the days of the Industrial Revolution. It is fortunate for us today that political democracy was so imperfect from the fifteenth to the eighteenth centuries because an enlightened, politically emancipated working class would likely not have permitted the extreme inequalities which were imposed on workers in the early stages of capitalism. Yet these inequalities led to the large capital accumulations upon which modern capitalism is based.

Lately, however, saving, for many, has become an end in itself, and now that workers have tasted the fruits of capitalist production, they are likely to want ever-higher consumption which can only be achieved through greater income equality. This need not destroy capitalism. In fact, once the capitalist productive machine has been constructed, great inequalities are not so essential to further progress. Production now tends to outrun consumption, and inequality hastens this process. The Marxian remedy for this was to socialize all income-producing property (capital goods). Keynes saw no need for this because he thought property income was due to scarcity of property. Public works could make capital goods more abundant, and hence, the profits to be made from them would fall. Eventually all incomes would go to labor (including "management") where they rightly belonged. Thus, Keynes concluded with a Classical-Marxist type of labor theory of value except that he defined labor broadly enough to include the functional labor of entrepreneurs or businessmen although not the contributions of landlords and money-lenders.

A policy of progressive income taxation combined with broad social services would reduce the existing inequalities of income and wealth and consequently raise the level of consumption. This would partly relieve the need for great public and private investment programs to fill the gap between that level of national income which is required to maintain full employment and the lower national income generated by businessmen in their attempt to maximize profits by investing in capital equipment which has a declining marginal efficiency for them. In the long run, then, capitalism would be purged of its speculations, financial abuses, and "unearned" incomes. Under government fiscal guidance, capitalism would emerge stronger, more progressive, more prosperous, and more stable.

SUPERKEYNESIANISM

Stagnation Thesis. The theory of guided capitalism which seems to unfold from the vast Keynesian literature is fairly widely accepted today. Often Keynes' own theory, however, is confused with the theories of some of his followers who tried to make long-run predictions about the economic system using Keynesian language and methodology but with different assumptions. Particularly, there was a group of Keynesian economists, with Alvin Hansen of Harvard as the leading spokesman, that studied savings and investment relationships in the United States in the late 1930's and concluded that American capitalism had reached "maturity" and that "stagnation" would set in unless Keynesian fiscal policy proposals were rigorously applied.[5] Although Keynes himself believed that depression would have to be avoided at all costs, his theory should not be confused with the stagnation thesis, which is not generally accepted by most economists today and goes considerably beyond what Keynes himself would probably have accepted.

The most unique and controversial feature of the stagnation thesis concerns a decline of investment opportunities, which, it was argued, would cause future private investment to be too low to offset the savings which would be forthcoming at a full employment level. The conclusion was that capitalism would develop a deep, chronic unemployment unless rather drastic government measures are taken.

In the 1930's, Hansen and others thought investment opportunities were disappearing. The "Depression Decade" was in obvious contrast to the golden nineteenth-century era of American economic expansion when the nation still

---

[5] The basic arguments of the stagnationist school are set forth in several books by Hansen including *Fiscal Policy and Business Cycles* (1942) and *Economic Policy and Full Employment* (New York: The McGraw-Hill Book Co., Inc., 1947). The principal criticism is found in George Terborgh, *The Bogey of Economic Maturity*, Machinery and Allied Products Institute, 1945. An even partial bibliography of the literature on this subject would fill many pages.

had vast, rich areas inviting exploitation. Capital had been easily absorbed in the nineteenth century because of the tremendous population growth. England's population quadrupled, Europe's trebled, and the United States' population increased fifteenfold during the century. In contrast, the depression of the thirties posed an apparently permanent surplus of capital and a shortage of markets and purchasing power. Dominant industries like railroads, steel, and electricity have been extremely important in the economic growth and relative decline of certain periods during which these industries ran their course. The original Industrial Revolution was accompanied by a great rise in output and incomes followed by a leveling-off period. Then the railroad age arose with an initial period of great capital outlay only to be followed by eventual saturation of capital investment in this area. The electrical and automobile industries had followed similar patterns, according to Hansen.

Recent innovations in the electronics and telecommunications industries illustrate that investment outlets are still available and to be hoped for, but they do not appear to be in a steady stream, and there is no assurance that they will continue.[6] George Terborgh, who is Hansen's leading critic, called this the "great guessing game," and it is doubtful whether the point is worth belaboring. It is never possible to prove in advance that undiscovered opportunities will be adequate to insure a continuance of the current rate of economic development. Furthermore, once a nation has completed the construction of its basic industries and its transportation and communications systems, new industries are more likely to become oriented toward the production of consumers' goods. These latter industries are not the primary determinants of growth because they do not absorb investment at the high rate that the basic capital goods industries do. Nor is there any assurance that their growth will continue. A widespread prewar prediction was that airplanes

---

[6] W. R. McLaurin, "The Process of Technological Innovation," *American Economic Review*, March, 1950.

would soon replace automobiles as a means of private transportation, yet this prediction seems even farther from fulfilment than it did in 1935.

One reason why stagnationists doubted whether new industries would arise at the same rate as in the past was based on the declining rates of population growth in the thirties. Hansen estimated that between 50 and 60 per cent of the net capital formation in the past had been due to the growth of population or the opening of new territory. If population trends between 1920 and 1940 are projected into the future, an absolute decline sets in about 1970. World War II and the years following witnessed a reversal of prewar trends, however, and population is now exploding apparently without bounds. As a consequence, the major problems of the future may be associated with overpopulation rather than underpopulation. This is no insurance against stagnation (as witness some Far Eastern nations) but may offer increasing expansion opportunities in the form of additions to existing capital equipment and rising consumption levels and, hence, living standards, if full employment and productivity growth continue.

Opponents of the stagnation thesis could not understand why declining population trends should affect the economy of the thirties when the rates actually began to decline seventy-five years earlier. In Sweden, for example, economic progress has occurred despite an apparent stability of population. Terborgh argued that countries with a rapid rate of population growth have not increased their per capita production more rapidly than those with slow population growth. Anyhow the rate of population growth has little to do with the level of investment opportunities.

Another reason for declining investment opportunities cited by the stagnationists was the closing of the geographical frontier. Terborgh noted that if the disappearance of the frontier in 1890 with the end of the era of westward expansion and expiration of the Homestead Acts was going to trouble us and have any effect at all, it should have begun to trouble us long before now. Hansen's reply to this was that the development of new lands in the West greatly influenced capital formation in the older sections of the United States and consequently a time lag was to be expected. Stagnationists admit that opportunities for investment did not begin to decline immediately when the frontier closed. It was not until the 1930's that the disappearance of investment opportunities reached a scale large enough to cause great unemployment. It takes time to consolidate the springing up of new industries and cities and the forging together of a national transportation system. The rate of increase in per capita man-made wealth was greater in the East than in the West during the first thirty years after the passing of the frontier in 1890, but this was caused, said Hansen, by the great production stimulated in the East as a result of enlarged Western markets. Since the major insurance companies and manufacturing industries had their main offices in Eastern cities, Western orders for new capital investment were placed largely in Eastern trade centers which were already developed for this task and could produce more efficiently.

The antistagnationists answer that the world beyond American borders does not lack investment opportunities. If political restrictions could be lessened, bold and imaginative programs of investment could be undertaken. The Truman Point Four program, for example, could be an effective weapon for combatting the stagnationist pessimism about domestic investment opportunities.

The stagnationists have also been concerned about the decline of foreign markets which threatens to exhaust the opportunities for development which led to the great economic expansion of the nineteenth century. This cannot be completely refuted by pointing to the great poverty both at home and abroad in the world and concluding that the elimination of low living standards will require centuries of high-level production. The stagnationists are not unaware of the opportunities to build houses for the millions of homeless people in the world and of the great prosperity which such a program would induce for possibly a century, but they doubt whether such programs can be undertaken by private businessmen without substantial government assistance because of the high commercial risks and low profits involved. Unfortunately, there has usually been more profit in housing lower-income people poorly than in housing them well.

In addition to the domestic and foreign frontiers, the stagnationists argued that another kind of frontier had been closing. Technological development at this stage of the evolution of capitalism cannot absorb the volume of savings being offered, and technology, they say, is becoming increasingly capital saving rather than capital using. Two important concepts are used in connection with this program of the effect of technology on the demand for capital investment. One is the "deepening of capital"; the other is the "widening of capital." The deepening of capital means the use of more capital per unit of output. Some economists hold that since our industrial machine is largely completed, the need to substitute capital for labor is past, and future demands for capital will be largely for modifications and replacements. New technical improvements tend to be capital saving more than labor saving. In other words, less and less capital goods will be needed to produce a given unit of output.

Opponents point to certain new industries which have recently experienced a deepening of capital, such as television manufacturing, where heavy investment has been made to improve the quality of the product. Other industries which would not be capital saving are awaiting exploitation, such as plastics, electronics, aeronautics, and, of course, atomic power. But this brings us back to the first complaint of the stagnationists—that new industries are not sufficiently forthcoming. The stagnationists would seem to be wrong here although there is no doubt that as industries grow older they often tend to become more capital saving.

The widening of capital means the utilization of more capital as a result of increased demand. Some studies have shown that capital formation in the twentieth century in

England and the United States has apparently been due to a widening of capital whereas capital formation in the nineteenth century consisted largely of deepening of capital. If labor-saving inventions are used to tap a potential consumer demand through flexible price policies, a widening of capital would probably follow since lower prices would stimulate purchasing power.

There is an interrelatedness of economic factors which the stagnationists underestimate. Not only do frontiers, population growth, and opportunities affect economic expansion, but this very expansion may stimulate the conquest of new frontiers, foster increased population growth and create its own opportunities. It may be true that capitalism develops the causes of its own stagnation, but it may also influence its own external environment and, hence, create or stimulate conditions conducive to further economic expansion.

Keynes once said that his ideas would still be followed by some people a hundred years after they had become obsolete. This statement may be applicable to the stagnationists. Certainly if the stagnation thesis had to stand on the argument of exhaustion of opportunities alone, it would probably not be a contender for serious consideration today. However, when it is bolstered with other, but less original, arguments, it becomes a rather complete theory of capitalist development which may be considered as a logical outgrowth of one phase of Keynesian theory. Following Keynes, the stagnationists foresee a falling profit rate due to a saturation of capital which reduces the profit rate on each additional investment. Underlying this argument is the assumption that demand is not unlimited and that, hence, it is possible for capital to become redundant. It is true that wants are limited in some primitive societies and that basic needs are satiable in a great many more. However, it is generally recognized that human wants greatly exceed capacity to satisfy them in all industrialized countries and that the capitalist economic system tends to create new wants constantly. Economic and political freedom, a high level of education, a materialistic and rationalistic philosophy, and, of course, billions of dollars worth of advertising have all contributed to this.

But unlimited needs or wants are not necessarily equivalent to effective market demand. The desire must be there, of course, but there must also be the ability to pay the price that is likely to be asked by manufacturers in what may be increasingly monopolized markets. It is difficult to imagine an economy in which there is a saturation of every kind of imaginable goods, but it is not difficult to remember the general insufficiency of demand of the Great Depression. It is even easier to imagine a surplus of capital because most industry today depends on mass markets, and a contraction of demand due to inadequate purchasing power may easily render capital equipment idle. This is especially true where production occurs under conditions of monopoly or semi-monopoly, and the businessman has it within his power to reduce output rather than prices.

This possibility leads directly to another stagnationist argument based on the old underconsumption theory that excessive income inequality will cause a rate of consumption which is too low to insure an adequate demand for consumers' goods. This argument, when taken with the declining investment opportunities argument, leads to the conclusion that there tends to be an ever-widening gap between savings and investment and, hence, an ever-increasing unemployment. The rate of investment falls with the profit rate because of declining opportunity and capital saturation. The rate of consumption falls because lower income groups cannot afford to consume as much as they would like. The inadequacy of consumption leads to a decline in sales and, hence, production and employment so that there is a cumulative decline of profits, investment opportunities, and employment.

Even if consumers have adequate incomes, they may refuse to spend enough to maintain full employment because of pessimism. Consumers may prefer to save because of unemployment, fear of unemployment, or expectation of lower prices. If enough consumers behave this way, they will bring on the unemployment they fear and, perhaps later, because of monopolistic rigidities, the lower prices they seek. Unfortunately the lower prices are likely to follow so far behind the unemployment that they will be of little benefit to consumers when they finally come.

This general line of reasoning is more sophisticated than the early socialist and other underconsumption arguments and has gained considerable professional acceptance. To the contrary, it can be argued that if stagnation occurred there would be little incentive to save, and this would increase consumption. It has also been maintained that unemployment gives people a chance to seek new job opportunities and that idleness stimulates innovation which may turn the tide toward prosperity again. It has even been argued that lower costs are finally reflected in higher profits and the depression will end as optimism follows the upturn. However, there has never been much convincing evidence to substantiate these counterarguments.

One stagnationist argument is neither Keynesian nor a logical extension of the Keynesian system. It concerns the metamorphosis of business organization. As the economy becomes older and more "mature," it becomes less flexible and less adaptable to change, thus causing maladjustments to continue indefinitely or grow worse. This reasoning is based on assumptions concerning competition and monopoly which Keynes did not consider at all. It owes more to the institutionalists, the historical school, and Marx than to Keynes. Because it attempts to tie together the Keynesian system and the theories of capitalism which are based on the evolution of market systems, this question will be considered in subsequent chapters.

NEW HORIZONS FOR PROSPERITY. The general underconsumption theory in its more refined and sophisticated form has survived its attackers fairly well. As Kenneth Boulding has pointed out, "A rich society must be equalitarian or it will

spill its riches in unemployment." [7] The underconsumptionists have been theoretically correct, but they failed to anticipate that capitalism would be able to attack income inequality with sufficient success to insure full employment. The
permanent reliance on the highly progressive income tax, the
increasing power of organized labor to raise wages, and the
effectiveness of compensatory fiscal policy (under both
Democratic and Republican administrations) have helped
avoid the situation which the stagnationists, and underconsumptionists in general, feared would come about.

In addition, the consumption function has not remained
stable. Four stimulants to consumption tend to dispute
Keynes' original thesis that as incomes rise consumption will
rise less than proportionally. First, the older age groups,
which are increasing in the United States and Great Britain,
consume more proportionately and save less than younger
people. Second, industrial countries become increasingly
urbanized, and city dwellers consume a higher percentage
of their incomes than do their rural neighbors. Third, the
fabulous growth of consumer credit since World War II
threatens the economy with overconsumption, undersaving,
and consequent inflation more than stagnation. Fourth, expanding world trade, if it continues, increases consumption
potentials. With these stimulants to consumption, the investment necessary to offset savings and fill the employment gap appears now to be much less than the stagnationists
thought. Yet, although consumption rates have risen more
than Keynes expected, the principle of consumption declining proportionally with higher incomes still holds. A
ten-volume study of the consumption habits of 12,500 families, made at the University of Pennsylvania and published
in 1956, shows that families making $3,000 to $4,000 spend
102 per cent of their incomes (thanks to easy credit), families making $5,000 to $6,000 spend 97 per cent, those making $7,500 to $10,000 spend 83 per cent, and those above

[7] *Economics of Peace* (Englewood Cliffs, N. J.: Prentice-Hall, Inc., 1945),
p. 111.

$10,000 spend only 69 per cent. The average of all was 95 per cent of disposable income.

Keynesians and stagnationists have argued, contrary to the neoclassical view, that savings and investments are not reciprocally motivated. The neoclassicists had believed that changes in the interest rate would equate savings with investment at the full employment level. Keynes, however, assumed that consumption was a function of income level and that interest rates had very little effect on consumption habits. Stagnationists point to the conclusions of the Ezekial study of the 1921-1940 period which showed income and changes in income to be the major factors related to movements in savings and consumption.[8] Some of Keynes' followers contended that a free-market interest rate would not fall to the point that investment would become profitable. They advocated low, controlled rates of interest. The evidence seems to show that as a means of installing a recovery atmosphere in a depression economy, a low rate of interest is relatively ineffective. In depression, when new investment has no profit at all, low interest rates certainly will not induce capital expansion. If existing plants are idle, a businessman would not borrow, even at no interest, to expand his capacity. When the RFC offered low-interest loans to depressed businesses in 1932, the railroads and others used the money to pay off their existing high-interest debt. More important for inducing capital expenditures than the cost of money are such things as the prospective volume of business, the economies resulting from the introduction of new machinery, and the anticipation of probable success of new ventures.

Many stagnationists and others confidently predicted a depression shortly after World War II. The failure of these predictions appears to be because the economists projected depression level consumption rates into the future when actually pent-up demand caused consumption to be much

[8] Mordecai Ezekiel, "Statistical Investigations of Saving, Consumption and Investment," *American Economics Review*, March, 1942.

higher after the war. For other reasons also the propensity to consume may rise. People may become convinced that prices are going to increase for a long time to come and may thus increase their expenditures percentagewise. The awareness that inflation will erode savings away may cause a progressive and permanent increase in current consumption. The failure of the postwar predictions of a severe slump tended to discredit the stagnationists although it does not significantly alter their basic arguments except to emphasize that the propensity to consume is less stable than it was once thought to be. Stagnation is still a possibility although not as immediately as was believed in the 1930's.

In summary, the evidence for the stagnation thesis is inconclusive although some of the individual arguments of stagnationists seem well founded when considered by themselves and not as conclusive evidences of general stagnation. The arguments on both sides are often dramatically presented, and this, unfortunately, has led to a popularization of the controversy which on occasion has deteriorated to the point of casting aspersions on the loyalty, or at best the good intentions, of the stagnationists, and on the social conscience of the antistagnationists. It is true that the stagnation thesis reflects unfavorably on the continuing vitality of some of our most hallowed institutions, but this should not be allowed to obscure the real issues which certainly deserve full and fair consideration regardless of whether they are pleasant to comprehend or not.

However, at best, the stagnation thesis is far from being proved. In assuming a stable or declining relationship between consumption and income, it clearly failed to foresee the trends following World War II which have shown a rising percentage of income spent for consumption. Furthermore, the prewar decline in the rate of population growth has been sharply reversed with consequently stimulating effects on many industries, particularly home construction. Finally, in recent years there has been a tremendous reduction in the great income inequality which early Keynesians regarded, along with insufficient investment outlets, as the basic causes of unemployment.

It is not likely that the immediate future will witness any great movement toward further equality. In fact, there has arisen a considerable amount of feeling that the progressive income tax which has accomplished the leveling process of recent years has gone about as far as it can go without seriously affecting investment incentives. Undoubtedly, highly progressive tax rates deter investment by eradicating the wealthy classes who are able to save in large amounts. British experience since World War II where income tax rates are much steeper than in the United States has demonstrated this. However, the fact that there is considerable concern about inflation and overinvestment and that credit controls and higher interest rates are being employed to keep expenditures under control is evidence that the problem is not yet a serious one in this country.

It may well be that the corporation income tax will stimulate the growth of new sources of investment capital which will offset any possible adverse effects which the personal income tax will have on private investment incentives. For example, three-fourths of all new capital already comes from sources internal to the corporation, and, consequently, it is subject to a positive rather than negative effect from taxation. High tax rates encourage expansion from profits since the expenditures are tax deductible. Capital expenditures thus reduce the tax load. More progressive corporate income tax rates with deductions for approved capital expenditures might stimulate more new investment than the complete abandonment of all corporate income taxes. Of course, personal income taxes tend to discourage risk capital put up by individuals, but industrial expansion does not rely heavily on this any longer.

Furthermore, there has been a trend toward replacing individual savings by automatic, collective, "forced savings" devices. Pension funds have grown enormously in recent years, and the funds have been invested more heavily in common stocks. This increasingly important source of investment capital is not affected directly by high personal income tax rates since the investors are institutions, not individuals, and may in fact be stimulated by high corporate tax rates since the company's contribution is deductible. This further militates against the possibility of stagnation.

POST-KEYNESIAN THEORY OF DYNAMIC CONSERVATISM

Two principles seem to underlie the "conservative revival" which was culminated by the Republican victory in 1952. One was that the government should be "neutral" in its effects on the economy. This meant that taxes for all purposes should be kept to a minimum and, where necessary, designed so as not to affect incentives, or savings of production. Government spending should follow the same rules. In the area of monetary policy, the quantity of money in use should be determined by its demand by the private economy. The supply of money should correspond to the volume and velocity of transactions so as to exert no influence on prices. The administration apparently accepted this principle initially. The second principle is accepted wholeheartedly only by the extreme "right wing" Republicans. This is that the government should have no economic functions at all—as distinguished from military and political responsibilities. This group feels that any productive economic activity of government is due to a conspiracy on the part of politicians and bureaucrats to enhance their own personal power and prestige.[9]

If there is any positive economic function underlying the Republican administration, it is expressed in the seemingly contradictory slogan, "dynamic conservatism." Symbolized by the Presidential Economic Assistant, Gabriel Hauge, it recognizes that the government must take some responsibility for the general economic climate but would control

[9] Arthur Schweitzer, "American Competitive Capitalism," *Schweizerische Zectschrift für Volkswirtschaft und Statistik*, XCII, No. 1 (1956).

mainly by monetary policies and, failing there, by traditional Keynesian fiscal policies. The Federal Reserve Bank is relied on heavily to restrict credit and raise interest rates. The fact that the federal budget remained unbalanced in three of the first five years of the Republican administration is evidence that fiscal orthodoxy has not been achieved. Also, the fact that the nonmilitary budget has risen substantially and steadily since 1952 shows that high government spending has not been abandoned altogether.

The slump of 1953-1954 forced a reversal of the Administration's monetary and fiscal policies. Quick action was taken to reduce interest rates, increase government spending, and thereby bolster the sagging economy with Keynesian policies. This action dramatized the facts that (1) there is no self-regulatory mechanism in the private market area and (2) the public sector of the economy is so well established that it cannot easily be discarded. Thus, the concept of a government without economic functions was readily abandoned by the "conservative" administration as soon as trouble threatened.

CONCLUSION

It is perhaps too easy to stress the similarities between the old European, particularly English, mercantilism and the modern Keynesian concept of capitalism. The similarities do exist, and a comparison of them is striking. However, the growth of democratic institutions in the last four hundred years and the appearance of general unemployment as a threat to economic stability have combined to change the emphasis of modern mercantilist-type thinking. The methods of state control remain, but the ends have changed. The sixteenth- and seventeenth-century monarchies used regulation to increase the national power of the state, to foster business enterprise, and to maintain the aristocratic alliance between capitalists and royalty.

The new mercantilism exists in a framework of new economic knowledge and popular government. The goals, therefore, have become increasingly consistent with the economic necessities of the times as well as with political expediency. True, private property and private enterprise remain generally unchallenged, but they are subject to regulation, not in their own interest alone, but in the interests of a community which is broader in scope than early mercantilists envisaged. The common welfare is still the goal of government policy, but now it is the masses of the people, rather than a privileged, propertied few, who determine what the common welfare is to be and how it is best served. Furthermore, Keynesian economics demonstrates that a high level of effective demand is necessary for full employment, and this can best be secured through maintaining a high level of consumption. Thus, economic security and higher living standards for everyone have become the goals of government policy, rather than the expansion of business enterprise in the nation and the government's prestige in the world. The knowledge that the prosperity of consumers (and hence labor, for the most part) constitutes the key to national wealth and, consequently, to political supremacy in the world has furthered the process of democraticizing the goals of mercantilist policy.

The Keynesian theory is certainly no rejection of the neoclassical economic system, but it is relevant under more possible sets of circumstances and is easier to implement from a practical policy standpoint. The Keynesian system does reject the "harmony of interests" assumption of orthodox economics which led to an automatic full employment equilibrium. But once the state, through its fiscal policy, has created the right environment for private self-interests to operate, then the neoclassical system is assumed to function properly.

In one important sense the Keynesian theory strengthens the neoclassical theory by resolving one of its most perplexing dilemmas. In the neoclassical system, maximum welfare can be achieved only with a more equal distribution of income because of the principal of declining marginal utility.

Transferring income from the rich to the poor increases the welfare or utility of the poor more than that which is lost by the rich. But this same equalitarianism prevents the savings from accumulating on which new investment, and hence economic progress, is based. Thus, in the neoclassical system a policy of greater equality to increase welfare would defeat its own purpose in the long run. In the Keynesian system, new investment is autonomous and not a function of savings. Maximum welfare requires full employment which is dependent on greater effective demand and, hence, consumption. The decline in savings and increase in consumption which results from greater equality of incomes leads to higher total income and greater investment in the Keynesian system. In the neoclassical system, welfare comes from equality and progress comes from inequality. It is not possible to maximize both. In the Keynesian system, both come from greater equality.

If the Keynesian concept of capitalism seems radical to some, it is because the history of economic thought is not generally understood. The goals of modern Keynesian mercantilism are economic corollaries of the goals of modern political democracy. In fact, they are the goals of the classical economics itself. Some of the means of achieving these goals are even more "conservative," if time and tradition are the criteria of conservatism, because they are basically the methods and devices of the early preclassical mercantilism. Modern "conservatives" who oppose Keynesian policies would do well to ponder Keynes' remark: "I do not know what makes a person more conservative, to know nothing but the present or to know nothing but the past." The essence of Keynesianism lies in its fusion of the two time-honored traditions of mercantilism and classical economics by adopting the viewpoint of the former to achieve the goals of the latter. Those who fail to recognize this conservative heritage are overlooking an important distinction which must be understood if modern economic policies are to be seen in their proper context. Fortunately, most of those who oppose and deplore the fiscal policies of Keynesian capitalism (policies which seem to be demanded by present-day international circumstances) are reconciled to the view that the goals, and for the most part the methods, are in no important way inconsistent with the best democratic traditions.

7

Organized Capitalism:
Monopoly Theories

The monopolists, by keeping the market constantly under-
stocked, by never fully supplying the effectual demand,
sell their commodities much above the natural price. . . .
The price of a monopoly is upon every occasion the highest which can be got.——Adam Smith

We demand that big business give people a square deal.
——Theodore Roosevelt

MONOPOLY DEFINED

Economists usually think of monopoly as the control, by
one seller, of a supply of identical commodities. When
there are two sellers controlling the market, the condition is
called duopoly, and when there are few sellers, but not
many, oligopoly. Monopoly in this restricted sense is as rare
as pure competition. In only a relatively few cases do single
producers exercise complete control over an entire supply
of goods. There industries are usually either (1) regulated
public utilities, such as transportation, power, and communication, (2) artificial local monopolies, such as milk distribution and barbering, or (3) monopolies based on patents such
as ethyl fluid, glass containers, and shoe machinery. Yet,
even these products are exposed to a degree of competition
provided by real or potential substitutes.

William Nassau Senior, an early English classicist, defined monopoly as "anything which confers upon those who
enjoy it a special and peculiar economic privilege, whatever

this special and peculiar economic privilege may be." Thus, to Senior, monopoly accounted for situations in which equal talents or efforts produced more than equal rewards. This broad definition, while neither precise nor generally acceptable today to economists, lends itself to use in analyzing the anticompetitive elements of modern capitalism. Adam Smith had used this broad definition by implication when he argued that rents were essentially monopoly profits paid to those who, by virtue of their status, controlled the land. He maintained also that high business profits were due substantially to monopoly and, hence, were not necessarily in the best interests of society. This broader definition of monopoly in terms of economic privilege rather than single sellers has the advantage of being functional. It describes monopoly by its results on the economy, not in terms of static market structure. It is, thus, relevant to a large area of modern industrial capitalism which is beyond the scope of the more generally accepted single-seller definition of monopoly.

The enormous increase which has occurred in the relative size of economic organizations and to a lesser degree in the concentration of wealth and incomes poses a most serious problem for capitalism. The role of the giant firm in a capitalist economy has become one of the major unsolved problems of our time. There have been many theories about monopoly and the large corporation, but most of them begin with the classical assumptions of pure competition—small, independent enterprises, free entry, high mobility of resources, etc. Then they proceed in a logical and ordered manner to concepts of giant firms, organized labor, and the role of government as a participant in economic processes. The classical concepts of value, self-interest, scarcity, supply and demand still underlie these theories. The methodology does not lend itself easily to a variation of market conditions or to cooperative business efforts. Most of these theories come back to the belief that neoclassical competition is the normal state of affairs, or at least the only relevant starting point. Monopoly invariably represents the exceptional case.

There has been too little attention given to developing theories of firm and industry behavior which start with a recognition that significant elements of special privilege are inherent in modern economic systems. In industrial capitalism, for example, the use of the corporate form of business organization itself confers many privileges such as limited liability, continuous life, transferability of ownership, and delegation of management. All these can lead to anticompetitive behavior. The growth of business corporations into national institutions permits many other types of action, such as corporate price control, output restriction, and suppression of inventions, which competition would eliminate. Hence, we use here a broad definition of monopoly which embraces most of what has been loosely called economic privilege. It is this very element of privilege which is directly contradictory to the consequences of pure neoclassical competition and which provides an explanation of some of the dynamic action of capitalism. The single firm concept of monopoly is the opposite of pure competition in *structure,* but the economic privilege concept is the opposite of pure competition in *performance* or *results.*

It will be the function of this chapter, and the following one, to explore, classify, and evaluate some of the major theories or fragments of theories which deal with the relation of the large firm to the capitalist economy. An attempt will be made to distill the results which have been achieved in solving the problems raised by the giant firm in the economic system and to evaluate those aspects of big business which are most important in determining the major goals of capitalism. Of course, the roles of other organizations such as labor, agricultural, and political groups are important, but emphasis is placed here on the business firm because of the belief that the capitalist system, in the United States at least, is still sufficiently intact to permit the major economic decisions to be made by private businessmen. This chapter will be concerned with those approaches to the large firm which emphasize the most strictly monopolistic elements. The following chapter will deal with the same problem from the standpoint of oligopoly, in which monopolistic elements may be present to various degrees but in which competitive practices of sorts are relied on for solving most pricing and distribution problems.

GROWTH OF THE CORPORATE ENTERPRISE IN AMERICA

So strongly has the competitive tradition of the classical school become embedded in our thinking that it has become almost a heresy to advance even a limited case for monopoly. A few early twentieth-century businessmen came out openly for monopoly, but public reaction was swift and devastating. Yet forces undermining the reality of the assumptions of pure competition were under way even before Alfred Marshall's first statement of the neoclassical economic system in 1890. Before the Victorian penchant for economic freedom had run its course, collective action, both government and private, was being employed to protect individuals and groups from the very forces which were supposed to give the classical capitalism its impetus and direction.

Before 1815, American enterprisers, mainly in the role of merchant capitalists, had prospered from a diversified foreign trade. Although this trade continued to flourish after 1815, a temporary postwar decline in mercantile profits encouraged a shift from commerce to industrial pursuits with a tendency toward specialization. As the economy expanded, business thrived with the aid of liberal federal government policies with respect to land grants, immigration, and patents. As late as 1890, for example, less than 3½ per cent of the land west of the Mississippi River had been given to actual homesteaders. Railroads and speculative land companies had acquired the rest for sale to settlers at huge profits. Immigration was free until World War I so unlimited quantities of cheap labor could be imported from Europe at any time that it was thought that wages were getting too high or workers too unruly. A steady stream of inventions throughout the nineteenth century led to a higher degree of specialization in both production and marketing.

Meanwhile the market was being revolutionized by the branch and chain store movement which, by broadening competition to a nationwide basis, brought prominence to customer service, the single national price, product differentiation, and mass advertising. Standardization and interchangeable parts aided techniques of mass production to supply this market. An unbridled land speculation soon led to banking excesses, a rapid exploitation of national resources, many technological developments, and an unwholesome degree of political corruption. As a result certain industries, particularly the railroads, reached a state of temporary overexpansion which culminated in the panic of 1873. Gentlemen's agreements and cartel contracts to limit competition, being unenforceable in the courts, broke down, and prices fell drastically. The trust, and later the holding company device, emerged as more effective formal devices for restraining competition.

In 1800, there were only about 335 corporations in the United States, and most of these were banks, insurance companies, canals, turnpikes, waterworks, and toll bridges. However, businessmen soon saw in the corporate form the great advantages of continuity of life, opportunity to raise vast sums of capital, and the privilege of limited liability. Under pressure of the rapidly growing business class, general incorporating laws were quickly passed in all states, and the formation of business corporations soon became a routine matter. As business expanded there was less reliance on individual forms of business enterprise, such as the proprietorship and partnership, and more emphasis on collective devices, particularly the corporation. It is now estimated that the total assets of all unincorporated businesses in the United States are only about one-tenth as great as the assets of corporate enterprises even though the number and assets of unincorporated firms has grown in recent years.[1] Over the

[1] A. D. H. Kaplan, *Big Enterprise in a Competitive Society* (Washington, D.C.: Brookings Institution, 1954), p. 238.

last twenty-five years private corporations have been the source of over half of the national income and two-thirds of all payrolls. By the mid-twentieth century there were over 550,000 corporations in the United States but with more than two-thirds of the wealth of all of them controlled by about 250 of them.

The period of 1888 to 1907 was one of widespread business combinations. In 1888, the New Jersey legislature empowered corporations chartered in that state to own and vote the stock of other corporations. Previously only "natural persons" had been allowed to hold corporate stocks. This revolutionary act was soon followed in all other states, and the door was opened for a flood of holding companies which could be used to secure control of other corporations without changing the internal organization of any of them. Sometimes this control was effected by securing only a small fraction of the stock. Some holding companies secured control of an unbelievably large number of separate plants. The U.S. Steel Company (chartered in 1901 in New Jersey, a state which has since become notorious for its loose incorporating laws) is reported to have secured an ownership interest in 785 separate plants. In 1903, it was estimated that seventy-eight corporations controlled 50 per cent or more of the production in their respective fields and that twenty-six of them controlled 80 per cent or more.[2] By 1932 the growth of economic concentration had progressed to the point that 200 (or 1/25 of 1 per cent of the total number of corporations) of the larger corporations controlled some 50 per cent of all corporate wealth and exercised even greater dominion by means of interlocking directorates, formal agreements, dealerships, secret understandings, and other devices for securing unity of action.[3]

This feverish economic activity which established the trend toward concentrated industrial and economic power

[2] John Moody, *The Truth about the Trusts* (New York, 1904), pp. 453, 486-87.
[3] A. A. Berle and G. C. Means, *The Modern Corporation and Private Property* (New York: The Macmillan Co., 1933), p. 32.

prospered in the prevailing atmosphere of laissez faire. As envisioned by the businessmen of the late nineteenth and early twentieth centuries, laissez faire was a much different policy from that advocated by Adam Smith in 1776. Smith had maintained that government interference which encouraged monopoly should be stopped, but that government interference which promoted the general welfare was good. In the twisted late nineteenth-century version, laissez faire was held to mean that business interests should be privileged to conduct their transactions as they pleased without any outside interference at all. Laissez faire and competition, in the view of the leading corporation lawyers, called, in effect, for a policy of anarchy in the conduct of economic affairs. Herbert Spencer, the British philosopher, found a large and receptive audience among American businessmen in the late nineteenth century, although his extreme laissez-faire philosophy led him to oppose even sanitary regulations. The death of the ignorant would improve the race, he had argued.

Yet, when businesses are left alone to do as they please without any restrictions, they often, and quite normally, develop all sorts of monopolistic devices to exclude competitors, curb production, and raise prices. Not infrequently they have called on the government for assistance in these matters. Between about 1860 and 1910, businessmen not only looked on resistance to the state as a patriotic and civic duty but at the same time that they were denouncing government intervention in general, they were also trying to get the state to assist them in every possible way.

However, two more subtle forces than overt collusion were at work to restrain competition in the late nineteenth century. One such force was economic, and the other was legal. The economic force was the technological progress which led to rapid industrialization, greater specialization, and an increase in the investment outlay necessary to secure the capital equipment for industrial production. A single specialized machine today may cost several millions of dollars. Overhead costs have accounted for an increasing share of total costs in industry and these costs require a high level of output to be sustained. In several basic industries the increased use of mass production machinery has apparently resulted in continuously declining unit costs as output is increased. Naturally the enormous production which necessarily follows depends on mass markets and, thus, a high level of purchasing power for the bulk of the population. This pursuit of the profits and economies of large-scale production has also been the basic economic justification for mergers and the growing concentration of wealth. Unfortunately the evidence seems to indicate that such tendencies toward monopoly do not necessarily cease even if the economies of large size are finally achieved.

The legal force leading toward monopoly was less obvious than the economic force. From the beginning, American business grew up around a rigid legal framework which had been inherited from England and stabilized by the Constitution. These foundations of economic life—such as private property, contract, credit, and the forms of business enterprise—are largely legal abstractions, but the origin of common law in custom and tradition has led to a doctrine of supremacy and reality of the law which has become so deeply ingrained through the evolution of court interpretations that it will probably persist indefinitely. Business monopoly has grown up under the essential protection of a legal system which has actually developed into an ideology. This has occurred in spite of the fact that common law forbids restraints of trade, and many statutes have reinforced this position.

The explanation of this apparent paradox lies in the fact that the law somewhat contradicts itself. The means it grants are not always conducive to the ends it seeks. This is especially true where the law, in the short run, expresses the will of pressure groups.

The business corporation itself is a person under the law and as such has all the rights and protections and obligations which the common law grants to natural persons. These legal privileges have greatly facilitated the efficient operation of commercial enterprises; in fact, without the use of the corporate entity the present scale of business operation would be impossible. The corporation itself may own, rent, buy, sell, or lease property; lend, borrow, spend, or save money; hire, promote, or fire employees; sue and be sued; engage in any legal contract; in fact, it can do nearly anything a natural person can do except vote in a civil election.

However, these rights sometimes permit individuals to evade their responsibilities by hiding behind, or manipulating, the corporate fiction. As Walton Hamilton so dramatically pointed out, the corporation "like the amoeba," can . . .

in a twinkling resolve itself into two corporations; like the queen bee's mate it can, living only for one brief moment, exhaust its life in a single creative act; like the phoenix, it can cease to be yet resurrect itself from its own ashes. It can, like a player on the stage, assume the person of many characters. It can in fact appear as any number of persons and at will shift from one personality to another. Nor does it, like you or me or Henry VIII or Banquo's ghost, have to remain itself. It can, like a celestial host, spiral itself into a hierarchy of corporations; and, like an amorphous spirit, fuse itself with other corporations in such a way as to confuse its own integrity. It can at any moment be alike one and many, remain itself or give way to a successor, demonstrate the truth of the resurrection, and present to the law which attempted to grapple with it the evasive identity of the angel with whom Jacob wrestled all night yet of whom he could get no hold.[4]

In addition to corporation law, three types of legislation can be distinguished which are directly inimical to a thoroughgoing competitive economic system. First are the public utility statutes which outlaw competition in certain areas where high capital costs, the need to use public domain, or the nature of the product manufactured would lead to wasteful duplication of facilities if product competition were permitted. Regulation of some sort normally is substituted for competition in this area which, although normally limited to the transportation, communication, fuel, and power industries, has included banking, stockyards,

[4] "The Economic Man Affects a National Role," *American Economic Review Supplement*, May, 1946, p. 737.

warehousing, liquor, and many other industries. During the NRA period (1933-1935) the public utility concept was extended to business in general.

Second, social legislation to protect disadvantaged groups, such as labor, farmers, and consumers, has grown enormously in recent years as the general population has become more acutely aware of its economic difficulties and of the possibilities of democratic political action. Usually this legislation takes the form of putting in a floor below which competition is prohibited but allowing competition to operate more or less freely above this floor. For example, minimum wage, child labor, maximum hours, and safety legislation all outlaw competition where it leads to undesirable types of cost reductions.

The justification of such laws is in the belief that competition can be carried to such extremes as to be wasteful, destructive, or degrading to human dignity. If all firms in an industry or area are required to comply with the same rules, then prices will be raised by all and competition will have to assume other forms. It is not considered to be in the public interest for lower prices to be due to child labor or other exploitation of helpless groups. Actually, the general case has long been made that such cost reductions are usually not economical anyhow. Slave labor, for example, may be the cheapest in terms of wage rates, but it is also the least productive and, hence, the most expensive in terms of total gain from its employment. Likewise, the cost savings from operating without adequate safety devices and the assignment of long hours are usually not financially justifiable.

The third type of particularly anticompetitive legislation is that which promotes monopolistic pricing and output practices. This type of legislation is justified largely on the grounds that certain monopolistic practices are necessary in order to combat other, more serious practices which are not easily outlawed themselves because of their close association with the economies of large-scale operation. Among these fairly anticompetitive laws are (1) the "fair trade" laws which permit price maintenance agreements among manufacturers and retailers, (2) laws which prohibit price discriminations which may favor monopolists (notably the Robinson-Patman Act of 1936), and (3) the many state laws fixing the prices of such items as gasoline, milk, cigarettes, and haircuts.

In addition to these specific exceptions to the competitive purposes of the law, some of the practices of large corporations may be inconsistent with the maintenance of a competitive economy in the traditional sense. The growth of large producing enterprises and sprawling holding companies has not been adequately controlled nor has the alarming amount of legislative lobbying by corporate and other interest groups yet been effectively curtailed.

Yet the folklore of pure competition, reinforced by its economic and legal ideology, has persisted, and the worst excesses of monopoly are sometimes still defended as being of the very essence of competition. The possibility of an inseparable concentration of economic and political power capable of destroying or perverting the system which gave it birth was at first shrugged off with an appeal for faith in the integrity and public spiritedness of the business community. Some writers, like Arthur J. Eddy in *The New Competition,* which appeared in the 1920's, argued that competition was destructive. Eddy advocated price fixing and market allocation agreements enforced by business combinations or trade associations. Significantly, he opposed labor unions and farmers' cooperatives on the grounds that their functions were only to raise prices whereas business associations were intended mainly to increase productive efficiency and, hence, reduce prices. This view did not gain much professional respectability, however, and orthodox economists continued to search for competition as an ideal.

The neoclassical case against monopoly was as strong theoretically as the case for competition. It had long been demonstrated logically that pure competition would result in maximum efficiency, rational allocation of resources, production to consumers' order, maximum output, and the lowest prices which could be maintained. Likewise, it could equally be shown that monopoly would raise prices, restrict production, and, in the static model which was used, fail to produce the incentive required to increase efficiency.

Under the neoclassical assumptions of competition no firm would be large or influential enough to exercise any control over the total supply or the selling price of the goods it sold. Goods would be sold much as at auction with buyers bidding and sellers having to take the highest offer. Thus, a firm could increase its output, or even its capacity, without increasing the total supply of goods on the market enough to depress prices. Conversely, restriction of output could not raise market prices. Under these conditions a firm would normally increase its output to the point where rising costs of production, due to diminishing returns on its resources, would equal the market price. This would be the level of output at which the firm would make the greatest total profit. The last unit produced would cost just as much as it sold for. The next to last unit would cost less than its selling price, and any additional units would cost more than their price since prices would be constant regardless of output and costs per unit would be rising. If a firm found its unit costs still falling when it reached its capacity production, it would find it profitable to increase its capacity until diminishing returns finally set in and unit costs rose to the market price.

If many firms found it profitable to increase their capacity, then the total supply of goods on the market would rise appreciably and in this "long run" period market prices would fall. Firms whose unit costs were above the market price would have to contract output or maybe even go out of business altogether unless they could increase their efficiency and thereby reduce their costs. Thus, competition would force firms to seek maximum efficiency, and increasing production in the industry would force prices down to the lowest which the most efficient firms would take. At this equilibrium price, the industry would be producing exactly the quantities and qualities of goods that consumers wanted at the lowest price the producers would take, which would be, simultaneously, the highest price at which consumers would be willing to buy this amount of output.

In contrast, neoclassical theory assumed a monopoly to be the only seller of a commodity, and, hence, the firm would be an industry in itself. Since the firm could control the total supply of its product, it could increase prices by reducing its output. Likewise, it could only sell more by reducing its prices. The point of maximum profits could logically be demonstrated to be at an equilibrium of price and output where the price was higher than it would be under competition and the output was less. Nor would there be any economic incentive to increase efficiency, expand capacity, or develop new products. On this kind of reasoning the classical theorists based their case against monopoly.

SCHUMPETER'S THEORY OF MONOPOLY CAPITALISM

ECONOMIC THEORY. The late Joseph Schumpeter, of Harvard, analyzed the relationships between monopoly and technological progress and formulated a theory which may have permanently altered the whole tenor of economic thinking about competition.[5] He began with the assumption of a *kreislauf*, or "circular flow," of economic life which is analogous to the circulation of blood in an animal organism which follows the same channels year after year. Under conditions of normal equilibrium the flow of incomes in the economy adheres to these courses which have long been established by businessmen. Through a process of trial and error businessmen learn how much labor, capital, and natural resources to use in different employments to satisfy the wants of consumers.

But the capitalistic system does not remain stationary because it contains within itself forces that make for change and development. According to Schumpeter it was constantly being revolutionized from within by a small group of

[5] *Capitalism, Socialism and Democracy* (New York: Harper & Bros., 1942). *The Theory of Economic Development* (Cambridge: Harvard University Press, 1934).

rare and exceptional people called "entrepreneurs" meaning literally, "undertakers," or those who undertake or venture to assume the uncertainties of enterprise. Using credit provided by other capitalists who have accumulated savings, the entrepreneurs attack the circular flow with innovations, seeking to divert the factors of production to other uses. Schumpeter defined innovation to include the introduction of new goods or new qualities of goods, or new methods of production, the opening of new markets, the conquest of new sources of materials, supplies, and products, and the reorganization of business activities. Thus, innovations were more than merely inventions although it was not necessary that they be world-shaking events. They included any improvements in products, techniques, or the organization of production which, however minor, upset the established economic order.

According to Schumpeter, the assumed tendency toward static equilibrium in the capitalist economy was due to a natural resistance to change. The social environment reacts against novelty, and the ordinary businessman is strongly inclined to continue along traditional lines rather than to venture into the unknown. Only the exceptional person, said Schumpeter, attempts innovation and then only when the chance for reward is very great. Patents or other monopoly protection are needed so that profits will be high enough to write off new investment quickly or to provide excess capacity in order to engage in price wars with rivals. Otherwise the high capital requirements of modern industry will not be forthcoming because the uncertainty of profits is too great in a dynamic economy. Thus, certain monopolistic practices are necessary so that entrepreneurs will take the risk demanded by a dynamic, capitalistic system.

Monopoly, to Schumpeter, was not the villain it had been to the classicists. Instead, he claimed it to be responsible for much of the glory of capitalism because large-scale organization makes the most efficient use of brain power. It places innovation on a production line, producing innovations either routinely or to order. This helped to stabilize the economy from the "perennial gale" of technological progress. Monopoly, which Schumpeter regarded as ultimately unstable itself, furnished some insurance against the risks of long-range investing under rapidly changing conditions.

Schumpeter advanced other arguments for monopoly. He claimed that monopolies have superior methods available to innovate and create even greater technological progress. In fact, the largest firms make gigantic expenditures on research and can afford to take chances. Thus, DuPont is said to have spent $27 million and thirteen years of research on nylon before it could be successfully marketed. R.C.A. has spent over $65 million on television development. The so-called competitive industries, like textiles, are among the least progressive. In agriculture, which is usually considered to be the most competitive industry of all, virtually all the technological progress which has occurred has originated in federal agencies and state experiment stations.

Schumpeter also argued that monopolies and cartels produce slow, but steady expansion. Rigid prices help to prevent obsolete industries from collapsing all at once under the impact of progress or external disturbance and thereby causing cumulative unemployment. He argued that consumers are pessimistic during recessions so price cuts would not increase spending and employment anyhow.

On the other hand, Schumpeter maintained that what may appear to be monopoly in the short run is actually a form of long-run competition. The prices set by monopolies and cartels are not as rigid as they sometimes seem, he said. For one thing, the constantly improving qualities of goods tend to offset price rigidities. Also there is constant competitive pressure from other industries and from new goods and processes. The entrepreneur builds his empire on "sinking sands" as innovation constantly renders his investments obsolete. Entrepreneurs exploit only what they themselves have created. Even for natural resources this is true because the gifts of a bountiful nature have no value unless they are recognized, developed, and put to constructive use.

While creating new values the capitalist entrepreneurs are simultaneously destroying old values by their innovation, according to Schumpeter. No firm can long be protected from the competition of innovation which comes from other firms and even other industries far removed in the economy. Furthermore, so-called free entry into an industry can make permanent entry of new firms impossible because of the limited profit opportunities. Only in industries where entry is impeded and prices can be manipulated is enterprise possible, according to Schumpeter. Competitive firms cannot be expected to have the quality and quantity of output of the giant firm. Thus, to Schumpeter the really significant force in economic development is not price competition but the "creative destruction" of old methods and goods being replaced by new, and it is not the flexible prices of competition but the short-run stability of monopoly which effectuates this dynamic force.

It is true, as Schumpeter argued, that the rewards for commercial undertaking, although going ultimately to a few, can be gigantic. However Schumpeter credited the huge rewards to a lack of competition and argued that without such incentives there would have been no capital accumulation and no enterprise. Competition, he said, is predatory, and it is fortunate for capitalism that it never existed to any significant degree. Furthermore, he said, competition would have been wasteful and costly and even at that would not have guaranteed full employment.

This analysis, though brilliant, novel, and provocative, oversimplifies the organization and operation of the large firm, misinterprets the role of monopoly, and overestimates the importance of the entrepreneur. It may be that there is little competition today in the neoclassical sense of small producers, homogeneous products, and market-determined prices and outputs. But, as the following chapter will show, more subtle forms of competition are at work to determine market behavior. Schumpeter's complete reversal of the neoclassical arguments to justify pure monopoly is a misinterpretation of market forces. The case against the perpetua-

tion of economic privilege by monopoly is too strong to be
so easily dismissed with the reminder that "even this shall
pass away."

The entrepreneurial function, which is the mainspring
of economic activity in the Schumpeterian system, is particularly vulnerable to attack because of its oversimplified
presentation. There is no evidence, for example, of the
existence of any elite class of entrepreneurs. There are no
special entrepreneurial qualities which are the exclusive
possession of a few people. In the large firm the entrepreneurial function may be differentiated among many salaried
managers or it may be spread out to the entire workforce
if some kind of group incentive can be developed to elicit
the workers' participation. Some entrepreneurial functions
are being shared by employers with unions, and some are
disappearing altogether. In any event the risks are not
ordinarily borne by those who innovate since the professional managements which operate most large firms do not
fire themselves for making wrong decisions.

In some instances the large firm or other organization
may actually take extraordinary risks simply because it is
so difficult to hold any particular individuals accountable.
In other cases the firm may provide an anti-entrepreneurship
by setting up obstacles to the acceptance of good ideas. The
well-known examples of Western Union, which turned down
the radio, the Odorless, the largest ice box manufacturer,
which rejected the refrigerator, are illustrative of this point.
The entire concept of entrepreneurship is so complex that
a vast amount of research still needs to be done before
Schumpeter's pioneering theory can be successfully evaluated.

HISTORICAL THEORY. Schumpeter's economic analysis of
capitalism is supplemented by a theory of the history of
capitalist development. It begins by showing that the
early capitalist class arose through business success. Unlike
the feudal lords whose success was due to their status, the
capitalists achieved success through exploiting their own
talent and initiative. The outstanding intellectual charac-

teristic of capitalism was the principle of rationality which, while possibly weakening the fear of God, strengthened interest in the betterment of mankind. It is possible, as Schumpeter asserted, that capitalism produced a spirit of rationality. Certainly capitalism and rationality arose at about the same time although this does not necessarily prove that one caused the other. Capitalism exalted money and there developed a general scientific attitude of asking questions and seeking answers to them. So it could be that capitalism produced an increasing rationality, and rationality in turn produced a more efficient and rapidly growing capitalism.

Capitalism, as it exploded into an economic system which was to engulf the entire civilized world, contained, according to Schumpeter, the seeds of its own destruction. Progress, he argued, tended to become mechanized as the large research laboratories of the giant firms created technological change automatically. Society gradually became accustomed to rapid change and resisted it less and less the more it became routine. Thus, because innovation became mechanized and resistance to change became more accepted, the personal effort involved in revolutionizing the economic structure from within began to disappear. The capitalist entrepreneur, said Schumpeter, found his principal function in society becoming obsolete.

Small businesses are absorbed by large firms, and the giant unit of control, said Schumpeter, "socializes the bourgeois mind," narrows the scope of his motivation and aspirations, and further impairs his prestige. As firms grow larger, ownership and control become divorced and all life is drained out of the concept of property. Power no longer requires legal ownership of property and even free contract loses some of its meaning in the informal agreements among the communities of interest which control economic resources. The capitalist enterprise tends to break to pieces under the impact of its own success. The monopolist bureaucracy, which Schumpeter claimed the development of the capitalistic system requires, is not only destined to oust its smaller rivals but ultimately to oust the entrepreneur himself.

The over-all conclusion of Schumpeter's analysis of the history of capitalism seems to be that the apparent advantages of classical competition are illusory, existing in the short run only. The long-run growth of capitalism depends on monopoly and short-run restraints of trade. Monopoly profit to enable a rapid amortization of capital investment is a prerequisite to the very existence of capitalism because capitalism, being essentially dynamic, depends on the technological progress which only monopoly can create. Nevertheless, monopoly simultaneously destroys the capitalistic system itself by reducing entrepreneurship to a laboratory routine and causing industry to socialize itself.

Although Schumpeter was not a socialist and indeed advanced the most academically respectable arguments to date for monopoly-capitalism, he was more persuaded by his logic than his convictions. He found capitalism to have served the human race exceedingly well. It had raised the volume of output and standard of living tremendously, enough in fact to make the complete elimination of poverty a real possibility for the first time in history. However, somewhat nostalgically perhaps, he envisaged democratic socialism as being the natural heir to capitalism. Security and stagnation, though not necessarily dictatorship, would accompany the peaceful transition.

SOCIOLOGICAL THEORY. A larger sociological theory adds impetus to the collapse of the capitalist economic system. The growing obsolescence of the entrepreneur, and the capitalist function, is hastened by an evolution of social attitudes. Capitalism, according to Schumpeter, produced a labor movement and a system of social legislation because it required a high degree of specialization of functions which left workers interdependent and without any personal security. It also produced an industrial middle class which, unlike the Marxian stereotype, was both highly moral and peace-loving. Capitalism, said Schumpeter, creates a vested interest in social unrest. It subsidizes a hostile group of intellectuals who, while living on unearned incomes from capitalist undertakings, nevertheless infiltrate labor and other social movements and undermine the basic institutions of capitalism.

Personal freedom, particularly freedom of the intellectual to criticize the economic system that feeds him, an uncensored press, toleration of criticism by the leading classes, and a popular sympathy for the real or fancied sufferings of others are also direct products of capitalism, according to Schumpeter, but the rationalist attitude which capitalism created in order to control and exploit nature proceeds to question the rights of property and all other capitalist values. Having permeated the minds of a class of radical intellectuals, rationalism goes on to destroy the economic system which it created.

Schumpeter advanced four reasons why capitalism is bound to lose the struggle for survival to the radicals. First, he said, the logic of capitalism would bow before the emotional case for socialism. Second, capitalism's case is both a long-run case and a complicated one. The masses of the people put short-run interests first and do not possess the insight to appreciate or even understand that the individual's fate may well have to be subordinated to the continuation of the capitalist system. Third, capitalism offers little emotional appeal, and people are likely to attribute their daily troubles to the impersonal capitalist economic system rather than to their own personal faults. Fourth, continually rising living standards allow people to have an increasing amount of leisure time which they may employ largely in adding to and exploiting social unrest.[6] He suggested also that widespread public education adds to the supply of people who are potentially hostile to capitalism because they are trained to be executives and other white collar officials, and there are never enough of these jobs available in the capitalist system. Hence these people become disillusioned with capitalism and favor socialism.

[6] *Capitalism, Socialism and Democracy,* pp. 144-45.

The first and second arguments above seem to contradict Schumpeter's general thesis that it is rationalism itself, and not emotionalism, which is the chief contributor to capitalism's suicidal impulses. The main argument upon which Schumpeter bases the decline of capitalist institutions is that the rationalism of science will spill over into the social structure and whittle away at the capitalist framework. Yet he says socialism will win because of its emotional appeal. Apparently, free education and the rational, scientific spirit are unfavorable to capitalism; yet an excess of emotionalism is also.

The third argument, that capitalism offers insufficient emotional attraction to insure popular loyalty, fails to consider the great appeal to the insecure and frustrated elements of society which any economic system has when it represents the status quo. Unlike Europe, where its benefits were reserved for a few, capitalism in the United States has been enjoyed by many. Consequently, it has demonstrated an amazing ability to attract almost fanatical devotion from a large segment of the populace, partly because of its proven benefits and partly, no doubt, because of its being a symbol of traditionalism.

The fourth argument, that rising living standards and public education stimulate social unrest, is also subject to question. It is a serious indictment of capitalism to suggest that it cannot bear close scrutiny or be justified by its own fruits. If education and enlightenment were all that were necessary to expose capitalism, it must be considered a fraud from the start. Fortunately for capitalism, the evidence does not support this portion of Schumpeterian sociology.

Undoubtedly Schumpeter's European background colored his thinking about the social framework and its evolution. In Europe the benefits of capitalism were so long reserved for a relatively small proportion of society that capitalist values never succeeded in having much attraction for the masses. Working people became emotionally attached to socialism, communism, or fascism. However, in the United

States the individualism of the frontier was almost directly replaced by a form of capitalism which, because of the expanding economy, offered opportunities for most of those who aspired to commercial success. Later the acceptance of profit motivation and private property became so ingrained that even modest social reforms became difficult to popularize except in periods of extreme economic crisis.

Probably as a consequence of his remarkable intellectual honesty, Schumpeter never succeeded in attracting any organized group of disciples. Yet he was one of the most profound and original economic thinkers of the twentieth century. His arguments for monopoly are still being broadcast by conservative businessmen although the word "monopoly" is rigidly avoided and terms like "dynamic conservatism" and "the new competition" are used instead. On the other hand, Schumpeter's predictions for the future of capitalism have been welcomed by socialists. There have been few, however, who could accept his theory completely. Nevertheless, if economic privilege has any place in modern capitalism, Joseph Schumpeter will have provided the most important clues for its justification.

OTHER ARGUMENTS FOR MONOPOLY CAPITALISM

A vigorous defense of big business as a necessary mainspring in our capitalistic system has come from David Lilienthal, former chairman of the Tennessee Valley Authority and the Atomic Energy Commission. Going beyond a defense of bigness as such he made strong arguments for certain types of monopolistic practices.[7] His primary thesis is that government's expanded role in economic affairs provides a strong check on the danger of abuses by big business. Hence bigness can be encouraged rather than viewed with apprehension.

Lilienthal argued that the public now looks to the government for aid and protection in many fields which formerly were considered off limits for government intervention.

[7] *Big Business—A New Era* (New York: Harper & Bros., 1953).

Many "temporary" or "emergency" measures have endured for more than two decades and show few signs of being abandoned. This provides a formidable obstacle to future corporate abuses of power. Organized labor also provides a check on big business in this respect. Lilienthal contended that the antitrust laws are based largely on an outmoded prejudice against big business which grew out of corporate abuses which have long been corrected. Corporations, he alleged, are becoming responsible to the public for their actions because of the diversity of stockholders in the largest firms.

Lilienthal also stressed the importance of interindustry competition such as the struggle between railroads, trucks, and airlines, between coal and oil, and between synthetic and natural fabrics. This kind of competition, he said, is an important long-run adjuster of economic inequities particularly since interindustry collusion is fairly rare. Firms faced with severe competition from outside the industry often turn to producing the product which is competing with them, thus increasing the total supply and creating a downward pressure on the price structure. Where this is impossible, the original industry may be forced to become more efficient. For example, the trucking industry has probably done far more to increase railroad efficiency than all government regulations put together.

Like Schumpeter, Lilienthal emphasized the important role which research plays in big corporations. Expenditures for research are known to have increased 500 per cent in the last twenty years. Unlike Schumpeter, he claimed that this research actually increases competition. Diversity of products, which is a consequence of research, is likewise becoming a strong competitive force, according to Lilienthal, even though diversification is easier for large firms than for small. The consumer is also benefited by the development of new products as, for example, "wonder" drugs developed by the Schenley Distilling Corporation as a consequence of that firm's extensive knowledge of fermentation. Big business was defended as necessary to serve national defense, for example,

A.T.&T.'s atomic research in the Bell Laboratories, and because of the superior ability of large firms to conserve natural resources properly. Lilienthal contended that abuses of corporate power were checked by internal competition among divisions or products of the same firm and by competition of products from other industries. These, he felt, were more important than the orthodox concept of competition among the products of firms in the same industry.

Lilienthal presented a strong and convincing case, but it minimizes the role of organized economic power groups. It is true that government and organized labor provide effective checks to corporate power, but there are many instances in which governmental power is invoked to protect business monopolies or in which unions join with employers to raise prices or restrict output to the detriment of the general public. Lilienthal also seemed to overlook the role which the antitrust laws have played in correcting corporate abuses. He seems to assume that the social conscience of businessmen has changed so greatly in the past twenty years that the antitrust laws can safely be ignored. Furthermore, while it is true that stock ownership in many corporations is so widely dispersed that no individual stockholder controls the corporation, this does not necessarily diminish the need for the corporation to make the largest profit possible but may even increase it. It is only in recent years that an oil or steel producer might be called before a Congressional committee to explain the necessity of a price increase, but this is due to the awareness of Congress and not to the diversification of stockholdings. Closely-owned corporations are no more immune from Congressional or public pressures than widely owned ones.

It is probable that research increases competition, as Lilienthal claims, to the extent that rivalry to develop better methods and new products is intensified among large, established firms. However, the growing need for expensive research facilities can discriminate against small producers and impede entry into industry from the outside. Most economists would probably agree that research and diversification promote more competition than they eliminate. However, Lilienthal argued that the integration of processes within industry also increases competition. Here there is likely to be controversy. Vertical integration can benefit consumers by eliminating middlemen and hence making lower prices possible; yet this may reduce competition among firms at the same time because the large integrated firm can consistently undersell independents and squeeze them out of the market altogether.

One of Lilienthal's strongest arguments for big enterprise was that the federal government now has the power to protect the public from the abuses of monopoly capitalism. Whether the government will actually do so is an issue which he did not squarely face. There has been an enormous growth of protective welfare legislation since 1933, which shows few signs of reversal. Furthermore, there were several major antitrust decisions after World War II which condemned, or at least deplored, the *power* to raise prices or exclude competition, whether exercised or not. All of these give hope that Lilienthal's faith in the government is not misplaced. More recently, however, a Boston Federal judge won the Supreme Court's endorsement in saying "The defendant may escape statutory liability if it . . . owes its monopoly solely to superior skill, superior products, natural advantages . . . low margins of profit maintained and without discrimination of licenses." This doctrine, if followed, would make consumer benefits the only test of monopoly. Since the actual cost data for providing monopolistic superiority in efficiency is controlled by the firms themselves and not generally available for outsiders to appraise except in the form presented by the corporation's public relations department, single firm domination of many industrial product markets might well be defended on purely economic grounds.

The inherent danger in this doctrine is all too clear. Granted for the sake of argument that the most efficient producer is the monopoly and granted also that the monopoly benefits are all passed on to the consumer, what assurance is there that this will continue? Once a firm has secured control of an industry through superior efficiency, will a contest between big and little producers ever be permitted again? Will the monopoly continue to pass its gains to the consumer or keep them to itself or share them with employees under union pressure? Finally, is the democratic process of government itself safe in a nation of private industrial monopolies? The doubts which prevail in answering these questions suggest that efficiency is not the only goal of society. Some loss of short-run living standards might well be tolerated, rather than sacrificing the democratic system itself. The 1957 Supreme Court decision against Du Pont's 23 per cent ownership of General Motors seems to indicate that any combination of firms, regardless of specific market restraints, which threatens the public welfare may be adjudged an illegal monopoly.

Lilienthal advocated a "Basic Economic Act" to supersede the antitrust laws. It would emphasize the positive aspects of big business, its prime concern being not with competition but with productivity and ethical and economic objective. It cannot be denied that in the large and complex society which modern capitalism has become, more play has been given to the individual than in smaller, simpler, and more primitive societies. But the spare time and variety of products which big business productivity has produced still seems to be only a partial substitute for the rapidly disappearing opportunity to go into a "free enterprise" for yourself. This is not to weep for the small family blacksmith shop or the small farm or business which gave way to the large corporation. But the antitrust laws are still needed to prevent big firms from taking advantage of their political and strategic powers after their economic advantages have been fully exploited.

Kenneth Boulding has suggested that since the classical abstractions of pure competition have been abandoned, monopolistic practices of business and labor may be justified in order to provide some assurance against short-run recessions particularly since the government has thus far failed to insure economic stability.[8] However, a completely consistent and general case for monopoly still remains to be made. Fortunately, there has not been any urgent need to make a general, theoretical case for monopoly in the United States although a military victory for the fascist powers in World War II might have led to such a necessity. Probably this explanation would have had to come in terms of politics rather than economic theory since the state, in these fascist nations, ultimately got control of the capitalist enterprises whose managements supported fascists and militarists initially in order to secure short-term economic gains.

The decline of the nearly pure monopolies of the early twentieth century, the more effective regulation or government ownership of public utilities in recent years, and the rise of the federal government as a positive force dedicated to the protection of general, as against special, interests, have all combined to reduce the threat of monopoly-capitalism in the United States. These developments were probably inevitable in view of the inherent conflict between any significant degree of private economic monopoly and political democracy. Although in many specific instances a clear case can be made for a single firm monopoly (in terms of high aggregate fixed costs, necessity for use of public domain, low rate of return on fixed investment, or providing a necessary public service) in such cases government regulation or ownership is recognized as necessary to prevent exploitation. Private entrepreneural motives may be abrogated to the extent that prices be required to be based on average rather than marginal costs, service be extended to all applicants without discrimination except by class of customer, and adequate service be provided to all who demand it.

Thus the more obvious cases of monopoly in the United States have been met with either public utility regulation, government ownership, or direct antitrust prosecution. It is in the industries of the "big threes" and "big fours" for which no clear public policy has been found. It is to these

8 *Quarterly Journal of Economics*, August, 1945.

oligopoly industries, which retain enough competitive behavior to escape the legalistically oriented antitrust prose-
cutions that look toward overt acts rather than economic
or market effects, that attention must now turn. It is the
oligopoly which fixes prices and then competes on quality
and service or gadgets and advertising. And it is those industries dominated by the "big three" or "big four" which
hold the key to contemporary American capitalism.

DIGRESSION ON FASCISM

Fascism is frequently identified as a form of monopoly-
capitalism. Latter day Marxists have been prone to argue
that as capitalism progresses toward the revolution it becomes increasingly monopolistic and fascist in character.
Non-Marxian socialists have made a similar though not
identical argument, and many nonsocialist liberals and conservatives as well have noted that monopoly capitalism often
displays fascist tendencies. The implication is that there is
some causal relation between monopoly and fascism.

Fascism is essentially totalitarian and, as such, is primarily a political rather than an economic system. However,
it is commonly assumed to be one of the major types of economic systems and does in fact have a close relation with
the economic system in the country in which it appears.
Particularly, it molds the economic system along totalitarian
lines.

Some discussion of the theory or at least principles of
fascism is important in any study of the concepts of capitalism for several reasons. First, fascism is more capitalistic
than socialistic in its economic organization even though
the German fascists called themselves "National Socialists"
(Nazis). This title was a misnomer, adopted for political
reasons. Second, fascism is still in considerable evidence
throughout the world in spite of the defeat of the Axis
powers in World War II. Third, there are fascist tendencies
in communist countries, possibly because the political, as
distinct from the economic, systems of fascism and com-

munism are so similar. Fourth, the recurrent waves of fascist-type hysteria in the United States, although probably representing the feelings of less than 20 per cent of the population, are nevertheless evidence that we are certainly not immune to the infiltration of fascist ideology.

Fascism is essentially a political system. The economic aspects are definitely subsidiary to the political as is true in any totalitarian scheme. However, every nation must have some sort of economic organization, and there are some economic principles which underlie fascism. It is just that in a fascist system the economic principles are especially obscure because of the irrationality underlying fascist beliefs.

Fascist political doctrine traces back to Nietzsche and, more recently, Georges Sorel, whose common ground consisted of a basic irrationalism or antirationalism. Fascism glorifies the fanatical and dogmatic attitude and openly employs lies and violence to achieve its aims of total subjection of all its adherents and complete annihilation of even the slightest opposition. It is more negative than positive. It is more sure of what it is against than what it is for. As Mussolini said, "We do not believe in programs, in plans, in saints, or apostles; above all we do not believe in happiness, in salvation, or in the promised land." Some American splinter political parties can be seen to share in this negativism. Their platforms emphasize what they are against, seldom what they are for in any specific terms. They are against the Federal government, taxes, socialism, or sometimes just against "Them." What they are for, if anything, is even more generally or obscurely phrased. Just what methods would be employed to accomplish their objectives are rarely stated. Fascists, like communists, avoid having to defend their positions by the implication that anyone who would oppose them is disloyal.

Fascism rejects individual rights and advocates government which is executed by force through a hierarchy of leaders, all of whom are subject to the whims of one heroic and idolized superleader. Any idea, whether true or utterly ridiculous, can be used to achieve this end of totalitarianism as a complete way of life. Racial supremacy, plunder, savagery, and murder are among the popular tools of fascism. Fascist ideology has a strong appeal for the megalomaniacal mentality. It is a perfect fuel for pent up fires of grandiose delusions. It inspires excitement, awe, fear, hysterical self-worship, heavily fortified isolation and psychopathic hatreds of imaginary enemies. It can only be met with calmness, courage, disregard, and, sometimes, ridicule.

Obviously the economic system of fascism is only one of the means of achieving totalitarianism and thus is not based on any independent, underlying principles of its own. Since there are no rational economic principles which are acceptable to fascism (indeed, free thought on any subject is discouraged or prohibited) there are no guides for reorganizing the economic system when fascists attain power in a country. Therefore the fascist economic system is most likely to be a continuation of the previous system with the fewest modifications which are required in order to achieve fascist purposes. There is no fascist blueprint for reorganizing the economic system itself. Fascism in the past has succeeded in achieving power in nations with a fairly high degree of technological and industrial development and where the economic organization is predominantly capitalistic. Therefore fascist political systems have normally operated through a capitalist economic order.

The basic economic unit in a fascist system is the corporation. The philosophy and psychology of individualism are rejected in favor of a corporate state in which all people except the ruling hierarchy participate in their economic capacities as producers but not in their political capacities as citizens. Entrepreneurs, workers, farmers, and professional people are assumed to understand their specific economic and technical problems, but as citizens they are not supposed to have any knowledge of, or participation in, the functions of government. Only the ruling class is qualified to govern. Consequently, the economic system is organized along functional lines with membership compulsory in the appropriate organizations such as cartels, chambers of commerce, trade unions, youth corps, farmers' collectives, lawyers' guilds, etc. Of course, all of these organizations are strictly controlled in the interests of the state.

In Nazi Germany, for example, business firms had to belong to two types of economic organizations. One was a horizontal type consisting of organizations such as regional manufacturers associations. These were called "Chambers." The other was a vertical type consisting of functional organizations such as specific industry cartels. These were called "Groups." The appropriate chamber for membership was determined by political geography. The appropriate group was determined by raw materials used, finished product, or type of productive process. Since political democracy is specifically denied under fascism, free labor unions, opposition political parties, unregulated free enterprise, free contract rights, and civil liberties were necessarily abolished. The old saying that under fascism everything which is not compulsory is prohibited was literally true. For example, in Nazi Germany, labor unions were abolished and their property looted. Labor lost all rights. All property rights of citizens were conditioned by race and political reliability. Jews were prohibited from entering certain kinds of contracts, such as partnerships, and tax assessments discriminated against them and other "inferior" or "disloyal" groups.

Unfortunately for the theory of the corporate state, it is impossible to separate economic from political functions. Therefore all economic control tends to become political control and price, wage, taxation, and material allocation systems, for example, fall under the authoritarian regulation of the elite. There is no way to prevent the rapid growth of centralization and bureaucracy so there is a consequent loss of efficiency. If there is any truth in the popular notion that dictatorial government is more efficient politically than democratic government then the loss of *economic* efficiency and flexibility in production and distribution due to bureaucratic centralization must be set against it.

As in Nazi Germany in the 1930's, economic freedom is rapidly replaced by forced labor, trading is replaced by regulation, and free association by compulsory organization. Although private property remained technically intact and national and municipal ownership of utilities were replaced by private ownership under the Nazis, controls and regulations multiplied until finally businessmen had no policy-making authority at all. By 1936 the Nazi party had ousted both the military and the industrialists from the fascist partnership which had been formed in 1931. Private profits remained for incentive purposes, but price controls fixed profit margins. Eventually the market system (except the securities market) was replaced by a coordinated, but unplanned, system of government intervention.

Fascism differs from nation to nation in its specific organization of production and distribution although the basic principle of the corporate state seems to hold generally. The most complete fascist economic system was found in pre-war Nazi Germany. The Nazis organized their entire economy for the purpose of waging war. For this reason, a study of its economic system is of interest mainly as a system of war economy.

Although fascism is correctly identified as being the extreme right, politically, the same classification is not precisely valid when considering the purely economic aspects. Even ancient Rome had its bread and circuses for the masses, and modern fascist systems have usually developed a rather advanced welfare state. Often, however, welfare measures are adopted as devices to forestall more urgently needed reforms or to take the edge off possible uprisings against the state. The specific welfare measures adopted are dictated either by political expediency or by national goals other than maximizing human welfare. For example, food subsidies are used to stimulate population growth, or public housing is used to encourage employment in armament industries.

Some convincing arguments have been advanced that political and economic institutions in the Soviet Union have been more fascist than Marxist. On the other hand, more recent developments suggest a growing democratization in the Soviet Union, possibly in the direction of return toward democratic capitalism or democratic socialism. Unfortunately, information is not available to prove or disprove any of these hypotheses. If future research indicates that the Soviet Union has abandoned its Marxist principles (assuming it ever adopted them or tried to) then some reappraisal of socialist and capitalist theory will be in order. In the meantime both theory (Marxist and otherwise) and experience support the appropriateness of classifying fascism as monopoly capitalism with a totalitarian political framework.

It is not safe to generalize about the conditions which lead to fascism because some are political and historical and hence do not lend themselves easily to quantitative expression. However, some attitudes clearly seem to create environments in which the seeds of fascism can grow. One such attitude is fear, especially the fear of some alien threat to the status quo. Nearly every successful fascist revolution has followed the careful and calculated cultivation and exploitation of a real or imaginary fear of communism. Fascism is usually held by its promoters to be the patriotic defender of all true and cherished values against the threat of communism. All who oppose fascism are said to be communists, communist sympathizers, or at least subversives. Of course fascism or fascist movements may use other names; in fact they usually do. Although it is dangerous to judge any organization by its name alone, fascist organizations frequently adopt names which are designed to appeal to an irrational patriotism, nationalism, religious mysticism, or racial superiority. Terms like Nationalist, Christian, American, and Constitutional are commonly used by fascists in America.

Another kind of terror which fascists regularly exploit is the purely irrational fear of either racial or other "inferior" minority groups. Sometimes the scapegoat is a clearly definable Negro, Jewish, or "foreign" element. In cases where the blame for insecurity or economic disadvantage cannot easily be shifted to some identifiable group, a general appeal to nationalism often suffices. Peron's Argentina and prewar Japan, for example, relied largely on creating a fear of British and American imperialism and nurturing a loyalty to national traditions. Actually fascism usually exploits all the prejudices which it can find anywhere, even when these prejudices directly contradict each other as they so obviously did in the Axis alliance.

In addition to fear, another attitude which favors the growth of fascism, and which fascists cultivate, is cynicism. Impatience with an ineffectual democratic government can lead to a longing for a strong leader who will "get things done." Despair with the immensely complicated problems of economic recovery or international relations can cause a general anti-intellectual attitude which seeks to substitute force for reason and action for orderly but slow democratic processes. Intense frustration creates a desire to unburden all responsibilities on some heroic leader who will demand conformity, reduce worries by prohibiting free thought, and inspire such devotion that all of his orders can be obeyed without question and his utterances believed on faith.

It is often said that monopoly-capitalism leads to fascism. It is true that fascism, in recent years, has arisen in countries where there was monopoly-capitalism to a high degree and that fascists depended on big business and banking interests for their principal economic support. Monopoly-capitalism is a fertile breeding ground for fascism, and some big industrialists are easy marks for fascist propaganda. However, a careful examination of actual experience indicates that the relation between monopoly-capitalism and fascism is much more complex than is often thought. The Marxist doctrine of competitive capitalism evolving inevitably through a stage of industrial trusts into finance- or banker-controlled monopoly-capitalism and finally into a gangster-fascist phase just before collapsing in revolution is a vast oversimplification if indeed it describes what happens at all. Fascist tendencies are peculiar to situations where monopoly capitalism exists, but it is less likely that monopoly necessarily leads to fascism than that monopoly and fascism are both products of some other set of conditions which may appear in an advanced capitalistic system. Fascism is, at most, the logical extreme of one of many possible capitalist developments.

There seems to be some evidence that where totalitarian trends get started and continue in wealthier and more industrialized countries they tend to assume fascist forms. For example, fascism came to power in Italy in the 1920's, in Germany and Japan in the 1930's, and in Argentina in the 1940's. Conversely, totalitarian tendencies often take communist forms when they persist in poorer or less highly developed countries. For example, communism came to power in Russia in World War I, in China after World War II, and in Guatemala (temporarily) after World War II. Obvious exceptions to this pattern include fascist Spain (an economically backward country) and communist Czechoslovakia (an advanced industrial country). However, in these exceptional cases, fascist or communist systems were politically or militarily imposed from the outside and did not arise as a direct result of internal economic developments.

Therefore the main point appears to be clear. Fascism seems more likely to occur where there has been both a fairly short experience with democracy, especially under a weak and ineffective central government, and considerable industrial development. Conversely, and contrary to orthodox Marxism, communism seems more likely to occur where there has been neither a democratic political tradition nor industrial economic development. At least these generalizations would seem to follow from experience to date.

The argument should not be pressed too far, however, because a *long* tradition of democracy and industrialization which has brought high living standards seems to produce a mature and sophisticated citizenry that resists totalitarianism in all forms, whether fascist or communist. Great Britain, the United States, Sweden, and Holland are examples in point.

There seems to be no inherent tendency for a system of capitalism to become fascist and then, following a revolution, become communist as the Marxists have so long predicted. This, of course, may happen. Any extremist tendencies, whether of the left or right, may provoke an opposite extremist reaction as South American and Central American experience so amply demonstrates. But the conditions governing such an occurrence are political and institutional, not inherently economic as Marxist doctrine holds. No economic system has ever followed the Marxist prediction of development from capitalism to fascism and on through a revolution to communism even though the stage for such a sequence of occurrences has been set many times.

8

Organized Capitalism:
Oligopoly Theories

Once oligopoly entered the picture, to prescribe the elimination of monopoly became tantamount to demanding a wholesale revision of the economic order.——J. K. Galbraith

Competition between cats and mice can only result in the elimination of the mice.——T. K. Quinn

RISE OF THE BIG FEW

Monopoly, in both its single firm concept and in its economic privilege concept, reached its height in the United States in the first decade of the twentieth century and has been gradually declining since that time, although not without interruption. Hardly any of the nearly one hundred major trusts which exercised virtually absolute control of their respective industries in the first years of the century still enjoyed their exclusive market control twenty years later. Of the seventy-eight corporations which controlled over 50 per cent of their markets in 1903, including twenty-six which controlled over 80 per cent, hardly a handful still dominate their industries today. Some, such as Standard Oil and American Tobacco, had been dissolved under the Sherman Act by World War I. Others had collapsed because of overcapitalization. Most of the rest had allowed additional firms to enter their markets and were depending on means other than exclusive control over supplies and markets for achieving their goals. Of course, the public utilities of transportation, communications, fuel, and power—the "natural monopolies"—have continued to be "one firm" industries, but recent years have seen them subject both to increasing government regulation and growing inter-industry competition.

President Wilson's "new freedom" from Wall Street domination was partly realized in the Federal Reserve, Clayton, and Federal Trade Commission Acts. Although later experience indicated that these laws barely scratched the surface of the problems they were designed to solve, the general opinion which gave rise to them tended to discourage further experiment with the more refined techniques of monopoly capitalism. After World War I the combination movement was resumed, but the results of these industrial mergers were different. A more rational kind of industrial organization began to appear in the form of vertically integrated corporations which, while gigantic in size, were more functional and conducive to efficiency and economic growth than the great financial oligarchies which had thrived in the pre-Wilsonian era. It is true that the consolidations which have featured so prominently in the creation and growth of most big firms today were not always motivated specifically by the desire for greater productive efficiency, although this frequently resulted. Most of the business combination took place in periods of national prosperity when competitive pressures to reduce costs were not pronounced. Many of these combinations were promoted by investment bankers with an eye toward making speculative securities profits in a rising stock market rather than production efficiencies. However, the general pattern was usually either to combine smaller firms so that they could compete more effectively with larger rivals or to vertically integrate successive stages of a productive process so that supplies could be assured or coordination achieved. Except possibly for the holding company movement in electric and gas utilities, the purpose of business combinations of the 1920's seems to have been rationalization and efficiency more than monopoly. In many industries, the most efficient size for firms is reached at a level of output which can supply a large portion of its effective market. Hence the existence of a few large firms supplying most or all of the market may, in large part, be due to the capital requirements and the technology of production.

An attempt to secure the economies of large-scale operation does not seem to offer a complete explanation of the emergence of what is now called oligopoly, meaning the control of an industry by a few large firms. According to J. S. Bain, who recently made a study of twenty large business corporations, the economies of multiplant operation are in considerable doubt. In half of the firms studied there was apparently no *economic* justification for the large size of the operation, and in most of the remainder the economies were very slight.[1]

There are many motives for corporate combinations which are not directly related to production cost efficiencies. For example, an awareness of the advantages of pooling patents, concentrating access to raw materials, centralizing banking and legal facilities, or simply eliminating price competition in a market can all lead to mergers resulting in control of an industry by a few firms. Therefore, firms may be created which are much larger than that required for maximum efficiency or progressiveness. Giant holding companies such as U. S. Steel and A. T. & T., which themselves engage in little or no direct production, must be economically justified on grounds of the efficiencies of centralized management. One factor which does seem to be highly correlated with size is *power* and behind many of these motives can be seen the desire for large size because of the obvious political and other advantages which bigness alone entails.

The depression decade of the 1930's witnessed an exposure of some of the worst abuses of corporate managements. The consequent public indignation led to a flood of reform legislation, most of which, such as the Securities and

---

[1] J. S. Bain, "Economics of Scale, Concentration and the Condition of Entry in Twenty Manufacturing Industries," *American Economic Review* (March, 1954), 15-39.

Investment Banking Acts, were designed to bring publicity, rather than punishment, to bear on unethical business practices. At first, the New Deal seemed to promote monopoly with the National Industrial Recovery Act and other restrictive and self-regulatory schemes. Later, the wind changed and a unified and concentrated antitrust policy began to be applied under the able direction of Thurman Arnold. When World War II intervened and the demands for rapid industrial expansion and dependable supplies of war materials took first priority, the tide again turned in favor of the giant concern. Long-run economic policies normally suffer under the pressure of military expediency.

Since World War II a series of antitrust decisions by the U.S. Supreme Court against the Cement Institute, the National Lead Company, the American Tobacco Company, the Aluminum Company of America, and others has added a new dimension to the concept of the large corporation. It was held in these cases that the "conscious parallel action" of several giant firms in an industry might constitute illegal collusion under the Sherman Act even though no specific intent to monopolize had been proved. Furthermore, the power to raise prices or exclude competition was condemned even though it had not been used. However, there seems to be little likelihood that these new concepts will be applied very vigorously because no remedial action was postulated by the Court. As in previous antitrust cases, the convicted firms changed their particular methods, and their lawyers found other ways of accomplishng essentially the same objectives.

The majority of basic American industries are now organized in such a way that three or four firms control the market for the industry. The repeated refusal (in most cases) of the Supreme Court to dissolve convicted firms, or even chronic violators, under the antitrust laws indicates that market control by a big three or four is not seriously threatened. Effective policing to prevent tacit collusion and control through potential market power would require commission regulation, nationalization, or some other equally drastic reform which most American voters do not seem likely to support. Consequently, if American capitalism finds its future in the hands of a relatively few private firms which make most of the basic economic decisions for the nation, any unified theory of the economic system's operation will have to analyze fewness, or oligopoly, as such.

The problems posed by oligopoly have been described as the ticket of admission to institutional economics. Certainly the institutional and historical context is far more important for understanding the market behavior of oligopolies than it is for pure competition, monopolistic competition, or even pure monopoly. An economic system in which most basic economic decisions are made by oligopolists must be analyzed by the use of some kind of institutional methodology.

Several recent studies have indicated that the basic assumptions of classical economics require substantial modification if models of markets or the economic system itself are to be based on them and have any relevance for modern capitalism. Serious doubt has been cast on the marginal calculus as a rationale of businessmen's behavior, and the classical profit maximization motive itself has come under attack.[2] The giant firm of today is said to be motivated by a desire to attain reasonable profits rather than maximum returns. Security of income, prestige, and maintenance of some established share of the market may well be equally important determinants of firm behavior. Furthermore, the decline of atomistic markets and price competition has to some extent been offset by competition among substitute products, quality and service competition, and an enlightened philosophy of management.

The survival of modern capitalism requires a reasonable amount of competition for four reasons. First, resources must

[2] R. A. Lester, "Shortcomings of Marginal Analysis for Wage-Employment Problems," *American Economic Review*, March, 1946; H. M. Oliver, "Marginal Theory and Business Behavior," *American Economic Review*, June, 1947. But for a strong defense of marginal calculus see Fritz Machlup, "Marginal Analysis and Empirical Research," *American Economic Review*, September, 1946.

be allocated objectively, according to needs and costs, for the system to operate at all. Second, prices must remain flexible enough to withstand self-generated cyclical pressures or the system will break down in a depression or an inflation. Third, unless capitalism remains highly progressive through competition, it will lose its world economic leadership to other systems, decline for lack of new investment opportunities, or both. Fourth, only competition can prevent the already unequal distribution of wealth and income, much of which capitalistic incentives may require, from becoming crystallized into a concentration of power which would seriously threaten political democracy. Competition is thus needed to prevent income inequalities from leading to an aristocracy.

Fortunately it seems unnecessary to dwell on the possibilities and consequences of either old-fashioned monopoly-capitalism or fascism. American industry has outgrown these concepts and may even have bypassed socialism as well. No traditional economic models, whether of neoclassical atomistic competition, Marxist monopoly-capitalism, or old-fashioned socialism, are adequate to explain or even describe modern capitalism. The dominant industrial pattern is oligopoly, and the form which competition takes is unique in history. The main question today is whether the "new competition" of oligopoly is an effective substitute for the neoclassical system or whether it is merely a new window dressing for old-fashioned monopoly.

Under neoclassical competition, it is assumed that there are so many rivals that the business firm is at the mercy of impersonal market forces. Thus the businessman concentrates his attention on his costs and tries to produce, for sale at the market price, that volume of goods which nets him the greatest aggregate profit. As an additional policy, he may try to insulate his firm against the rigors of competition by such devices as advertising, product differentiation, restrictive agreements with competitors, or lobbying for protective legislation. If the competitive firm is successful in any of these endeavors, its position becomes to some

extent monopolistic. If it fails, the only weapons for securing a competitive advantage will be commercial and productive efficiency. The simplicity and determinativeness of
the price and output solution of this system contributed
much to the popularity of neoclassical theory. When demand
and cost conditions can be assumed as given, prices and
production are the outcome of impersonal forces and can
be easily determined theoretically.

The firm in monopolistic competition (many sellers but
of differentiated products) also has too many rivals to think
about their reactions to his specific market decisions. However, the sale of a differentiated, rather than a standardized,
product provides some limited scope within which prices
may be raised. Nevertheless, the effect on the firm is essentially the same as in the neoclassical system. Market forces
determine firm behavior rather than vice versa, and the
monopoly profits go to the salesmen's and advertisers' expense accounts as tax-deductible selling costs. The consumer
gets essentially the kind of product which he thinks he wants
although it may be jazzed up by the product designers and
packagers and served with a liberal portion of ballyhoo.
Prices are higher than necessary, but profits are kept down
by competition. Selling costs account for the difference.

Even the hypothetically pure monopolist who has no
rival in his product market competes with other industries
for the consumer's dollar. Actually his competition is likely
to be much more specific and, consequently, real than this.
Examples include the railroads' problems with road and air
transportation and the industrial power alternatives offered
by electricity, gas, oil, and coal producers, most of whom
are single firm monopolists in their own particular industries and market areas. The single firm monopolist may think
he has no rivals, in which case traditional economic theory
offers a simple, determinate solution to his pricing and production problems. On the other hand, the monopolist may
feel that he has so many rivals in the form of other alternatives on which the consumer may spend his money that
he is forced to ignore them and concentrate on maximizing

his aggregate profits by manipulating prices and outputs. If he *does* consider the reactions of firms in other industries, as the railroads have finally got around to doing, we are back in an essentially oligopolistic situation again.

Thus the most important single characteristic of oligopoly —and the characteristic which no other market structure can claim—is that prices and outputs are determined not by consumers' ability to pay (as in monopoly) or by production costs (as in competition) but by the specific, anticipated reactions of rival firms. The pattern of expected reactions to price and output decisions is conditioned by such circumstances as the number and relative sizes of rival firms, the political power structure of the industry, the motives of entrepreneurs, and their knowledge of market conditions. To some extent, all of these conditions are determined by the stage of historical development of the industry and the institutional structure which has evolved.

Each oligopoly is likely to contain some peculiar characteristics of its own. There does not even seem to be any general tendency for an optimum number of firms to exist. The only element sure to be present in all situations is uncertainty. Oligopoly, being thus inherently unstable, may lead to a formal cartel, a pricing scheme like the basing point system, cost accounting uniformities enforced by trade associations, price leadership, secret collusive agreements, cutthroat price wars, gigantic output, or defensiveness and conservatism. Consequently, generalization from abstract economic models, such as those of pure and monopolistic competition and pure monopoly, becomes extremely hazardous. It is therefore not surprising that major emphasis has been laid on the institutional aspects of particular market structures and that no general theory of oligopoly has appeared.

For analytical purposes, oligopoly can be simply defined as an industry composed of few enough firms that mutual interrelationships become a determinant of price and output behavior. There is not even a theoretically determinable demand schedule as in competition or monopoly. In pure competition, demand facing the firm is completely elastic; a firm can sell any amount from nothing to its capacity without affecting the market-determined price. In monopolistic competition, demand facing the firm is almost completely elastic; each seller can exercise some small control over his price, but he is limited in price increases to an amount which measures the premium which the public will pay for the presumed additional quality which advertising and product differentiation have created. In monopoly, the choice of price-output combinations available to the firm is large, but nevertheless determinate, so that the firm can maximize its profits by considering only its demand and cost schedules. However, in oligopoly the demand facing any one firm is related to the demand facing its rivals. The uncertainty produced by this interdependence creates a strategic problem the solution of which is not immediately obvious or even easily calculable. Thus a further simplification and abstraction is necessary before an approach to oligopoly behavior is possible.

Oligopolies can be classified according to two sets of criteria which are relevant to an analysis of economic behavior: product characteristics and interdependence. Whether the product sold is standardized or differentiated provides one basis for classification, and whether there is independent decision-making or collusion provides the other. Thus four major types of oligopoly can be distinguished:

1. Pure oligopoly (standardized product with independent action)
2. Differentiated oligopoly (differentiated product with independent action)
3. Pure collusive oligopoly (standardized product with collusive action)
4. Differentiated collusive oligopoly (differentiated product with collusive action)

For the purpose of analysis here the last two categories will be combined because collusion creates problems which are common to all oligopoly situations.

Even though there is a strong institutional flavor in oligopolistic industries and traditionalism plays a recognizable role in determining managerial decisions, it still appears reasonable to assume that rationality of businessmen persists to a significant degree and that the profit motive and related economic considerations are the overriding forces driving the firm. In oligopoly, the existence of a large fixed investment, a rapid rate of technological change, and businessmen's awareness of interrelationships with rivals combine to add another motive to that of profit maximizations. This is maximization of security of investment and income. The oligopolist can be assumed to seek some optimum combination of the two goals, profit and security.

PURE OLIGOPOLY

AGGRESSIVENESS: THE PRICE WAR. Two types of pure oligopoly may be distinguished on the basis of general managerial attitudes—aggressive and defensive. Aggressiveness is the situation which oligopolists fear the most because it is the most dynamic, unstable, and uncertain. If this uncertainty cannot be mitigated, aggressive firms will turn almost inevitably to price wars designed to increase sales and relative market positions at the expense of rivals and to reduction of unit costs by utilizing excess capacity. Except in the oil industry, oligopolists seem to have this kind of situation pretty well under control at the national level. However, disastrous price wars are not unknown in local markets. Recently, motel rates in Miami, Florida, got as low as 50¢ for the best double rooms, and in an Oregon town bread prices reached 1¢ per loaf for a short while. Usually these price wars among local oligopolists are ended by mutual agreement before any actual bankruptcies occur.

Sometimes a policy of large output and low prices, as Ford followed in the Model T days of 1912-1927, can effectively forestall new entry. Oligopolists sometimes deliberately undertake expensive diversification of products so as to minimize the uncertainties of selling one or only a few types of goods. This proliferation of production can become almost a fetish. Many big firms today are seeking protection in trying to satisfy as many different needs as they can think of. This is motivated, among other things, by a desire to avoid or localize any price competition which might break out.

There can be no doubt that price competition in a pure oligopoly, if carried to the logical extreme which the absence of market controls would permit, would become cutthroat and hence disastrous to the industry. Where there are only a few firms engaging in price competition, rivals become the object of personal attack with the purpose of inflicting losses and causing bankruptcies, rather than merely protecting one's position in an impersonal, competitive market. Prices may be reduced below cost for the express purpose of destroying a specific competitor. There are countless examples of this, including the recent A & P case, but a classic one is the freight rate war between the New York Central and Erie railroads. In the early nineteenth century, a rate war between these two carriers resulted in rate reductions so drastic that even the out-of-pocket transport costs were not being covered, to say nothing of depreciation and other fixed costs. The Central, knowing that the Erie was taking a loss on every pound of freight carried, hauled all its own freight over the Erie line and thus forced the Erie to terms by swamping it with unprofitable business.

Critics of competition who object to the impersonality and sometimes inhuman brutality of competitive market forces would do well to remember that legal and social safeguards against extreme personal hardships, such as factory legislation, minimum wages, safety regulations, pure food laws, etc., can be built into an otherwise objective price and distribution system without adversely affecting its operation. On the other hand, the worst abuses of power arise specifically where the personal element is allowed to creep in, as in oligopoly and monopoly, and it is far more difficult to circumscribe the power of a dictator than to regulate an impersonal market. Regulation by law is easier to accept than dictation by persons. Conversely, assistance, such as social security, from a remote federal agency causes less loss of pride and morale than the same aid administered by a local welfare department, private charity, or a benevolent philanthropist.

Since pure, aggressive oligopoly creates so much uncertainty, there are strong tendencies for product differentiation to be introduced to give some protection to the various firms. However, most of our basic raw materials industries (such as metals of all kinds and building materials like cement, glass, and roofing) are not sold to ultimate consumers but to other producers whose demand is derived, through the profit motive, from an ultimate consumer demand for a final product. These buyers are influenced more by prices and specifications than by advertising and product differentiation. Therefore, most pure oligopolists have had to rely on patent monopolies, and as these have expired they engaged increasingly in restrictive activities and general collusion with rivals to maintain prices. Thus pure, aggressive oligopoly is usually soon replaced by defensiveness, product differentiation, or collusion.

DEFENSIVENESS: KINKED DEMAND AND GAME THEORIES. The second type of pure oligopoly is characterized by the defensive or conservative attitude of letting well enough alone. Prices tend to be rigid, and relative market positions change slowly if at all. A classic case is the duopoly (an oligopoly of two firms) in the sulphur industry where prices remained unchanged for over thirty years (through depression, prosperity, and war) at a level reputed to be three times the average cost of production.[3]

One of the most significant contributions to the theory of pure oligopoly was made a number of years ago by Paul Sweezy, who asserted that in a pure oligopoly the sales of any one firm would be affected more by price increases than

[3] R. H. Montgomery, *The Brimstone Game* (New York: Vanguard Press, Inc., 1940).

by price cuts.[4] In economists' jargon, the demand curve was elastic above the market price and inelastic below it. Thus it had a "kink" in it at the market price, meaning that an increase in price would result in a more than proportional decline in sales while a decrease in price would result in a less than proportional sales increase. Regardless of where the market price happened to be, the kink would be there.

The explanation of the kink is that in a pure oligopoly uncertainty pervades the market. Any price cut will be matched by rivals because if they did not meet the lower price quotations of their competitors, sales would decline drastically. On the other hand, a price increase will not be matched by rivals, if demand is constant, because the rivals could sit tight and take away most or all of the price-raiser's business. Thus a firm will lose revenue if it initiates any price change either up or down. This ingenious theory admirably explains some price rigidities and the reasons why some trade associations have instituted price reporting systems which insure that the prices of all firms in an industry move upwards or downwards simultaneously, but it gives no clues as to how the market price was originally established.

Some of Sweezy's critics, such as George Stigler, modified and refined the original theory, but the main argument is valid under certain limited conditions. The difference in elasticity, or responsiveness, of the two parts of the demand curve is influenced by the number and relative size of the firms in the industry and their degree of independence of action. If there are relatively few firms, say three or four, a price increase as well as decrease by one is likely to be matched, thus erasing the kink and leaving the demand inelastic, or unresponsive, throughout, as in a single firm monopoly. This could occur in any case if there was an increase in demand and rivals were operating at or near capacity.

[4] Paul Sweezy, "Demand Under Conditions of Oligopoly," *Journal of Political Economy* (1939), 568.

On the other hand, price cuts would probably not be followed when total demand is increasing. A reverse kink might even develop, price increases being matched and price cuts ignored. In this case a price cut would give a more than proportional stimulation to sales whereas a price increase would cause a less than proportional sales decline. However, the fear of ultimate retaliation for grabbing a larger market share through price reductions could effectively forestall such a lower price policy. For example, a major oil company recently made a public announcement that a lower gasoline price which had gone into effect was being rescinded and the old higher price reestablished because other oil companies had not followed suit and lowered their prices also.

If there are relatively many firms (say twenty), rivals are less likely to match a price cut because of imperfect knowledge, regional markets, etc. This also erases the kink, leaving demand facing the firm elastic throughout as in pure competition. Thus the kink theory seems most valid for a middle group of perhaps five to ten firms, all of which are selling a homogeneous product.

If there is a single dominant firm in the industry, there will be no kink because its price leadership will contol and there will tend to be a single demand curve for the industry. Of course, if there is collusion, the kink will not exist either because the entire industry will be following the pattern of a single firm monopoly and again no firm will have an individual demand for its product.

When the demand, or average revenue, function has a kink in it, the marginal revenue will have a discontinuity in it due to the abrupt change in the average revenue at the kink. This means that if the firm tries to maximize its profits by equating marginal revenue and marginal cost (increasing output to the point where the last unit produced brings in revenue just equal to the cost of producing it) there exists a whole range of marginal costs which can equal marginal revenue at its discontinuity without requiring any change in price. Although it is doubtful whether any businessman ever worked this out and acted on it, this presumably explains the familiar phenomenon of fluctuating costs in a firm which nevertheless maintains stable prices or else changes prices in ways which otherwise have no relation to costs. This explanation is logical, but, since ignorance of costs and marginal revenues is likely to result in the same type of behavior, it is easier to believe that lack of knowledge, rather than close and detailed reasoning, is the explanation of these price policies.

An alternative type of analysis which can be applied to pure oligopoly is commonly known as the theory of games and strategy. As K. W. Rothschild has pointed out, "The oligopoly theorist's classical literature can neither be Newton and Darwin nor can it be Freud; he will have to turn to Clausewitz' *Principles of War*." [5] Oskar Morganstern and the late Atomic Energy Commissioner von Neumann developed a new approach to oligopoly which employs game theory.[6] Assuming perfect rationality and knowledge of their own demand and costs, oligopolists would seek for, and attain, a determinant solution to the problems of production and pricing, following mathematically predictable paths. Basically the concept of strategy between two or more parties, where each has free choice, incomplete knowledge of rivals' activities, and awareness that rivals will react to moves, provides a method whereby an optimum solution can be reached. This optimum, called a "minimax," is a final position in which every participant achieves the greatest gain for himself which he can be certain of irrespective of what his rivals do. It is neither the best possible outcome for him nor the worst, but it is achievable and unbeatable.

First, assuming that his strategy may be found out by his rivals, each player follows a particular series of moves

[5] K. W. Rothschild, "Price Theory and Oligopoly," *Economic Journal*, 1947.

[6] *The Theory of Games and Economic Behavior* (Princeton: Princeton University Press, 1944).

and countermoves, some of which are in direct response to rivals' actions and some of which are purely random for the purpose of deceiving the rivals. The particular game, if rationally played at all, will maximize the total rewards of the group (called the "value of the game") and distribute them according to the potential value of each player's resources without risk of loss. If any player tries to maximize his individual gain while the others play for the optimum, he will lose everything to the others. If he takes this risk and the others do likewise, the result is unpredictable and he may either win a fortune or lose it.

In an oligopoly, a most complex classification of possible types of games can be made because there can be many variables (price, output, selling costs, etc.) and many assumptions concerning relationships among firms. For example, each firm can be assumed to ignore its rivals' moves, to expect no reaction at all from rivals, to expect a given reaction, such as matching price cuts and ignoring price increases (the kinked demand curve theory), to engage in collusion, which will maximize either group or individual profits, or to form temporary coalitions with some firms in order to achieve specific objectives in a game with other firms.

A great deal has been written describing the possible outcomes of various types of games which firms in oligopoly might play with each other. Analysis of this kind of behavior is most rewarding intellectually, but the dreams of most of those who expected game theory to provide a new theory of capitalism, or even oligopoly behavior, have gradually evaporated. When applied to actual oligopoly situations, game theory has been most disappointing.

Of course there are always the objections to game theory that businessmen do not really know their costs and profits and do not act rationally anyhow, but these objections will not be considered because they apply equally to all types of price output theory, and considerable abstraction is always necessary to analyze firm behavior at all. There is plenty of value to abstraction and logic in economic analysis even though the predictions are often not too accurate.

However, there is a sounder basis for questioning the applicability of game theory to oligopoly. For one thing, game theory has not yet been extended to even consider cases of more than three or four participants. Yet buyers in most markets of pure oligopoly, being other producers and not ultimate consumers, are also players in the game of business, so most oligopolistic situations contain more participants than game theory can accommodate. Furthermore, game theory has thus far been applied with reasonable precision and determinativeness only to strategies between two players, and the occasions for practical applicability of such analysis are extremely rare.

Secondly, there is considerable doubt whether oligopolists play games with each other anyhow. Even at a third or fourth level of abstraction it is hard to find anything that resembles even the unconscious playing of games by businessmen. The typical businessman tries to avoid costly conflicts if at all possible. In those few instances where resemblance to a game of strategy has existed, it is noteworthy that collusion almost immediately followed. Each firm in an oligopoly usually knows what to expect from the others and avoids acting in an unexpected way which might lead to open price competition.

A good, recent example is that of two leading pen and pencil manufacturers who both announced almost simultaneously that they had developed, independently, a new type of "liquid lead" pencil. Before speculation about possible strategies or price competition could get very far, both firms announced that an orderly plan of sales coordination had been worked out involving cross-licensing and the distribution of each other's products. Both firms emphatically denied that this obvious collusion indicated any possible merger plans. Apparently this was a short-term arrangement designed to avoid the uncertainties of oligopoly price competition.

Rather than trying to hide his moves from a rival, the oligopolist may readily inform everyone of his plans so as to avoid a misunderstanding which would lead to costly conflict. Often there seems to be little regard for possible antitrust violation. While an antitrust case was pending before the U.S. Supreme Court in 1955 to require DuPont to divest itself of its 23 per cent common stock holdings in General Motors, DuPont openly began purchasing more G.M. stock in the market. DuPont's existing holdings could have been sold at a handsome profit, but apparently the capital gains on the new purchases were expected to offset any possible fines which might be incurred for law violations. The adverse decision finally rendered by the Supreme Court in 1957 will force Du Pont to take its profits, get out of G.M., and invest elsewhere.

DIFFERENTIATED OLIGOPOLY

Every producer, whether of oranges, coal, lipsticks, or locomotives, would like to differentiate his product from that of his competitors, at least in the minds of his customers. Sellers of consumers' goods have had considerable success at this although at the cost of expensive advertising and a multiplicity of designs and models which accelerate obsolescence. Sellers of producers' goods have had less success because their products are normally sold to other business firms through professional buyers who are more impressed by low prices and adequate quality than with brand names and psychic or hairsplitting product differences. Nevertheless, there is evidence that goodwill, established commercial relationships, and communities of interest do play a considerable role in the sale of raw materials and capital equipment. And some success is claimed for branding and differentiation even for such prosaic goods as coal and building materials.

Most of the consumers' goods in America are produced, if not sold, under conditions of differentiated oligopoly. Production is now characteristically done by a few firms producing for national markets. Retailing usually takes place under conditions where there are few enough firms in any one local market area that oligopoly conditions are approximated. The differentiation of the product may be real, as in some electric appliances, imaginary as in aspirin and most cigarettes, or a combination of real (though perhaps superficial) differences and strong consumer preferences developed through advertising, as in automobiles. The nature of the differentiation is less important than the extent to which consumers prefer the product. Regardless of the reason— whether it is real or imagined superiority, services which accompany the product, the reputation of the firm, or the feeling of prestige which the purchaser enjoys—differentiation causes sales to be less sensitive to price changes and hence gives producers some control over their prices. Effective differentiation permits the seller either to raise his price within limits without a corresponding loss of sales or to increase his sales without having to reduce his price. The stronger the consumers' preference, the more discretion the firm has over its prices.

Price policy in a differentiated oligopoly may be subject to over-all agreement even though the differentiated products of the various firms do not sell at identical prices. One type of policy may be an agreement favoring mutual respect. In this case no firm would change its prices without consulting the others. This protects all firms against the rigors of the kinked demand curve.

A second type of price policy involves agreement on price differences which are based on the "margin of substitution." Prices of more preferred products are kept just enough above those of less preferred products so that consumers generally have no incentive to switch to the cheaper product. This practice has characterized the sale of gasoline where the two cent differential between the major brands and the independents is supposedly the value of consumers' preference. This type of policy tends to maintain fixed market shares for the various firms although there may be no tendency toward uniform prices.

A third type of policy ignores prices as such and concentrates on the division of the market. Where demand is fairly elastic, nonprice competition, such as advertising and the offering of services, may be used to determine the market share for each firm. Prices will be rigid, and there will be a strong incentive to advertise up to the point where the last dollar of advertising justifies its cost in profits from additional sales. This may result in huge advertising outlays for two reasons. First, selling expenses are tax deductible as business expenses. This can save most firms fifty-two cents in taxes for each dollar spent on advertising or other selling expenses. Thus a dollar in expenditure may cost the firm only forty-eight cents—or even less if the expense shifts the firm to a lower tax bracket.

Second, overhead costs may have been written off on a lower budgeted output so that the new gross sales induced by advertising may be almost entirely profit. The cigarette industry has probably been in this kind of situation. In any event, advertising efficiency is most difficult to evaluate. One executive recently stated, "We know half of our advertising expense is wasted. We just don't know which half."

A fourth policy may permit minor price competition as in discounts, trade-in allowances, one cent sales, contests, coupons, etc. These may be permitted by rivals as long as the price structure itself remains intact. When a buyers' market arrives, however, these minor concessions to price competition may spread and grow until the price level is forced downward. The recent collapse of fair trade standards in the face of the enormous growth of discount houses has brought lower appliance prices in many markets, for example.

Other types of policies could be postulated, but there is one factor which is inherent in all policies of differentiated oligopolies. That is nonprice competition, and its most prevalent form is in advertising. When a firm can convince buyers that its product is superior, it can charge a higher price for it. If a rival firm retaliates by further advertising and raising its price, then the first firm can differentiate from the rival and may even be able to raise prices again. Thus product differentiation can be used as a lever to jack up prices.

More likely, however, prices will stabilize at a level high enough to protect all firms in the industry, with price cuts coming occasionally when demand is temporarily depressed or technological obsolescence forces certain lines to be discontinued and cleared out at low prices.

Nonprice competition unfortunately does not *necessarily* lead to the results which competitiveness is supposed to achieve: lower prices, better quality, maximum efficiency in distribution, rational allocation of resources, maximum want satisfaction, progressiveness, etc. Consumers' Union and other product-testing organizations have repeatedly shown that there is little correlation between prices and quality. In extreme cases, as toothpastes and bathroom scales, the highest prices at one time accompanied the products having the lowest quality while the lowest prices were for products with the highest quality.

It is true that in some instances there are real consumer benefits from nonprice competition. If, as doctors claim, about half of all physical complaints are purely psychic (though they may lead later to actual physical disabilities) patent medicines undoubtedly cure many ailments in the same way that faith healers do. However, reliance on such nostrums often results in the neglect of symptoms having physical causes. Yet the feeling of importance attached to the use of certain "prestige" goods may really be a contribution to human happiness. Advertising often broadens knowledge, and it will make costs lower if the total market for the advertised product increases enough to permit the introduction of machines which create manufacturing economies.

Another type of nonprice competition is in collateral terms of sale—such as guarantees of performance or service. Probably real benefits accrue to consumers through this medium because it has focussed considerable attention on the maintenance of service and replacement facilities. This type of nonprice competition is very important in some industries. Mileage guarantees backed by appropriate refunds have exerted a strong influence on the market for automobile tires. At least one line of agricultural implements and two automobiles have been seriously handicapped because of an inadequate service organization.

In other fields, nonprice competition may facilitate, rather than forestall, rational consumption. In women's dresses, for example, well-defined price lines are often established as the result of convenience and custom. Wholesale, and to some extent retail, prices are fixed at different levels, and competition takes place in varying the character of the garments. Buyers are probably better able to make rational comparisons and choices under this arrangement than if quality, style, and prices were all subject to fluctuations.

However, it is no less likely that excessive diversification of models, styles, and brands will confuse the consumer. For example, manufacturers faced with a decline in demand may introduce new grades or lines of products rather than cut prices. When competitors create similar grades, the process will be repeated. Many states have passed laws limiting the variety of fertilizers and other products that can be sold in order to reduce buyers' confusion. For some products an undue emphasis on quality has forestalled the introduction of low price, utility merchandise for budget conscious or low income consumers.

For some people the satisfaction gained from acquiring a greater quantity or better quality of goods for the money may well exceed the satisfaction of imitating the "Man of Distinction." Furthermore, nonprice competition results in expenditures which are not divisible among consumers. Free financing and free delivery only mean that the costs of these services have been absorbed in the price and that the consumer must pay for them whether he wants them or not. Likewise, the cost of advertising falls on all buyers. The "useful" expenditures on television entertainment bene-

fit the television viewer, but there is no reason to expect
that the shows which the consumer does not watch but pays
for through buying the sponsor's product will be balanced
by the shows which he watches but does not pay for.

Nevertheless, nonprice competition has led to great improvements in quality and in a useful experimentation with
customer services. It has created, for the most part, an
attitude of respect for the consumer and a catering to his
wants. Furthermore, most consumers are not usually price
conscious and seem to prefer the advertised brands and the
leading firms. Some large firms which have reduced both
advertising and prices have lost their markets. A recent victim, Chrysler Motor Company, lost nearly half of its sales in
two years through continuing to produce a high quality,
utilitarian automobile while its rivals were going in for an
imitation space ship for creeping around in heavy traffic.
On the other hand, the recent rapid growth of discount
houses selling household appliances indicates that many customers would rather have reduced prices than trading
stamps, money back guarantees, credit terms, or other
"extras."

Actually, price competition is superior to nonprice competition from a strictly economic viewpoint because lower
prices provide greater economic freedom. A lower price
permits the customer to do as he pleases with the money he
has saved whereas nonprice competition requires the customer to accept useless gadgets or valuable services whether
he wants them or not. Nonprice competition, even an improvement in quality at no increase in price, does not permit maximization of total satisfaction because there will always be a minority of consumers who will prefer a lower
price even if it requires lower quality. The best way to insure maximum consumers' freedom and satisfaction would
be to offer the customer a choice of a lower price or advertised quality, fancy packaging, services, etc. As the
Temporary National Economic Committee observed, "If but
a small fraction of these economically useless expenditures

were translated into reductions in the price level, the gain in public purchasing power and the resulting stimulus to production and employment would be material." [7]

Any price set above the competitive equilibrium price must be followed by (1) a reduction in the goods offered for sale, (2) an increase in the demand, and/or (3) price competition between sellers which reduces the price level. Present antitrust laws only prohibit the first of these— agreements among firms to restrain trade. Thus the result of monopolistic pricing is likely to be further nonprice competition, which may be good or bad depending on the form it takes.

Part of the problem is one of management and communication. Market research tries to convey to management what the majority of people want, and producers then try to satisfy the majority. Hence the minority, which may prefer lower prices and standard quality or fewer gadgets, has no opportunity for satisfaction. Furthermore, market research is far from being very reliable. The questions asked by market polls are frequently leading ones. They ask the consumer if he likes what amounts to a better product. The answer, of course, is "yes," since the alternative of a lower priced, utility product may not be suggested. Or the consumer is asked to compare something real with something hypothetical. He naturally chooses what the producer already has, rather than something he knows nothing about. Thus producers often do not know what even the majority of consumers want so they produce what they think is wanted and then advertise to create a demand. If all producers in an industry do this, there may be little genuine choice for consumers. Therefore all new cars are about alike, being "longer, wider, and more powerful," meaning harder to park, more expensive to operate, and more dangerous. There is no choice offered to the consumer who might prefer a low priced, utilitarian automobile. A possible solution has been suggested by the British. When they finally

---

[7] Temporary National Economic Committee, Monograph No. 1 (Washington, D.C.: U.S. Government Printing Office, 1941), p. 55.

came around to new models of automobiles, they continued to produce the old model for sale at a lower price for those who might be more conscious of price than style.

Probably all that should be expected for preserving the advantages of price competition is that every market have some source of price flexibility and hence lower prices available for those who want them badly enough to make a reasonable effort to secure them. A big department store bargain basement, some discount houses, or a Sears & Roebuck outlet keep the hardware, clothing, and notions markets fairly competitive in most big cities. Price competition has a resilience which is hard to hold back when some real threats to price fixing are lurking around. But consumers' rationality should be constantly promoted. As George Bernard Shaw once said, "People should get what they want or they will end up wanting what they get."

COLLUSION

Both pure and differentiated collusive oligopoly can be considered under the general heading of collusion, since agreements supersede the behavior distinctions between the two types of situations. Any adequate attempt to analyze the history of collusive activities in America, its current extensiveness, or its economic effects would occupy an entire volume and perhaps several. Nevertheless, collusion in one form or another is widespread in spite of being specifically illegal under the antitrust laws.

Price leadership, an almost unconscious form of collusion, is a characteristic of many American industries, from newsprint to tin cans. It may exist where there are many small firms who belong to a trade association, but it is most likely to occur where there is one firm which produces at least 25 per cent of the output of the industry.[8] In some major industries, particularly those characterized by one dominant firm, price leadership may be the final step before a merger

8 George Stigler, *The Theory of Price* (New York: The Macmillan Co., 1953); J. W. Markham, "The Nature and Significance of Price Leadership," *American Economic Review*, December, 1951.

or the installation of some system of formal collusion. Many oligopolies have one member which regularly initiates price changes for the industry. Usually there are some smaller firms who shade their prices at every opportunity but are ignored by the dominant producer because the entire output of all of them combined is insignificant.

Those industries in which price leadership exists may be divided into three general classes.[9] First, there is a small group of industries in which there are two or more companies having similar costs but controlling different, though unchanging, shares of the market. Second, there is a much larger group of industries in which there is one producer, not necessarily the largest, who because of superior knowledge of market conditions regularly initiates price changes and is followed confidently by his competitors in that industry. Third, there is a smaller group of industries in each of which there is one dominant firm that, either arbitrarily or by common consent, has become the price leader. This latter group is the most important of the three, and the most dangerous from the point of view of the manner in which competition is stifled and the rights of the consumer threatened.

The first of these groups is comprised of a relatively small number of firms. The gasoline industry provides a typical example of this group. Ordinarily it might be thought that large companies such as Standard Oil of New Jersey would set the price throughout their entire market areas. However, this is not true of each section of the country in which Jersey Standard operates. Scattered about are independent producers of petroleum products who, though they sell to only a small portion of the market, nevertheless are able to retain their portion of the local market regardless of any increases or decreases in prices. Selling only in their local area, their costs are about as low as those of their larger competitors. Though a small producer might be expected to sell at the same relatively high price as set by the dominant

[9] The author is indebted to Mr. H. Lynn Miller for compiling some of the information included in this section.

producer in that area, it is not uncommon for the small producer to set the lowest possible price which will provide a
return on his investment. Thus there are isolated cases in
which the smallest producer in a given area can impose his
price upon all the other producers in that area. Standard
Oil of New Jersey has implied this was the case with the
Richfield Oil Company in the New York City area several
years ago. Jersey Standard claimed inability to combat such
practices. To the extent that such practices on the part of
the smaller producers result in the lowest possible prices to
the consumers, it would hardly be fair to criticize price
leadership of this particular, albeit uncommon, type.

The second group is composed of many industries in each
of which there is one producer who acts as a sort of business
barometer, quick to recognize changes in supply and demand in the industry. This producer, who is usually one of
the larger firms in the industry, regularly takes the lead in
making price changes. Often the producer does not consult
his competitors before making the change but passes the
word along as soon as the new price has been determined.
In a majority of cases the competitors will quickly adjust to
the new price although there have been instances where the
other members of the industry have adopted a wait-and-see
attitude, feeling perhaps that the new price was out of line
when compared with the current prices of close substitutes.

Under this barometric type of price leadership, the leader
is frequently a low cost, high capacity firm, and its competitors are higher cost producers. Thus the leader could sell
profitably at a price below the costs of his rivals if he wanted
to risk some unpredictable forms of retaliation.

Frequently, a number of firms in a given industry have
similar demand and costs. Although none of these companies
may have an overwhelming share of the market, one will invariably institute most of the price changes within the industry. Such is the case in the copper industry where, during
a recent two year period, Phelps-Dodge, a medium-sized
producer, took the lead in three out of five price changes,
with its larger rivals following suit. Also, in the rayon indus-

try recently, the American Viscose Company, a producer of about 30 per cent of the total industry output, has been responsible for three-fourths of all the price changes within the industry. In a good many cases, the price leader has attained its position not by producing substantially more than its competitors but by possessing a marketing division so well informed that its recommendations are readily accepted by most of its rivals. In cases where a well informed price leader occasionally takes advantage of its extensive knowledge of coming changes in market conditions, it would be difficult to punish it under the antitrust laws. Such a company probably has a legal right to do as it pleases with whatever advance information it can obtain. Of course, if it should consistently withhold such information from the rest of the industry and always keep it for its private use, then the leader might be said to have attained a position in the industry from which it could use its vast knowledge to restrict competition.

The third group of price leadership industries mentioned above appears to be the most dangerous to competition. In each of the industries in this group, there is one dominant producer along with a number of smaller firms. Here it is only natural for the largest firm to take the lead in setting prices. In general, prices are less flexible under dominant firm leadership than they are under barometric price leadership, although there are definite limits, based on demand elasticities, to which any price leader can go. The price may be a relatively high one, as in the case of the U.S. Steel Corporation, or a comparatively low one, as in the case of the International Harvester Company.

The case of the U.S. Steel Corporation is particularly interesting because it illustrates to what extremes a high cost producer will go in order to maximize its own profits, all the while allowing more efficient competitors to enjoy proportionately higher earnings of their own. U.S. Steel seems to have maintained its prices at a relatively high level whenever demand slackened and at a point below the highest possible price during periods of increased demand. One might argue that such a pricing program would tend to even out over the long run and should not be construed as injurious to the consumer. This would not be altogether true, however, for U.S. Steel usually waits as long as possible before instituting a general decrease in the price of steel, whereas its competitors, anxious to develop new business during periods of recession, tend to shade their prices or resort to secret price cuts at every opportunity. On the other hand, during periods of peak demand, the prices charged by U.S. Steel do not lag very far behind the highest prices charged by any member of the industry. This price leadership policy on the part of U.S. Steel has kept prices unduly high. For instance, from 1922 until 1932 the price of steel rails remained virtually unchanged. It was only with the greatest reluctance that the corporation agreed to lower the price, even though the depression was long under way. The chief argument given by U.S. Steel in stabilizing prices over such a long period of time was that once the market for items such as steel rails has been disturbed it becomes unpredictable and may disappear completely until conditions become less chaotic and the major producers can once again agree on a stabilized price. This points up more clearly than ever the dangers of price leadership by a dominant firm. Smaller competitors may wish to sell at lower prices, but, except within very narrow limits, they dare not do so. New producers might well hesitate to enter the industry because of the allegiance which they would have to pay to the dominant firm.

Similar conditions may be said to exist in the farm implement field, where the International Harvester Company has long been the price leader. Its leadership, however, has differed somewhat from that of U.S. Steel, for International Harvester has been a low cost producer. This has enabled it to set prices at such a low level that its competitors have been forced to meet International's low prices or go bankrupt. In fact, in the early 1920's the company had set its prices so low that 150 of its competitors were forced out of business, and only three managed to survive. During that period, however, International Harvester continued to earn substantial profits. Thus we have a case of an oligopoly in which the dominant firm did not choose to set high enough prices to allow established competitors to operate profitably and new firms to enter the industry. On the contrary, it drove out competitors by its efficiency and low prices.

Price leadership may eventually lead into one of a large variety of more formal collusive agreements. The more explicit the agreements become, the greater the likelihood of government antitrust attack so, in this country at least, formal cartels have been rare. Formulas such as the basing point system and price reporting schemes have been successfully prosecuted also, so that about all that is left is the gentleman's agreement. Communities of business interest in oligopolies make the unwritten understanding a potent short-run weapon against price competition, however. The enforcement of standard percentage markups over cost, for example, has been effective in many industries.

Ultimately, agreements which raise prices abnormally tend to drive consumers to seek substitutes, and agreements which raise profits as well entice new entries into the industry. The Great Depression finally broke most of the world's international raw materials cartels simply by causing such a great disparity between supply and demand at the high cartel prices that new, noncartel supplies came into the market in huge quantities and at lower prices. When new entry can be effectively forestalled by patents or other legal restrictions or by high capital costs, collusive oligopoly can be perpetuated. When the danger of new entry is immediate, however, the protection of product differentiation will be eagerly sought.

THEORY OF COUNTERVAILING POWER

One of the most notable and courageous attempts in recent years to set forth a general theory of capitalism has been that of J. K. Galbraith of Harvard University and *Fortune* magazine.[10] Starting with a recognition of oligopoly as the dominant market structure, Galbraith developed an ingenious theory of "countervailing power," which is supposed to replace and accomplish the objectives of the traditional neoclassical competition. Assuming that neoclassical competition is largely extinct and free markets, with their automatic, built-in regulators of economic activity, have given way to producer-dominated, administered-price markets, then there is tremendous "original" market power for oligopolist producers. They may elect to produce or not and to set their own prices. Galbraith contended that the very existence of producers' market power gives rise to countervailing power which comes from the other side of the market, rather than on the same side as in competition, and controls or checks the original power of the producer.

Sometimes countervailing power appears in the form of large integrated buyers, like A. & P., who bargain with producers and force down prices for the thing they buy. In other cases, strong labor unions are stimulated by low wages and poor working conditions, and they force needed corrections. In some instances, the lack of common interests among individuals or groups who are exploited by original corporate power prevents any effective organized private resistance so the government is called in to protect the weak. Farm price supports, public home building and financing, and social security are conspicuous examples of this kind of countervailing power.

Actually, the concept of countervailing power, while new to economics, appeared in ancient Indian and Chinese religious philosophies which explained the forces of nature in terms of the inevitable creation of opposites. Newton's law of motion ("to every action there is an equal and opposite reaction"), Hegel's thesis and antithesis, Toynbee's theory of history, and the modern sociological concept of interest groups in society generating their own opposition are all

---

[10] *American Capitalism: The Concept of Countervailing Power* (Boston: Houghton-Mifflin Co., 1952). The following section is based on several portions of this book; specific references will not be made.

applications of the force which Galbraith calls countervailing power.

The description of large power groups as often acting politically and strategically is accurate, but, unfortunately for the theory, pressure politics is likely to lead to inflation if the government tries to resolve conflicts in favor of both, or all, sides. Since countervailing power is actually bargaining power, the holders of this power must be in a good bargaining position. But when demand is greater than supply at existing prices (which is the situation in times of inflation) the ability of countervailing power to regulate original power is diminished. Thus inflation may effectively nullify countervailing power by creating a permanent sellers' market so that conflicts of interest can be settled at consumers' expense. Countervailing power may be latent, but it can never get off the ground when inflation keeps the original power holder, the producing corporation, in the driver's seat. Benefits of inflation may trickle down to other groups, but the first beneficiary is the large corporation, and the first returns on inflation are frequently business profits.

Galbraith believes it is the duty of the government to make possible the growth of countervailing power by not prosecuting economic power groups indiscriminately under the antitrust laws. He favors repeal of the Robinson-Patman Act because this act prevents the operation of countervailing power by prohibiting manufacturers from giving discounts to large buyers in excess of actual cost savings. As it is, the countervailing power of large buyers which could force manufacturers to reduce prices is limited by law.

Since countervailing power only functions effectively when business conditions are stable or deflationary and since recession is now universally opposed, it is reasonable to ask why the government should support this power and use it to regulate business as Galbraith advocates. Galbraith answers, correctly, that government support of countervailing power will enable the continuation of decentralized economic decision-making. But economic stability, without inflation, will be required for countervailing power to be effective.

Galbraith uses Schumpeter's arguments that the technological progress which has produced such high living standards in America has been due to corporate giantism. The great expense of modern invention and the development of new products, markets, and techniques of production and distribution could only have been borne by firms which are so large that one to four enterprises are sufficient to supply the needs of most markets.

This argument is valid up to a point, but there is no substantial evidence to prove that the size of most, or even many, of the largest firms is justifiable on the basis of the technical economics of production or even research. Not all of the six to seven hundred mergers which have been occuring in the United States every year since the end of World War II have been to achieve operating economies. Many are undoubtedly promoted by management who are concerned with acquiring market power in order to secure discounts from suppliers, higher prices from customers through control of supplies, or a better bargaining position with labor for control of employment. Galbraith would probably see countervailing power created by these mergers, but the increased size which comes from acquiring more and more of the same kind of facility, such as steel plants or retail outlets, does not necessarily lead to any significant operating economies.

Galbraith somewhat underestimates some of the more important economies which do not lie in technical production, centralized management, possessing multiple units of production and distribution, or even in a great diversity of output. These economies lie in the growth of the entire industry and in the growth of all industries. An expanding market permits the introduction of new techniques of production and distribution. However, the growth of the industry and its market is largely independent of the size of particular firms.

Furthermore, Galbraith seems to have somewhat misinterpreted the function of neoclassical competition, which was never intended to be a cutthroat struggle for existence in which no holds were barred and only the strongest survived. Competition provided an arrangement whereby coordination and cooperation among numerous opposing and diverse economic interests could be attained. If all buyers and sellers had the same demand and cost information, each would have to adjust his position and actions to objective, market-determined conditions. There would be no place for coercion of rivals or bargaining over prices. Competition assured that economic power would be highly decentralized, unorganized, and severely limited in scope. It is the oligopoly—the market of the few large firms—which can degenerate into a struggle for economic power that may lead to irresponsible power concentrations.

The examples cited by Galbraith to show the development of countervailing power seem to prove his point that the power does exist and indeed has replaced competition in the American economic system. Growth of chain and department stores during the depression years of the thirties was cited as a prime example of the way in which retailers were able to control prices. But to explain the growth of these institutions as examples of countervailing power and to neglect the other influences present at the time seems unrealistic. There are other causes for this growth which cannot be overlooked. How can the tremendous expansion of chain and department stores during the postwar inflation be explained? In Galbraith's theory, this new growth could not be due to countervailing power; yet Galbraith claims the prewar growth was due to the development of this power.

Galbraith's theory does not give adequate weight to the possibility that a large firm may choose to bypass the powerful group opposing and seek out weaker, unorganized opponents. Some large retailers do not purchase from the largest suppliers who have original market power but instead use their power against smaller, weak suppliers, leaving the powerful manufacturers free to deal as usual with smaller retailers.

Possibly the most unorthodox aspect of countervailing power is that it depends on the growth of cohesive economic groups. Americans are individualistic and have not traditionally tended to identify themselves with economic interest groups. There have been too many conflicting interests to enable many large single-purpose groups to arise. Groups may grow, people may join them; yet the members will still do as they please in areas of self-interest. For example, many people belong to unions, believe in them, and support them; yet they do not always vote as the union leaders urge them to. In the case of farm cooperatives also, members regularly drop out and sell their crops on their own when they feel it is more profitable to them personally to do so.

Countervailing power has received a lot of serious attention from economists. The theory has been brilliantly and persuasively presented, and it does open the door for a new kind of market analysis which permits ingenious reasoning to bear some fruit. However, it is not likely to be acceptable either to the liberal view, which is suspicious of oligopoly, or the conservative view, which holds that the economy is still essentially competitive and is in no danger from business monopoly anyhow.

The view of liberal economists trusts neither countervailing power to work at all nor the political oligarchies which might result if it did work. The view of conservative economists is also suspicious of countervailing power since even if it were effective and the results were superior to those of neoclassical competition it would not prove that the economy was competitive just because the results came out the same. Nor does countervailing power protect the nation from the centralization of political power of giant economic units. In fact, it promotes large units itself.[11]

Perhaps the most basic objection to the growth and support of countervailing power as a replacement of competi-

[11] E. W. Swanson, "Review of American Capitalism," *Journal of Public Law*, Spring, 1953.

tion is the question of who benefits under this condition and who suffers. Countervailing power groups representing consumers have remained conspicuously absent. Only producer groups have ever developed it. Hence manufacturers may bargain with labor, suppliers, and retailers and share business profits in various ways, but the consumer seldom stands to gain directly. Thus the theory of countervailing power does not lead to the same results as competition and cannot be considered as a substitute for it as a regulator of the economic system.

THE SIGNIFICANCE OF OLIGOPOLY CAPITALISM

The importance of oligopoly in modern capitalism is probably underestimated. Many people tend to assume that cheap transportation, mail order houses, nationwide advertising of products, and the statewide advertising of large urban department stores prove that there are effective national or regional markets for most goods. It is frequently asserted that the decline in the number of firms in an industry has been accompanied by an increase in the number of firms competing in any given market because the size of the market has grown. This is certainly true to a degree, but the argument can be easily overdrawn. Long distance transportation and freight costs have not declined appreciably in the last 50 years in terms of purchasing power. Mail order houses have seen their local retail business grow more rapidly than their mail order business, although, on the other hand, chain stores have grown rapidly. Nationwide advertising may increase the demand for particular products, but they are still purchased mostly in localities where three or four firms dominate the market and small, independent sellers follow a leader. There is no conclusive evidence that the barriers between local or regional markets have been significantly reduced.

Even the generally accepted assumption that an original state of pure competition has over the past 150 years evolved into oligopoly is subject to considerable qualification. The great combination movements of the 1880's, the 1920's, and the post 1945 period have enormously increased the size of the typical industrial and financial enterprise, and in recent years many markets have come to be dominated by giant enterprises. However, the combination movements have, in large part, merely offset the competitive tendencies which followed from the growth of transportation during the nineteenth century.

There were many cartels in England by 1800, and oligopoly was typical of many markets as early as the seventeenth and eighteenth centuries. Even Alfred Marshall doubted if there was a free labor market in the 1880's. Thus oligopoly may have been a major characteristic of capitalism since the very beginning with the exception of a period between the development of nationwide transportation in the mid-nineteenth century and the great combination movements which began in the 1880's. Anyhow, the duration of relatively pure competition was brief compared to the emphasis it has received in economic theory. If oligopoly had received as much attention from economists as pure competition has, there might be a general theory of capitalism today which would deserve the respect of all social scientists.[12]

Economic theory has long sought to explain economic processes through an explanation of price and output determination. It seems reasonable to expect that any future economic theory of capitalism will necessarily have to be constructed on this solid foundation of price and production theory. Without an explanation of price, determination of the level, character, and distribution of production and income is impossible. Without an explanation of the productive and distributive system, an over-all theory of capitalism is impossible. The rise and persistence of oligopoly and the dominant role which it plays in modern American capitalism therefore requires a more adequate theoretical explanation before any workable theory of capitalism can appear.

[12] For one of the best studies of this subject, see Fritz Machlup, *The Economics of Sellers Competition* (Baltimore: Johns Hopkins Press, 1952).

Part III

THEORIES OF SOCIALISM

9

Development of
Socialist Economic Theory

When society requires to be rebuilt there is no use in attempting to rebuild it on the old plan.——John Stuart Mill

EARLY THEORIES OF SOCIALISM

PRE-ECONOMIC IDEAS. There are many concepts of socialism, and no single definition can embrace them all. To Lenin, it meant a dictatorship of the proletariat; to British Laborites, it means an economy of public and private enterprise with a democratic government that guarantees minimum living standards and full employment; to Scandinavians, it means all this plus cooperatives; to Christian Socialists, it means the Kingdom of God on Earth; and to some Americans, it apparently means government controls.

In spite of these and many other differences, there are some features which are common, to varying extents, in all varieties of socialism. First, socialists have always protested against the existing order of things. Second, socialists have always believed in the cooperative nature of humans and have advocated some kind of collective solution to human problems. Third, socialists have demanded a greater degree of social and economic equality than has ever before existed. There has been a voice of protest since Adam, and if socialism is defined broadly enough to include the ideas of all people who want to change existing institutions, then socialism has existed for a very long time.

There have also been many groups throughout history who believed in cooperative living—certainly most major religious movements in their early phases. And relative equality has been stressed by various schools of economic thought, including the English classicists. Since there is no well-defined starting place for studying socialist economic thought, a beginning might best be made with thought which was neither socialist nor economic but which contained some of the emotional content which has been carried forward into all socialist and other reformist literature.

One of the main features which distinguishes modern socialist ideas from progressive or liberal economic thought is the desire for greater *social*—as distinct from *economic*—equality. Socialism has distinct ethical implications in addition to its economic content. The call for social and economic reform is an echo from the most remote past. Going back to the eleventh century B.C., the voices of Amos, Hosea, Isaiah, and Jeremiah are heard crying out for a better world in which class conflict and exploitation are eliminated. These early radicals called down the wrath of God on ill-gotten gains. Wrote Jeremiah, "Woe unto him . . . that useth his neighbor's service without wages, and giveth him not for his work."[1] Isaiah also envisaged a new society in which "they shall not build and another inhabit, they shall not plant and another eat . . . mine elect shall long enjoy the work of their hands. They shall not labor in vain . . ."[2]

The ancient Greeks, in the fourth to third centuries B.C., contributed to man's longing for, particularly, political reform. Plato's *Republic* described a communistic society in which private property was abolished and perfection in government was achieved through a combination of eugenics and education. However, class distinction, even slavery, was permitted as part of the system.

Somewhat later Jesus described the "Kingdom of God" as an ideal society in which service to others, humility, and disregard for material things were the basic principles of

[1] Jeremiah 22:13.
[2] Isaiah 65:22–23.

life. By sermons, parables, and deeds—in fact, the example set by His entire life—He taught a philosophy of social service. Through the parable of the talents and the account of the widow's mite, He taught payments according to ability. Through the parable of the Good Samaritan and by reported miracles, He taught to give according to need. Always, He emphasized social equality, and, as an example, He mixed freely with inferior social classes. The hero of the Samaritan parable was of an inferior social caste which illustrated, as did many of His other utterances, that it was the inner man— the spirit—which was important, not outward superficial distinctions. Jesus never lost an opportunity to reiterate that the accumulation of material wealth, far from being a motivating force in the ideal society, would be a positive deterrent to living a spiritually significant life.[3]

Jesus advised the rich young ruler to give all of his possessions to the poor or face a probability of salvation which could be illustrated by a camel going through a needle's eye. Early Christians apparently took this advice a step further by abolishing private property and taking vows of poverty. The Roman persecution of these early believers, it is reported, was more for their communal living than for their subversive activities. The Book of Acts describes these early Christian customs: "And all that believed were together, and had all things in common; and sold their possessions and goods and parted them to all men, as every man had need." [4] The importance of the teachings of Jesus can hardly be overemphasized in this context in view of the tremendous influence which they have had on socialist thought. Not only have the entire Christian Socialist and Social Catholic movements in Europe been based on the social philosophy of Jesus, but virtually every brand of socialist thought except Marxism owes a recognized debt to the founder of Christianity.

Many secular writers have exhibited the emotional spirit of social reform held by the early Christians. Sir Thomas

[3] See, for example, Matthew 19:24–25 and Mark 6:8–9.
[4] Acts 2:44–45.

More's famous book *Utopia,* published in the early sixteenth century in England, was the first of a long line of books (now all called "utopias") which have indirectly criticized existing society by painting a picture of a better, or ideal, state. The typical form was a description of something that does not exist but stirs men's imaginations toward the possibility of human progress. Most utopias criticized private property and profits, emphasized that social institutions are subject to controlled change, and held that happiness was the goal of human existence. To achieve this goal, they stressed economic and social equality, education, development of science, and international organization for peace.

The utopians were usually able to avoid suppression by letting their picture of the ideal society speak for itself without actively participating themselves in reform movements. The utopias were so vague in their specific recommendations that it was hard to pin the authors down on any particular point. While this may have prevented outright suppression and persecution of the utopians, it likewise resulted in the failure of the utopias to directly inspire any practical reform movements.

Some utopias did have significant indirect effects. The Royal Society was inspired by Bacon's *New Atlantis.* Harrington's *Oceana* is said to have influenced political scientists who became aware of the dangers of centralized government and succession of power and tried to prevent these through systems of checks and balances such as the U.S. Constitution provides. Other utopias, such as Bellamy's *Looking Backward,* Campanella's *City of the Sun,* and H. G. Wells' *New Worlds for Old,* have had enviable reputations of literary success, while still others, such as Swift's *Gulliver's Travels,* have enjoyed continuing popularity because of the plot alone.

ASSOCIATIONISM. The associationists were a group of social theorists and reformers living in France and England in the seventeenth and eighteenth centuries who believed that society could be improved through collective organization and cooperation but who did not have any national reform platforms or political ambitions. Unlike the utopians, the associationists tried to put their ideas into practice, but since they considered basic economic and social units to be in small, autonomous groups rather than the national state their activities were on an insignificant and harmless scale. The associationists were mostly individualistic themselves and feared state-imposed collectivism so their associations were voluntary and not enforced by authority. It is hard to draw a line between pure associationists and the more politically active socialist reformers of the day because some individuals had basically associationist ideas but pressed for wide national reforms at the same time. But associationism can well be considered as an attempt to reconstruct society along equalitarian lines with self-contained communities or cooperative productive organizations as the basic unit. Although the ideas are more important than the people who had them, it is nevertheless desirable to consider associationism by individuals since the various associationists recognized and analyzed different aspects of the growing pains of industrialization.

The political fact of the French Revolution and the economic fact of the Industrial Revolution inspired the first genuine socialist movements. Among the leaders in these movements were Henri Saint-Simon, Charles Fourier, Etienne Cabet, Sismondi, and Louis Blanc in France and Robert Owen and William Godwin in England.

Saint-Simon (1760-1825) was an eccentric French aristocrat who is credited with founding French socialism. Although not strictly an associationist in the sense of advocating self-sufficient communities, he did start a movement which had wide influence on socialist thought. His followers in later years advocated national collectivism rather than local association although Saint-Simon himself had much in common with the associationists discussed here. His chief contribution lies in the fact that he was one of the first people to recognize some of the consequences of industrialization. To Saint-Simon, the basis of everything was industry. As Veblen was to point out a century later, Saint-Simon held that economic and industrial institutions were more important than political institutions in determining historical events. He advocated a system of scientific and industrial leadership to replace the old political and religious hierarchy. France was to be turned into a factory, organized like a single, model workshop, and the right to work was to be recognized as greater than the rights to own or inherit property or engage in business. He advocated distribution of capital and income on the basis of talent and effort only. Although his followers went on to oppose all forms of private property, Saint-Simon maintained that private inheritance was more the real clue to inequality and poverty than property itself.

Louis Blanc (1811-1882) was a French historian, statesman, economist, and author of an outstanding study of the French Revolution. Like Saint-Simon, he saw industry as the basis of society but, in more typical associationist fashion, tried—and succeeded temporarily—in having government workshops set up in Paris to alleviate unemployment. He asserted that competition was the main cause of poverty, moral degradation, and wars and advocated voluntary association as the foundation of social life. His associations, called "social workshops," were to be along craft union lines rather than being self-contained communities, however.

Another French associationist was Charles Fourier (1772-1837), who had an enormous influence for a time in spite of the fact that he is generally thought to have been insane because of the extravagant ideas and direct contradictions which characterize his writings. At times Fourier appeared to advocate communism, free love, and religious fanaticism although the communities he founded had strong capitalistic features such as stock ownership, interest payments, and dividends. Nevertheless he had a remarkable insight into the sociological problems of communal living.

Fourier dreamed of a world of apartment hotels and subsistence farms in which everyone would perform the tasks for which he was best suited. He suggested that children should be in charge of garbage disposal and dish washing since they seem to enjoy getting dirty. They would also march at the head of all parades.

Over forty cooperative communities in the United States can be traced to Fourier's influence alone, the most famous being Brook Farm, Massachusetts, which was supported by Ralph Waldo Emerson, Nathaniel Hawthorne, James Russell Lowell, Horace Greeley, John Greenleaf Whittier, and others.

Fourier directly contradicted Saint-Simon in some respects. Particularly he advocated a "back to the land" movement which would reverse the trend toward industrialization. Autonomous communities of fifteen hundred people all living in huge resort-like hotels and working and eating together would provide the necessary environment for a kind of social living that would reduce the unpleasantness of work. Private property would be retained through private stock ownership in the community, and an elaborate profit-sharing plan was supposed to harmonize conflicting interests. The Radical Socialist party in France (a right wing, nonsocialist group) follows Fourier in some respects to this day.

Robert Owen (1771-1858) was probably the most outstanding of the associationists and is sometimes referred to as the greatest of the utopians as well. Although he had a passion for utopias, Owen actively engaged in social reform movements and, being a wealthy industrialist, financed and carried out a number of experiments in community cooperation and factory reforms which served as models for new legislation for half a century. This famous British economist and social theorist not only made significant contributions to progressive education theories, social welfare programs, and industrial relations but is credited with being the father of the cooperative movement, the profession of welfare work, factory legislation, and British socialism itself.

Probably Owen's greatest theoretical contributions were in education and sociology where he recognized the role that proper training, good environment, and decent treatment play in making factory workers not only into good citizens but into valuable contributors to the industrial enterprise. Owen noted that machinery is more productive and efficient if cared for properly and reasoned that human beings, being infinitely more complex and delicate, would respond likewise. He reduced the work day from 17 to 10 hours in his factory, put all of his workers under the age of 10 in model schools, which he built for them, rather than employing them in the shops, and abolished fines for infractions of rules. These experiments were highly successful both commercially and socially.

Owen placed great faith in the beneficial effects of proper surroundings. To him, a man was entirely the product of his environment, and, consequently, neither ability nor effort, to say nothing of status, entitled him to any greater reward than any other man. If the individual is not responsible for his talents or efforts, argued Owen, then why reward him for them? Hence when Owen went out and founded communities they were absolutely equalitarian and subsequently failed for lack of adequate incentives to produce.

In Owen's new society all profits would be abolished because they were thought not only to reflect injustice—the excess of selling price over cost or the medieval "just price"—but to cause underconsumption (and hence relative overproduction) which in turn leads to unemployment. Owen denounced competition, declaring that even perfect competition would not abolish profit as the classical economists claimed because some profits are included in the cost of production in the form of interest. The only elements he would permit in selling prices would be labor and depreciation of capital. (Raw materials, supplies, etc. can be broken down into labor and depreciation also, of course.)

Since profits are realized in money, Owen advocated replacing money with labor notes as measures of value. He recognized a contradiction here since payment in labor notes (presumably in proportion to labor value created by ability and effort) is not consistent with absolute equality. But apparently Owen considered the labor note system of payment as a step toward his ultimate equalitarian goal.

An interesting experiment in substituting labor notes for money was tried when the Labor Exchange was set up by Owen's associates in London in 1832. Nearly one thousand members were allowed, at first, to value their merchandise in labor terms. However, the members found it profitable to exaggerate labor value so this function had to be turned over to independent brokers. These brokers, however, either did not understand or did not accept Owen's philosophy so they valued the goods at current prices and then expressed the values in labor at the rate of six pence an hour. Thus instead of labor value determining market value, market value determined labor value.

Eventually, the Exchange became flooded with useless goods. The members found themselves buying goods whose labor cost exceeded their market value and selling goods whose market value was greater than their labor cost. When a group of outside merchants cornered the supply of labor notes, the Exchange collapsed.

A principal weakness of the system appears to be the identification of money with profits. Far from being synonymous with profits, money actually reduces profits by providing an accurate, homogeneous measure of value and a definite rate of exchange. Money thereby prevents the exorbitant exploitations of ignorance and uncertainty which occur in barter systems. Another weakness was, of course, the assumption that labor cost determines exchange values to the exclusion of demand.

In summary, the associationists can be credited with three major contributions to economic thought. First, they recognized the necessity for justice in distribution. The classical economists had described the mechanism of distribution of returns to the factors of production, but it was for the associative socialists to inquire into the ethics of the system. Second, the associationists recognized that production is social as well as economic—that man is a human being as well as a producer. Much of our modern social legislation has its roots in these two concepts. Third, they saw the evolving nature of social institutions and advocated organized efforts to adjust to it. The German historical school, later socialists, and the American institutionalists can trace their methodology to its first feeble beginnings here.

The associationists contributed little to any positive theory of socialist organization, but their negative contributions were significant. By actual demonstration with hundreds of cooperative communities, all of which later failed, they proved that utopia is not easily attainable because human nature is difficult to change. From these experiments has come the conclusion that any fundamental reforms in industrial society will be unlikely to succeed without the aid of government. True, Catholic and Buddhist monasteries organized on essentially associationist principles have persisted for centuries, and Mormon and other religious communities have a history of remarkable accomplishments. In these cases, however, there has always been a transcendental motivating force which inspired ordinary people to extraordinary achievements. The more subtle humanistic and ethical challenges may have provided sufficient incentives and philosophies for a few highly intellectual individuals but have never proved adequate to the task of inspiring large numbers of ordinary men and women to devote their lives to social improvement.

SYNDICALISM. It was perhaps inevitable that there would be reactions against any socialist movements, such as the utopians and associationism, which were led entirely by middle- and upper-class intellectuals. One such reaction was Marxism (which is discussed in Chapter 5 because it concentrated on a criticism of capitalism). Another reaction was syndicalism which, in some respects, was directed against Marxism also for not offering a positive substitute for capitalism.

Syndicalism, which became a significant movement in France, Italy, and Spain between 1890 and 1918, was influenced in considerable measure by the early nineteenth-century French anarchist, Pierre Joseph Proudhon (1809-1865). Proudhon's attacks on socialists were hardly less vicious than his diatribes against property and capitalism. He attacked the existing institution of property, calling it "theft," and condemned interest, rent, and profits as well. On the other hand, he condemned communism also because he thought individuals should be allowed to own the property for which they had labored. But he did not want people to be able to use their property to exploit others or to benefit from another's efforts. Proudhon scorned the associationists and evolutionary socialists for believing in peaceful reforms and hoping that the government might be used for democratic purposes. Instead, he proposed voluntary, independent workers' organizations to carry out all productive purposes, using force if necessary to achieve their goals.

The final form of syndicalism, however, was shaped by the French engineer, social theorist, and revolutionist of aristocratic background, Georges Sorel (1847-1922). To Sorel, all government, whether capitalist, socialist, or communist, was bad. The only thing that counted was what he called a "social myth." This myth was an idea which, even though false or unattainable, would generate a new social energy by arousing a fanatical loyalty to it. In the struggle, and even martyrdom, which attainment of the mythical goal attracted, men would realize their noblest potentialities and hence would achieve what he thought to be true moral greatness.

Sorel, like Proudhon and Marx, had no more use for intellectuals and social reformers, who were considered to be traitors to the "true" revolution, than for capitalists, who were pitied for being more decadent than evil. Also like Marx, Sorel rejected parliamentary methods and believed in an inevitable class struggle leading necessarily to a revolution. The revolution, however, was one of Sorel's social myths and took the form of a general strike which would overthrow all existing order. In the general strike, violence would flare, blood would flow, and the souls of the strikers would be purged of evil. This highest expression of human values would be realized in this triumph of blind emotion over reason and order.

The conditions following the revolution were to be different from those envisaged by Lenin and more contemporary Marxists. Sorel believed that the new society would be controlled by voluntary, self-governing workers' organizations called *syndicats,* and, except for these, anarchy would reign. He rejected the Leninist "dictatorship of the proletariat" as being a resurrection of the same soul-stifling organizationalism which caused capitalist society to decay in the first place. Sorel's aversion to rationality and order clearly shows that he believed not only that the ends justify the means but that the ends themselves are unimportant except to inspire the means which alone are the key to the true life. The goal was in the social myth which was a lie existing solely to inspire the soul-purifying violence of the general strike.

Sorel was successively a Catholic conservative, democratic socialist, revolutionary syndicalist, nationalist, monarchist, and finally a reactionary conservative. Probably his influence was greatest on fascism because in spite of his wandering among philosophies he never lost his pessimism, his glorification of chance, free will, and arbitrary power, and his passion for violence as the supreme, heroic act of rebellion against civilization.

It is not surprising that while the star of syndicalism shone brightly, it soon died out, especially when the specific objects of its fixation were modified or reformed. The syndicalist glorification of violence for its own sake soon became too much even for the Marxists. Sorel's contempt for reason, his criticism of science, and his reliance on impulse as a means of reaching truth were ultimately rejected by all revolutionary groups and, oddly enough, seem to have made a lasting impression only on the young, super-conservative royalists who became Sorel's strongest supporters. Out of the decline of syndicalism fascism, not socialism, ultimately arose.

SOCIAL CHRISTIANITY. The nineteenth century also produced strong socialist movements based on both Catholic and Protestant religious doctrine. The Catholic variety, Social Catholicism, and the Protestant variety, Christian Socialism, had tremendous influence throughout Europe and, to a smaller degree, in the United States. The Social Catholic movement received great impetus from the famous encyclicals of Pope Leo XIII (1890) which strongly supported collective action to achieve social justice. The Protestant Christian Socialist movement received substantial support from high church officials in several countries, particularly England.

Both groups condemned classical competition as being oppressive to the weak, and both believed cooperative social and economic organizations were more consistent with achieving the brotherhood of man than laissez faire individualism. Consequently, labor unions and social, educational, and welfare legislation were strongly advocated. Except for opposing some of the more comprehensive nationalization of industry proposals, these Christian-based movements agreed with non-Marxian socialists on the general pattern of the welfare state.

The strong Christian Democratic parties of Western Europe and much of the rest of the world are either the ruling party or the official opposition to the more doctrinaire socialists. Based more on Social Catholicism, the Christian Democrats are more conservative than their nineteenth-century counterparts but hold to most of their welfare state ideals, nevertheless. In Great Britain, where the Social Christianity movement was predominantly Protestant, the Christian Socialists moved to the left to merge officially with the Labor party. The late Sir Stafford Cripps, famous post-war Chancellor of the Exchequer, was but one of a long line of illustrious Christian Socialists, which even included the late Archbishop of Canterbury.

The World Council of Churches itself derives its social philosophy partly from Christian Socialism although not without some modification. Private profit has been opposed as a proper mainspring of activity in an economic system by the leading Protestant denominations, and the rugged individualism of capitalistic folklore has been repeatedly condemned. The right of every man to a job and the duty of the state to guarantee minimum standards of welfare and social justice are essential parts of this semiofficial Protestant social philosophy. In this the World Council of Churches is in close agreement with modern social Catholics who draw their inspiration from Pope Leo XIII's forceful and unmistakable stand for positive social action to remedy the injustices of laissez-faire capitalism.

In spite of the great social and political contributions of these religiously inspired movements, it is necessary to look elsewhere for a theoretical basis for the *economics* of modern socialist systems. Theologians quite naturally are more occupied with the problems of the spirit. The problems of the flesh have been more of a challenge to those scholars who, while often deeply religious, are not full-time religious philosophers. Without intending to detract from the great impact on ethics and general philosophy which Social Christianity has produced, it is not inaccurate to say that the stream of economic thought has flowed almost entirely from secular sources. For this reason it is necessary to turn to the humanist Fabian Society of Great Britain for the economic foundations of modern non-Marxian social theory.

ECONOMICS OF THE EARLY FABIAN SOCIETY

ECONOMIC AND POLITICAL BACKGROUND. Modern democratic socialism arose in Great Britain, and British socialism arose largely from the Fabian Society. Formed in 1889 by Bernard Shaw, Graham Wallas, Sidney Webb, and others, this remarkable organization devoted to the advancement of socialism through education and propaganda has grown until it could boast, after World War II, that practically the entire Cabinet from the Prime Minister down were Fabians. Although the Fabian Society is not a political party and has never run candidates in elections, the postwar Labor Parliament contained a majority of Fabians. The Fabian Society with only about seventy thousand members is one of the most influential single organizations in Great Britain.

There is no official position or policy of the Fabian Society. However, the founders of the society made substantial contributions to political, economic, and sociological theory, and these were published by the society although not necessarily accepted by all of the members. To the Fabians, the problems of socialism were never distinctly economic, political, or sociological, and the theories advanced and studies made were usually a combination of all three. Therefore, it is not possible to analyze the economic elements of Fabian writings without considering the sociological and, particularly, the political elements as well. Since from the very beginning the Fabians assumed that the state could be used as a tool for achieving economic goals, it is necessary to examine the Fabian theory of the state before proceeding to purely economic considerations.

The socialism of the Fabian Society has always differed markedly from the socialism which developed on the Continent. Until World War I, the governments of France, Spain, Italy, Russia, Germany, and other European countries maintained repressive attitudes toward labor unions and working-class movements. Consequently, the governments in these countries incurred the reputation among workers as being exploitative and evil. It is not surprising that the movements which had the widest appeal in these countries called for the elimination of the state itself by extralegal methods and the establishment of either some kind of workers' self-government or else no government at all. Since the workingman's principal experience with laws involved their use to suppress his interests, he was inclined to have little respect for legal procedures. A possible exception would be the Germans who have always had more respect for the state than other Continental peoples. As early as 1862 the German economist Ferdinand Lassalle had insisted that the state could and ought to be used to enable individuals to attain higher standards of living and a higher degree of culture than they could attain individually or through anarchic collective organizations. Marx had a greater appeal to German working classes than Lassalle did, however. In Europe generally, labor movements could usually trace their political ideologies to Marxism, syndicalism, and or some kind of anarchism. Except in Scandinavia, Austria, and Switzerland, Communism gained considerable working-class support all over Continental Europe.

In Britain, the political climate was altogether different. Here the government was not generally regarded as oppressive but rather as an instrument of progress. True, there had been periods of discontent when socialist-inspired political movements, such as the National Union and Chartist organizations, had been able to thrive on syndicalist ideas, but such movements were usually narrowly devoted to agitation for a particular kind of reform and did not attract much serious attention. With the extension of the franchise, the accomplishment of economic reforms, and the growth of trade unions, the targets for syndicalist attack largely disappeared. After the repeal of the Corn Laws in 1846, general prosperity further strengthened the working people's faith in the effectiveness of parliamentary methods for achieving freedom and progress. Thus the Fabians were treading a well worn path when they entered the scene advocating democracy and progress to be achieved through the transference of authority to a paternalistic government.

To the Fabians, the state was potentially good and could be used as an instrument for abolishing "unearned" incomes, meaning rents, interest, and certain types of profit. The government could also be used for owning and managing industries, for promoting justice, and for mitigating the existing extremes in economic well-being. The Fabians were cautious, however, and spoke in terms of the "community" or "society" as being potentially good. They avoided glorifying the state as many German writers tended to do. The Fabian benevolent state was not nationalistic or aristocratic, nor did it have any mystical significance. In no important sense did it resemble the fascist concept of the state as a supreme guiding spirit. The Fabians have never worshiped the state or even pretended that it was a separate entity apart from the pressures of many individual interests.

To the Fabians, Parliament represented the will of the majority. It was, therefore, democratic and should be retained, not overthrown. Parliament had simply never before represented the working people. But if enough workers' representatives could be elected, then Parliament would obviously express the workers' wishes. Thus the task to be done was political and educational but not revolutionary.

Another outstanding characteristic of the Fabians was their profound respect for experts. Possibly because the Fabians were for the most part middle- and upper-class intellectuals rather than representatives of the working class they did not hesitate to recommend that economic and other problems be attacked by committees of trained or experienced specialists rather than by delegates or workers. Basically, Sidney and Beatrice Webb (who, more than anyone else, molded Fabian political theory) were planners. Their orderly minds were more revolted by inefficiency than by the loss of personal or political freedom. The Fabians, particularly the Webbs, were among the first to recognize that administration, both in business and government, was becoming a highly complicated profession. They saw that elaborately trained specialists would have to take over much of the burden of business management from property owners and much of the task of public administration from elected officials.

In addition to political thought, the early Fabians made a distinct contribution to socialist economic theory.[5] Rejecting the Marxist theory of distribution, the Fabians, particularly Sidney Webb and Bernard Shaw, preferred to pursue the classical economics of Adam Smith, Stanley Jevons, and John Stuart Mill to a socialist conclusion. Sidney Webb had read and mastered the principal works of Mill, who at that time was the universally recognized authority on economics, and Webb often quoted Mill against the opponents of socialism. Actually this was not hard to do since the necessity for public property and relative equality could be made to stem directly from the most respected of the classical economists. Classical economics had made its goal the greatest

[5] Shaw, et al., Fabian Essays in Socialism (1st ed.; London: Fabian Society, 1889), chaps. i, ii, vii. Reprinted 1950.

happiness for the greatest number of people. To the Fabians, nonrevolutionary socialism was the logical means of achieving this utilitarian end.

Wealth, declared the Fabians, was social. This was a necessary conclusion because modern industrial organization made it impossible to distinguish the contribution made to the final product by each factor of production or each individual person. Thus the Fabians denied the labor quantity theory of value of Ricardo and Marx. Any attempt, they said, to distribute wealth according to the pure labor expended is also impossible. The only alternative is to make wealth public property. This is also in contrast to Marx who had argued that labor should receive all income because labor produced all value.

By implication, the Marxist doctrine of class struggle and eventual victory of the working class is denied. There is a sort of class struggle in Fabian thinking, but it is a struggle of lower classes to receive their rightful share of the national product along with other groups rather than a struggle to overthrow a privileged class as in Marxism. Confiscatory taxation and nationalizing of rents are means to this end but are not ends in themselves as they are to Marxists. Expropriation of landlords and capitalists is incidental to the achievement of a fair distribution of wealth to all. The free medical service now in effect in Britain, for example, gives the upper classes the same treatment as the lower classes. Class prejudice exists, of course, but only as a political device. It has no real place in Fabian economic theory.

The Fabians agreed with Ricardo that rent is a differential payment which accrues to the owners of any land that is more productive than the poorest land in cultivation. If equal labor is applied to different lands, some land will produce more than other land because of its inherent fertility. If all labor receives the same pay for the same type of work and all like products sell at the same price (pure competition in both labor and commodity markets) the payment for the surplus product of the better lands will go to the landowners as rents since, under competitive conditions in labor and product markets, landowners can and will charge the economic rent to a tenant or cultivate the property themselves. The tenant gets subsistence and no more.

According to the Fabians, this was sufficient in itself to justify nationalization of land and the abolishing of landlords. The orthodox economists, said the Fabians, argued that price is determined by the cost of production at the margin. Since rent is a differential payment based on the relative productivity of different pieces of land and hence does not enter into the cost or production at the margin, the orthodox economists concluded that (1) rent does not enter into price and (2) the value of commodities is fixed by cost so that commodities exchange in exact ratio to the labor cost spent on them. The implication of this was that private land ownership costs the community nothing. But the Fabians, following the Austrian school rather than the classical (and Marxian) labor theory of value, stressed the fact that commodities do not exchange or tend to exchange in proportion to the labor expended in their production or any other costs. It is a fact that commodities produced well within the margin bring as high a price as commodities produced at the margin with much greater labor. The Fabians thus concluded that landlords, instead of costing the community nothing, cost all the difference between the lowest and highest costs of production.

This same analysis of land rent can be applied to capital and other resources and factors of production. An admired and respected contemporary of the early Fabians, Alfred Marshall of Cambridge, had introduced the concept of the quasi-rent, meaning the excess income which some resources receive over that amount which they would yield at equilibrium in pure competition. The Fabians went beyond Marshall to argue that all kinds of capital, and even skills and ability, are rewarded by the same differential payments which, like Ricardo's land rent, are based on the price of the product at the "margin of cultivation." Thus labor working with marginal capital or marginal knowledge and skill would only produce subsistence while labor working with better tools or talents will earn a rent for the owners.

The Fabians proposed to tax away these bonuses where they could be found but to permit, for incentive purposes, income differentials based on productivity. Unlike Marxist distribution which would return surplus products to the workers, Fabian distribution theory would collect surplus for society as a whole. Labor would then continue to receive its subsistence as before, but the state, which owned the wealth, would use the surplus, or rent, to provide social services such as education, medical care, and insurance or else to provide certain basic goods free of charge. In this way, the living standards of wage earners would rise above subsistence.

The early Fabians were also concerned with the problem of economic power and its effect on the distribution of income and wealth. They maintained that those who possess power use it, consciously or not, to appropriate the economic surplus for themselves, leaving the majority of the population with no more than subsistence. These people, since they are able to control and exploit the more favorable land, industrial sites, capital equipment, and even human talents, are able to control the economic rents which accrue to them. Private property was condemned because it led to private monopoly which held prices unreasonably high, restricted production, caused great extremes in economic well-being, and led to recurring and perhaps permanent unemployment. The state was always envisaged as preventing these unhappy consequences by playing an ever larger role along the lines of (1) regulation of industry, (2) municipal ownership and administration of industry, and (3) taxation of rent and interest.

The Fabians' penetrating analyses of private power always led to restriction or abolition of private property and a corresponding expansion of the role of the government. Unfortunately the Fabians' rather naïve faith in democratic institutions blinded them to the fact that government ownership and regulation does not abolish power but merely transfers it to the state. In a mature, democratic society, power may be safer in the government than in private hands, but it certainly continues to exist and to pose serious problems of control or dispersal.

In addition to economic arguments, private property was rejected by the early Fabians on philosophical grounds. Virtue, it was said, is relative to circumstances. Poverty and misery lead to a low moral code. The argument for relative equality (which was felt could come only through public property) was made complete by Shaw's conclusion that excessive wealth also leads to low moral standards.

The Fabians did not reject the Marxian doctrine of the inevitability of socialism, but they supplemented it with a belief in gradualism. Socialism could be "helped along." They promoted all kinds of progressive legislation such as inheritance taxes, social security, income taxes, labor legislation, and the like on the theory that a step toward democracy must be a step toward socialism and vice versa. This gave rise to an odd contradiction which permeates Fabian literature. Socialism to the Fabians was to be earnestly desired and worked for. Fabians consciously permeated all levels of society armed with logical arguments, emotional appeals, and a detailed knowledge of facts; every opportunity was taken to advance the cause of socialism and democracy. The society's motto even suggests a final coup: "For the right moment you must wait, as Fabius did; but when the right moment comes you must strike hard, or your waiting will have been in vain and fruitless." This is hard to reconcile with what they called the "irresistible glide into collectivist socialism" and "the irresistible progress of democracy." The Fabians were not bothered by this contradiction, however, and continued to work ceaselessly for what was to them inevitable.

Although the Fabians borrowed their name from a Roman general, their outlook and attitude toward political economy were more typical of certain of the ancient Greeks. These freethinking, radical intellectuals had a deep reverence for democratic processes, an assurance that public ownership of property would solve much of society's ills, and an almost naive faith in the administration of the philosopher-kings who would be produced by the civil service. No doubt, many Fabians would not have felt far out of place in the public square of Athens during the days of Plato.

TRANSITION FROM CAPITALISM. The Fabians in general and the Webbs in particular carried on most of the research on social problems in Great Britain from about 1885 to 1925. It was largely due to Fabian activity that the British Labor party was able to take over the leading place in the Western European socialist movement from the German Social Democrats, who had held that position until World War I. As soon as it was organized, the Fabian Society recognized a trend toward municipal ownership of utilities which existed in the 1880's. Until this time, direct municipal operation of industrial enterprises and even local services had been very limited. In the seventeenth and eighteenth centuries, many small statutory trusts had been organized to operate sewers, poorhouses, turnpikes, and other local services which since ancient times had been administered by appointees of the justice of the peace. In spite of the fact that these trusts had been notoriously inefficient, it was not until about 1850, with the reform of local government, that they began to be absorbed by democratically elected municipal governments. Operation of these local services together with some port facilities was about the extent of municipal commercial activity until late in the nineteenth century. Public utilities were owned almost exclusively by private enterprise.

During the 1870's, however, several English cities discovered that there were numerous advantages to be gained through municipal ownership of gas and water companies. Apparently the leader in these experiments was Birmingham.[6] In the next three decades, a large number of munici-

---

[6] Pease, *History of the Fabian Society* (London: Fifield, 1916), pp. 81-82. Oddly enough, this experiment in municipal socialism which had such far-reaching effects was motivated by the highly antisocialist objective of reducing the tax burden on local property owners through municipal business profits.

palities began or took over and developed utilities, including gas, electricity, water, and transportation. Municipal services were, as they still are, operated by city officials usually through committees to whom the permanent staff of the enterprise answered for the conduct of the business. Revenue passed through the municipal accounts, but surplus could be used for improving service, retiring indebtedness, or lowering rates. There was no compulsion that this had to be done, however. Municipal services were normally self-supporting, charges being adjusted according to the revenue, and many eventually became debt free by redeeming their bonded and funded indebtedness through sinking funds chargeable to the enterprise. Sometimes they operated at a profit to the city, surplus revenues going to meet other city expenses. When this occurred, citizens paid a disguised tax through their gas and water rates.

Quickly seeing the possibilities of promoting public ownership on this basis, the Fabians began such a vigorous campaign to extend municipal industries that for many years they were referred to as "gas and water socialists." (In Germany, the even less inspiring term "sewer socialists" was used.) In addition to ordinary utilities, municipalization (which means the transfer of ownership and operation of private property to a municipal authority) was advocated for such diverse undertakings as pawnshops, hospitals, steamboats, bakeries, and fire insurance underwriting. Although Fabian tracts also appeared concerning state ownership of the Irish railroads and the possibility of municipalization by provinces rather than by local authorities, the general socialist feeling at the turn of the century was that public ownership of enterprise in a socialist state would be predominantly municipal in form.

The early Fabian theory of the transition to socialism involved the transfer of private industry to public ownership through bankruptcy, forced sale to municipal governments, or threat of municipal competition. Increased labor union organization and political agitation by labor and socialist groups would lead to increased political awareness and activity by working people. This, together with the gradual extension of the franchise to propertyless classes and women would lead to a demand for economic security and social guarantees provided by the state. These measures would be expensive and could only be financed through higher taxes on income, property, and inheritance. These taxes would not only be necessary but would be demanded by the working class in order to ameliorate the existing extremes in income. Thus rent, interest, and profits would be confiscated by the state. This transfer of unearned income would not occur in a lump sum but gradually by installments.

As the profits of private industry were reduced by taxation, the situation would become more favorable for the transfer of productive resources from private to public ownership. Cities would therefore be alert to the possibilities of acquiring property from private owners where the price had fallen below equity values, assuming, of course, that city officials were properly "educated" to take advantage of opportunities to acquire private property.

City officials would see that a municipality could construct factories or stores, using either tax revenues or funds borrowed at low interest rates because of government guarantee, and operate on the basis of minimum average cost for an entire area, excluding rent and quasi-rents. A private firm could not hope to compete on this basis since it would have to sell at a price equal to the "full cost of production at the margin of cultivation." A favorably situated firm could compete only by ceasing to pay rents while an unfavorably situated firm would have to sell out immediately. In other words, a private firm in a situation in which its cost per unit continued to fall with increasing output could compete with the city on a no-rent basis while a firm whose costs were rising due to diminishing returns could not compete under any circumstances. Thus by threatening to build a plant and compete on a nonprofit basis the municipality would force the private firm to sell out at a price equal to the capitalized value of the interest payments available to the municipality.

Probably the forced sale would not involve a cash payment but rather an exchange of securities, the private stockholders receiving, for their stock, city bonds paying an interest rate equal to the rate at which the city could issue bonds to the public and construct its own plant. For example, if a private firm earned 10 per cent for its shareholders while a city could sell bonds at 4 per cent to construct a similar plant, the private shareholders would have no choice but to turn over their stock to the city and receive 4 per cent bonds in return. The amount of income going to these new municipal bondholders could gradually be diminished through a highly progressive income tax which might even discriminate against interest income with rates higher than those applying to wage income.

This process would be cumulative. As the public sector of the economy grew, the private sector would find it harder to compete. Wages would be higher in the public sector (due to governmental policy), and private firms would consequently have to raise wages in order to get labor. This would bring further downward pressure on profit margins, which were already squeezed by taxation, and would lead to a demand on the landlords for lower rents. The city, which was taxing rental income, would experience a decrease in revenue as rents fell and would then raise the tax rate. The landlord class, squeezed from both sides, would gradually disappear. The business capitalists would be disappearing at the same time through the process of municipalization.

In fairness to the Fabians, it should be pointed out that whether such methods are "fair" or not depends on one's concept of justice. To the Fabians, private interests and rents (especially the exorbitant ones charged in those days) were tools of exploitation and had no justifiable basis. Hence the taxing of interest and rent to the point of confiscation was considered to be a perfectly just and logical conclusion.

Bernard Shaw advocated the expropriation of all land and capital. However, since expropriation would have to be accomplished gradually, justice required that the owners

be adequately compensated. If all property could be ex-
propriated at once, then everyone would find himself working in municipal industry and compensation to former property owners would be unnecessary. It would be paid by
property owners, through taxes, to themselves. In other
words, if compensation were paid to all property owners for
their acquired property from funds raised by a tax on property, this would lead to a mere income transfer, and the net
effect would be no different from outright expropriation.
The basic aim of socialism, said Shaw, is the transfer of all
unearned incomes from the landlords and capitalists to "the
people." The Fabians also spoke of the possibility of expropriation by means of the highly progressive income tax
used to finance the construction of new state industries to
compete with private industry, with disastrous consequences
for the latter.

Although the House of Commons was envisaged as developing into a central government which would be the
organ for consolidating the municipalities and "nationalizing
intermunicipal rents by an adjustment of the municipal contributions to imperial taxations," it is clear that the socialist
society was to center around the local government board or
city council. The Webbs, in their gigantic study of local
governments, had this in mind. Since rapid transportation
and communication, national advertising and nationwide
markets, businesses, cartels, and labor unions had not developed in that day nearly to the extent that they exist today, it
was quite reasonable to imagine a socialist Britain economically organized on a local basis. The Fabians, therefore,
emphasized the reorganization of local government so as
to attain a maximum of democratic participation in municipal affairs and to approach the ideal of maximum democratic self-expression of the individual desire for freedom
through the medium of the local government. Parliament's
principal duties would be to provide for national defense,
supervise international trade, and equalize economic rents
for the nationwide network of socialist municipalities by
confiscating, through taxation, all rents above the national

average and subsidizing all municipalities whose rents were, for natural reasons, below the average.

GUILD SOCIALISM

From the earliest times socialist thought has contained two contradictory doctrines regarding the management of public industries. One is the syndicalist principle of workers' control; the other is the principle adopted by the Fabian Society of centralized, expert control in behalf of the entire community. In the years following the formation of the Fabian Society, the conflict between these two doctrines was never resolved and both continued to develop concurrently.

The faith in parliamentary methods and the perhaps exaggerated belief in the benevolent state held by most of the early Fabians was not shared by all socialists at that time. A different or special kind of socialism, based in part on syndicalism, arose and became known as guild socialism or guildism. The leading economists who were exponents of guildism, such as J. A. Hobson, R. H. Tawney, and G. D. H. Cole, looked toward quite a different form of industrial organization than most of the Fabians envisaged. While the Fabians relied on the worker as a citizen who could create and maintain a democratic state, the guild socialists tended to rely on the worker as an economic producer who would offset state power.[7] However, some of the strongest exponents of guildism were also Fabians themselves, and all were deeply influenced by the environment of British politics; so guildism resembled the reasonable, nonrevolutionary Fabian reformism more than the revolutionary anarchy of continental syndicalism.

Relatively mild as it appeared, however, guildism contained two germinal ideas which closely resembled continental syndicalism. One of these was a conviction that workers' interests could be properly represented in Parliament only by workers' delegates themselves. The second

[7] G. D. H. Cole, *Self Government in Industry* (London, 1922), chap. i.

was a conviction that *direct* control over production by the workers, in addition to public ownership, was a necessary requisite of a democratic socialist state.

The first conviction was formulated by G. D. H. Cole, who developed a pluralistic basis for the socialist state. To Cole, the individual was a consumer, a producer, and a citizen as well as a worker; since he belonged to several interest groups, he could hardly be properly represented by one geographically elected delegate. To Cole, true democratic representation had to be functional. Man could only realize expression of his highest aspirations if he took part in both political and industrial management functions himself. Several representatives, one for each of his several interests, would be necessary, and this would involve a reorganization of both Parliament and the electoral system on a functional basis.[8]

The other belief, that of direct workers' control over production, was based on a traditional conception, which had been expressed by Robert Owen and John Stuart Mill, of the worker as a self-governing craftsman. To the guildists, socialism could not satisfy the desires of workers by merely transferring property titles to the state. This would only substitute bureaucrats for capitalists, and workers would still have no control over their working conditions. There could be no such thing as harmonious labor-management relations in either private or public enterprise. The mere existence of any kind of management made labor-management strife inevitable. Labor would have to assume positive control over the operation of the industrial enterprise and eliminate management as a function separate from labor.

Guild socialism was thus highly idealistic. Its challenge to orthodox socialism was based on the idea that power and responsibility should be widely dispersed among working people, not centralized in a state bureaucracy. Freedom had to be based on free organization at every level of economic life in order to be real. Like Marx, the guildists argued that

[8] G. D. H. Cole, *Guild Socialism Restated* (London: Leonard Parsons, 1920), pp. 31-35.

man's economic status would determine his social and political status. Unlike modern Marxists, they concluded that a political democracy could not coexist with an autocratic system of economic control of industry. Unlike non-Marxian socialists, they distrusted both state controls and large labor organizations.

In order to attain their objectives, guild socialists exhorted workers to press for a larger role in the control of prices, production, and product quality in privately-owned firms as well as for more control over working conditions. By slowly wresting managerial power away from employers through collective bargaining, workers would eventually secure control of the firms and industries in which they worked. Ownership was to be vested in the state, but administration was to be on a federation principle of workers controlling through their guilds. These firms and industries would then be operated "as a trust" for the public.[9]

Thus economic control by labor was to be secured independently of political control of the government although there was hope for eventual control of political institutions as well. The movement for control and eventual ownership by the workers would be more rapid in such industries as the building trades where the smaller amount of capital involved would strengthen labor's bargaining position. Also it would either facilitate the gradual usurpation of management functions or make possible direct, nonprofit competition by workers' guilds with private building firms.

Guild socialism thus advocated a different kind of "socialization." In industries such as building construction, expropriation would be unnecessary since workers could force private enterprise out of business by bargaining pressure or competition. For industries such as coal mining, guildists demanded nationalization by the state just like other socialists. Ownership was to be vested in the state, but control and administration were to be by the workers through their guilds. G. D. H. Cole pointed this out.

[9] *Ibid.*, p. 39. See also Cole, *Chaos and Order in Industry* (London: Methuen & Co., Ltd., 1920), pp. 39-60.

The miners have to demand public ownership, not because they want the State to manage the mines, but as the only way of getting rid of the mineowners and at least clearing the path for the creation of a Mining Guild. They know that State management would be inefficient and bad both for the consumer and the miner; and they therefore couple with their demand for public ownership a demand for democratic control.[10]

Guild socialists were active in the Fabian Society and the Labor party during the first quarter of the twentieth century, and although they supported nationalization of industry along with these groups they constantly emphasized the need for joint control. Their proposals usually took the form of demanding the largest possible direct representation of workers (at least one-half) on the directorates and executive staffs of nationalized firms. The guildists hoped eventually to oust the state from the partnership. To quote Cole again:

The real aim . . . must be not merely the expropriation of the capitalist, but the supercession of his economic functions and his replacement by the workers in every sphere of his economic and social power. For it is by this capture and assumption of social and economic functions that the workers will alone make possible an equitable distribution of the national income and a reasonable reorganization of Society as a whole.[11]

In the economy envisaged by the guild socialists, each producing firm would be owned and managed by a guild of workers. Industries would be organized into guilds representative of the firms, and, finally, all would be organized into a national producers' guild. Even the professions and civil services like health and education would be similarly organized. Individuals in their consumer interests would be organized into a system of guilds not unlike the existing consumer cooperatives although producers' and workers' interests were assumed to be more important and would have preferences over consumers' interests.

Replacing the market system as a means of allocating materials would be bargaining between guilds. The tradi-

[10] Cole, *Guild Socialism Restated*, p. 205.
[11] *Ibid.*, pp. 206-7.

tional functions of government would be performed by local, regional, and national "communes" which would represent the people in their various capacities, members being elected by producers, consumers, civil service guilds, and the like. For example, the guild which distributes a commodity would base its selling price on the price it paid to the manufacturing guild plus its own costs of distribution. It would submit this price to the cooperative society representing the consumers. If the price were not accepted or if the two could not agree on a price, the question would go to the local, regional, or national commune (depending on the type of market involved) which would act as arbitrator. If it were decided, for social reasons, to sell a particular commodity at either more or less than its cost of production, then the commune again would determine the allocation of the resulting surplus or loss.

The issue of workers' control versus expert control in behalf of the community ultimately brought the guildists into disagreement with each other. Guildists expected workers to assume all the actual management functions themselves. This was inconsistent with the joint control with the state which they advocated for nationalized industries, for this latter meant workers' participation only. Many socialists who were not guildists accepted this principle, but most of them defined it to mean workers' consultation, which guildists strongly rejected as being a sham device with no real meaning except to delude the workers into thinking they had control when they did not. Words like "participation," "joint control," and "management by workers" were so loosely defined that the guildists themselves could not agree on what they meant or how they could be carried out.

Guildism furthermore was too highly theoretical and, like communism, assumed too much ideal rationality. Guildism was charged with emotion; yet it had to include a strong faith in human abilities to assume that striking workmen could take over and operate a complicated business. Some guildists argued that the state should continue to exist as an organ of democratic action for the nation. Others envisaged the state's replacement by a sort of federal structure representing functional organizations of producers, consumers, civic interests, and cultural interests.

Cole, writing in 1920, observed in Russia "a marked bureaucratic tendency by no means in harmony with guild socialist ideas," but seemed sure that this was a temporary trend caused by the necessities of war and the need to prevent failure of the revolution. He was sure that Lenin was right in saying that the "state-like soviets will together atrophy so far as economic functions are concerned leaving the trade unions and the consumers' organizations in possession of the economic field." [12]

By 1921, when the New Economic Policy was introduced in Soviet Russia, the weaknesses of industrial management by workers were becoming obvious to many guildists. Cole and other stout defenders of guild socialism gradually began to face the problems of workers' control more realistically by recognizing that management was rapidly becoming (if it had not already become) a profession which required special abilities and long training to master. Furthermore, the hope of separating economic and political functions in a complex modern society was appearing increasingly unrealistic. For these reasons, guild socialism as a separate movement within British socialism declined after 1921.

As a political movement, guild socialism split into three groups. The extreme syndicalist wing went over to communism. A right wing group followed the social credit doctrines of C. H. Douglas and became a splinter party, which still has remnants in some countries such as Canada. The center group quickly dissolved for lack of popular support.

A "CONSTITUTION" FOR SOCIALISTS

Although guild socialism was short-lived, it effected a change in socialist thought which resulted in modification of the early Fabian premises of parliamentary democracy,

[12] *Ibid.*, pp. 212-13.

state ownership, and disinterested, expert management. The position of the Fabian Society and the main stream of socialist thought in general was restated in 1920 by Sidney and Beatrice Webb.[13] This famous study was the first serious attempt by professional social scientists to deal directly with the problem of transforming Great Britain into a socialist state. In this study, the influence of several different movements (such as the guild socialists, Henry George's Land Nationalisers, cooperatives, and labor unions) merged with Fabian thinking into a practical handbook for social reformers. This book, probably more than any other, was the cornerstone for the future socialist Britain. Here the nationalization program of the Labor party was put on solid ground for the first time. The relative merits of various types of industrial organization were discussed, and a framework for a socialist policy was developed.

Not unlike the guild socialists, the Webbs assumed a pluralistic psychology. They felt that a man was actually several persons at the same time. He had four separate personalities or four major interests, and a democratic organization must satisfy them all. He was at once a producer, a consumer, a citizen concerned with defense and internal order, and a citizen concerned with promoting civilization. The functional parliament of the guildists was rejected, however, in favor of a bicameral legislature consisting of a political parliament which would perform the traditional governmental functions of defense, foreign affairs, and justice and a social parliament which would have jurisdiction over publicly owned industries and services and other economic and social problems.

Although eventual national or municipal public ownership was advocated for the largest sphere of economic life, gradualism was preferred over any attempt to socialize, through direct action, large segments of the economy at one time. In this way each situation could be studied carefully,

[13] *A Constitution for the Socialist Commonwealth of Great Britain* (New York: Longmans, Green & Co., Inc., 1920). The following section is based on portions of this book.

and the most suitable form of organization could be chosen. Three general types of industrial organization were recognized, all of which could be used. Nationalization and operation through a national board were suggested for large basic industries which were nationwide in scope. Only about half a dozen industries met this standard in the Webbs' estimation although they included mining, railways, banking, forestry, insurance, and perhaps iron and steel. Municipalization was considered adequate for the bulk of British medium and light industry. Operation through cooperatives was recommended for wholesaling, retailing, and small consumer goods manufacturing. Certain areas of economic activity such as agricultural enterprise (as distinguished from land which would be publicly owned) and craft service industries would remain under private enterprise.

For the nationalized industries, direct ministerial responsibility as in the Post Office Department was rejected in favor of operation through a national board appointed from above but representing interest groups. Furthermore, the various interest groups themselves would make the nominations although the final appointments would rest with the social parliament. This was a significant compromise with the guild socialists and trade unions.

The Webbs recommended the tripartite national board with tripartite district councils where necessary. One suggestion called for a board of sixteen members consisting of five representatives each of consumers, labor, and the former private management with an independent chairman. Recognition of the need for consumers to play a direct part in the management of industry was a novel concept at this time because it was an abandonment of the traditional idea that the government naturally represents the consumer. This idea has not been followed in the recent nationalization program in England, but in Western Germany the codetermination plan of labor-management directorships is a variety of the Webbs' proposal for management by interest groups. The British Labor party, since 1933, has rejected interest group representation of all kinds on the boards of nationalized industries because of the inherent conflict with political responsibility and economic planning.

Municipal ownership was thought by the Webbs to be particularly well suited for most manufacturing and utilities except the few nationwide basic industries. Here local pride and the advantages of healthy rivalry play an important role in securing democratic participation of all citizens in the production of goods and services and the promotion of welfare and culture. Great emphasis was placed on the reorganization of local government.

Small consumer goods manufacturing and distribution functions would be organized into producers' cooperatives. Cooperatives could not manage large monopolistic industries or services where there are many consumers as well as other interests involved. Imagine, suggested the Webbs, a railroad being cooperatively owned and operated by a "mob" of commuters. However, cooperative organization was considered to be appropriate for small firms which need flexible management. Producers' cooperatives also had proved effective, from past experience, in controlling quality in several small-firm industries.

To the Webbs, the growth of nationwide producers' associations, labor unions, and professional organizations, all of which tend to become vested interests, seemed to make the guild idea impractical. Yet central administration was not desirable either because of its impersonal nature. A worker would see no difference between working for a capitalist and working for a distant government manager. Central control would merely substitute one bureaucracy for another, hence the emphasis on municipal and cooperative ownership in all but the few basic industries mentioned.

The market system would be supplanted by controlled pricing. Publicly owned industries would fix their own prices, in the absence of competition, by paying the producers an agreed standard rate arrived at through bargaining and fixing the price at the level of accounting costs so far incurred. In the case of consumers' cooperatives, price could exceed cost somewhat, the surplus going to members as a dividend. The entire cost and pricing system would be based on accounting and statistics in much the same manner as in Soviet Russia at the present time.

Some prices need not have any relation to cost. Services such as health and education could be free; others such as water and transportation could be priced above cost as an alternative to taxation. Some goods might be priced on a scale having little or no relation to cost, such as in the postal system, or use could be according to need with payment coming through taxation, as public highways are financed. Some goods could be priced above cost to discourage consumption (liquor, for example), while others were priced below cost to encourage consumption (milk, for example). One industry could price above cost and thus subsidize another industry in which public policy encouraged pricing below cost. The social parliament would exercise final judgment in these matters. If in its opinion a price was too high, it could set a price ceiling. This would discipline inefficient firms. In all cases, however, "freedom of socialized enterprise" would be encouraged by a minimum of government control, and in this way true "production for use" could be attained.

The transition to this socialist state, as set forth in the *Constitution,* would be gradual and peaceful. The social parliament would have the power to expropriate without compensation where a benefit to the public could be shown, but this power was never to be used if it would deprive a former owner of his livelihood. If the owner were a manager or an employee of the business, he would continue in that capacity as before except that he would no longer receive any "unearned" income. If he were not employed by the business and if the rent or profit income he received from it comprised his only source of income, he would be compensated.

Expropriation would ordinarily take the same form as when a city now widens a street or takes over a gas company. A fair market value in cash, government securities, or an annuity for a term of years or life would be paid and financed through taxation. Because the Webbs believed unequal income to be caused by unequal property distribution, and thinking that one necessarily implied the other, they visualized the bulk of tax revenue as coming from property taxes. The fact that income might be disassociated from property did not seem to occur to them. Thus they assumed the property tax fulfilled the basic socialist, and orthodox classical, requirement that taxes be based on ability to pay. High inheritance taxes would be levied, but the income tax would be only moderately progressive so as not to have any adverse effects on incentives. The burden of expropriation would still fall on the property owners since most of the revenue which would be collected to purchase private property or pay the interest on government compensation securities would come from property taxes. After expropriation the community would be neither richer nor poorer; the difference would be that a formerly private firm would be transferred to public ownership. The long term advantage would be in redistribution on income from the higher to the lower income groups.

The Webbs recognized throughout that the composition of the boards, the methods used to raise funds to compensate owners, and the criteria by which the efficiency and service of the public enterprise would be judged would vary in time and in particular situations; yet their program did establish a general pattern of public ownership which was to guide the Labor party policymakers for years to come.

CONCLUSION

From earliest times the central theme of socialist philosophy had been the establishment of an economic system which would end the exploitation of workers. However, the period following World War I was characterized by an entirely different economic climate in Great Britain than the one of the preceding several centuries. Britain surrendered world leadership, became a debtor nation, and began to suffer from declining basic industries, shrinking world trade, and mass unemployment.

By 1933 factory legislation and favorable labor laws had removed many of the abuses which had given rise to the socialist movement in the nineteenth century. By this time the working class was suffering less from intolerable working conditions, child labor, and long hours and more from the general unemployment of the Great Depression. Working conditions had improved, but the jobs themselves had disappeared. Consequently, since that time socialism's principal indictment against capitalism has not been exploitation of workers but failure to provide full employment and economic stability. As a consequence, "economic planning" has gradually become an integral part of socialist economics.

Since the theories of economic planning originating in the nineteen thirties are still in the process of being developed and refined, they belong in the classification of contemporary socialist theory and are consequently treated in the two following chapters.

10

Theory of Liberal Socialism

Socialism is about equality. A passion for equality is the
one thing that links all Socialists; on all others they are divided.——W. A. Lewis

BACKGROUND OF LIBERAL SOCIALISM

Socialism is not the negative, or opposite, of capitalism
even though it has often been represented as capitalism's
principal alternative. As previous chapters have shown,
there have been serious criticisms of capitalism from many
quarters almost since the dawn of the Industrial Revolution,
and many of these criticisms have come from people or
groups who called themselves socialists. However, a criticism of either the theory or practice of capitalism does not
constitute a theory of socialism.

In the development of modern socialism, practice and
experimentation have preceded theory to a large extent.
Since World War I socialist economic systems have become
a reality in the world although there were no clear blue-
prints or theories of socialism upon which these systems
could be built. In part, the classical economists were to
blame for this lag in the development of socialist economic
theory because their interest in the pure science of economics led them to disregard institutional problems. They
assumed either explicitly or implicitly (1) that economic
principles were universal, (2) that the institutional framework of capitalism was the only one within which the

313

economic problems of an industrialized economy could be rationally solved, and (3) that since the regulating forces of a free-market system operated automatically there were really few, if any, practical economic problems which needed to be solved by conscious action. Therefore socialism was either assumed away or else was considered unimportant to the solution of economic problems. Some leading neoclassical economists even went so far as to suggest that the substitution of socialist for capitalist institutions would not have any great effect on the actual mechanical operation of the economic system.

The German historical economists and American institutionalists also must share the blame for the very belated rise of positive socialist economic theory. Going to the other extreme from the classicists, they were largely content to describe economic institutions and sometimes even denied the existence of economic laws. This results also in a lack of interest in any abstract socialist theory.

Because of its rather late arrival on the scene as a definite, theoretical economic system, socialism is still in the stage of definitional and semantic confusions. The term socialism means all things to all people, and considering the diverse background of modern socialist thought, it is not surprising that contemporary socialist theorists show but little more agreement among themselves than their forerunners did. Still, the experience of socialist governments in recent years and the trend of socialist writing permit a classification of socialist economic theories based on two more or less distinct concepts of the assumptions, methodology, and goals of the socialist economic system. One group of theories, or fragments of theories, is based on the evolution of traditional economics along equalitarian lines but retaining most of the major assumptions and methodology of classical economic theory. The theorists of this group look to the experience of Great Britain, Scandinavia, and other Western European countries for verification of their deductions. In fact, these economists and philosophers have played a significant role in the development of socialist institutions in these nations. These theories display enough uniformity to be considered under the single heading of "liberal socialism" and will be discussed in this chapter.

The second major group of socialist theories is based, in part, on an evolution of Marxist doctrine. The writers who are associated with this viewpoint look to some extent to Soviet experience for empirical reinforcement of their theoretical arguments. Although complete and well-formulated theories of this group have nowhere been set forth, there is a large body of fragmentary writing which can be analyzed under the heading of "central planning," and this is the function of Chapter 11.

The classical economics, which began with Adam Smith in the late eighteenth century and ended with John Stuart Mill about a hundred years later, contained many of the seeds of liberal socialism. The neoclassical economics from Alfred Marshall's *Principles* in 1890 to the present has provided some more. The classical utilitarian ethic maintained that the goal of society should be to secure the greatest good to the greatest number of people. This put the burden of proof on the requirements of incentive to show that wealth and income should not be distributed equally. The unseen hand of competition required that all monopolies and combinations defend themselves against the assumption that they quite naturally raised prices and restricted ouput. Adam Smith had not anticipated the needs of modern industrialization which have been met through the rise of the large corporation with its professional management.

The classical labor theory of value put the return to labor above that of all other factors of production. Adam Smith had contended that labor alone was "productive," that landlords were essentially monopolists, and that the interests of those receiving profits were often inconsistent with the interests of society. However, he expected competition to reduce or abolish these "unearned incomes" in the long run. Smith also argued that any unfilled social need should be undertaken by the government although he expected these unfilled requirements to be few if private enterprise were allowed free reign. Later classical economists, however, were not sure that private enterprise could always be depended on. In Chapter 1, socialism was defined as embodying four principles: (1) public property, (2) relative equality, (3) participation by workers in economic decisions, and (4) economic planning. To this general definition the liberal socialist variety adds the use of a market system which permits free consumers' choice to guide production within the limitation of costs.

The liberal socialist theoretical model of the ideal economy differs from the modern capitalist model largely in the substitution of public ownership for private enterprise. The other three socialist goals have all been attained to a substantial degree in modern capitalist countries and apparently without crippling the capitalist institutions of profit motive, private property, and market system. In most modern capitalist nations a considerable redistribution of income towards the universal socialist goal of greater equality has been effected through progressive income and inheritance taxation and social services. In most basic industries workers have been able to gain a large degree of participation, through collective bargaining, in the decisions which affect them. Economic planning by government has become commonplace in all capitalist countries. It is only in the retention of private ownership of most of the nation's capital that modern capitalistic systems differ markedly from the socialist model. However, it is private property which underlies the competitive market system. Without private ownership of the means of production the comprehensive pricing and costing system which is essential for rational economic calculation does not automatically operate. Hence, any alternative to capitalism must be able to provide some mechanism to perform this function artificially.

It is fairly obvious from contemporary experience, if not from the chapters on theoretical capitalism, that an economic system can achieve relative equality, workers' participation, and economic planning without abolishing private property in the means of production. The question for liberal socialism thus becomes whether or not the rational pricing process can be reproduced without private ownership of capital equipment and, hence, without any genuine economic profit motives or market competition. Liberal socialism proposes to substitute an artificial mechanism for the capitalist free market.

As Chapter 1 also pointed out, the goals of any economic system include the optimization of (1) employment, (2) stability, (3) consumers' welfare, (4) efficiency, and (5) progressiveness. In recent years liberal socialism has tended to emphasize consumers' welfare, maximum employment, and stability at the expense, where there is a conflict, of efficiency and progressiveness. Emphasis on public ownership and workers' control as means to these ends has noticeably declined.

As Chapter 9 showed, the harbingers of modern liberal socialism were the Fabians who, early in this century, began to apply the accepted tools of economic analysis to achieving the goals of social welfare and distributed justice. They argued that the goals of classical economics would not be achieved through laissez faire and private production but only through (1) government policies to redistribute incomes and (2) government ownership of industry to insure better wages, working conditions, and workers' control over their means of livelihood.

Since the 1930's the trend of socialist thought outside the Soviet Union has been steadily to the "right," toward liberalism. (Since Stalin's death, the trend has gathered momentum in Russia, too.) The failure to provide full employment and stability have recently overshadowed all the other alleged evils of capitalism in the Western socialist viewpoint. Since the "Keynesian Revolution" called attention to achieving full employment and stability through monetary and fiscal policies rather than nationalization of industry, most Western socialists have been "converted" to this view leaving only a small minority which considers further government ownership to be of any great importance any more. Nationalization is still advocated by Western socialists, but economic planning for full employment and greater equality is given higher priority. Thus, to liberal socialists, economic planning is expected to regulate prices, production, and distribution of incomes on the one hand and the level of employment and rate of economic growth on the other. Since this planning involves the use of prices and a market mechanism and since it consciously seeks to preserve individual freedom and values, the term liberal socialism is appropriate to analyze the economic planning system envisaged by these non-Marxian socialists.

The magic term "economic planning" has also been used by institutionalists, Keynesian and others, and is often used to mean quite different things. To Keynesians it means fiscal policies designed to maintain full employment. To the socialists of Eastern Europe and the U.S.S.R. it still involves direct controls and government ownership of all industry. Hence, a definition is necessary. As the term will be used here, economic planning will mean merely the coordination of production and distribution by means of a conscious effort as distinguished from the "automatic" coordination which occurs in the pure competitive market of neoclassical theory. For liberal socialists, economic planning utilizes a market system for achieving planned results.

ECONOMIC PLANNING UNDER LIBERAL SOCIALISM

ORGANIZATION OF PRODUCTION. The theory of liberal socialism does not attempt to offer an explanation of the principal economic phenomena in a given society since the liberal socialist society is an ideal one and has never existed in actuality. In recent years economic and social reforms have been instituted in several countries, notably Great Britain, Sweden, Norway, and Australia, which make the theory of liberal socialism at least partly applicable as a generalization about activities in certain sectors of actual working economic systems, but the usefulness of the theory for explanation is still extremely limited. The theory of liberal socialism still mainly offers what is alleged to be a superior solution to the fundamental economic problem of all countries, the allocation of scarce economic resources so as to attain their best and most efficient use.

In sharp contrast to traditional social thought, modern liberal socialists have repeatedly emphasized that socialism is not to be identified with the nationalization of property. They say they are concerned about property at all only because private property in the means of production is supposed to be a major cause of inequality.

One way of dealing with industrial property is to turn it over to workers to be operated cooperatively on either a profit-sharing or nonprofit basis. The "workers council" system in Tito's Yugoslavia is being called the only true socialist organization by its supporters. Such a system, without as much governmental control, was used in Socialist Czechoslovakia after World War II until the Communist coup substituted direct state control on the Russian plan. The British socialists of the late nineteenth and early twentieth centuries, as well as the present day Cooperative Party (which is associated with the Labor Party), have supported arrangements of this type. Recently the Labor Party advocated "mutualization" rather than nationalization of insurance companies.

Another method of organizing public property is municipalization (see Chapter 9) while still another method is nationalization. Within the framework of nationalization itself there is still a variety of alternatives available. For instance, there can be government monopolies, government competition with private enterprise, nationalization of one or more stages of a productive process, or competing government-owned enterprises. Furthermore, the public firms can be autonomous as to policy or centrally controlled.

Although most liberal socialists favor nationalization of public utilities and a few other basic industries such as steel, there is considerable disagreement as to how much further public ownership need go in order to achieve socialist goals.

A rather extreme view is that of Oskar Lange who contended that the main weaknesses of capitalism ("monopoly, restrictionism and interventionism") are barriers to equality and can be removed only by government operation of all production except agriculture and small-scale industry.[1]

Emil Lederer noted that "the line of demarcation between those processes of production to be directly managed and those to be only indirectly influenced would not be easy to fix and would no doubt be altered from time to time."[2] Nevertheless, Lederer advocated nationalization of basic industries and "indirect" control of others through a government controlled credit system. Others, like Eduard Heimann, have emphasized governmental control over investment and credit but would allow units of production to be otherwise independently managed.[3] Private ownership with some indirect financial controls, of the Keynesian type, over investment has been fairly generally accepted by nonsocialist economists as well as socialists.

The liberal socialist view of public ownership is somewhere between these two poles. Nationalization of basic industries and public utilities is usually advocated uncompromisingly, but the general view is that economic planning rather than public property is the main device for achieving socialist goals and that, except for these essential services, planning does not require public ownership. British Labor party leaders have repeatedly proclaimed that modern economic activity "naturally" divides into two segments, public and private. The public sector, about 20 per cent of the economy, would consist of the area of "natural monopolies" or "public utilities." The other sector, consisting of the bulk of the industrial economy, would remain indefinitely,

---

[1] Oskar Lange, "On the Economic Theory of Socialism," *Review of Economic Studies,* October, 1936 and February, 1937.

[2] "National Economic Planning" in *Encyclopedia of the Social Sciences* (1936).

[3] Eduard Heimann, "Planning and the Market System," in MacKenzie (ed.), *Planned Society* (Englewood Cliffs, N.J.: Prentice-Hall, Inc., 1937), p. 704.

and perhaps permanently, in private hands.[4] This reasoning provides an explanation for the Labor party's anti-monopoly law as well as for other portions of the Labor party program (such as overseas developments) which definitely resemble capitalist legislation.

This view is not limited to British socialism. The *Sozialistische Internationale* has adopted a new manifesto calling not for public ownership of the means of production but for "planning for production in the interests of the people as a whole." Furthermore, it stated, "Socialist planning does not presuppose public ownership of all the means of production. It is compatible with the existence of private ownership in important fields. . . ."

More recent proclamations of official socialist organizations (outside the Soviet bloc) have reiterated this view. G. D. H. Cole, longtime leader of the more orthodox wing of British socialism, stated in late 1955 that socialism was "dead." He went on to point out that there was no longer any threat to private property in the Western world. Capitalism had been saved by liberals, Keynesians, and other "progressives" who had demonstrated that unemployment, instability, and gross inequalities could be reduced without adopting the uncertainties or dangers of vast but untried institutional changes. This is not an official socialist position, but it is certainly indicative of the eclipse of nationalization theory. The recent decisive victories of the moderate wing of the British Labor party and the refusal of the party to demand further government ownership are further proof.

GOALS OF PLANNING. Liberal socialists, and other critics of the orthodox price theory, have correctly pointed out that the purely competitive market only maximizes individual satisfactions under one condition. There must be equal incomes. Otherwise there is plural voting for consumers' goods

---

[4] J. E. Meade, *Planning and the Price Mechanism* (Allen and Unwin, 1951); *Labor and Industry in Britain*, September-October, 1947, pp. 200-212; Labor Party, *Let Us Face the Future* (London: Tothill Press, Ltd., 1945).

since it is money that votes, not individuals and their wants. Of course, there is an implied assumption here that individuals have identical capacities for enjoyment. This cannot be proved, but the converse cannot be proved either, and to assume that some people have greater sensitivity and need than others because of inherent human differences is repugnant to the ideals of Western democracy. It is well established that individuals have widely differing capacities for production, and income differentials are ordinarily justified on this basis. But to argue that some people deserve higher incomes because of their status or their claim for having a greater capacity for enjoyment is to lay the basis for an aristocracy whose whims must be catered to before the basic food and shelter requirements of less sensitive classes. Socialists have a strong argument here for using the classical demand theory to justify greater equality of incomes.

The liberal socialist argument for greater equality has two corollaries, individual liberty and human welfare. In neoclassical economics individual political liberty is assumed to be provided by government while individual economic liberty is to be achieved through laissez faire. Liberal socialists do not assume that people are necessarily free if they have a democratic government because they believe that poverty and unemployment can exert greater control over free choice of goods, occupations, and movement than political dictators can. Nor do they assume that laissez faire creates even economic freedom except for a small minority of wealthy people. Real freedom must be achieved through a conscious, positive policy and cannot merely be assumed to exist. Liberal socialism does not separate economics and politics to the degree that neoclassical economics ordinarily does, so political and economic freedom are considered by liberal socialists in their relationships with each other.

The goal of individual liberty requires that workers be permitted to choose their own jobs. This means that there must be a labor market as well as a consumers' market and that the planning authority's task of allocating labor to the right jobs in the correct proportion must be achieved by inducement and not by direction. Free occupational choice can be maintained in two ways. First, wage differentials could be used which attract workers to less desirable occupations or discourage them from entering overcrowded occupations. Second, the professions or trades which are particularly attractive, because of prestige, power, or extra leisure which they offer, could be restricted through high educational and examinational requirements. Fortunately, the necessity of choosing an occupation in advance is fairly easily discernible, and the planning authority should not have too much difficulty in determining the number of aspirants for all types of work.

The pursuit of maximum consumers' welfare also requires that consumers be free to spend incomes as they please and that workers be free to choose their occupations. This consumers' free choice should not be confused with what is often called consumers' sovereignty. Consumers' sovereignty supposes that the qualities and relative quantities of goods produced are actually controlled by the choices of consumers whereas consumers' free choice requires only that consumers be free to choose among those goods and services which producers offer for sale although the original output might be independent of consumers' desires. Some liberal socialists actually envisage a high degree of consumers' sovereignty although in a practical sense there is no need to go very far beyond consumers' free choice since many consumers have little more freedom than this in existing capitalist economies.

Although consumers' sovereignty is a worthwhile ideal, there are many practical considerations which may prevent its operation even where producers and consumers are all free to pursue an unlimited self-interest. For example, expenditures for education, health, and housing may be in the social interest but, unless provided for by some central authority, might be insufficient to satisfy social needs if individual consumers are allowed free choice. Many consumers lack the education, knowledge, and foresight where such long range goals are concerned. Thus in some cases, the individual under capitalism is likely to be overruled by the state which, presumably, is looking after his long-run interests.

Some liberal socialists realistically admit that full consumers' sovereignty is not compatible with economic planning—that these are alternative ways of determining economic priorities. Nevertheless, most of them argue that planning is in many ways superior to consumers' sovereignty and consequently should replace it in some instances.

Social welfare, a broader concept then consumers' economic welfare, is also an implicit part of liberal socialist theory. Much like the institutionalists, liberal socialists do not try to draw a very fine line between economic and social values. Hence, social welfare is a specific goal of liberal socialism. Although welfare is also a goal of the neoclassical economics, it is not usually stated as such because it is assumed to follow automatically from self-interest, laissez faire, and competition.

To varying degrees liberal socialists assume that people do not know what is really good for them and that if they are left to their self-interests may build race tracks instead of schools and drink more liquor than milk. Consequently, there is a strong bias in favor of providing free some necessary social services like education and health; others, like basic housing, milk, and medicines at low cost through subsidies and prohibiting or taxing highly some less desirable human activities, such as gambling or buying mink coats. Of course, all countries have provided some free social services and taxed or prohibited undesirable activities, but liberal socialists go somewhat further than nonsocialists would go. Particularly they sometimes assume that the burden of proof is on an industry to show that it should not be restricted whereas neoclassical economists put the burden of proof on consumers to show that certain activities should not be left free.

Time preference is a particular area in which individual and social interests may diverge. Individuals usually show interest in economic well-being only throughout their lifetime or, at the most, during the lifetime of their children. However, society is an entity existing for a much longer time. If pure consumers' sovereignty existed it is quite possible that aggregate savings would be less than that which is socially desirable in the long run. The centralist socialists insist that consumers' sovereignty be abrogated as far as savings are concerned and, instead, that the state save at a rate determined by valuing future satisfactions equally with equivalent present satisfaction. However, liberal socialists now usually favor only some form of government control over private investment for the Keynesian reason of insuring enough spending to maintain full employment.

An additional problem of maintaining capital investment arises when an economy achieves a relatively equal distribution of income. In countries with considerable income inequality the rich do most of the saving. It should be remembered, however, that while great inequality *permits* savings by the rich, it by no means *guarantees* that this saving will occur or that if it does occur there will be any capital investment from it. As in Saudi Arabia, for example, only a tiny fraction of the king's enormous wealth is used for capital. Most goes into fleets of air-conditioned Cadillacs and for the maintenance of palaces and hosts of servants. While there is economic justification in retaining considerable inequalities if they lead to capital growth, there is little economic reason for inequalities if they lead only to extravagant consumption for a few. Inequality has led to economic growth in the United States. It is probably impeding it in many other countries, especially in the Near East.

Nevertheless, reducing high incomes and raising low incomes decreases the possible saving of the rich far more than it increases the possible saving of the poor. As income inequalities are abolished and savings decrease it becomes increasingly necessary to plan for the correct amount of investment. W. A. Lewis suggests three principles of investment planning for the socialist state. First, the government must have a budget surplus large enough to fill the gap between the investment that is planned and the voluntary savings that are available. Inflation may otherwise occur. Second, there must be adequate provision for stocks of raw materials, work-in-process and finished commodities. Third, investment must not be planned beyond the limits of available physical resources.[5]

Carl Landauer treats the problem of over and under saving in both a long-run and short-run sense. In the long run there may be an excess or deficiency of savings contrary to the intentions of the planning authority. In the short run, more or less may be saved during the current planning period than was anticipated by the authority. In either case Landauer envisages an active role for the government to alleviate these disturbances by fiscal policy, interest policy, or allocation of investment expenditures.[6] Since the determination of savings and investment is an area in which liberal socialists admit that decision-making must be largely arbitrary, this subject will be dealt with in greater detail in the following chapter on central planning.

The goals of liberal socialism are often given different emphasis by different writers. Thus, Oskar Lange says the fundamental objective of a socialist economy is the "maximization of the total welfare of society," while Burnham Beckwith states that the only purpose of socialism is the "maximization of average net utility income."[7] W. A. Lewis places equality of income above all other objectives, while the late E. M. F. Durbin wanted to remove inequalities based on inheritance and the "institutions created for the

[5] *The Principles of Economic Planning* (London: George Allen and Unwin, Ltd., 1951), p. 55.

[6] Carl Landauer, *Theory of National Economic Planning* (Berkeley: University of California Press, 1947), pp. 114-20.

[7] Burnham Beckwith, *The Economic Theory of a Socialist State* (Stanford, Calif.: Stanford University Press, 1949), p. 22.

service of the rich." [8] These writers frequently discuss
equality without adequately defining it. Yet, equality has
a variety of meanings. It may mean no differentials in either
income, wealth, class, or opportunity. Income equality itself may mean equal money payments to all households,
equal rates of pay per hour for all work, or it may allow
differences in skills to be compensated with wage differentials but not permitting differences due to ownership or
social status. British socialist thinking seems to favor allowing the highest incomes to be about ten times the lowest
but with a maximum of about $25,000 per year. [9] Further-
more, they feel that all incomes should be earned by work
(physical or mental) so it is the *source* of income that is of
concern. For example, British tax rates are higher on rent,
interest, and dividend income than on wages and salaries.
Most management, being salaried, is thus not discriminated
against by British socialists.

Sometimes liberal socialists assume a measurable scale
of values just like many neoclassical economists do. In this
case the goal of equality is based on the neoclassical Mar-
shall-Pigou concept of total welfare as the sum of all utilities, or satisfaction, of individual households. Because of
the principle of diminishing marginal utility, any income
payment to a man with a small income will give greater
satisfaction than the same payment to a man with a large
income assuming that both persons are equally sensitive.
Thus, greater satisfaction can be obtained by increasing
lower incomes than by increasing higher ones, and this condition will continue to exist until all incomes are equal.

Objections have been raised to this argument. Orthodox
critics have rightly maintained that interpersonal comparison
of satisfaction cannot be assumed because individual enjoyment and well-being cannot be measured. Lange is aware

[8] E. M. F. Durbin, "The Problems of the Socialized Sector," in *Problems
of Economic Planning* (London: Routledge & Kegan Paul, Ltd., 1949),
p. 42.
[9] Francis Williams, *Socialist Britain* (New York: The Viking Press, Inc.,
1949), p. 113.

of this weakness but maintains that differences in sensitiveness of individuals are mainly due to artificial social distinctions which would disappear in the "relatively homogeneous social stratification of a socialist society." This would leave only differences of "purely individual character" such as age, family status, health, etc., and these he assumes will be distributed according to the normal law of error.

Two Italian economists, Vilfredo Pareto and Enrico Barone, circumvented the Marshallian "welfare" concept by setting as a goal the conditions under which it would be impossible, in reallocating resources, to increase the welfare of one household without reducing that of another.[10] Thus, optimum allocation of resources was defined without assuming that total welfare is the sum of individual measurable utilities. The inference—that incomes would have to be equal—remains. However, neither Pareto nor Barone could solve the problem of determining how to make allocations of resources which result in some households being better off and others worse off, and, unfortunately, most decisions would fall in this category.

Abba Lerner made a further advance by building an economic model which avoided measuring utilities quantitatively yet permitted a determinate solution.[11] The optimum distribution of goods would be attained when "marginal substitutability" is equalized among consumers for the various commodities. This means consumers would attain maximum satisfaction when there was no longer any incentive for any consumer to substitute an additional unit of any commodity for something he already possessed. Thus, if one consumer would give two units of A for one of B while another would give two units of B for one of A it would be possible to increase total satisfaction by transferring some of commodity A from the former (who has a lower marginal substitutability for A) to the latter (who has a higher one)

[10] See articles by Pareto and Barone in Hayek (ed.), *Collectivist Economic Planning* (London, 1935).

[11] A. P. Lerner, *Economics of Control* (New York: The Macmillan Co., 1944), chaps. i-iii.

in exchange for some of commodity B for which the latter has the lower marginal substitutability. This transfer would continue until each was unwilling to substitute further. Thus, by exchange total satisfaction is increased. If there is a free market the money prices of all goods would tend to reflect their rate of marginal substitutability and therefore optimum allocation will be approximated qualitatively.

In order to establish an optimum *quantitative* distribution the added assumption of diminishing marginal utility of income is necessary. There is no way of comparing one person's marginal utility of money with another's. Therefore, while it is impossible to prove that different people's marginal utility of money is the same, it is equally impossible to prove that it is not. Although the maximization of total satisfaction by equalizing marginal income can never be attained, Lerner contends that *probable* total satisfaction could be maximized if incomes were divided equally.

FUNCTIONS OF THE PLANNING BOARD. To liberal socialists, economic planning is the indispensable preliminary means for creating a society in which men are free, equal, and secure. Although planning must be done by a central authority there need not be a "plan" in the sense of an arbitrary economic budget which sets in advance the physical volume of output for different industries. Planning does require, however, taking a broad view of the consequences of economic decisions. It also requires the setting and attaining of intermediate goals which are, in effect, means of attaining the basic goals.

An example of an intermediate goal is full employment. To some groups, including some labor unions, full employment is an ultimate goal in itself because of the well-known psychological and physiological effects of enforced leisure and because the goals of the particular group (union membership and power, for example) are not necessarily coincident with the goals of society. However, from a total social standpoint full employment is desired as a means toward greater production and welfare. Liberal socialists, like the Keynesians, doubt that uncontrolled markets in a dynamic economy can guarantee a stable, high level of employment. The wartime and postwar years of full employment have reduced the concern about unemployment to some extent, and now inflation has become a possible danger. Thus, the goal of full employment requires modification to prevent undue inflationary pressures.

Planning, to liberal socialists, is to supplement the free market, not replace it. If a particular market is allocating resources reasonably well, if prices are generally proportional to costs, and if social needs are being adequately met, then there is no need to interfere. But if adjustments are too slow, as in most markets in wartime; if the market appears unable to attain its social goals, as in low-cost, rental housing; if bottlenecks exist; or if monopoly has stifled the market by restricting entry, then planning can be injected. However, liberal socialist planning is designed to serve the same purpose that the free market is supposed to serve. Planning can never be complete because consumption would then have to be controlled, and this would frustrate the goals of individual liberty. It should also be noted that in liberal social writing there is a distinct bias in favor of using the market mechanism. This could be due in part to classical tradition and partly out of fear of inefficiency, bureaucracy, and centralized political power.

Liberal socialists imply that economic planning is to be undertaken by some kind of central planning authority composed of experts appointed for definite terms of office in the manner customary for administrative boards or commissions. It would have at its disposal all the resources for statistical fact-gathering which are normally available to the government. The function of the planning authority would be to see that resources, goods, and services are allocated in such a way as to achieve the socialist goals. In order to do this it would first have to survey the entire economy. The planning authority would be in a position to see things that no individual enterprise could ever see and could also give consideration to matters of social interest that do not enter the calculations of private firms in an unplanned economy. Furthermore, it is argued that it would have foresight not ordinarily enjoyed by private producers. For example, it is said to be able to foresee the exhaustion of raw materials, the wastage of human resources, or the sacrifice of esthetic values like beautiful scenery or historic landmarks which result from particular industrial policies but which cannot adequately be considered by individual firms seeking short-term gains.

The planning board would have statutory authority to (1) give general directions to the boards of directors of national- ized basic industries, (2) control to some extent the policies of the larger private sector of the producing economy, and (3) control credit, investment, and fiscal policy.

In this way all economic policy decisions would be con- centrated in a single agency. This would avoid the difficul- ties frequently experienced in which several government agencies plan simultaneously on different assumptions and for different goals. Of course, the concentration of policy- making might also cause errors to reinforce each other rather than cancel out. The planning authority could make and execute plans as much as it wanted but would depend on manipulating the market except in emergencies when it might have to resort to direct controls.

Where this type of planning differs from laissez faire, then, is not in rejecting the market economy controlled by demand but in asserting that demand itself is not sacred but some- thing that should be manipulated by the state. Therefore, if the planning authority wants firms to produce more of cer- tain kinds of goods which are ordinarily purchased by lower- income groups, there is no need for a cumbersome machinery of allocations and controls. It could increase the tax rates of higher income groups and reduce rates on lower groups; or it could subsidize the production of the goods to be en- couraged and tax those it wishes to discourage. For example, the production of peanuts could be increased at the expense of other commodities by raising the peanut subsidy or the guaranteed price for peanuts. Or exports could be expanded by subsidies at the expense of domestic consumption (or at the expense of inefficiency!) without giving each firm a direct export quota or allocation. Taxes could be increased to reduce purchasing power; the foreign exchange rate could be altered; tariffs could be reduced to enable foreigners to secure the exchange to purchase more domestic products; a purchase tax could be placed on goods sold in the domestic market; or subsidies could be paid on imports. Capital investment could be promoted at the expense of consumption by taxing consumption and/or subsidizing investment (through fast tax write-offs, for example) or direct government investment itself.

Manipulating demand by inducement is not always possible. There are problems of supply that also must be corrected. One real source of concern is the immobility of resources that sometimes occurs. Manipulating demand by inducement presupposes that a supply large enough to meet market demand can be obtained. For example, if it is desired to increase the consumption of milk and the method chosen is to distribute free milk to schools, the total demand for milk is thus increased, and its price tends to rise. If a small price rise induces a large flow of resources into milk production, supply will keep pace with demand. However, if there is immobility of resources (say, not enough cows), there will be a large increase in the price of milk, or a shortage for the ordinary consumers of milk. In either case action must be taken to keep the price at a reasonable level or to allocate the limited supplies fairly, or both. The proper action to take would be to eliminate the inadequate supply. In the interim, however, price control and rationing may be necessary. But these are stop-gap measures necessary only for so long as the shortages last. The quality and success of planning are to be measured not by the excellence of price and rationing controls but by the speed with which shortages are eliminated and by the effectiveness of the measures taken towards that end.

Liberal socialists are fully aware of the dangers of direct controls. Not only do direct controls tend to create enormous administrative problems of expense, inefficiency, and corruption but controls tend to multiply. Price controls, for example, lead to rationing, and both lead to further controls as producers tend to concentrate their output on uncontrolled commodities in order to increase profits, and consumers having extra, unspendable income tend to seek out uncontrolled uses for it. Under price controls, the gambling, entertainment, and luxury goods industries may expand during periods of the most intense shortages of necessities. A good, though extreme, example is the reaction of troops on a transport ship. With their basic needs provided free, soldiers find nothing immediate on which to spend their pay. Hence, exorbitant prices are frequently paid for souvenirs, and poker games involving thousands of dollars may flourish.

Effective price control is impossible unless the commodity or service can be described in exact terms. Otherwise, suppliers can escape control by changing quality. Also there may be shortages and black markets because price control leaves demand in excess of supply at the controlled price. Furthermore, price controls may make long-run adjustments impossible because new investment is not attracted to industries where prices (and hence, profits) are controlled. The long experience of Britain and France with rent control illustrates the point. In any event, liberal socialists generally accept direct controls in temporary crisis periods only and prefer to control indirectly through the manipulation of demand.

PRICING AND ALLOCATION IN THE PLANNED ECONOMY. In a socialist economy the allocation of goods and services could be determined in a number of ways. There could be (1) free public storehouses (associationism), (2) rationing, (3) special purpose of restricted money systems (typically advocated by a wide variety of fringe groups like the Social Credit party in Canada, Townsend Planners, etc.), (4) representative assembly, (5) public opinion poll, or (6) free choice of consumers using money incomes as in free-market capitalism. Liberal socialism relies most heavily on the latter—free choice through money incomes—because this method of allocation (1) gives an indication of the relative attractiveness of goods as reflected in their prices, (2) allocates the available supply in accordance with consumers' own estimates of their needs, and (3) serves as an indication of what would be most worthwhile to produce without sacrificing the goal of individual liberty. Also, it is more practical in an industrial society where individuals cannot participate directly in government except through representatives. The only completely planned economy, the U.S.S.R., uses a combination of methods (2), (3), and (6) although that country does not have a liberal socialist economic system as defined here. In part, this is because the Soviet planners apparently do not attempt to maximize individual liberty as liberal socialists do.

Decisions as to the quantities and qualities of goods produced would be made largely by consumers except for education, defense, health, housing, social security, and such similar needs which, as in capitalist economies, are often provided for collectively and financed through taxation because of pricing difficulties or the divergence between individual demands and a clear public interest. Thus, the arbitrary element in total economic decision-making would not be much greater under liberal socialism than in the more advanced capitalistic countries in which the government underwrites basic living standards.

Since freedom of choice is maintained, demand would play much the same role that it does in a capitalistic economy, and liberal socialists allege that it would do far more. In a liberal socialist economy, the theory of demand would not be necessary to aid in explaining the operation of a market which would continue to function regardless of whether or not attempts were made to explain it. Indeed it would play a more positive role. In a capitalist economy, demand theory explains why entrepreneurs and consumers act the way they do although most entrepreneurs are only vaguely conscious of the refinements of demand theory, and most consumers are altogether unaware of it. In a liberal socialist economy the theory would do more than explain the phenomena. It would be used by the planners to help determine what should be produced, how much should be pro-

duced, and what prices should be. Estimated demand schedules would actually be drawn up from the vast statistics
available to the planners, and important production decisions
would be based on them.

Traditional value theory in recent years has been based
on two assumptions, first, that resources are scarce relative
to needs and desires, and second, that consumers possess an
ordered scale of preferences. Neither of these assumptions
is affected by the introduction of liberal socialist planning as
defined here. If the goals of society are known, the problem
becomes one of selecting the best means toward achieving
those goals using the given scarce resources. If some definite
relationship is not established among these resources then
no rational allocation can occur. The operation of the capitalist free market tends automatically to allocate resources in
the best and most efficient manner, given the framework of
assumptions used in the usual capitalistic models. Through
the mechanism of price, resources tend to be rationally allocated. A competitive economy, then, tends to (1) minimize
all costs and (2) cause production of all goods to be continued to the point where the net revenue received from the
sale of the last item equals its cost (marginal revenue equals
marginal cost). If a socialist system using the price mechanism is to merit consideration at all, it must show a reasonable presumption of doing these same two things. Otherwise it will not be able to economize the factors of production or increase human welfare.

The planners are faced with two immediate problems.
The first is to dispose of the goods that have been produced
so that the most intensive wants of consumers, as indicated
by their preferences in spending their income, are satisfied
first. The second is to produce goods in such proportion that
the prices at which they are sold are equal to the cost to
society in terms of other goods which might have been made,
i.e., their opportunity costs. The difficulty of this second problem is that of calculating marginal products of factors of
production in alternative uses.

If we assume that the liberal socialist system replaced a capitalistic one in such a manner that the industrial machine remained intact, the most practical thing to do would be to keep production going in the same amounts and proportions as before and keep the same managers and laborers in the same jobs. In this way workers would be using their acquired capacities and producing approximately what the consumers want. This would be a reasonable starting place anyhow.[12]

The selling agencies of nationalized resources and basic industries would offer their commodities at arbitrarily fixed prices (no doubt based on historical prices under private ownership), and the planning authority would raise the prices of those goods which are in short supply. Probably the selling agencies themselves would have this authority delegated to them in order to make price changes more flexible and aid in the decentralization of government functions. The selling agencies would try to keep stocks of goods on hand to meet current needs by ordering from the producing agents and paying "wholesale" prices as determined by the planning authority. These "wholesale" prices would vary with the selling prices so that goods whose prices were raised due to excess of demand would show a profit to the producer and goods whose prices were lowered due to excess of supply would show a loss.

Estimated retail demand schedules of consumers' goods would be drawn up by the selling agencies on the basis of observations and wholesale demand schedules would be drawn up by the producing agents on the basis of orders sent in by the selling agents. The planning authority would draw up estimated demand schedules for the factors of production on the basis of the bidding for them by the producing agents. The planning authority would then adjust the prices of the factors of production in precisely the same manner as the selling agents adjust the prices of consumer goods. Prices would be raised or lowered according to demand schedules

12 R. L. Hall, *The Economic System in a Socialist State* (London, 1937), pp. 105-6.

so that all factors of production would be fully employed, consumers would decide, the quantities and qualities of goods produced, and there would tend to be an equilibrium in which demand and supply would be equated.

The demand schedules would have to be estimated, and no claim could be made for perfection. However, by taking groups of goods in composite supply or joint demand and considering them separately it does not seem impossible to draw up schedules of reasonable accuracy. Probably no greater accuracy is obtained in the imperfect free-market society.

It can be seen that the production process is "free" at both extremes. On one end both public and private agents bid for the factors of production and on the other end consumers bid for the finished product. Before these two loose ends can be tied together and the function of the production-distribution process completed, however, the matter of costs must be considered.

Calculations must be made regarding the relative economic significance of resources if efficient use is to be made of them. The primary factors of production must be evaluated in a rational manner. In a free, competitive economy, these factors are valued in a market where buyers bid against each other for their use. The prices which emerge indicate the relative importance of the factors in the minds of firms which are trying to maximize their own profits. In spite of widespread talk about the "automatic" operation of the market it should be remembered that the prices which emerge are the result of the actions of people, not of any supernatural machine which announces the prices of goods like a stock-market ticker. It is true that the market price registers collective behavior, but it is human behavior nevertheless. If costs are defined to be coefficients whose magnitude is a function of the good relative to the wants whose satisfaction depends on it, then there is no necessary reason why prices could not exist in the absence of a free market.[13]

[13] H. D. Dickenson, *Economics of Socialism* (London: Oxford University Press, 1939), chap. iii.

Nationalized producing agents would be required, first, to employ productive resources in such ratio and the amounts as to maintain output at the point where marginal revenue equals marginal cost (maximize profits or minimize losses) and, second, to keep average unit costs at a minimum. For the private sector of the economy, monopoly would be discouraged through some form of antitrust policy so that competition would regulate these firms in this same manner. If prices are considered as indices of the terms on which alternatives are offered, minimizing average costs would minimize alternatives sacrificed. Requiring marginal revenue to equal marginal cost means that the marginal significance of each satisfied preference equals that of the best alternative preference. This rule is necessary to insure that higher preferences are satisfied before lower ones.

Some socialist economists prefer average costs rather than marginal costs as a basis for determining the output of firms in a planned economy. This would mean that the firm should produce additional units which must be sold at a loss as long as their total revenue is enough to cover the total cost of producing all of its output. This principle is frequently followed by regulated public utilities in capitalist countries.

The prices of the basic factors of production (management, labor, capital, and natural resources) would be fixed by the planning authority using some average of historical prices as a guide. These prices would be the prices which are included in the cost of production. By further assuming here that the wages paid to labor are fixed like the prices of other resources, and are raised or lowered by the central planning body on the basis of demand, then production would logically cease for those goods which have a selling price below cost and shift to goods whose price is above cost. Since there are usually alternative ways to combine the factors of production and since the producing agent must produce to the point where marginal revenue equals marginal cost, then low-cost productive factors will be substituted for high-cost factors, and through this adjustment a true economic price can be determined which can be used as a cost of production. Of course the use of cost adjustment would lead to considerable wage differentials, but modern socialists are reconciled to this.

The cost of producing a certain commodity can be determined by adding up the costs of the various factors used and dividing by the units of output using conventional cost-accounting techniques. The cost of a consumption commodity being the sum of all the prices of production goods used in making it, the demand prices for given quantities of production goods can be derived and reflected forward again to consumption goods in the form of costs. For private producers or public corporations competing with private producers agreed profit and tax equivalents could be included as part of the cost.

Critics have argued that the planners would require complete lists of the quantities of all goods that would be purchased at any combination of prices and that the planners would have to solve millions of simultaneous equations before making any economic decisions. However, as Lange has pointed out, the trial-and-error method of determining prices under socialism would be much the same as in an uncontrolled competitive market. The only equations to be solved would be those of consumers and businessmen, and these are solved in a capitalist market by watching quantities demanded and supplied and raising the prices when demand exceeds supply at the existing price and lowering the prices when the reverse is true. Now if the producing agents under socialism treat the prices of resources set by the planning authority as though they were objectively determined free-market prices and if they base their cost calculations on them, then the adjustments in prices and outputs which follow will not be any more arbitrary than those in a free market. If in their efforts to equate marginal revenue to marginal cost the producers use the prices which are assigned to the factors by the planning authority, then the adjustments made on the basis of demand will make it possible for consumers' preferences to be reflected all the way back to production decisions. If the government-owned producers try to maximize their accounting profits by equating marginal revenue with marginal cost and try to keep their average costs at a minimum by shifting resources from low- to high-profit goods and using the most efficient methods and resources, then a pricing and distribution pattern will emerge which balances supply and demand as rationally and objectively as the one produced by a free market.

One might well ask at this point why the free-market system should be abandoned if this system of planning by consumers merely tries to imitate it. Indeed, the liberal socialist planning authority would be quite as neutral as a telephone switchboard, merely translating and relaying messages. Liberal socialists have several answers. For one thing, they argue, the entire consumption pattern would still fit into a national economic plan. The use of many goods and services (like education or medical care) could be encouraged by being supplied free or at low cost through subsidies while the use of others (like liquors or mink coats) could be discouraged through the use of consumption taxes which raise prices. But of course all this can be, and is commonly, done in private capitalist economies. Even socialists admit today that democratic planning is possible under private capitalism.

Another answer is that consumers would have a greater degree of freedom of choice than would exist in a theoretically free, unplanned market because liberal socialist planning would provide a more equal distribution of income so that demand prices would more nearly reflect actual needs and not the whims of high-income groups. Furthermore, it is argued that more reliable product information could be substituted for the misleading or false advertising now prevalent, and this would further increase consumers' freedom and the reliability of prices as guides to actual wants, needs, and costs. However, there seem to be no insurmountable reasons why a capitalist system could not achieve these results by further regulation of free markets as, for example, the United States has done in recent years through the Federal Trade Commission and Pure Food and Drug Laws.

A more substantial argument for liberal socialist planning is that the adjustment of prices to consumers' demand would be much quicker than in an unplanned competitive market because the planners would have a much wider knowledge and more information than any private entrepreneur could have.

A final argument is that free markets tend to become monopolized unless their operation is planned. In other words, planning through the market is superior in technical efficiency to free-market distribution because free markets are said to be inherently unstable and tend to become privately controlled for the benefit of monopolists. Hence, public control in the consumers' interest would increase production, efficiency, and welfare. Thus, liberal socialist planning is advocated as a supplement to, or substitute for, capitalist antitrust policy. This argument needs to be taken seriously although it should be remembered that the comparison is between a *theoretical* socialist market and *actual* capitalist markets, and so far there is no way of knowing exactly how such a planning system would operate in any given institutional environment.

The most substantial arguments against liberal socialism are the traditional arguments for private property and initiative. Private management, it is contended, is simply more efficient. In most cases this is probably true although there are many other considerations which are not strictly economic and which will be considered in greater detail later.

THE SOCIAL DIVIDEND. Socialists generally feel that if supply and demand are allowed to operate in a free market with wages and employment left to the self-interest of employers, the result will be employment instability and exploitation of wage earners. However, liberal socialists generally agree that workers must be paid in money wages in order to insure freedom of choice in consumption. Furthermore, they admit that competitive wage differentials must be permitted as in a free market or else rational pricing and allocation of resources is impossible, and there would not be adequate incentives to work efficiently. They are fully aware that this will lead to considerable income inequality, but it should be remembered that nothing resembling absolute equality is seriously advocated by socialists today.

It is believed by socialists, and many others for that matter, that if income were based solely on earnings (as distinguished from inheritance, monopoly, etc.), inequality would be much less than in capitalist countries at present. Nevertheless, some income payments on the basis of need, in addition to earnings, would decrease the inequality, particularly the poverty which is due to competitive wage differentials. If incomes were based solely on productivity, there would always be some people who could not produce enough for a living wage and others who might be able to support themselves but who have family responsibilities beyond their ability to provide even in the absence of any wage exploitation by employers. These payments on the basis of need could be carried out to some extent without seriously affecting incentives and productivity.

To achieve this result, liberal socialists propose a double wage system. In addition to his earnings every worker or household would receive a "social dividend." This dividend, paid by the government, would attempt to achieve socialist goals of welfare and liberty without sacrificing labor productivity and the incentive for innovation or distorting the price structure as requiring producing firms to subsidize workers would do.

The social dividend could be distributed in several ways. It could be in the form of an enlarged area of free (or nominal cost) goods or services. The accepted "free" services, such as education, roads, and social insurance could be extended to medical care, basic housing, or even further. Water rates in parts of Great Britain, for example, are levied on the basis of property evaluation rather than consumption, and throughout the world public transportation has been widely subsidized by taxpayers. There have been proposals from some liberal socialists in Great Britain to provide electricity free as a social service. The provision of free services cannot be extended far into the area of general industry, however, without destroying the rational pricing and distribution system. Free electricity, for example, would cause a vast increase in demand relative to other forms of heat and power, and the resulting expansion of electrical producing facilities would bear no relation to the relative costs of production.

Another method of paying the social dividend would be in the form of freely disposable purchasing power. Certain payments according to need, such as family allowances and pensions to old or disabled persons, would come under this heading. Or a certain minimum income per person might be paid also. In any event the social dividend would have to be distributed in such a way as to have no influence on personal ambitions, costs, or prices of specific goods or the choice of occupation. For example, if workers in certain occupations or regions received a larger dividend, labor would be diverted, and this would of course interfere with the optimum distribution of labor services among industries, occupations, and regions.

The social dividend would be paid out of a fund accumulated through a progressive income tax system. For low-income groups social dividends would exceed income taxes while high-income groups would pay more into the social fund through taxes than they received. Most capitalist countries are using this system in some form already.

GENERAL CRITICISM OF LIBERAL SOCIALIST THEORY

A great controversy has raged in many books and countless articles in economic journals for the past thirty years over whether a socialist state could allocate its products and resources rationally and whether, or to what extent, economic planning was consistent with personal freedom. One viewpoint, which might be called the extreme "left," asserts that economic planning requires explicit, complete, and detailed plans with equally comprehensive controls for achieving them. This view rejects the market mechanism for allocating resources, claiming that planning (as specially defined) is more efficient than the price system and that the highest degree of personal attainment can be obtained only through centralized control. The market system is held to be an impediment to, not a vehicle for, planning. This viewpoint is called "central planning" and is considered in detail in the following chapter.

Another viewpoint, which might be called the extreme "right," is one which has been most prominently expounded by two Austrian economists, Ludwig von Mises, now of New York University, and Frederick von Hayek, of the University of Chicago. This view maintains that planning will not work, that it is necessarily totalitarian (regardless of the institutional environment), and that, like pregnancy, it cannot exist in degrees. Consequently, anything that interferes at all with the freely operating, perfectly competitive market (which is based on private ownership of all capital) will ultimately and inevitably lead to totalitarian economic control by the central government.

Furthermore, according to this view, totalitarian and centralized economic control lead to totalitarian and centralized political control. If private property is abolished or if the government attempts to control or influence private markets, the results will be the same. Without private, competitive markets a national planning board must decide what is to be produced and how much. These decisions must be based on the needs of government, and the people have to accept them. It is said that no consumers' sovereignty, free choice, or even democratic political institutions could survive. Since planning of this dictatorial variety has developed in the Soviet Union, the critics of socialism who hold to the Mises-Hayek view argue that all planning, public property, or government controls must necessarily lead to a similar situation where democratic institutions do not exist. This is a curious argument for such outspoken anti-Marxists since it seems to be based squarely on the Marxian thesis that the methods of production (whether public ownership, controlled private production, or laissez faire) determine the political environment, regardless of the cultural, institutional influences.

The assumptions underlying the Mises-Hayek theoretical attack on socialism are, however, too extreme. It is assumed that all rational economic behavior depends on a pricing system. The pricing process, it is claimed, must be based on markets for all goods (both capital and consumers') and for all factors of production (labor, capital, management, and land or natural resources). In order to have markets, it is then argued, there must be private ownership of all property, and producers and consumers must be in possession of this property. They must also be motivated by a desire to acquire profits to add to this property, and their actions must be regulated only by a thoroughgoing competition. Thus, it is argued that goods produced under public ownership, controlled markets, or less than pure competition cannot have any objective monetary values, and no costs or demand can be calculated for them.

Mises and the others associated with this view use the term "price" in too restricted a sense. Actually, prices are not absolute measures of the value of resources but are merely terms on which alternatives are offered. Hence, they are relative measures of demands and scarcities and as such do not depend on the existence of such rigorous, ideal conditions as this argument assumes. It is not necessary to assume that buyers and sellers cannot act rationally unless they own the means of production or own the firms they represent. Actually, it is needless to refute this assumption theoretically, because it has been contradicted by everyday experience in most capitalist countries for the past sixty years. It is the exceptional, rather than the usual, case where economic calculations are made by the legal owners of resources any more. The growth of the institutions of proxies, professional managements, holding companies, agencies, even the corporate device itself, have shown that an economic system can operate in a democratic political environment without the direct owner-trader relationship assumed by Mises and Hayek.

Furthermore, it is erroneous to assume that in democratic countries, particularly in the United States and Great Britain, the government is an entity separate from the citizens of the country. Rather than being an independent agency with a mind of its own, the government is more likely to be a conglomeration of diverse groups and interests which responds more or less directly to the pressures which are brought to bear on it. Rather than being an expanding organism which seeks to increase its scope and power, it is more likely to be a loose confederation of many agencies which often pursue conflicting or inconsistent policies and frequently seek to limit their own jurisdiction or authority.

The current controversy over economic planning, at least in the Western world, largely rejects both extremes. The central planning concept of direct controls, which is considered in the next chapter, is still considered necessary in wartime but is not otherwise a serious contender for consideration as an economic system in peacetime even by the socialists of Britain and Western Europe. The Mises-Hayek economic system has also been fairly generally repudiated and is not under serious consideration because of its vast oversimplification of the real world. Some political writers, such as Henry Hazlitt of *Newsweek*, still cling to this extreme position, but it is little more than an impractical ideal.

Economic planning is thought of by liberal socialists, and many nonsocialists too, as a healthful tonic which is not necessarily habit forming but which could be dangerous in overdoses and should be prescribed according to the condition of the patient. The debate centers around the diagnosis of the patient, not around the medicine. There is not even any serious attempt to define planning or distinguish it from mere government interference with the economy. There is, in general, a profound respect for the government in the United States and the rest of the Western world. There should be no alarm lest it step out of its role as protector of individual rights and undermine traditional freedoms. Many British socialists and American liberals agree that direct controls threaten personal freedom and breed corruption and inefficiency. They would rely on a "guided" market economy to allocate resources, with the steadying hand of government felt in the areas of fiscal policy and, of course, through the agricultural program, the public sector of the economy, and the welfare services. The debate is over how much planning there needs to be. There must always be a national budget, the control of which necessarily has decided effects on employment and investment. All governments today go at least this far since this is hardly more than policy-making in the economic sphere.

Most economists admit that democratic economic planning based on consumers' free choice is at least theoretically possible. The practical feasibility of the theory has been accepted by liberal socialists generally and even by many orthodox economists who recognize the economic advantages of liberal socialist planning but prefer an imperfect capitalist economic system because of the psychological and sociological values which attend the institutions of private property and the profit motive.

CONCLUSION

Under liberal socialism the government is assumed to be in a position to plan for the whole nation. However, this poses a dilemma for the planners. Having discovered the basic economic causes of existing economic trends, their professional duty as economists would clearly be to facilitate these trends by providing information, improving the mobility of the factors of production, and interfering with economic developments only where temporary steps were necessary to mitigate the hardships caused by tentative conflicts between social and commercial or economic goals.

Thus, although the planning authority would have the power to mold economic activity to fit any given social ends, it would (if it chose to exercise its powers rationally) limit its activity to creating a framework within which individual incentives and freedom to pursue them could operate most efficiently and with the least social hardship. Of course, the planning authority would have to remain, for who else could gather the information necessary for discovering the economic goals of industrial movement and protect the innocent from the relentless attack of economic forces?

Once the trends are known, however, the planning authority would defeat its purpose if it tried to arrest them unless clearly recognized hardships cried out for special treatment in the form of subsidies or other protection. The ultimate goal of liberal socialist planning is to require firms to bear their own social costs, but if this goal could ever be attained, planning would be unnecessary.

This chapter has concentrated on the economic planning aspects of liberal socialism as they work through the market mechanism. The field of liberal socialism is much broader than this as it includes such areas as distribution of labor, public utility pricing, monopoly, financial policy, and foreign trade. Here all that has been attempted is merely a summary and an explanation of the case for planning through the market as its advocates have presented it. In the past liberal socialists have offered their system as a substitute for capitalism. More recently, collectivist trends throughout the world (stimulated in part, no doubt, by the possibility of atomic war) have caused liberal socialism to be considered more and more as an alternative to the Soviet type of central planning. Thus, Eduard Heimann says, "The traditional reasons for wholesale unification of all economic activities under a socialist government . . . are obsolete, because they lump together in one stroke of revolutionary change different objectives which can, but need not be logically lumped together; but can be dealt with by different sets of measures and must be so dealt with if totalitarian control is to be avoided." [14] The following chapter considers the alternative, and totalitarian, form of socialism—central planning —and a critique of some of the problems raised by both forms of socialist economic systems.

[14] Heimann, "On Economic Planning," *Social Research*, 1950, p. 275.

11

Authoritarian Socialism: Theory of Central Planning

> There are two kinds of socialists, those who put the accent on liberty and those who care most for the class struggle.
> ——Giuseppe Saragat

AUTHORITARIAN VERSUS DEMOCRATIC PLANNING

The concepts of authoritarian socialism trace their ancestry to the erratic genius of Karl Marx. As Chapter 5 showed, the first genuine theory of economic process came from Marx. Although Marx had no theories of either socialism or planning, nor did he even speculate about the post-capitalist society, it is on the Marxian idea of economic process that modern theories of authoritarian socialism are based. There has been much expansion, distortion, and confusion of Marxian theory, however, so that precise definitions of the concepts underlying authoritarian socialism can best be derived by contrasting modern authoritarian socialism with the contemporary liberal socialism which was discussed in Chapter 10.

At the heart of authoritarian socialism is the concept of central planning. Of the four basic principles of socialism set forth in Chapter 1—public ownership of capital equipment, participation of workers in economic decisions, relative equality, and economic planning—the authoritarian socialists emphasize public ownership and planning over participation and equality. If equality or workers' control ("industrial" or "economic" democracy) are ever in conflict with planning, then equality and workers' control are readily sacrificed. Thus the Marxist central planners are, at best, only partly socialists even in theory since equality and economic democracy are abandoned if they conflict with public ownership or planning. Since legal ownership of capital assets has become subordinated to the need for professional management, and planning can be effective under capitalism, it seems that the centralists have forsaken the more important principles of socialism and clung to the more insignificant ones.

Experience in Soviet Russia bears out the Marxist renunciation of the basic socialist principles in practice. Economic inequality is as pronounced as in any capitalist country with key bureaucrats and favored scientists receiving over fifty times the average wage of workers. Free labor unions are not permitted, and workers have much less control over their wages and working conditions than in any existing capitalist country. There is almost no consumers' free choice. Politically the government has displayed strong fascist tendencies. Everything has been so sacrificed to the rapid growth of capital goods industries that many observers are tempted to classify Russia as "capitalistic." [1] Certainly, practical reality has forced the Russian rulers to make many concessions toward capitalism, but since they still seem to be wedded, ostensibly at least, to a theory of authoritarian socialism based on Marxist-Leninist assumptions, it still seems best to classify the Soviet Union as the best example in practice of centralist socialism.

Central planning theory differs from liberal socialism in two important respects. First, it does not use the orthodox economic concepts of marginalism, competition, equilibrium, and value theory but employs "average" concepts of cost and demand and "dynamic" process analysis. Second, it contemplates either abolition or modification of consumers' free choice. This leads to the necessity for a more or less arbitrary central authority to make basic economic decisions.

[1] For example, Gilbert Burck and S. S. Parker, "The Crisis of Soviet Capitalism," *Fortune*, February, 1957, pp. 102-7, 242-48.

Hence, the price system is relegated to the distinctly subordinate role of allocating resources after decisions as to their use have already been made. This is in contrast to the liberal socialist economic model, which allows consumers' preferences to determine the economic plan in large part and uses an artificial market mechanism to translate consumers' desires into producers' decisions. Both liberal socialism and central planning attempt to abolish the entrepreneural profit motive by substituting public ownership for private ownership of capital, but central planning also aims at abolishing consumers' free choice while liberal socialism tries to retain it.

METHODOLOGICAL DIFFERENCES. Underlying the theory of central planning is a belief that the accepted concepts and analytical devices of both capitalist economic theory and liberal socialism (such as the marginal analysis, competition, and equilibrium) are inadequate either for explaining the operation of an existing economic system or for creating a new theoretical system. Central planners, along with institutionalists and others, claim that the more important problems of growth and development are frequently overlooked by most economists' preoccupation with the problems of allocating given scarce resources among competing ends. Whereas liberal socialism employs mostly the tools of capitalist economic theory, central planning claims to rely on the labor theory of value to develop new concepts or give different stress or usage to existing orthodox economic concepts. Stalin is supposed to have said, "We have replaced the law of value with the planning principle."

A criticism of orthodox theory, as well as a trenchant analysis of the theoretical concepts of central planning, has been well-formulated by Maurice Dobb, and by some other socialist economists such as Paul Sweezy and Paul Baran, who either reject traditional methodology or who have been strongly influenced by the recent development in the U.S.S.R.[2] This criticism deserves careful attention because

2 *Soviet Economic Development Since 1917* (New York: International Publishers Co., Inc. 1948), pp. 1-33, 324-36, 348-62.

it is the principal theoretical explanation of the operation of the Soviet economy.

The adherents of central planning look to a considerable extent to Soviet economic planning experience for their theoretical arguments, although it should not be concluded from this that all central planners are necessarily Marxists. However, many of the more outspoken central planners outside of the U.S.S.R. are associated with extreme left wing movements, such as the followers of Aneurin Bevan in England. They usually distrust the price system and advocate direct controls over the economy and physical planning through government agencies rather than the indirect controls and financial planning advocated by liberal socialists, Keynesians, and most other economists.

Central planners doubt whether the producers in classical capitalist or liberal socialist economic systems can be expected to use the marginal revenue and marginal cost concepts for determining their most profitable price and output combinations. Of course this criticism is shared by many diverse groups of economic theorists, such as institutionalists, so central planning concepts should not be confused with the rejections of orthodox methodology advanced by non-Marxian or nonsocialist economists.

Marginal revenue and marginal cost functions are admittedly estimated, but central planners doubt whether they can be determined with sufficient accuracy to be used as a basis for decision-making. But if it is assumed that neither private businessmen nor state enterprises can use marginal reasoning to determine their price-output levels, it is hard to see how a central planning authority could make marginal calculations for a future period. Since the market system provides no automatic guide to the production of *new* commodities, producers must necessarily rely on rough calculations. Central planners, along with other critics of marginalism, believe that average costs and revenues could be more easily estimated for the future than marginal functions because accurate data concerning existing output levels are more readily attainable than data concerning other hypothetical levels, which would necessarily be extremely rough estimates at best.

Marginalism, both in theory and as a practical economic tool, has been attacked on both the demand and supply sides of the production equation. From the demand or revenue aspect, Dobb points out that the items which comprise consumers' demand are not random or independent of, or competitive with, each other as orthodox economics has usually assumed. Sociological research has shown that the goals of society itself are not unlimited nor are the wants and needs of individuals unlimited as the neoclassical economists had assumed. In fact, the wants and needs of individuals are both limited and related to each other. They exist in sets of closely related goods and services bound together by social convention or conditions of technology. The consumer, according to Dobb, is not faced with the problem of choosing one of an infinitely large number of possible combinations of goods and services which are available. Wants are arranged into groups, and a person living under one of a relatively few possible sets of conditions will be in the market largely for the items which comprise the group. For example, city dwellers tend to demand rental apartments, public entertainment, restaurants, and stylish clothing in a group while suburban dwellers demand household services, furniture, bulk groceries, and gardening equipment as a set of goods more in keeping with their mode of living.[3] If group demands are more significant than individual demands, the concept of marginal revenue is weakened. The sales of those firms which supply several items demanded as a group would tend to move unilaterally in one direction or the other, and any one marginal unit or sale would be difficult to find.

The marginal principle has been questioned from the cost as well as the demand side. Some recent studies seem to show that, in the short run at least, marginal costs in many

---

[3] Dobb, *op. cit.*, p. 5. *See also* Abram Bergson, "Socialist Economics," in Ellis (ed.), *A Survey of Contemporary Economics* (Philadelphia: The Blakiston Company, 1948), I, 414-16.

industries are relatively constant and that the proportions of labor and other variable costs are consequently likely to be fixed.[4] Historical, social, and technological conditions frequently tend to limit the practical choices available. Indivisibilities in production, particularly, may grow as the scale of output increases so that the producer does not have a choice of many levels or combinations of output but must choose among the relatively few which are dictated by the capacities of his specialized machinery.

Not only do technological factors limit the choice but limited resources impose restrictions also. The production of a certain product may necessitate such a level of output and therefore such a utilization of scarce means of production (labor, raw materials, etc.) that the number of different products that it is possible to produce simultaneously is considerably reduced.

However, this point can be pressed too far. Productive factors may be both immovable and interdependent, and the minimum scale of output for technical reasons may be high, but the variety of quantities and qualities of output may still be very great. In the United States, with all of its mass manufacturing methods, the average production run is still under twenty-five items of any one type. It is true that a steel mill with two furnaces has a choice of but three output levels—zero, half, or full production. But, as in the case of automobiles, manufacturers frequently vary production by increasing or decreasing the number of eight hour shifts worked. This permits far more flexibility and variability in output than the centralists admit because of many possible combinations of shifts worked. Even the total productive capacity of the plant can frequently be varied by small improvements without constructing an entirely new plant comparable in size to the original.

[4] Summarized in *Cost Behavior and Price Policy* (New York: National Bureau of Economic Research, Inc., 1943). *See also* W. Leontieff, *The Structure of the American Economy* (Cambridge: Harvard University Press, 1941) for a similar view. Oskar Lange, however, believed that this condition of "fixed coefficients" was the exception in modern industrial society. Lange, *op. cit.*, p. 94.

If marginal cost is constant over a considerable range of short term variations in output, the possibility of choosing an optimum scale of output would be eliminated. Lange (who must be classified as a liberal socialist) recognized that "if the amount required of all factors of production is simply proportional to the quantity of the product . . . or to the quantity of another good used . . . marginal cost is independent of the scale of output." [5] Lange thinks of this condition as a special case and is thus in disagreement with Dobb who believes that indivisibilities are quite common.

In spite of the arguments for cost or supply indivisibilities, the grouping of consumers' demand is probably the main factor limiting variations in the relative proportions of different goods which can be produced. The demand for one product may be dependent on the demand for others, and when all the goods in one group are produced simultaneously there may not be sufficient resources left to produce an unlimited variety of other goods. But convincing evidence to dispute marginal demand calculations is still lacking.

The main theoretical problem to the centralists is determining how any given situation or state of technology, with its available resources, limits the number of ends from which it is practical to choose. This is in contrast to the classical (and liberal-socialist) problem of allocating limited resources among unlimited ends. The emphasis is shifted to the characteristics of any situation which limit and determine the kind of development which can occur. According to the centralists, economists have been too much concerned with conditions of equilibrium and not enough with those of growth, change, and development. The goals or ends which orthodox economists (both capitalist and socialist) considered as "given" are themselves changing forces which determine, and are in turn determined by, the entire economic and social process. It is therefore useless, they say, to prescribe in terms of an "optimum" allocation of resources since any optimum requires given, fixed ends among which means can be adjusted.

[5] Lange, *loc. cit.*

This might be the case in a socialist society where complete collectivization had occurred and atomistic individual decisions no longer existed. The problem the central planners would seek to solve would not be how to find an optimum combination of factors of production from an infinite variety of possible combinations but would be discovering what conditions determine the present state of development and how can they be utilized to achieve the most desirable rate of growth.

If insufficient attention has been given to problems of growth, then an important aspect of economic systems has been neglected. Certainly the transition from one economic situation, with its political and social institutions and state of technology, to another is of great importance. Dobb suggests that the success of such a transition, as from a feudal, agricultural economy to a capitalist or socialist industrial economy, might even be a more meaningful indication of the accomplishments of an economic system than the achievement of equilibrium or the maximization of short-term welfare. But the abandonment of the marginal calculus as a rationale for economic decision-making does not necessarily follow from this.

ROLE OF CONSUMERS' PREFERENCES. Central planners generally disagree with both neoclassical capitalist economists and liberal socialists on the role of consumers' choice. To centralists, there is nothing sacred about consumers' preferences. They prefer expert or "scientific" study to determine needs rather than relying on individuals to know what is best for themselves even when properly educated and informed. Some go to the fantastic length of proposing that those goods which are found by research to be essential (such as water and electricity) should be made available to all at no direct cost. Although sound economic and social arguments can be made for providing some goods or services free (as education, roads, pensions, funerals, and lighthouses), there can be no rational economic calculation in these cases. The costs must be borne somewhere, and, if not by the users, it becomes hard to estimate needs and wants objectively.

While not advocating the complete elimination of consumers' preferences, central planners envisage many instances in which the planning authority would have to ignore consumers' professed desires. For example, in the development of new types and qualities of goods or the encouragement of new wants, the market is often an inadequate guide to production, and the centralists expect the planning authority to overrule consumers' preferences in many such instances. Of course, time preference decisions involving savings and the rate of capital accumulation would also be proper areas for arbitrary central decisions in view of the alleged shortsightedness of individuals.

Abram Bergson is of the opinion that central planning is neither tied to a system in which consumers' preferences are overruled nor to any particular ends. The ends could be freely varied by the planning authority. Dobb disagrees, contending that too much emphasis has been attributed to consumers' sovereignty. He emphasizes the fact that in a capitalist economy there is usually a great inequality of income which permits some consumers to have much more purchasing power than others so that luxuries can be demanded by (and hence produced for) some before necessities are provided for others. But going beyond this, he claims that even assuming pure competition there would never be either a maximization of satisfaction or an optimum allocation of resources. Thus capitalism would not even theoretically achieve its goals.

In addition, the centralists assert, technology limits the choices available to consumers. Goods must be produced on a fairly large scale, and this, they insist, reduces the genuine variety which might otherwise be possible. This is probably true to a degree, but many product variations are still possible with relatively few basic types. Furthermore, under existing forms of capitalist imperfect competition, firms are independent enough from market forces to be able to produce first what they think consumers want and then, through sales promotion, convince the public to buy what is already produced. It is true that to some extent large producers can anticipate aggregate consumers' wants more accurately than individual consumers can anticipate their own desires. Producers can also advertise and mold consumers' demand so that goods can be sold. However, the mere fact that goods are produced for inventory rather than for a specific customer's order does not mean that consumers' sovereignty is necessarily eliminated, leaving producers unaffected by consumers' wants. Patterns of production may be altered constantly to meet expected consumers' wants, and advertising may be used merely to sell goods for which there is no demand because producers miscalculated consumers' wants.

Dobb is of the opinion that consumers' sovereignty has never existed to any significant degree in capitalist economies. He sees no great loss if it is eliminated in the centrally planned economy. Furthermore, he expects that consumers' free choice (of goods already produced) will have to be curtailed to some extent in order that planned quotas can be achieved. This does not mean that the planning authority would be completely arbitrary in its decisions. However, it would mold consumers' demand in the interests of the over-all plan through advertising and manipulating prices and output and would follow consumers' expressed desires only insofar as they did not conflict with the plan. Here centralist theory may be more relevant to monopoly and oligopoly capitalism than to classical competitive capitalism or liberal socialism.

GOALS OF CENTRAL PLANNING

Although liberal socialist goals are generally consistent with those of orthodox capitalist economics, central planning envisages a social and political reorientation far more complete than anything that reformist or liberal socialist theories anticipate. Like liberal socialists, centralists advocate nationalization of industry as a means of achieving their objectives. But they usually go beyond the liberal socialist program of nationalizing only public utilities or basic industries and advocate public ownership for all or most manufacturing, mining, and trade. Unlike liberal socialists, they are often dogmatic about government ownership and may even deny that compensation be paid. They sometimes confuse ends with means, pursuing nationalization as though it were a goal in itself.

Central planners have advocated the political ascendancy of labor *as a class* and the development of new organs of control which will substantially modify existing social institutions and relationships as well as economic arrangements. Thus central planning is radical, not reformist. This is not to imply that illegal or unconstitutional means are necessarily to be used to achieve such revolutionary ends. Even for the more revolutionary Marxists, anticipation of any violent overthrow of government has largely been abandoned in favor of more sophisticated techniques.

Dobb contends that the dominant aim in a centrally planned socialist economy is the rapid increase of wages.[6] Since he undoubtedly has reference to real wages (the purchasing power of money wages), this objective could be logically translated into an appeal for an improved standard of living for the individuals in the economy, inasmuch as wage earners comprise by far the largest single economic group in all industrialized countries—up to 90 per cent in some. This would thus roughly approximate the welfare goal of neoclassical and liberal socialist economics. However, the objectives of central planning diverge from those of neoclassical capitalism and liberal socialism on the issue of precise measurement. Since central planning theory is not based on marginal analysis, there is no place for the

[6] Dobb, *Political Economy and Capitalism* (New York: International Publishers Co., Inc., 1940).

maximization of total welfare or consumers' want-satisfaction.

Another goal of central planning is in the traditional socialist attempt to achieve a condition approximating economic equality for the individual members of society although, in conformity with centralist doctrine, no mention is made of an optimum position. Thus Dobb notes only that the fundamental character of socialism consists of its abolition of the class relation which forms the basis of capitalist production. Actually nothing resembling equality is pursued very vigorously by most central planners.

Friedrick Engels, writing in 1878, suggested another objective that is more consistent with modern centralist theory than is equality. It was "the completely unrestricted development and exercise of their (members of society) physical and mental faculties." This is certainly not the same thing as economic equality but resembles more the "equality of opportunity" concept of traditional American capitalism. It is certainly not inconsistent with rather substantial economic inequalities.

The experience of central planning systems in practice suggests that the major goal is a rate of economic development (through rising labor productivity) which is more rapid than that of capitalist countries, accomplished by a social transformation to a "classless" society. To accomplish this, consumers' welfare is expendable. For example, the U.S.S.R., under the Stalin regime at least, has sacrificed consumption to capital growth and industrial expansion.

The central planners disagree with both classicists and liberal socialists on the issues of freedom and welfare. Since central planning does not consider maximum individual freedom as a long-run goal, short-term problems are to be met by using varying degrees of compulsion. The reasoning behind this is that social development in the direction of long-run higher living standards, greater capital accumulation, and particularly an improved social structure are not ordinarily achieved through maximizing individual liberty. Individuals allowed to pursue their self-interest without restriction, it is contended, would sacrifice their own long-term interests in favor of short-term gains. Vested interests would try to protect their special privileges, and the middle classes might well oppose all revolutionary social measures. As Aneurin Bevan has aptly admitted, the Industrial Revolution might never have occurred if perfect democracy had existed. The masses of the people would not likely have supported those policies which were required for capital accumulation because they involved a temporary reduction in the security and even the living standards afforded by medieval society.[7]

To the central planners, liberal socialism merely leads to maximization of present satisfaction in any given set of circumstances without permitting any economic or social progress. Centralists argue that any genuine improvement in the capacity to produce and any genuine social reform must be carried out through central decisions without regard to consumers' immediate desires. Authoritarian, centralist socialism, they say, must plan for economic growth in much the same way that any nation plans to win a war in which it is already engaged. Accordingly, present Russian industrial policies resemble those used by the United States and Britain at the height of World War II.

In the case of consumers' satisfaction, central planners reject the welfare concepts of neoclassical and liberal socialist economies. The capitalist and liberal socialist formula of balancing price with marginal cost is unacceptable, they declare, because the policy of enforcing such a criterion would eventually lead to an economy in which the planning authority's only function would be to allocate resources in accordance with consumers' desires.

If planning is to have any real meaning, according to the centralists, it must be possible for the planning authority to make policy decisions on such matters as defense, industrialization, and cultural development where the short-run desires of individuals may conflict with their best long-run interests. Of course, it is possible that maximum total welfare would

[7] *Democratic Values* (London: Fabian Society, 1950), Tract No. 282.

be more nearly achieved through central planning than through consumers' sovereignty or consumers' free choice. Ignorance, custom, and human vagaries are notoriously influential in preventing rational consumer decisions. However, central planning does not even try to maximize total consumers' satisfaction in the first place so the marginal revenue and cost criteria are not applicable anyhow. Central planning theory is to some degree a logical extension of Marxism since it seeks to create a society in which certain types of "exploitation" are eliminated and in which social relationships are radically changed. These changes are thought to be realizable only to a greater or lesser extent (depending on the characteristics of the people) through authoritarian government controls.

CENTRAL ECONOMIC PLAN

The central economic plan is an immense, all-inclusive blueprint that attempts to govern the economic activities and interrelationships of all persons and institutions in the economy as well as economic relations with other countries. It is a physical plan (as distinguished from the "fiscal" plan of liberal socialism and the budget of the Keynesians), and its components are stated in terms of actual quantities of goods, services, manpower, and the like rather than in money terms. Of course the aspects dealing with hiring or otherwise securing the use of factors of production, with savings and capital investment, and with foreign balances of trade have to be in money terms since a monetary system is now considered necessary for all industrialized countries. However, money is used only as a means for achieving the ends of physical planning and not as part of a semiautonomous market system as in free-market capitalism or liberal socialism. The Russian five-year plans follow this general pattern.

The centralist theorists put great stress on the influence of given supplies of resources and a given state of technology. These limitations are believed to aid in accomplishing the goals of central planning to the extent that they narrow down the practical choices to more workable proportions. Because of the alleged indivisibilities in production and the complementarity and groupings of consumers' and producers' demand for goods, the economic calculus of orthodox theory is assumed to be inapplicable and, instead, an elaborate system of cost accounting is to be used. Accordingly, in Soviet Russia, cost accountants and statisticians are given a higher status than they receive in capitalist countries.

Costs and prices, as well as money, would be used to effectuate the fundamental decisions, but they would be tools, not yardsticks, consequences, not causes of economic activities. The final decisions of the proper channels of action would not be the result of precise, objective monetary calculations. Rather they would be determined by a scale of preferences set up by the planning authority. Relative purchasing power, for example, would be determined by the authority in fulfillment of planned requirements. This purchasing power takes the form of demand which itself is transformed into money payments with which costs are then compared. Thus cost data play a minor role, subordinate to the aims of the authority. They influence but do not determine the decisions of the planners.

To the extent that consumers' sovereignty, as reflected through price movements in the consumers' goods market, is abolished, it is necessary that the central planning authority assume responsibility for making basic policy decisions concerning what goods will be produced, in what relative and absolute quantities, where they will be produced, by whom, and such other decisions which are ordinarily accomplished to a greater or lesser extent by the market system.

Initially the goals of central planning must be translated into specific objectives of the plan. In keeping with centralist theory, great stress is placed on the present level of development of the economy. The central planners think in terms of what is desired and what is technically possible in a given situation. Thus a particular ratio between agricultural and industrial production might be planned (as the 37–63 ratio attempted by Soviet Russia in the 1930's), an extension of existing railroad facilities or an expansion of capital goods industries might be considered desirable although these would be possible only through the sacrifice of other, less important, objectives.

Objective and subjective conditions are thus merged into the concept of a "socio-economic optimum." What can be done in a given situation is combined with a desirable course of action. Once a policy is decided upon, technological conditions determine the resulting course of action and limit alternative possibilities. The criteria of capitalist profitability and automatic price adjustments are abandoned, and the economic optimum is conceived of as the combination of a unified and purposeful economic policy and a technical maximum.

The next step for the planning authority is to arrange for the allocation of the means of production. Traditionally, economists have believed that capital could be rationally allocated among industries only if the productivity of the investment in every use could be compared with the cost in the next best alternative use. The lowest cost (i.e. most productive) use for any invested capital would have to be found by calculating the cost of the opportunities which were lost because of the decision to use capital in a certain way. This "opportunity cost" requires evaluating capital goods in terms of labor power at current wages and a "capital cost" calculated as an interest rate expressing the scarcity of all capital goods in relation to the total of their potential uses.

Dobb maintains that it does not follow from this that some kind of market is required to provide this evaluation. He suggests a technique for the planning authority to make rational decisions if data are available about the comparative productivities of different investment projects and their construction costs.[8] He maintains that from this data the "net productivity" of each proposed project could be calculated. The net productivity is defined as the output of the plant at current prices over a given period of time less the

[8] Dobb, *Soviet Economic Development*, p. 14.

cost of production, expressed as a ratio to the construction cost of the plant in current wages and materials prices. Once this was known a priority list could be assembled in terms of the comparative yields of the projects, and allocations could be decided by working down the list. Exceptions could be made where social goals not expressed in the calculated productivities were to be pursued.

Dobb makes no claim for perfection for this technique. He admits that the imperfection of calculating instruments and a number of difficulties (such as where resources are not homogeneous and cannot easily be compared) cause his method to fall short of an optimum allocation. However, he believes that this priority list mechanism is capable of registering and correcting any considerable departure from an efficient allocation of resources. There is some evidence that financial arrangements concerning investment decisions in the U.S.S.R. use a method similar to this, although how it is done efficiently without a price system is hard to envisage.

It is apparent that the "price" and "cost" data upon which net productivity is calculated are themselves the product of the central planning authority. The current prices of output are the result of the preference scale of the authority which determines the allocation of purchasing power which, in turn, determines demand. The cost data are also the product of estimates of the authority so that the "raw materials" upon which Dobb's technique is based are really no more than the state's planning decisions themselves. Nevertheless this does not defeat the purpose of using prices in the first place because these prices translate qualitative decisions of the planning board into quantitative measures. Quantitative cost data so created may influence the authority's decisions but will not determine them in the final analysis.

Actually consumers' preferences themselves are both objective and subjective in this same fashion. Demand in a free-market economy consists of both desire (subjective) and ability to pay (objective, since it is determined by income and relative prices). Yet demand is translated into quantitative market data in the neoclassical and liberal socialist price systems, in spite of the fact that it is made up of these two dissimilar elements.

The economic problem facing the planning authority in the centralist scheme resembles a problem of military strategy. The choice of alternatives is limited by the technical indivisibilities of capital equipment which preclude small variations of output as well as production below a certain minimum. Because of the existence of high fixed costs, this minimum output is itself fairly high in relation to maximum possible output. Thus the alternatives have to be treated as organic units which cannot be combined with each other to produce many variations but which, having once been selected, must be carried out in their entirety because their very selection makes other goals impossible of attainment.

RATE OF INDUSTRIALIZATION. Central planning is more concerned with transforming the "constants" of traditional economics than with the allocation of any given set of resources. Thus the growth of technology, the location of industry, the development of new power sources, and the evolution of social institutions are all of prime importance to centralist theorists. These are also of concern to orthodox economists, but the solution to these problems is usually left to the operation of forces in a free market except where a case for exceptions can be made. Direct government planning (as in regional development or city planning), government regulation (as in fiscal policy or price controls), or government ownership and operation (as in defense plants or public utilities) are instituted under capitalism only where the free market system can be shown to be inadequate as a "natural" regulator of economic activity.

In the central socialist scheme, the basic decisions on resource allocation are not solved by the use of interest rates as in the orthodox capitalist system. In a decentralized, free-market economic system a firm can obtain the necessary funds for expansion (indeed it *has* already expanded by definition) when its receipts cover its total costs including interest on its borrowed capital and enough dividends on its shares to maintain their market prices. In a centrally planned economy, however, the criterion of expansion is physical productivity, not financial profitability.

The enormous difficulties of calculation and measurement in physical terms are, of course, a major stumbling block to effective central planning. One possible method has been suggested by Soviet economists for the planning of investments in a centralist economy.[9] The concept of a "coefficient of relative effectiveness" is used as a criterion for deciding between investment alternatives. The coefficients refer to absolute, not relative, effectiveness. They tell the planning authority how much a given alternative is more effective than another or more effective than the general average of investment returns.

The criterion of effectiveness of investments under central planning is the average effectiveness carried out and not the effectiveness of those investments which lie approximately on the margin between those to be undertaken and those to be rejected. This is because the apportioning of investments among industries and firms is not made solely on the basis of relative effectiveness but is made on the outcome of various social considerations with effectiveness playing an important, but secondary, role. As a result of these considerations, projects are sometimes undertaken which, considered singly, yield small immediate effectiveness or advantage yet guarantee huge indirect advantages in other branches of the economy. For example, an investment might appear relatively inefficient from a direct cost point of view but would produce great social advantages in utilizing otherwise unused resources or contributing to a desirable location policy, the advantages of which would not become apparent for years to come. The use of the criterion of relative effectiveness is necessary in order to

[9] Summarized by Holland Hunter in "The Planning of Investments in the Soviet Union," *Review of Economic Statistics*, 1949, pp. 54-62.

determine not the choice of projects to be built but the choice of the most effective projects for putting into effect the tasks provided for in the plan.

This kind of analysis requires knowledge of (or more correctly, an estimate of) the outlay for alternative investments, current expenses, maintenance and amortization of the investment alternatives, and the life-span of the potential investments. In addition there must also be an estimate of all indirect benefits, savings, and expenses that result from the alternative investments. Only then can the coefficients of relative effectiveness be determined.

Actually the result of an investment is not an increment of output but a money saving in operating expenses. Instead of a marginal product, there is a reduction in the money outlay required to produce the present volume of output. According to the labor theory of value, these operating expenses consist ultimately of wages alone, and if money wage rates remain constant the result of investment is to reduce the man-hours required to produce a given volume of output.

An appeal to practice in the U.S.S.R. does not shed much light on the criteria of investment choice actually developed in this centrally planned economy although one significant study of the Soviet literature on the subject has established a five-fold classification of proposals of Soviet economists for ascertaining the proper investment variants.[10]

The members of the first group denied that any single criterion existed for the choice among investment alternatives. They spoke vaguely of choice among investments being made in accordance with the total circumstances prevailing in the economy and those surrounding each alternative.

The second group attempted to formulate a standard to govern the choice among alternative methods of producing a given output. This method introduced a discount factor

[10] Norman Kaplan, "Investment Alternatives in Soviet Economic Theory," *Journal of Political Economy*, April, 1952, pp. 133-44.

to compare projects with different time patterns of capital outlays and operating expenses. This factor was determined by estimating current savings in operating expenses attributable to investment activities and dividing by an estimate of total investments in some preceding period which led to such savings.

The third group proposed scale of plant as the economic standard. This standard involved determining the minimum point on the average cost curve for the firm where average cost is defined to include the specified rate of return on capital.

The fourth group was concerned with the narrow problem of analyzing the economic efficiency of mechanization. The amount of labor released by different kinds of machinery was sought in order to determine which of a specified set of investment goods should be produced.

The fifth group sought to solve the problem of choice by a more or less reasonable facsimile of the internal rate of return on capital.

It is evident that most Soviet economists have used some kind of a calculation bearing a close relationship to the capitalist concept of the rate of interest. In the above study, it was found that the concept of the rate of return on capital was common to all but two of the writers examined. In addition, these Soviet writers exhibited a well-developed notion of opportunity costs, that is to say alternatives sacrificed when scarce resources are committed to a particular project.

A major aspect of the planning process is its role in the growth of wealth in the system. Soviet economists have long asserted that a principal concern of the five-year plans is the construction of additional plant and equipment (once called by Stalin: "starving to glory"). Thus it is assumed that at each stage of development an outlay of capital will be made which will lead to a steadily growing output of equipment and basic raw materials, to an increasing productivity of labor, and to an increasing economy in the use of physical resources. Therefore that which is technically possible at one period of time will be much greater than at an earlier period of time.

In a capitalist economy, investment and output decisions are made by many individuals. Economic theory in the capitalist economy concerns itself in large part with the securing of an optimum allocation of resources among alternative uses with both uses and resources assumed constant. Central planners are inclined to regard this emphasis on the attainment of perfect equilibrium in a given situation as inadequate for analyzing the real problems confronting the economic system. Central planning is sometimes called "developmental" because the successful development from one economic situation to another is considered to be more important than maximizing welfare. Central planning offers the prospect of coordinated and unified decisions concerning output and investment matters, to be undertaken by a single group.

Although the centralists have been inclined to disregard the orthodox concept of equilibrium (they consider it an apology for the status quo) the term "moving general economic equilibrium" has been used by Soviet economists to describe the inner consistency and orderliness of a moving economic framework at any given time. In spite of centralists' professed rejection of orthodox equilibrium theory, it is necessary, in any type of planning, to balance the different branches of the economy using some concept of equilibrium. Centralist theory uses "balances" described by Dobb as "a complex system of equations between the various magnitudes in a plan as the tests of internal consistency or coherence between its various elements." [11]

These balances may be in physical quantities, or they may be accounting balances. Physical or material balances are limited in their use either to a single product or to a group of similar products which permit homogeneous physical measurement. The synthetic, accounting, or money balances can be used to coordinate heterogeneous material

[11] Dobb, *op. cit.*, pp. 331, 348-52.

relationships but are less direct in their results. Both kinds of balances are designed to insure mobility of the factors of production and equating planned consumption with the available resources within the framework of a changing economy.

EXECUTION OF THE PLAN. The central economic plan is divided into sectional and regional plans, production, distribution, consumption, and investment plans, and individual industry output quotas. The targets of all these plans must be coordinated and reduced to a single system. To achieve this, the limits of the various tasks must be verified by the method of balances in order to see whether planned production corresponds with planned consumption. For example, the balance for steel must coordinate the stocks and output of steel with the consumption of steel by major steel-consuming industries. If the limits indicate an unbalance, it would be necessary to plan for either an increase in steel production or steel imports or a reduction in steel consumption. Additional, more general, balances are required such as a balance between prices and cost of production plus accounting profits and a balance among variations in the cost of production and the efficiency of labor.

Although the centralist theorists do not seem to be fully aware of it, much of their analysis of the physical planning process involves a framework which closely resembles that used for capitalist planning in wartime (or for the government sector at any time) using input-output tables and linear programming techniques. The main difference seems to be that centralists assume that only through government ownership of industries and direct control over management and labor can the central planning system be made to operate. It is here that they are probably farthest from reality.

It became apparent rather early from Soviet planning experience that money payments, interest rates, credit, profit margins, rents, and other financial institutions were not peculiar features of the capitalistic system but were necessary elements of any economic system. For example, differential wage rates payable in money which could be spent according to individual choice were found to be an absolute prerequisite to industrial incentive. In the early 1920's in Russia, it was discovered that equal payments in kind stifled initiative and that because of wide differences in taste even differential payments in kind provided inadequate incentives because of the impracticability of bartering except within narrow limits. The use of profit margins was also found to be the most useful test of efficiency (although admittedly not the only one). In fact, an entire system of financial planning became necessary in the U.S.S.R. (in spite of its capitalist connotations) simply because dissimilar physical quantities could be compared only in terms of money prices. A financial system is as necessary to an industrial country as an accounting system is to an enterprise.

At one time there were several groups of writers who proposed the abolition of money altogether and advocated the use of physical units of economic calculation. To the socialist writers in these groups, money, interest, foreign exchange rates, rents, and other price or cost calculations were tools of capitalist exploitation and should therefore be replaced with new concepts. Some of the nonsocialist writers advocated that certain physical qualities be added to money or that it be dated or otherwise qualified to control its use. These suggestions evidence only a confusion about the necessary functions of money which are to provide a standard unit of account, a store of value, and a means of exchange. Money itself is not the cause of economic maladjustments. In the old saying, it was not money but the love of money that was the root of all evil. Likewise rents, profits, and interest are not exploitative in themselves. It is only their misuse which can cause human suffering. A monetary system is as necessary to any specialized, industrialized economy as streets are to a city.

The mere existence of a monetary system and a fiscal budget do not necessarily mean that the solution of financial problems must take precedence over the successful completion of production plans or that traditional capitalist rules of fiscal orthodoxy must be observed in a socialist society. The allocation of productive resources under central planning is controlled by the planning authority and limited by the amount of resources and the state of technology. The mobilization of finance through taxation or savings is not necessary in order to allocate resources in a certain way. On the other hand, there is indeed a financial problem because the existence of a highly specialized industrial system precludes a barter economy, and the maintenance of incentives requires wage differentials and some consumers' free choice. The necessity for money payments to labor, with free disposal of consumers' goods as its corollary, requires the existence of some kind of consumers' market which is not subject to detailed regulation. Thus the central authority cannot control distribution of consumers' goods (as through rationing) except in emergencies, unless efficiency and incentives are to be allowed to deteriorate. When money is used, inflation and deflation become possible, but these are more easily controlled than economic activity would be without a monetary system.

In the central planning model, with production and investment directly controlled and distribution of consumers' goods largely free, there must be some over-all financial control in order to balance the volume of purchases at retail prices with the available supplies and provide for a smooth distribution of resources among the various sectors of the economy. Through fiscal policy the government can greatly modify the framework within which free choice operates. Consumers, indirectly, can be made to spend their incomes in a manner generally consistent with the objectives of the over-all plan although the control is less effective than the direct control exerted over production. Of course, many kinds of nonmonetary rewards and incentives can be added to the indirectly controlled market for consumers' goods. Without a monetary budget and a financial plan, however, there is nothing to prevent great shortages, inflated prices, and pressures on the productive system from developing. Thus a financial plan must be used to augment the more basic production plan.

So far the planning process has been discussed in future terms. It can be expected that perfect coordination will not be obtained, and errors must be corrected before they accumulate. In order that the central, over-all plan be elastic and adaptable, a system of reserves is provided for miscalculations or catastrophes. Also the plan is divided into a twofold period classification of current and perspective planning, both of which are interrelated. Finally there is a division into branch and regional plans. The managers of productive units participate in the planning process from beginning to end but not in the capacity of adjusting outputs to factor and product prices. They are only given instructions concerning the plan and the role of their particular units in it. The managers' participation is limited to giving technical advice.

The actual execution of the central economic plan is more a matter of practical policy-making than of economic theory. Furthermore, the methods of achieving planned goals can be expected to vary widely among countries having different political and social institutions and national characteristics. The centralist theorists generally hold that planning cannot be fully achieved in reality unless direct controls can be utilized and enforced. A plan which sets a definite physical quota for the production of wheat, for example, and which provides for enforceable orders for achieving this goal can properly be regarded as planning. The fixing of prices of wheat to stimulate production or the taxation of alternative agricultural products to achieve goals is more properly termed "production control" according to some centralists. The general control of consumption, investment, or industrial location through fiscal policy, as in Keynesian capitalist or liberal socialist systems, is considered by centralist socialists to be largely ineffective and not worthy to be called planning at all.

This does not mean that all, or even most, industries must be nationalized before effective planning can be undertaken. Experience in the United States and Britain in wartime has amply demonstrated that physical planning is possible with private ownership of industry and guaranteed private profits. Nor does nationalization insure that direct controls can be carried out. British experience with nationalization (notably the British Broadcasting Corporation) shows that an industry may be less easily controlled under public ownership than private. It is often remarked facetiously that there are two spheres of industries in Britain, the private sector, which is subject to the strictest controls, and the nationalized sector, over which the government has no control at all. Of course, many centralist socialists advocate nationalization as a prerequisite to effective planning, and some, as Aneurin Bevan of Britain, prefer a more direct type of industrial organization than the public corporation device, but this argument is largely ideological and is not well founded if applied indiscriminately to different situations. In some types of industrial organization, government ownership might be the easiest way to secure control, but in others it might be the longest way around. For example, some private American firms using atomic materials are more effectively controlled in some respects than some British nationalized industries.

VALUE THEORY IN CENTRAL PLANNING

In a capitalist or liberal socialist economic system, it is the free market, with its supply and demand schedules, which tends to give objective valuations to goods and services. There is no such mechanism in the centralist scheme so the question arises as to what kind of value theory can apply in such a system. Since many of the centralist theorists are associated with the neo-Marxist point of view, or are Soviet economists, it might be concluded that the labor theory of value would be considered applicable. Actually there is a dispute over this, and the role of the labor theory of value in the central planning system is uncertain.

Some leading Soviet economists have argued that the labor theory of value is just as applicable in a centralist socialist economy as in a capitalist one. Marx, it is claimed, intended the labor theory of value to regulate the allocation of resources under socialism. Although there would be no market, still the labor theory would guide the central planning authority.[12] Lange maintains that the labor theory of value is an inadequate guide as a basis for central socialist planning as it implies neglect to scarce resources other than labor. Its use would result in a wasteful allocation of resources if two goods which required the same amount of labor required different amounts of other resources. Other centralists maintain that the labor theory of value is based on "exploitation" and is thus not applicable in a centrally planned, socialist economy where "exploitation" has been eliminated.

Dobb pays lip service to the labor theory in his theoretical models of central planning but also appears to make some use of orthodox value theory. He apparently recognizes the inadequacy of labor in central planning because he resorts to the Marxian concept of "prices of production" in pricing goods rather than their labor value. The price of production makes allowance for the amount of capital used in producing the commodity. Those goods requiring more than the average amount of capital would be priced higher than their labor value, and those using less than the average would be priced lower. Although using prices of production rather than labor value, Dobb warns that equilibrium will be attained only when prices correspond to labor costs and receipts cover current wage costs.[13]

Implicit in all of the objections to the use of the labor theory of value is the assumption that other factors of production may exist as well as labor, and it is surprising that this fact is not recognized when the labor theory is applied by Marxists to capitalism as well as central socialism.

---

[12] Raya Dunayevskaya, "Teaching of Economics in the Soviet Union," *American Economic Review*, September, 1944, p. 519 and "Revision of Marxian Economics," *op. cit.*, p. 536. Paul Baran, "New Trends in Russian Economic Thinking," *American Economic Review*, December, 1944, p. 869. Oskar Lange, "Marxian Economics in the Soviet Union," *American Economic Review*, March, 1944, p. 128.

[13] Dobb, *Political Economy and Capitalism*, pp. 328-29.

CONCLUSION

The theory of central socialist planning constitutes a movement farther away from the typical economic system of capitalism than the half-way effort of liberal socialism. There is a much greater degree of centralization of functions under central planning than under capitalism or liberal socialism. Investment decisions are made by "experts," a plan is drafted, and all economic activities of the system are planned and coordinated for a specified future period of time. Central planning proposes a direct, although not too clear, answer to the problem of providing for the functioning of the economy. Basic decisions on the allocation of resources are made, funds are allotted, and the plan is put into operation. Dependence on the price mechanism is not necessary to perform the task of deciding what goods are to be produced, in what quantities, by whom, and with what methods. These questions have all been answered, and the answers have taken the form of directives in the all-inclusive, central plan.

The central planners maintain that it is impossible for independent producing units to plan ahead because they cannot predict the actions of other producers. The short-sighted and irrational behavior of independent producers, it is charged, leads to cyclical fluctuations and an improper utilization of the resources of the economy. The centralist substitution of advance coordination of the constituent forces in the scheme of development in place of hindsight coordination is one of the main differences between central planning and liberal socialism.

The central planners claim to be able to introduce advance coordination whereby a given objective can be reached more easily because of the elimination of much uncertainty. In the capitalist economy, say the central planners, the range of alternatives and its relation to a given time-horizon is not envisaged as an element in policy-making. The entrepreneur steers his business according to expectations and guesses because he cannot accurately predict the actions of his rivals. Thus, as Dobb says, "To discover what are the theoretically possible routes which the economy as a whole could take would be of little assistance in forecasting the actual path which a capitalist system will follow." [14]

Here is possibly the only clear theoretical advantage which nationalization and planning can offer over the free-market economy. In both the liberal and centralist socialist models, the basic unit of production is the industry, not the firm as in capitalism. Decisions concerning the location of new plants, the enlargement of existing plants, and other basic economic decisions which transcend the individual firm can be made more rationally on an industry-wide basis. In both liberal and central socialist models, the managers of industry can know the cost and demand schedules for the entire industry better than the managers of single firms can under capitalism except where the capitalist firm is a monopoly. Under capitalism, particularly where oligopoly is dominant, independent firms are faced with much uncertainty in their future planning because they cannot predict with any accuracy the actions of their rivals in the industry. If decisions could be made on an industry-wide basis, much of this uncertainty might be avoided.

As a corollary of this, economic planning can take account of social costs as well as economic costs. The wastes of competition could be avoided by having fewer overlapping distribution outlets, and the costs of river pollution, occupational diseases, and other industrial by-products might be more accurately calculated.

Central planning theory consciously substitutes the arbitrary decisions of a few planners for the aggregate desires of the population. Under capitalism, and to a considerable degree under liberal socialism, these decisions are made in a decentralized manner by countless individuals acting independently. Central planners consider planning of this kind as merely a kind of logistics and deny that planning under capitalism or liberal socialism is genuine. They consider such planners as mere planning technicians since they

14 Dobb, *op. cit.*, p. 8.

have little power to determine the goals of society but can only attempt to achieve, in the most efficient way, the goals as determined by people in the market place.

As a matter of fact, planners under capitalism and liberal socialism are likely to acquire a considerable amount of discretionary authority due to the lethargy of the bureaucracy which is likely to surround any national planning organization. So central planning, in practice, can develop to some extent under capitalism and liberal socialism. Conversely, the central planners, even in an authoritarian system, must give some consideration to peoples' wishes or ultimately they will be deposed. So liberalism, in practice, can grow in a central planning system. Thus the differences between authoritarian and democratic planning are not likely to be as pronounced in practice as they are in pure theory.

As Chapter 5 showed, neither Marx nor his immediate followers had any specific theory of socialism, but rather they concentrated on an analysis of capitalism which showed its basic inconsistencies and predicted developments which would lead to its downfall. Even as late as 1918, when a successful, Marx-inspired revolution was carried out in Russia, the Marxists had no notion of what the socialist or communist system which was to be established would be like. The Bolsheviks proceeded *ad hoc* without the aid of theories and consequently made many stupendous blunders. Their task was made doubly difficult because the traditional Marxist theory of capitalism (in which the revolutionary leaders were highly steeped) was largely inapplicable as a basis for proceeding toward establishing a communist system in Russia. Prerevolutionary Russia was not the highly industrialized capitalist economy upon which Marxian theory was based but was largely an agricultural, feudalistic autocracy.

Since that time there has been considerable progress toward developing a positive theory of authoritarian socialism or central planning. Such a theory is still far from complete, and progress is slow, possibly because in those countries where central planning is being tried the intellectual environment is not conducive to scientific inquiry.

In spite of the many years of experience with such a system in practice, relatively little pure theory has come out of the U.S.S.R. This may be due to the fact that Soviet economists are too concerned with the practical problems of planning to engage in theoretical generalizations. There has been some criticism in Russia recently of economists who are too engrossed in practical affairs to theorize. However, the fate of those Soviet economists who have advanced independent theories suggests that the political environment has stifled virtually all free expression and that economic theory has been one of the major casualties.

Part IV

TOWARD ONE ECONOMIC SYSTEM

12

Evolution of Economic Institutions

The next stage of technical advance was an increase in the scale of operations through the organization of mass production based upon slave labor. . . . The new plantation slavery was a far more serious evil than the old domestic slavery. . . . It was impersonal and inhuman, and it was on a grand scale. The social consequence was a depopulation of the countryside and the creation of a parasitic urban proletariat. . . . This social cancer eventually exhausted itself by causing the death of the society upon which it fastened.——A. J. Toynbee (describing the fall of Rome)

Today, the corporation is about the only example left of the old concept of an economic man. The consumer, according to the market analysts, is the victim of mass advertising, fads, prizes, and high pressure salesmanship; the laborer, only a little better, is captivated by propaganda and union loyalty; the farmer, like the teacher, is the follower of a way of life; and the businessman is now best known only as a Hollywood caricature. The only example of the real *homo economicus* still in existence is the modern business corporation.——E. H. Anderson (from presidential address to Southern Economic Association, November, 1956.)

EXPANSION OF INDUSTRIAL ORGANIZATION

CONCENTRATION OF AMERICAN BUSINESS ACTIVITY. The Industrial Revolution of the eighteenth century introduced the factory system, destroying feudalism and guild production by breaking labor up into many specialized functions and creating a new and separate role for the owner-manager, or capitalist. Likewise the "corporate revolution" of the late nineteenth and early twentieth centuries swept away much of the basis of classical competitive capitalism by breaking management up into many specialized functions, divorcing it from ownership and creating a new, professional, semiautonomous management. These two revolutions brought forth what is now called "big business."

The first collectivists to move in on the competitive, individualistic capitalism of the America of the 1870's were not socialists but the most successful capitalist entrepreneurs. The great trusts of the late nineteenth century succeeded pretty effectively in collectivizing the business world. It is true that the typical form for major industry has since changed from the single trust to the "big three" or "big four." It is also true that private control of markets is practiced today more as a matter of economics than as a conscious design. However, the typical market has become one which is dominated by the big few, and, furthermore, the size of the business units has grown enormously in recent years.

There is considerable evidence that competition in the classical sense has declined in the last fifty years. The Great Depression provided the first real proof. Theoretically, under competition a decline in consumers' demand would lead to a reduction of prices, with production remaining fairly constant. Total demand fell drastically between 1929 and 1933, and, while agriculture bore out this prediction, just the opposite happened in the industrial sector—prices stayed up and output fell—as Table 1 shows.[1]

TABLE 1

Markets Composed of Many Producers
1929–1933

	Prices	Production
Agricultural goods	fell 63%	fell 6%
Petroleum goods	fell 56%	fell 20%
Textile goods	fell 45%	fell 30%

[1] Stuart Chase, *Democracy Under Pressure* (New York: Twentieth Century Fund, Inc., 1945), p. 52.

MARKETS COMPOSED OF FOUR PRODUCERS OR LESS

	Prices	Production
Iron and steel	fell 20%	fell 83%
Aluminum	fell 4%	fell 41%
Sulphur	fell 0%	fell 62%
Cultivators	fell 3%	fell 90%
Iron ore	rose 1%	fell 93%
Automobiles	fell 11%	fell 76%
Plate glass	fell 5%	fell 65%

The most comprehensive study of economic concentration ever made indicated that by 1939, in over half of 1,807 manufactured-product markets, 70 per cent of production was controlled by four firms or less. A few typical industrial market structures, as found by the Temporary National Economic Committee, are shown in Table 2.[2]

TABLE 2

Product	Number of Firms	Per cent Output Controlled
Asbestos shingles	4	97
Aluminum	1	100
Automobiles	3	90
Cans	3	90
Cigarettes	3	80
Copper	4	78
Corn binders	4	100
Plate glass	2	95
Whiskey	4	58
Dry batteries	4	80
Refrigerators	4	77

Other industries controlled by four firms or less included typewriters, ammunition, linoleum, rayon, writing ink, automobile tires, chewing gum, locomotives, fruit jars, biscuits, electric motors, sewing machines, milk bottles, and matches. It was found that 65 per cent of all corporate income went to 2 per cent of all corporations while 40 per cent went to one-tenth of one per cent of them. Two hundred corporations at that time owned half of all the industrialized assets of the country.

Experience since World War II has not demonstrated any

[2] *TNEC Monograph 21* (Washington, D.C.: U.S. Government Printing Office, 1940).

significant decline in the degree of concentration reported
by the TNEC in 1940. Tentative estimates indicate that the
concentration of ownership and control may be increasing
while competition, in new forms, may also be increasing.
The necessity for quick and dependable production in wartime led the government to award over half of the basic war
contracts to 33 corporations. Ten corporations received 30
per cent of all contracts (by value) while 8 per cent of all
contracts went to the General Motors Corporation alone.
Of course, much of this was subsequently subcontracted to
smaller firms. In 1939, firms employing over 1,000 persons
had accounted for 30 per cent of all employment and 36 per
cent of all payrolls, but these had increased to 44 per cent
and 53 per cent respectively by the end of 1943. A 1951
Federal Trade Commission study, while not conclusive, indicated that concentration had increased during World War
II.[3]

In terms of assets, the membership of the billion dollar
club, by 1957, stood at 36 nonfinancial corporations, 21
banks, and 16 insurance companies. The ten largest corporations had combined assets of $99.1 billion or about 20
per cent of the capital assets of the country. The top two
firms, American Telephone and Telegraph and the Metropolitan Life Insurance Company (with $17.4 and $14.8 billion in assets respectively) each have more assets than the
total assessed property values in any one of 40 states.

Assets are not the only criteria of size or importance,
however.[4] Although ninth in assets, the General Motors
Corporation has led all others for several years in both gross
sales and net profits by a wide margin. GM has averaged
nearly $1 billion per year in net profits after taxes for the
last three years which is far above second-ranking Standard
Oil of New Jersey. In terms of employees, American Telephone and Telegraph led the field with 896,000 (including

[3] *Report of the Federal Trade Commission on Interlocking Directorates* (Washington, D. C.: U.S. Government Printing Office, 1951).
[4] The figures in the following three paragraphs are for 1956 and were
compiled in the *Fortune Directory* (New York: Time, Inc., 1957).
Original source: official company annual reports.

Western Electric of which AT&T owns 99.82 per cent of the capital stock) while GM came second with 599,000. General Electric was a poor third with 280,000.

Size alone does not measure concentration, of course. The 1957 *Fortune Directory* of large companies showed that the 500 largest industrial companies account for over half (53 per cent) of the nation's manufacturing and mining production, two-thirds of the after-tax profits and half of all industrial employees. Banking, utility, and insurance are even more highly concentrated. Only in merchandising is there a lack of any significant nationwide concentration of assets, profits, or sales in the hands of a relatively few firms. The Senate Antimonopoly subcommittee reported that the 50 largest corporations in the United States accounted for 23 per cent of all sales in 1957 as compared with 17 per cent in 1947. Firms having under $1 million in assets accounted for 19 per cent of the sales and 13 per cent of the profits from manufacturing in 1947. By 1956 the sales of these firms had fallen to 13 per cent and their share of the profits had sunk to 4.5 per cent. A survey by the *Wall Street Journal* showed, significantly, that these firms blamed rising raw material prices (especially of steel), tight money, and increased labor costs—in that order—for their plight.[5]

Corporate profits before taxes reached an alltime high of $43.4 billion in 1956, and many individual firms made fantastic records. Texas Gulf Sulphur, for the last two years, earned over 34 per cent return on its sales. The very largest of the big 500 are not the most profitable, however. GM, with an 18.5 per cent return on capital after taxes (far below its best year), was seventy-ninth in rate of profit. The greatest profitability, in general, was enjoyed by oil companies and consumer goods manufacturers of moderately large absolute size and in fairly highly concentrated industries.

There are some recent studies which suggest that the performance of large firms is not as monopolistic as the market structures would appear to indicate. An authorita-

5 *Wall Street Journal*, January 23, 1957, p. 1.

tive investigation by A. D. H. Kaplan of the Brookings Institution shows substantial turnover in the relative size of large firms. Of the 100 largest in 1909, only 36 were still among the group in 1948. Five of the ten largest industrial corporations in 1948 were not even among the largest 100 in 1909.[6] However, in rebuttal, it has been shown that, when these same firms are grouped according to industry, in nearly every case the same firm that led the industry in 1909 was still the largest in 1949.[7] This points to a lack of traditional interfirm competition in spite of what appears to be substantial long-run interindustry competition as evidenced by the turnover and flexibility among all industries.

On the other hand, since 1929 the ratio of self-employed persons (outside of agriculture) to total employment has remained about constant. Concentration seems to have persisted along with a continuing opportunity for self-employment or employment in small or medium sized firms. Nevertheless, the fact that there has been a certain long-run flexibility in the composition of the industrial concentration of the nation does not necessarily lead to a conclusion that modern capitalism is competitive in any orthodox or accepted definition of that term. In 1956, 77 per cent of all gainfully employed people in the United States were wage and salary workers and they received about 66 per cent of the national income.[8] Of the remaining 23 per cent who were self-employed, most were farmers. The employee group included most top management, however, and many employees of small businesses so this 77 per cent of employees does not necessarily define any distinctive industrial proletariat. Nevertheless, the professional top management group is too small numerically to be very significant, and further economic concentration would reduce the significance of the

---

[6] A. D. H. Kaplan, *Big Enterprise in a Competitive System* (Washington, D.C.: Brookings Institution, 1954).

[7] Book review by Jesse Markham, *American Economic Review*, June, 1955, pp. 449-51.

[8] *Survey of Current Business* (Washington, D.C.: U.S. Department of Commerce, August, 1956), XXXVI, No. 8.

"potential capitalists" who are employed by small businesses.

The actual statistics on size, profits, and concentration do not tell the whole story either. Most of the largest firms have influence far beyond their actual properties and employees. For example, thousands of independently owned automobile dealers and gasoline stations have their policies determined in part by the firm which grants them their franchise or agency. Another current *Fortune* study states that "one out of every four business employees in the country works for one or another of the 200 corporations with the largest assets" and that "at least one-half of the nonfarm, nongovernmental working force is tied directly or indirectly to the 200 largest corporations." It is estimated that these 200 firms "strongly influence, at the very least, more than half and perhaps as much as three-quarters of U.S. business life." [9]

The influence of business firms goes even beyond this, permeating many other local community activities. Business leaders often occupy positions of power in civic affairs which are considerably beyond the power of their formal corporate positions. The so-called power structure, consisting of leading business executives and bankers, has been shown to control local public opinion and sources of funds to the extent that civic drives and programs must meet with their approval or be lost.[10] Political candidates who fail to get the endorsement of the power structure face a difficult handicap since important sources of campaign funds and newspaper support may be lost to them. These invisible governments are often defended as being evidence of a desirable community responsibility on the part of corporate managements. Critics interpret this responsibility as domination of civic affairs. In any event, the existence of a large element of corporate influence in local political and civic matters cannot be disputed.

[9] Herrymon Maurer, *Great Enterprise* (New York: The Macmillan Company, 1955).

[10] Floyd Hunter, *Community Power Structure* (Chapel Hill: University of North Carolina Press, 1953).

BIG INDUSTRY'S CHALLENGE TO MANAGEMENT. In the modern world, the ancient Greek ideal of moderation has sometimes yielded to a sort of "Texan" attitude toward the virtues of sheer size. Achievement may be measured in terms of quantity rather than quality. In this environment, the large firm has occupied a peculiar position. The very existence of a big enterprise is often considered prima-facie evidence of success; the management of such a business has reached the apex of a successful career. Large size usually implies such conservatism, respectability, and responsibility that the firm is viewed with pride by the citizenry as the greatest achievement of the free enterprise system which fostered its growth. The higher management people typically occupy a position of prestige above all others in the community. Their advice is sought and publicized on important issues. Their practical approach to problems is emulated by the government, and frequently their administrative talents are brought directly to bear at some point within the governmental structure with anticipation of efficient and sound results. If a top manager can claim the handicap of simple beginnings, the story is complete. Expanded into legend, it fits neatly into traditional folklore.

But the basis for this business aristocracy has not remained constant. That romantic figure, the nineteenth-century entrepreneur, has largely vacated the American industrial scene, having been relegated to a portion of the service and retail areas. The man of daring and imagination who relied on intuition and vision or, perhaps more accurately, hunch supported by experience, is fast becoming a technological casualty. The self-made man is already a rarity. The individualist is yielding to the bureaucrat. The businessman of this century avails himself of an ever-expanding body of knowledge to aid his decision-making. Periodic statements and reports emanating from the accounting, sales, legal, and other departments pour onto his desk. Conferences with lesser executives increase the scope of his knowledge. The development of the more rational economy has brought into being a new concept of business organization. The top executive can no longer have knowledge of all the details of his firm's operations. He has been forced to rely on his subordinates.

One of the most significant differences between the businessman of today and his nineteenth-century counterpart lies in the improved knowledge of the contemporary executive who has superior means at his disposal which permit him to more accurately predict the future. Evidence to buttress this contention of increasing rationality and enlightened planning is easily found even in the unlikely field of accounting. Standard cost accounting makes possible much closer executive control over plant operations because of the existence of variance reports which reflect efficiencies and inefficiencies in operations. These reports can be prepared daily or weekly according to the wishes of the management, precluding the necessity of waiting until the end of the month for operating information. However, not only has management been placed at an advantage by receiving more useful data more quickly, which appears to have been the most plausible explanation for the original development of standard costs, but comparison of actual figures with standard figures is simpler, quicker, and usually more reliable than historical comparison.

The introduction of mass production has also affected the character of industry. Business has ceased being an operation that can be stopped and started with small loss. Rather, it is often necessary that it be thought of as a flow of goods, sometimes requiring a twenty-four-hour operation. Concurrently, the task of management has changed. The shrewd bargain has lost its significance, and regulation of the flow has become the dominant concern of the firm. In effect, there has been a steady movement away from the authoritarianism of the Robber Baron era, so that the present day executive views his task as more than the mere manipulation of men and materials. Rather he thinks of his functions as consisting of planning, coordinating, and controlling the operations of the firm and harmonizing the interests of employees, investors, suppliers, and customers. The full consequences of this new concept of management have not yet begun to be realized.

One possible consequence of the trend toward rationalization of business and industrial management has been repeated often in recent years. This is the fear, expressed by many science fiction writers, that the rationalistic philosophy of the Renaissance, which has proved so fruitful in the advance of science, would spill over into business management and finally into the social system itself. A superrationalism in the business world, it is feared, would lead to the commercialization of everything. The economic and social system would be transformed into an exact mechanism in which all elements of chance, risk, capriciousness, free will, and even all esthetic and spiritual values would be eliminated. Only a cold and deadly efficiency would remain, and the destiny of man would become wealth, security, and slavery.

There have been widespread predictions that such developments would radically alter the form and essence of capitalism. Some writers have pictured a new feudal baronage which controlled all economic and political life and provided security and a permanent low status for labor. Others have predicted a society in which a vast self-perpetuating bureaucracy of managers made the important decisions. Schumpeter thought that capitalism would crumble under the impact of its own success as the entrepreneurial function grew obsolete and progress became automatic. Aldous Huxley's *Brave New World* and George Orwell's *1984* projected present tendencies toward security, conformity, and loss of freedom to similar logical extremes.

Although the distant future can never be known, it would seem that if such conditions as these are ever to exist they will not likely arrive by 1984 or even in the following century or two. Speculators and logical extremists often oversimplify the causes of social changes and vastly underestimate the enormous complexity and variability in the world. Deducing the future history of the world is a risky occupation even with far more evidence than is now available. Actually some of the first results of the rationalization of management seem to point in the opposite direction from that predicted by popular alarmists. They may seem to indicate more wealth and possibly even greater security but not necessarily anything resembling dictatorship.

The attempt to rationalize human relationships in the early twentieth century resulted in a hard-boiled cult called scientific management, and for a time it appeared that efficiency experts and standardizers might try to dehumanize civilization by fractionalizing all production activities into trivialities. However, the sect vanished almost as rapidly as it appeared and has been replaced by a far more sophisticated approach which integrates many separate disciplines into high level, "operations research" teams. Over-all management problems of large enterprises are being rationalized cooperatively by economists, sociologists, psychologists, engineers, and physical scientists.

This approach promises to solve complex management problems much more successfully than the earlier, abortive scientific management movement since the contemporary professionals have the richness and depth of each others' disciplines to broaden their comprehension. Furthermore, some startling breakthroughs in theory and techniques have presented many new opportunities. Some incipient advances in linear programming, input-output analysis, communications and organization theory, and electronics have made it possible to translate many previously developed principles into practical significance for the first time. But the new theories are advanced more cautiously, the new practitioners are more conservative and critical, and the limitations of the new theories and technologies are being explored more realistically. Thus there are no alarming consequences in immediate prospect. Management has raised its sights considerably. Long-run considerations have become more influential as interdependence in the economy has become more obvious. Top business and labor leaders are showing an increasing concern about the over-all state of the nation, particularly the economic aggregates of income, production, employment, consumption, investment, and taxes.

The growing preoccupation with the broader, long-run problems has not caused modern management to ignore the more traditional concern with problems of output and price. These individual or firm problems, which also include costs, product demand, and interfirm competition are still considered important, but the solutions to these problems, as well as others, are being turned over to professional staff specialists. Policy makers in business, government, and labor organizations are relying more heavily on staff specialists, and the influence of these groups is reflected in their enormous growth. Separation of functions and specialization have even been instituted at the top management level so that policy making and policy execution are now often distinct and separate responsibilities.

Regardless of what may have been an increase in inter-industry competitiveness, there will likely continue to be tendencies within any large organization for individuality to yield to conformity, risk-taking to give way to security-consciousness, and initiative to evolve into administrative routine. As Justice Brandeis long ago feared, we are tending to become a nation of clerks and employees. There is a great amount of individuality, risk-taking, and initiative left in the economy, and new techniques of management could encourage more, but so far the basic conditions under which these forces thrive best have continued to deteriorate. Only a sustained economic expansion such as has followed World War II and a positive, objective, and continuing managerial self-appraisal can hope to stem the tide of industrial bureaucracy.

TRENDS IN INDUSTRIAL FINANCING

The growth of corporate giantism has been accompanied by a separation of functions of which the most notable is the divorce of control from ownership. In 1939 (the most recent authoritative date) only forty-two of the two hundred largest nonfinancial corporations were controlled by a majority of their voting stock.[11] These included the large family-owned and controlled firms like Ford Motor Company, Jones and Laughlin Steel Corporation, and Singer Manufacturing Company. In three-fourths of these cases, control was vested in another corporation such as control of Western Electric and the Bell Telephone companies by the American Telephone and Telegraph Company.

Thirty-seven of the two hundred were controlled by 30 to 50 per cent of the voting stock. Included here was DuPont (44 per cent of the stock family-owned) and the Aluminum Company of America (34 per cent of the stock owned by the Mellon family). Forty-seven of the two hundred were controlled by 10 to 30 per cent of the voting stock (the Standard Oils of Indiana, New Jersey and California, Pullman, International Harvester, Firestone, Colgate, Gimbel, U.S. Rubber, etc.). Again many of these were controlled, as they still are, by other corporations (General Motors controlled by DuPont's 23 per cent interest, for example).

In some cases, family ownership of less than 10 per cent seemed to assure control as in American Can Company, Swift and Company, and Warner Brothers Pictures, Inc. In sixty-one of the two hundred corporations, there was no evidence that ownership had any relation to control. The management perpetuated itself largely through the proxy device. The classic case of divorce of ownership from management is the American Telephone and Telegraph Company, which had over 1.4 million shareholders in 1956 with the largest single shareholder owning less than one-thirtieth of one per cent of the stock. Sixty-five thousand shareholders owned only one share each.

Reliable statistics are not available to indicate any definite trend in the concentration of stock ownership. Today about

---

[11] TNEC, *The Distribution of Ownership in 200 Largest Nonfinancial Corporations,* Monograph 29 (1940). The following data are from this study.

8 per cent of all adults in America own some corporate stock compared with about 6 per cent in 1952. But 1 per cent of all adults owns two-thirds of all the individually-held stock. Another 1 per cent owns most of the rest. Thus about 2 per cent of the nation's adults own nearly all of the corporate stocks not held by institutions.

But regardless of the concentration of stock ownership it is apparent that stockholdings are of diminishing importance in an economy where ownership of the means of production is largely divorced from control. In fact, the capital market itself is rapidly losing its influence over corporate affairs. Fifty per cent of all corporate profits are plowed back into expansion today in contrast to about 30 per cent in the 1920's. In the decade following World War II, over three-quarters of all private corporate investment was financed from "internal funds" meaning depreciation allowances and retained earnings.[12] Of the remaining quarter, most was financed through short-term bank credit and bonds. Less than a third of this was from stock sales. Since it is estimated that about half of all equity financing was in the form of nonvoting preferred stock, this leaves about 4 to 5 per cent of all new capital investment being financed by the so-called "risk capital" which is supposed to be the mainspring of capitalist enterprise. Some studies put this percentage as low as 3 per cent.[13] So there may be plenty of new private capital (over $400 billion added in the last decade), but it is becoming harder to find the capitalists.

One effect of the tendency to finance corporate expansion out of profits, rather than from the sale of securities, would seem to be that capital investment would be less dependent on interest rates. Accordingly, government monetary controls (as distinguished from the fiscal controls of taxation and spending) would tend to be of less value in preventing inflation or depression. Capital expansion from profits is

---

[12] John B. McFerrin, "Financing Corporate Expansion During the Postwar Decade," *Georgia Business,* October, 1956.

[13] A. A. Berle, *The Twentieth Century Capitalist Revolution* (New York: Harcourt, Brace & Co., Inc., 1954), pp. 37-40.

costless to the corporation in the sense that no interest is paid for its use, whereas the use of capital which is borrowed or which comes from the sale of stock must be paid for with interest or dividends. The cost of capital which comes from surplus or profits is partly borne by the consumers whose purchases at prices which were higher than the competitive equilibrium led to the excess profits which permitted the expansion in the first place. To some extent, then, consumers may make an involuntary investment in the firm for which they receive no interest, principal repayment, or profits except indirectly as such corporate expansion may lead to lower prices in the long run.

The cost of this capital expansion from surplus is also partly borne by the stockholders whose dividends ordinarily amount to only about half of the company's profits plus possible capital gains if they sell their stock. Of course, the long-run interests of the stockholders and customers may well be served by the corporation's growth in this way, but the point is that neither the stockholders nor the customers have any direct voice in the decision to reinvest the company's earnings. The board of directors has substituted its judgment for the judgment of the capital market, and although this expert opinion may be superior to that of the market place the fact remains that this is more in the nature of central economic planning than a competitive market system.

Clearly the provider of risk capital is no longer the decisive market force he once was. Instead, most important investment decisions are ordinarily made by boards of directors of large corporations who do not have to raise the money in the market but merely have to decide what to do with the firm's profits. Only in the regulated public utility industries have large amounts of new capital been raised in the market in recent years. Even here, AT&T, the largest utility by far, customarily announces its financing decisions to the stock market after they are made rather than relying on the market to determine the needs, desires, risks, and profit potentialities of the nation's communications system. The newer and more dynamic industries seem to be practically immune from the control of the investment market altogether. The present tax structure, which encourages wealthy investors to seek capital gains rather than income, has probably protected the corporate policies of piling up surpluses rather than distributing earnings. Here the law, by taxing incomes more heavily than capital gains, attracts investors to corporations which plow their profits into capital expansion rather than distributing them to the owners to whom paying an income tax is the cost of the privilege of deciding for themselves what to do with their profits.

Another recent development in capital financing has been the phenomenal rise of private pension funds. About 12.5 million U.S. employees—over a fifth of the labor force—are now covered by some twenty thousand pension funds with total assets of over $30 billion. These funds are growing at a rate of about $3.5 billion per year. While these funds have been invested traditionally in government bonds and most of the smaller funds are insured by life insurance companies, the trend is toward larger investment in private industrial bonds and even preferred and common stocks.

Westinghouse, for example, has about 45 per cent of its $100 million fund in preferred and common stocks; Sears Roebuck has 60 per cent of its $600 million fund in its own shares and much of the rest in mortgages on over 700 domestic stores. Standard Oil of Indiana, which once had 60 per cent of its fund in government bonds, recently reduced this to 20 per cent, the rest being invested in private industrial bonds and stocks. So far, however, these stock investments have been confined to the safe "blue chip" securities, particularly of the largest utility companies. Furthermore, these funds are managed by corporation executives or union leaders so even the switch to stocks does not indicate that the private risk capitalist is reappearing on the scene. The real owners of the stocks, the employees, typically have no say in their management.

A major problem for capitalism is arising over the relationship between institutional investors and the companies whose stocks they own. Investment trusts, insurance companies, and employee welfare and pension funds may soon own enough voting stock to control large segments of the economy if they want to. So far their atttiude has been one of "hands off," but several recent experiences indicate that if a corporation is mismanaged, or if its fortunes falter, the potential power of institutional investors may come to life. Undoubtedly this would lead to some kind of government regulation lest a new form of the old European finance-capitalism arise. There is now evidence of abuses in the management of some of these funds. This may also lead to some kind of regulatory legislation similar to that governing banks and insurance companies.

THE NEW CORPORATE STATUS

The rise of the giant corporation and its attainment of a semipublic status has been one of the significant developments of recent times. The technological advance of the last seventy-five years has permitted, for the first time in history, the manufacture and distribution of a volume of goods and services sufficient to abolish poverty in the world. This enormous production (which is just now beginning to get under way) requires the use of gigantic organizations. In some countries, the productive unit has been the semiautonomous, publicly owned corporation, as in Great Britain's nationalized industries. In other countries, centrally controlled state agencies have attempted to perform this function, as in the U.S.S.R. In the United States, the major instrument has been the giant privately owned corporation, although a few large cooperatives have been used, such as the great mutual life insurance corporations and the Rural Electric Membership companies. A few publicly owned regional development corporations, such as the Tennessee Valley Authority and the major port authorities, have also succeeded in organizing production on a large scale. However, by far the most important is the giant privately owned stock company.

Adolph Berle contends that "the two most notable achievements of the twentieth-century corporations have been their ability to concentrate power in themselves and their ability to increase production and distribution." [14] Some economists, such as Schumpeter and Galbraith, have seemed to imply that the productivity is due principally to the power, but most contemporary economists are probably more inclined to see the power as a result of the productivity. While the comparative success in achieving the efficient, large-scale production which the United States has enjoyed is probably not due solely to the type of industrial ownership (since productivity has risen following nationalization in British industries, for example), there is little doubt that this peculiar form of private corporation device has facilitated America's unprecedented industrial accomplishments.

In spite of a possible trend toward a broader distribution of corporate stock ownership, the typical executive of the large corporation seems likely to continue to be subject more to the traditions and customs of the firm and economic pressures from labor, government, and customers than from any legal control from stockholders. While some separation of functions between owners and management has undoubtedly been necessary in order to raise sufficient capital and concentrate the best managerial talent available for directing a large undertaking, there have been corresponding losses. Just as the specialization of labor which accompanied the industrial revolution deprived the craftsman of control over his livelihood, the corporate revolution has deprived the property owner and investor of the same thing. The investor, whether a bondholder or stockholder, is as dependent on the corporation's prosperity as is the employee, and he is even more helpless to control his fate since he does not even enjoy the protection of a union.

The satisfaction and security which come from being able to create, plan, produce, and express individuality in the use of property is as much lost to the modern dividend-

14 Berle, *op. cit.*, p. 25.

receiver as it is to the machine-tender. The investor may have some legal claim to property in the form of a bond or share whereas the worker has no legal right to his job, but the worker often has far more valuable rights in his position than the investor. The labor contract may provide for a grievance procedure and participation in decisions affecting the worker's livelihood whereas the investor usually has no practical control at all over his investment. The worker may through his union control all of the details of his day-to-day work assignment and be able to paralyze the entire enterprise through a strike. The investor's power seldom extends beyond the right to receive dividends at the directors' pleasure (or interest semiannually through a remote bank) or else to sell his securities at an unpredictable market-determined price if he is dissatisfied. Profit-earning is no longer identical with profit-receiving. The earning is controlled by professional executives; the receiving is done by noncontrolling investors.

As the firm grows larger its physical assets become more decentralized, its products more diversified, its processes more varied, and its employees more numerous. Consequently, the usual risks such as fire, accident, death, or even unwise management decisions tend to disappear. The large firm has so many components that they can be dealt with statistically with a considerable degree of accuracy. Insurance has become unnecessary as many large firms discovered that they have more widely separated risks within the organization to balance against each other than many insurance companies can secure from their policyholders. The large corporation can thus estimate its own losses from risks, set aside "reserves for self-insurance," and save the profit that a private insurance company would have made.

So far the corporate giant has successfully defied economic analysis. Legal and sociological investigations indicate that the large corporation may have a character of its own which is independent of its formal, legal status in society. A particular corporation may have a private ideology which is much more than its financial statements and legal titles show. The people who work within the organization's structure are molded by the corporation's ideology. They become part of a way of life, and their motivations are not based on the property investment but on the influence of the group itself.

The large corporation of today is not simply an enlargement of the small enterprise. The corporate giant has attained a specific status in society, and through its organization it solves its economic problems far differently than small firms do. The large firm does not have to rely heavily on property or contract rights or on the judgment of the market place in achieving its goals. It can draw on its human and technical resources, its vast knowledge and experience, and almost unlimited financing. In its position, it can rely on goodwill, established production records, customs and preferred banking, commercial and political connections.

The large corporation today has much in common with a modern central government. In fact, some American corporations have a scope of operations which exceeds that of some of the smaller European countries. General Motors' annual gross revenue, for example, is greater than the total national production of Yugoslavia or Sweden. International and interfirm contracts among these corporate giants partake of the nature of treaties which cover an enormous field of operations. However, the gigantic size of modern corporations entails a public responsibility which cannot be avoided. Large firms can no longer shut down their operations, move their plants, invest in foreign countries, or raise their prices without intimately affecting the lives of millions of people. They do not necessarily adjust their output and prices according to the economic conditions prevailing in the country. They help to create the economic conditions of the country by their price, wage, and output policies. Thus it has not been the individual entrepreneur or the legal owner —the stockholder—who has emerged from the process of mechanization as the basic economic decision-maker and the holder of economic power in the economy. It has been the corporate entity itself.

Just as the function of the businessman evolved from that of innovator process, so has the function of the government changed. A British statesman recently referred to the modern industrial economic system as being like a jet plane which cannot slow down without falling out of the sky. The interdependence of large corporations on each other, the government, and all other sectors of the economy has become so complete that unemployment and other maladjustments can no longer be tolerated without seriously threatening the entire framework of our economic system. Hence large corporations have become, of necessity, semipublic institutions with responsibilities extending far beyond their legal contracts. Since they can consciously control the level of production and employment through their wage, price, and output policies, they control the welfare of every citizen. In a democracy, then, it becomes a responsibility of business and the government to insure continued prosperity, high living standards, and social justice.

As in America, business organization has been undergoing a transformation in Great Britain and Western Europe. The form has been different, but the content has been much the same. The state has played a larger and more formal role as in outright nationalization of basic industries, but, in general, there has been no serious threat to the democratic political institutions which were already well established. The private sector in Europe continues to be fairly well monopolized, largely through the use of price-fixing and other trade restraint agreements. These devices are illegal in the United States, where market control has nevertheless been achieved but to a lesser degree than in Europe, through the formation of giant, integrated corporations. It is ironical that the American antitrust laws are partly responsible for monopolization of markets by the more subtle means of mergers. Combinations of ownership have been allowed to accomplish the same objectives which are strongly prohibited when independent businessmen try to achieve them through cartel contracts that control competition without the loss of identity which results from mergers.

As in the United States, the power of property owners and stockholders in other capitalist countries is passing to a class of hired managers. The traditional ideological justification of property rights, and hence management prerogatives, has been weakened by the separation of ownership from management and the decline of risks through diversification and dispersal. The old Roman doctrine of property as the invulnerable and sacred right of using, enjoying, and abusing is yielding once again to the medieval concept of property as the right of getting and spending. As a cynic might see it, public control has sometimes reduced the legal rights of property to little more than the privilege of paying taxes.

In England, organizational patterns are more formal than in the United States, but in the private sector the essential features of the development are comparable. The power of private economic interests has been limited more than in the United States. The power of the state has increased enormously and has been utilized in the form of direct government operation of commercial enterprises, fiscal policy, and, to a decreasing extent, direct physical controls. Unions and labor-management cooperation have further restricted traditional management prerogatives.

DILEMMAS OF NATIONALIZATION

Great Britain and many other industrialized, democratic countries have tried to cope with large corporations in basic industries, especially where the industries were highly monopolized or chronically depressed, by nationalizing them. While this has solved many problems, it has raised many others. The transfer of ownership may come about through compulsory purchase of assets or equity securities or through condemnation and seizure—the exact method depending on the legal powers and political traditions of the government.

In recent years, nationalized industries have been administered by publicly owned corporations. The corporate device has been frankly borrowed from capitalist countries where it has long been found uniquely suitable for owning and operating public utilities or other "natural" monopolies. The public corporation combines the autonomy and administrative efficiency of the private corporation with the public responsibility of the government agency.

One of the most difficult economic and political problems is knowing where to draw the line between private and public enterprise. For those who possess an ideology of some kind, the knot is easily cut. Socialists and antisocialists of various hues have their minds made up as to what industries should be publicly owned, or at least what tests should be applied to determine the answer. But those who would approach the problem objectively have two strikes against them. First, they are under suspicion from both right and left of being spies for the other side. Most of the attack, so far, has come from representatives of private property, since they have been threatened and are on the defensive. Private industry has been dominant so long that those with vested interests in it sometimes assume that it was established by natural law. Furthermore, there is nothing like a threat to one's income or prestige to kindle the fires of emotion and hence banish rational thinking. Of course, there is no reason to assume that a threat to restore private enterprise in a socialist economy would not evoke the same emotional wrath from those with vested interests in public ownership. British socialists are fighting the denationalization plans of the Conservatives with the same vigor that Conservatives used against nationalization. The second handicap against objective analysis is the tremendous difficulty in weighing the relative values of assumptions, alternative courses of action, and seemingly conflicting statistics.

Government ownership of industry is widespread outside the United States. Most electric and gas utilities, communication and transportation systems in other countries are publicly owned. In many cases these operations were begun by governments in the first place, but after World War II there was a tendency to nationalize private enterprises in Europe and especially in Great Britain. Now nationalized in Great Britain are central banking, coal mining, railroads, civil aviation, electricity, gas, and telecommunications. The steel and trucking industries were nationalized and subsequently denationalized. All of the remaining nationalized industries are characterized by (1) producing basic, necessary, and generally standardized products, (2) having developed under private ownership a uniform, centralized, or regionalized monopolistic structure, (3) being subject, before nationalization, to extensive government controls, and (4) being suitable to relatively routine and riskless administration rather than requiring a dynamic management. This is not to imply that important entrepreneurial decisions do not have to be made but merely that once a relatively few decisions have been made—such as a decision to build an electric generating plant or to close a railway depot—the day to day management, though often highly technical, tends to be largely routine.

Economic circumstances often place an industry in such a deplorable condition that everyone agrees that some drastic action is required. Whether nationalization should be tried depends on (1) how bad things really are (this is an economic question), (2) what untried alternatives there are (this is an administrative question largely), and (3) what kind of solution is desired by the majority (this is a political or ideological question). Both economic and ideological considerations enter into drawing the line between private and public ownership. In Britain, socialist ideology has secured nationalization in some cases where another solution might have been better. In the United States, a strong private property bias has led to the immensely complicated federal and state regulatory system which protects consumers from exploitation and the industries from the more destructive consequences of competition.

British experimentation since 1945 with some aspects of the theory of liberal socialism has brought some latent dilemmas into sharp focus. Nationalization has not established workers' control or equality, nor has it substantially increased efficiency by itself. On the other hand, it did not prove to be confiscatory to the former owners, nor has the public management so far been dictatorial or even unduly bureaucratic. Yet this is probably due more to the democratic political traditions and legal precedents of Great Britain than anything else. The citizens of a less mature society would undoubtedly have more to fear than the British from public monopolies in basic industries.

In Great Britain, the nationalized industries have embraced about 20 per cent of all economic activity and because of their strategic importance have formed a new economic aristocracy. In relative size and influence, they are comparable to the great lords of medieval times. Britain's future will, in part, be determined by the place which the new lords find for themselves in the new society. There are three directions in which the nationalized industries may move. (There is a fourth if one considers going back to private enterprise, but this seems to be unlikely.) First, they may form the central core of a "new despotism" which will crush human freedom and decency in its grip. This opinion is held by a few people, although it is hard to find many Britons who entertain such ideas very seriously. Second, they may supplement the existing social services, ushering in a system of paternalism. Based on the idea that a benevolent state can best determine and provide what people need, this is the true philosophy of the welfare state. It has wide support in Great Britain and elsewhere. Third, the new lords may become the servants of an enlightened people, responding to their wishes and imparting to them a genuine participation in making economic decisions for the community. This thoroughgoing economic democracy is the traditional dream of British socialists and is a major goal of the Labor party. It has not yet been fully achieved although a combination of this with the paternalistic welfare state seems to be the best appraisal of the results so far. The ground work for participation through joint consultation has been laid, however, and a real measure of participation may accompany Britain's economic recovery.

Economic planning was not accomplished automatically by the British socialist experiment. Traditionally, socialism required that workers should control, or at least participate in, the major economic decisions of production. In practice, workers and unions were excluded from control of the management of British nationalized industries for three reasons. First, basic union prerogatives would have had to be relinquished if labor were represented on the board. It was believed that in order to represent the workers' interests properly unions should remain independent, and not be placed in the compromising position of having to defend, or be responsible for, management. In practice, a few union officials were appointed to the boards of directors, but they had to sever all union connections in order to serve. Second, it was felt that board members should not have a divided loyalty. If they were responsible to workers and to the minister too, the board would become a negotiating committee in which the workers' representatives would be in an ambiguous position. Third, it was believed that, ultimately, complete control should be exercised by Parliament in order to effectuate economic planning.

The public corporations which own and operate the nationalized industries are instruments of national policy. Accordingly they have been made responsible to the public, through the cabinet and Parliament, for their activities. This was necessary to avoid delegation of power without responsibility. There is no question of the adequacy of the corporations' powers or of the ministers' powers to carry out the will of Parliament. Nor is there any question as to the adequacy of public responsibility. If there is any danger, it lies in the direction of too much power coupled with too much detailed responsibility—not too much responsibility for the power involved but too much responsibility to permit initiative and efficiency to thrive. Since it is the clearly expressed will of Parliament to grant wide and expansive powers to the boards, any objections must be based on the wisdom of that course of action or on the adverse effects of the responsibility which must accompany the power.

The British government exercises control over the nationalized industries in three ways. First, cabinet ministers control the board of directors of the public corporations through their power to appoint, remove, or increase the number of members. Second, ministers control public corporation policies through general powers of direction. In each of these areas, of course, the minister is, in turn, responsible to Parliament to the extent that the public corporations are responsible to him. Third, there are requirements that financial statements be presented or audits be permitted to give Parliament an additional measure of control through the Treasury and the minister.

Public ownership and responsibility does not remove all the adverse features of monopoly. The mere statements of intent in the nationalization acts and the appointment of public-spirited directors do not insure that the nationalized industries will not inadvertently or through fear of excessive criticism hide behind the cloak of monopoly and take the easy way out by granting wage increases and passing them on to the consumer. Nationalization merely removes the possible irresponsibility of private management by making it subject to ultimate public control. Hence there should be no objection to reasonable regulation by some other government agency or commission.

Nationalization in Britain may offer an opportunity for establishing a rational pricing system based on marginal or average costs and administered by a public-spirited management which honestly tries to maximize the public interest. There is some evidence of this. A typical remark was made recently by a high Coal Board official who said, "I am far more interested in costs than profits." Certainly the fifteen-year plan for the coal industry looks toward an objective price output solution. The nationalized industries are permitted to use profits for raising wages, reducing prices, or improving service (or some combination of these). Except for the currently subsidized airways, they are not expected ever to make payments to the Treasury from any profits which might arise. However, the opportunity which this broad discretion provides for the industrial managements is a two-edged sword which might equally be used for maintaining excessive establishments (empire-building) or conceding too easily to wage demands. Nor are nationalized industries exempt from seeing in every cost increase the necessity for raising prices. For example, the coal industry, faced with a deficit in 1948, raised its prices. The nationalized railroads, which buy huge quantities of coal, suffered an unexpected loss because of increased coal costs. The railroads consequently asked for a rate increase to offset these increased costs. Had the Transport Tribunal granted this increase it would have merely passed the deficit back to the coal industry since freight is a major item in the delivered price of coal. The inflationary potentialities in this kind of financial volleyball game are tremendous. Nationalization does not automatically solve this kind of problem although in a democratic society like Great Britain it may focus new attention on many old problems now that they have to be solved in the glaring searchlight of public knowledge.

British experience also demonstrates the necessity for relying on economic incentives. Granted that the devastation of World War II required the continuation of direct controls for several years after the end of hostilities, it is nevertheless true that an increasing reliance on the market system has been accompanied by almost spectacular economic progress. Western Germany's recovery was even more rapid and was accomplished with more dependence on the free price mechanism.

Another serious dilemma of socialism which has been displayed by postwar British experience concerns the role of labor in socialist society. In the nationalized industries there are no private capitalists, and the workers cannot claim to be fighting them. Labor is contending with a government which represents the entire consuming public. Even more significant to the worker is the fact that he is competing with his own fellow workers in other industries. For example, when coal miners strike for, and receive, higher wages this may raise the price of coal which, in turn, may increase the cost of production of railroad transportation (which depends on coal) and hence may raise the price of railroad fares. But the railroad worker has no capitalist to fight either, and an increase in his wages could lead to higher rail fares and hence to higher delivered prices for coal which must be transported over the railroads. This analysis leads to the conclusion that labor must alter its fundamental outlook toward the economy when industries are nationalized.

When its own government is substituted for the former private managements in the nationalized industries, labor is faced with three possible alternatives. One is to use the traditional labor weapons, just as before, to promote labor's own partisan interests in spite of the policies and plans of the government as expressed through the ministers and public boards. However, as mentioned above, the private profit motive has been removed in nationalized industries, and the old socialist demand for production for use instead of production for profit has finally been granted. The public corporations operating the nationalized industries are required by their statutes to produce and sell at reasonable prices so as to best further the interests of all sections of the community. Presumably the public corporations would be less resistant to wage demands than private employers since the latter have no responsibility to labor. But wage increases in the absence of income surplus or wage increases not justified by increased productivity or efficiency are not in the public interest. Any wage demand beyond that which strikes a reasonable balance between the interests of all sections of the community can only have one of two results. First, it can be granted with the result that the economic gain of one group of workers is the loss of another group. Second, it can be denied, which would presumably result in a strike which would tie up a basic industry and thus reduce the total national product to be divided among all groups.

A second choice is to go to the other extreme. With the profit system eliminated and production for use a reality, the unions could assume that labors' interests could be safely left to a Labor government which would necessarily reflect the interest of labor at all times. The unions would agree to accept, without question, the decisions of the Labor government and the boards of the nationalized industries, thus giving up a large measure of their independence. In this event, unions would have only an advisory capacity, and the situation would not be far different from the days before union organization except that management would ostensibly be in the public interest instead of devoted to the interests of a few property owners. This is the course which has been followed in Soviet Russia and has led some observers to the conclusion that without effective, independent labor organizations a new form of capitalism has arisen in which the interests of a few state officials have been substituted for those of private entrepreneurs.

The third choice available is to steer a middle course between these two extremes. The unions could remain independent and continue to represent labor's interests, getting the wages and working conditions possible through the traditional collective bargaining methods. At the same time they could recognize that, since a Labor government's long-term objectives are presumably in the interests of labor, unions must raise their sights and make their actions conform to goals more distant than short-run partisan objectives. They could allow the right to strike to become dormant. It could be reserved as a potential threat to any antilabor government which might wish to use its power toward ends not commensurate with labor's over-all objectives but not used by unions to wrest economic concessions from each other or from the general public. Labor could, in other words, pursue a course of "enlightened self-interest."

Experience since 1945 indicates that British trade unions are attempting to follow this middle course over the objections of a small but very vocal minority of the workers. The Trades Union Congress as well as the major unions have all officially espoused this position. In many cases, their words have been backed by actions. The National Union of

Mineworkers, for example, has pledged that its members will not tolerate any restriction of work and would cooperate fully in the upgrading and transfer of workers and other schemes to increase labor productivity. The National Federation of Building Operatives, speaking for 1,250,000 construction workers, agreed to use an incentive wage plan to increase productivity although this union has strongly opposed such plans for decades. Other similar examples abound.

In spite of official union recognition of, and action on, their new status, there is not yet much evidence that nationalization has created any definite feeling of partnership in the new public enterprises. To most workers, public boards staffed largely by men who are former owners and managers of the industry do not represent anything very concrete in the way of socialism. This is true even though the boards are not operating for private profit and are subject to policy direction from the government. In some ways the new managements are more remote than the old private ones since, in the case of coal especially, authority is more centralized and the worker finds himself more of a cog in a vast machine than formerly.

The fact is that nationalization has taken place in economic circumstances far different from those in which socialist nationalization policies were first evolved. In those times overproduction, maldistribution, and underconsumption appeared to be the principal defects of capitalism. Socialists had assumed that production problems had been largely solved and that the main problem to be considered was that of securing a better distribution. It was natural to assume that nationalization would immediately improve wages and working conditions. The real problem of the present time is not overproduction but underproduction. Instead of having an easier time, as he expected, the worker in the newly nationalized industries has been asked to work harder and longer than ever before. Since 1945 Britain's principal need has been for more production. Schemes which might have produced a greater measure of worker participation have had to be postponed in the interest of greater efficiency.

GROWING LIMITATIONS ON CORPORATE DOMINANCE

In America, the problems of giant enterprises are being worked out within the framework of private property and profits. The increased collectivization of private business has emphasized the fact that a commercial enterprise is necessarily organized along lines of authority and responsibility which are not at all like those of a democratic government. In a political democracy, needs and wants of people begin at the bottom, are translated into demands and pressures on legislators or government agencies, and are finally expressed as political policies at the top levels of governments and political parties.

In a commercial or industrial enterprise, economic policies are formulated at the top and enforced all the way down through the structure. This is necessary. Efficiency of production and distribution requires that authority and responsibility be concentrated at the top and definitely determined. The commercial enterprise is essentially an autocracy and cannot be anything else if it is to be successfully managed. It can be benevolent but not democratic. If it is to be efficient, it cannot be run by its workers, its customers, or, in the case of large firms, even by its owners.

As long as business enterprises remained small and decentralized, competition prevented the autocratic power required for economic efficiency from being translated into political power and subverting the democratic state. The rise of giant corporations, however, has raised the serious dilemma of private, economic "governments" existing in a democratic political framework and having the power to strongly influence the democratic political government. But the largest corporations of today are now powerful enough to ignore many of the judgments of the competitive market. Like the Treasury, they can control the level of employment in their communities or, collectively, in the country by their price, production, and investment decisions. Like the State Department, they help conduct the nation's foreign relations. Along with the Federal Government itself, they shape the destiny of the country. What are the limits of this power? Fascist and communist efforts to have the state swallow and digest this kind of private economic power have failed either economically, politically, or morally. In the democratic capitalism of the United States, ways are being developed without resort to basic changes in the existing capitalistic institutions of private property and profits.

First, a powerful federal government, particularly the executive and its administrative branches, has arisen partly in direct response to the virtually uncontrolled power which business exercised prior to the Great Depression of the 1930's. Social security and labor legislation, banking, insurance, and securities regulation, enforcement of antitrust laws, and a host of direct controls designed to reduce the power of big business or increase its public responsibility grew out of the depression. Some of the laws and regulations were inconsistent with each other, but one principle underlay most of them. This was that private groups should not again be allowed to escape the social consequences of their economic activities. This principle seems likely to continue to underlie business legislation although not without exceptions.

A second limit to corporate power is organized labor, which has arisen with direct aid from both specific protective legislation and a government-sponsored full employment policy. The legislation has protected labor's constitutional rights, for the most part, and the prosperity has given workers, in general, a sellers' market.

It is debatable which of these conditions, legislation or full employment, has given labor the most power. Legislation has undoubtedly broken the resistance to unionization, but since 1929 unorganized workers have increased their wages by more than union workers, and this has been almost exclusively due to the full employment since 1940. The unskilled (and largely nonunion) workers usually benefit relatively more than skilled union workers in times of labor shortage if only because they were unemployed before the shortage occurred. There is some doubt as to whether union organization has succeeded in raising real wages for its members. Tentative studies seem to show that the share of national income going to all workers is only slightly above what it was fifty years ago.

Undoubtedly the status of many workers has improved immensely as a direct result of unions. There has been a general increase in organized workers' control over working conditions, job security, and protection from employers' arbitrary power and capriciousness. The vast noneconomic improvement in labor status may have more far-reaching consequences on the structure of capitalism than any of the more debatable economic benefits which may have been incurred.

Yet the power of labor is not a completely satisfactory balance to that of business. For one thing, the interest of labor does not completely and necessarily coincide with that of the public although it represents an overwhelming majority of the population. Furthermore, labor's interest is that of a producer, not a consumer. Consequently labor and management may often tacitly combine to share monopoly profits between them at the expense of the more general consumers' interest.

Also that portion of the labor force that is organized and effective as a political and economic force is only about a third of all workers in the United States although it is much higher in some other countries. However, labor leaders are becoming increasingly public minded. Many programs advocated by the AFL-CIO are more in the public interest than in organized labor's interest. For example, if the low rent public housing legislation which labor has fought so long for should ever be enacted, hardly any organized workers would be eligible for it because their incomes are too high. Furthermore, since the labor force represents by far the largest single group of people contributing to the productive process, it follows that the rise of a powerful labor movement has helped to shift the balance of power from a relatively small group of businessmen in the general direction of the public.

A third check on business power is public opinion, which has become more acute and critical in recent years. Many large corporations can hardly move without considering the public relations consequences of their actions. Actually the gold fish bowls which many corporation executives claim to live in may be rather clouded by publicity agents, yes men, and general public ignorance or apathy, but it seems probable that public opinion has become more enlightened and critical in the last twenty-five years. The rise of an enlightened public opinion is partly due to improved public education and educational opportunities. It is also partly due to the rise of large-scale government which, through its multitude of agencies and services, has created a general awareness of government and of what can be secured or accomplished through the use of democratic political procedures. An increasing percentage of the population has come to view the government as a benevolent friend to those in need. Since 1933, all U.S. presidents have tried, and succeeded, in fostering an attitude of personal affection and devotion to the federal government, particularly to the chief executive himself.

Many business executives learned too late that adverse public opinion could be severely damaging. Private power companies have had to endure the enormous growth of rivals in the form of government-financed, cooperatively-owned electrification projects. Even today the threat of furthur government-sponsored competition has caused some electric power companies to make huge investments in rural areas which they otherwise might not have entered at all. The below-market price policy followed by General Motors after World War II, which permitted a black market to develop in their new automobiles, was partly, if not wholly, due to a fear of adverse public opinion which would express itself in congressional investigation, antitrust action, or loss of future sales from consumers' dissatisfaction. Steel production increased over 20 per cent in the five years following President Truman's threat, in 1949, to build government-owned steel mills to alleviate the postwar shortage. No doubt tax concessions in the form of five-year amortization of new plants helped to encourage this increase, but the fear of government competition probably contributed considerably to this expansion of capacity. President Eisenhower also has used the threat of controls in an attempt to induce self-regulation and prevent inflation but with less success.

Because public opinion has become more easily translatable into political action, many corporations have become highly sensitive to criticism. They therefore attempt to forestall government pressures and public antipathy by mobilizing corps of public relations experts, trade associations, and "independent" foundations. These organizations prepare and distribute a flood of advertisements, pamphlets, films, and books designed to enhance the prestige of the particular firms or create a "healthy business climate," meaning, usually, a public attitude of faith in, or at least tolerance of, unrestricted business activities. Most of this literature is highly sophisticated, frequently realistic, and undoubtedly convincing to its readers. Some firms even employ citizens in selected communities to act as anonymous public relations men whose job it is to spread favorable information about the company, dispute any criticisms they may overhear, and report to the company on the attitudes which its policies create.

Significantly, the new look being presented today by large corporations does not claim that the American economy is characterized, in the neoclassical tradition, by small businessmen, none big enough to control their market and competing pricewise for customers. Nor is the manager viewed as a rugged individualist seeking to maximize profits for the firm and its owners. The new competition recognizes the existence of the large firm but pictures the control as being in the hands of a highly efficient team of enlightened business experts who manage the corporation's affairs wisely and fairly in the interests of its customers, owners, workers, and the nation at large. It is contended that these firms pay high wages, provide good working conditions and security, contribute heavily to worthy charities, and patriotically support the nation's best interests.

The new competition is not in price cutting, wage cutting, or trying to eliminate competitors. It is in research, enhancement of quality, and multiplication and improvement of customer services. It is in the use of the most advanced management and production techniques in order to increase productivity, open up new markets, create new products and uses for them, and otherwise gain strategic advantages over rival firms in the industry or in other industries supplying substitute goods. These arguments are convincing but, to the economist, must be considered as further proof that neoclassical price competition is now just so much ancient history. Still they are evidence that public opinion can be a real regulator of business activity unless business can control it first.

A fourth powerful check on the unrestricted exercise of corporate power is the rivalry which exists in oligopoly (see Chapter 8). The hidden hand of price competition, in the classical sense, does not act as an effective restraint on corporate power where there are only a few large firms in an industry. However, a restraint of another kind is likely to exist in the form of rivalry which expresses itself as maneuvering for technological, strategic, or public relations advantages. In an oligopoly, the desire to be the price leader, or the desire to have the largest output in one or more products, may lead firms to seize every technical advantage over their rivals that they can. For example, the frantic attempt of Ford and General Motors to outsell each other in the low price automobile field every month has become largely a struggle to attain what has become a symbol of leadership. This form of rivalry serves the public interest better than the horsepower race which has also developed among the automakers and which seems to contribute more to accidents and expensive maintenance than anything else. This kind of check on corporate power is indirect but nevertheless effective to varying degrees in different industries.

The fifth restraint on corporate power is genuine management enlightenment. While much of the change in management philosophy may be due to pressure from government, labor unions, and public opinion, it is certainly due, in part, to the unique position in which the large firm finds itself. This is not to say that large corporations can develop a soul or a conscience although this possibility is a currently popular speculation. The serious attention being given to the so-called corporate conscience or soul illustrates the danger of explanation by analogy. Corporations cannot possibly have such characteristics although it is sometimes useful to personify corporate behavior for illustrative purposes.

Still, great power has stimulated a growing sense of genuine public responsibility on the part of many of the individuals who are employed in corporate managements. It is possible that some of this responsibility has come from the corporations' own educational programs which were designed, in the beginning, to instruct employees or the public but ended by educating management as well. The sincere belief that unbiased research and free discussion would uphold management's case may well have been responsible for some of the modification of management's position in the last twenty years. Believing that the facts would justify its cause and prepared in advance to accept the results of research, management may have been persuaded by its own efforts.

The change in management's attitude over the past twenty years toward capitalism is indicative of the new enlightenment. In the 1930's American industrialists were almost unanimous in their claim that the New Deal had utterly destroyed the free enterprise system. Shortly after World War II, however, with the New Deal still unrepealed, American industrialists were heartily supporting what they called the existing free enterprise system. The official American policy of the European Cooperation Administration, enthusiastically supported by American industrialists, was to persuade European nations to dismantle their cartels and imitate our vigorous free enterprise economy.

As the units of economic activity in the United States grow bigger and more powerful, Keynes's prediction that the giant firm will socialize itself, making the issue of nationalization irrelevant, seems to be vindicated. Yet the substitution of semipolitical checks and balances for the neoclassical price competition should not be accepted uncritically. The economic system characterized by large, interdependent, collectivized groups rather than small, independent, atomized units needs to be thoroughly and systematically examined, using such relevant economic theory as exists to cope with it. It may or may not be a worthy substitute for traditional, free-market capitalism.

AUTOMATION: THE TWENTIETH-CENTURY INDUSTRIAL REVOLUTION

The economic and technological experience of the last few years has brought forth an unexpected development which may not only lay the Marxian thesis to rest once and for all but could help to pave the way for a single, worldwide economic system in the future. The Marxian view of industrialization was that the advance of machine technology split society into two distinct and irreconcilable classes— capitalists and workers. The experience of the early Industrial Revolution seemed to bear out this thesis. Right up to World War II there continued to be a latent fear that the Marxists might still be right. But the postwar years have done more than merely display the vitality of capitalism. The form which technological development has taken in the last few years holds the promise of converting the tendency of old-style mechanization to draw society into two opposing camps into a tendency toward a dispersion of functional groups. This particular form of industrialization has been called automation.

There are four distinguishable elements of automation, each of which has been erroneously considered to be the essence of automation itself. The first is mechanization. This was the basis of the original Industrial Revolution and consisted of using machinery to replace human or animal muscle, as the steam engine did, or to replace human brainwork at the lower, routine levels, as modern electronic computers do. Because of their compactness, speed, or power machines may often perform tasks which could never be undertaken by human beings alone no matter how well the work was organized and managed.

The second principle of automation is continuous flow or process. This was the basis of the mass production and assembly line techniques developed early in the twentieth century. In many cases, they led to the necessity for a continuous production operation which, because of its high fixed costs, could not be stopped, started, or even slowed down except at great cost.

The third element of automation is the unique feature of feedback, or automatic control, of machine inputs by their own outputs. Called "Detroit automation" by some, this principle has been the basis of electronic, automatic control of conventional assembly-line operations. A simple example is a thermostatically controlled heating system where the temperature operates the thermostat, the thermostat operates the furnace, and the furnace controls the temperature. Machines controlled by the feedback principle can start and stop themselves and regulate the quantity and quality of production automatically.

The fourth principle of automation is rationalization or the application of reason to the solution of problems or to the search for knowledge. In a production system, it means that the entire process from raw material to the final product is carefully analyzed so that every operation can be designed to contribute in the most efficient way to the achievement of the goals of the enterprise.

Following these principles, the direct consequences of

automation, as it advances rapidly in the economic system, can be summarized as follows:

1. Many direct production jobs are abolished. Some businessmen have reported a 25 per cent reduction in direct wages, and in twelve cases of automation studied recently the average reduction in employment was over 63 per cent.[15]

2. A smaller number of newer jobs requiring different, and mostly higher, skills are created. These new jobs include equipment maintenance and design, systems analysis, programming, and engineering.

3. The requirements of some of the remaining jobs are raised. For example, the integration of several formerly separate processes and the enhanced value of the capital investment increase the need for comprehension and farsightedness on the part of management. Also, greatly decreased inventories and more rapid change-over times create tensions which require more alertness and stamina.

4. Production in aggregate and per man hour is enormously increased. The twentieth-century industrial revolution promises to be more humanitarian than that of the nineteenth century. It is not that people are less selfish, but the tremendous capital accumulation already in existence makes it possible to produce far more goods to distribute.

5. The production of new and better goods of more standardized quality becomes possible. However, there may be a loss of variety. Many different models are made possible by combining a few standardized processes in different ways, but, as in automobiles, the final products are still likely to look much alike.

6. There is an increase in the quantity and accuracy of information and the speed with which it is obtained. Management can thus have a clearer picture of its over-all operation, and, by knowing the consequences of alternative courses of action, it can act more rationally.

7. In most cases, a more efficient use is made of all the components of production—labor, capital, natural resources,

[15] David Osborne, *Geographical Features of the Automation of Industry* (Chicago: University of Chicago Press, 1955).

and management. In a few cases, high operating speeds waste materials, but even here the loss is usually justified by saving other resources including time, which is a valuable component of production.

8. Mostly because of high fixed costs, a continuous pace is often set at which the plant must be operated.

9. Industrial location is affected by a shift in labor-oriented industries away from low labor-cost regions for two reasons. First, the smaller labor force reduces the savings from lower wages. Second, there is a smaller wage differential between the skilled workers of different regions than between the unskilled. The more highly skilled workers are likely to be retained if automation is introduced. For example, the new corn products plant at Corpus Christi, Texas, was located in an area which normally would not supply a large skilled labor force. However, since automation reduced the importance of a large labor supply, this plant could be located closer to its markets, sources of raw materials, and fuel.

Automation will probably be limited to industries which now employ only about 25 per cent of the labor force. Because automation creates many new jobs for which the necessary education and training will delay the entry of young people into the labor force, there would appear to be no reason to fear long-run mass unemployment. However, there is no automatic regulator in the economic system that guarantees full employment. Those who disparage fears of technological unemployment usually assume the existence of a perfectly adjusting labor market. Actually there is a real danger that imperfections in the labor market will delay absorption of the displaced workers. The great advantages of automation are likely to be insured only if there is a sustained economic expansion.

It has already been seen that the causes of unemployment are known and the tragedy of depression can be prevented. However, automation makes the need for vigilance all the more imperative because it has unstabilizing effects in the short run just like the original Industrial Revolution had. By greatly increasing the fixed costs of industrial plants and setting a continuous pace at which they must be operated, the adverse consequences of shutdowns are magnified. Unfortunately the very increases in efficiency and technological progress which automation brings are a potential threat to continued stability. Rising living standards permit more consumers to save if they desire. Thus prosperous countries are particularly vulnerable to cyclical changes since an ever greater proportion of consumers' spending is discretionary. It follows that a fairly equalitarian distribution of income is necessary to sustain mass purchasing power. The costs of economic instability are now too great for modern, high speed, industrialized economies to bear, and the public now looks to the central government for protection against what are now known to be the useless wastes of recession or depression.

Automation poses many short-run problems such as worker displacement, hidden downgrading, engineer and technician shortages, industrial location, management philosophy, and personnel relations.[16] The long-run prospects of this kind of technological development are of importance in connection with the evolution of economic systems. Particularly there seems to be a tendency for automation to lead to decline in the proportion of direct production workers and a rise in the proportion of technical, scientific, and other professional people. These professional groups are normally possessed of a middle-class psychology. They may be moderately liberal or conservative in their opinions, seldom going to extremes.

There are other elements leading to an expanding middle class in the long run, of course. Some of them are also due, in part, to automation, such as rapidly rising living standards, which tend to increase the proportionate demand for services and luxury goods over utility goods and necessities. Others may be prerequisite to full utilization of the technology we already have. Among these are both the spreading and in-

---

[16] See the author's articles in *Commercial and Financial Chronicle,* May 19, 1955, pp. 12, 30-31, *Monthly Labor Review,* May, 1955, and *Hearings of the Joint Committee on the Economic Report* (Washington, D.C.: U.S. Government Printing Office, October, 1955).

tensification of education. The lack of adequate education and knowledge is the principal short-run obstacle to both occupational and geographical labor mobility and to psychological adjustment to the new technology. Some factors leading to a growing middle class are not directly related to automation but are products of the same conditions which produced it. Among these are the growth of formal security schemes such as pensions and social legislation, the rise, expansion, and maturity of labor unions, and the adoption of full employment policies and built-in economic stabilizers, such as progressive taxation and unemployment compensation.

An expanding middle class tends toward moderate, middle-of-the-road political policies which reject both the extremes of the left and the right. Hence the similarity between both the platforms and the actual programs of both Democratic and Republican parties in the United States and the Labor and Conservative parties in Britain. The same could be said for most other leading industrial nations.

Whatever the short-run maladjustments and conflicts may be, automation favors the long-run improvements of economic well-being. The second half of the twentieth century seems likely to be dominated by an accelerating worldwide economic expansion carried out largely through gigantic organizations possessing an advanced, seemingly limitless, technology. No traditional theory of capitalism or socialism has so far been able to adequately forecast the consequences of this economic growth although the established theories have all made some valuable contributions. Furthermore, the growth process seems likely to unify the factual bases for all theoretical economic systems. The next chapter will evaluate the contributions of the principal theories of contemporary economic systems. The following, and final, chapter will recognize some of the powerful forces which drive contemporary systems and will venture a guess as to what the future holds for the theory and practice of political economy.

13

Integration of
Theoretical Economic Systems

But, above all, individualism, if it can be purged of its defects and abuses, is the best safeguard of personal liberty . . . being the handmaiden of experiment as well as of tradition and of fancy, it is the most powerful instrument to a better future.——J. M. Keynes

Private enterprise at private risk is a good ship and a ship that has brought us far, but it is a ship for fair weather only.——Sir William Beveridge

SURVIVAL OF THE CLASSICAL SYSTEM

The understanding of the recent spectacular developments in economic institutions is not complete without a system of theories to interpret and rationalize its causes and purposes. Probably the greatest contribution so far has been made by the classical and neoclassical theories which have provided a basic methodology for studying both capitalist and liberal socialist economic systems. Modern economic theory began with the classical vision of a world of perfect competition. Here every man would specialize exclusively in producing what best he could and exchange his products in a competitive market for the many things required to satisfy his wants. It was an abstract model of an ideal society composed of small, free, equal, and independent buyers and sellers. As in geometry, a large number of principles were deduced from a few axioms. Among these axioms are: (1)

that humans are rational beings who take positive action to satisfy their wants; (2) that human wants are insatiable; (3) that goods and the resources to produce them are scarce in relation to these wants (including needs, since a rational person would want what he needs most of all); (4) that in a free market humans would make choices in order to satisfy their wants according to their urgency.

According to some classicists, the whole fabric of economic theory is spun from the axiom of rational human action alone. This methodology has the enormous advantage of emancipating economics from psychology. The only psychology left is the minimum assumption that people have sufficient ability to make the choices that give them the most satisfaction out of a multitude of alternatives. The entire theories of demand and opportunity costs are based on this assumption.

It was necessary, of course, to make simplifying assumptions in order to strip enormously complex economic problems of some of their less essential trappings, to reduce them to a few basic variables and, hence, to manageable proportions. More specifically, in order for the classical theory to be valid for explanation and prediction, it had to be assumed, among other things, that markets are characterized by many small producers and consumers; that all economic units act rationally to maximize their self-interest; that there is perfect knowledge of alternatives; that all resources are highly mobile, flexible, and divisible; that goods and services in each industry are standardized; and that there is a continuing full and stable employment of all resources. Furthermore, many procedural assumptions were usually necessary, such as constancy of expectations, neutrality of money, permanence of institutions, equality of incomes, and so on.

Classicists recognize that these assumptions do not actually describe any real economic system, but it is generally believed that they are not unreasonable and that for procedural purposes they are necessary. From these basic premises, the classicists drew their conclusions about prices, allocation of resources, wages, rents, interest, and profits.

However, since the Great Depression it has become apparent that some of the conditions outlined above are not even approximated in the real world except in some agricultural markets, on organized security and commodity exchanges, and in a few industries like bituminous coal mining and cotton textile manufacturing. In most markets there are too few sellers to insure independent pricing, or lack of knowledge on the part of consumers to make rational choices, or products are highly differentiated. The nearer the market is to the ultimate consumer (as in retail trade) the more suppliers there tend to be but the less standardization of products and the less perfect is the buyers' knowledge and rationality. Conversely, the nearer the market is to the primary producer (as in jobbers' and wholesale markets), the more standardized are the products, the greater is the buyers' knowledge and rationality (since buyers are typically professional purchasing agents for other industrial producers), but the fewer are the sellers in any particular market area. Therefore, the significance of classical theory is subject to some dispute. Although there is fairly general agreement among contemporary economists—in America and Britain at least—that static equilibrium analysis of markets in pure competition has a considerable usefulness there is some difference of opinion as to what use it should be put. Five general classes of thinking can be distinguished here.

One view is that of a small but highly vocal group of extreme right wing economists and political writers. They insist that the assumptions of pure competition present the essential features of the only kind of economic system which will operate automatically and objectively without the control of a dictatorial government. They assert that without pure competition the economy must be "directed" or "planned" and that this interference with the system is incompatible with political freedom. They further argue that the neoclassical analysis can be applied with equal value to any economic system at any time with only minor supplements or modifications for institutional or historical differences. Because they often implicitly assume that only one condition or assumption varies at a time, they insist that the same theory can be applied with equal success to all kinds of different situations. Ordinarily any government influence on the framework of the economy, whether through fiscal policy, social security, or market restrictions, is considered by this group as a peril to human freedom and individualism.

Some of the more rigorous and uncompromising logicians of this faction, such as Ludwig von Mises, Frederick von Hayek, and Henry Hazlitt, the well-known journalist, deny the existence of any "middle way" between atomistic competition on the one hand and a centrally directed, dictatorial state on the other.[1] Typically their arguments are couched in vague terms which permit escape from the dilemma which the demand for security creates in a democratic, capitalist economy. Members of this sect often maintain that production and distribution are, in reality, highly competitive in the classical sense. They typically claim that they favor anti-trust laws yet show little interest in anything more than token enforcement. While ardently defending most big business activities, they usually condemn labor unions and government-sponsored security and welfare schemes as destructive of the competitive system and political democracy as well. Consequently, they do not seem to object to strict and detailed regulation of labor as long as business is left free from government controls. The inherent inconsistencies in this viewpoint have tended to limit its popularity as our population has become better educated and grown more intellectually mature.

A second view of the neoclassical economic system is held by more moderate, but conservative, reformers who believe that pure competition describes an ideal economy and that the theory must be followed by economic and social reform. This is better known as the traditional, or nine-

[1] F. A. von Hayek, *The Road to Serfdom* (Chicago: The University of Chicago Press, 1944); Ludwig von Mises, *Socialism* (New Haven: Yale University Press, 1951) and *The Anti-Capitalist Mentality* (New York: D. Van Nostrand Co., Inc., 1956). These are good examples of the view of this group.

teenth-century, liberal view. All of this group distrusts organized or concentrated power, whether of government, business, or labor. In general they favor a reduction of government controls including tariffs and subsidies. Many advocate dissolving large corporations, abolishing industry-wide collective bargaining, farm price supports, and vigorous antitrust action. The late Henry Simons, who was the most outstanding representative of this view, insisted that the role of government should be (1) to maintain active competition wherever possible and (2) to own and operate directly those industries which were inherently monopolistic. To enforce competition he advocated federal incorporation, an upper limit on assets, reduction of corporate securities to two types to minimize hidden control, and prohibition of holding companies, interlocking directorates, and industry domination by any firm.[2]

Another provocative contemporary economist who falls in this general group is David McCord Wright. Although he advocates some of the same contradictions as Mises and Hayek, condemning even the most modest government and labor welfare and stability programs while defending many forms of business restrictionism as necessary to stabilize capitalism, he nevertheless emphasizes perhaps the most crucial element which competitive capitalism requires—flexibility. In numerous books and articles, of which a recent volume called *Capitalism* is typical,[3] Wright has maintained, correctly, that prices, wages, and production must be free to fluctuate if necessary economic adjustments are to be made. Unfortunately, his policy recommendations are more provocative than precise. Without defining his terms very specifically, he seems to conclude that "planning" is bad when undertaken by government but good and necessary when done by businessmen. His influence has been based more on his critical insights into the dangers inherent in the institutionalizing of opportunities and incentives and the

[2] Henry Simons, *Economic Policy for a Free Society* (Chicago: The University of Chicago Press, 1944).

[3] Wright, *Capitalism* (New York: McGraw-Hill Book Co., Inc., 1951).

pitfalls of government planning than on any bold new program for restoring competitive capitalism. This view, as well as the more extreme ones of Mises, Hayek, and Hazlitt, has lost much of its influence in recent years as it has become obvious that no large, interdependent economy like the United States can be expected to remain balanced at stable, full employment without any substantial government influence.

A third view of the usefulness of competitive analysis of the economic system is that of left wing reformers who believe that the competitive ideal should be made the basis for liberal socialism. Oskar Lange and others have developed this idea which was discussed at length in Chapter 10.

A fourth view is that of some mathematical economists who hold that the assumptions of pure competition are set up in order to make use of a mathematical method. They believe that economics can become an exact science through the use of mathematics and that the neoclassical system is best suited to this kind of analysis. From this it would appear that they are more interested in the method than in the validity of the results. Nevertheless there promises to be a large, and probably fruitful, expansion of this kind of economic analysis in the future as electronic computers make possible the solution of many theoretical economic problems. Already much mathematical analysis based on the neoclassical system is being used, in conjunction with new, experimental evidence, to produce conclusions of great value.

Finally, pure competition is being viewed today by a large and growing group of economists as a norm for action. Without advocating large-scale reform of the entire economy many economists are investigating what might be called "normal" profits, "reasonable" wages, "workable" competition, and so on. Their recommendations for action are often in terms of what should be done if sound economic principles are to be followed. This view recognizes the existence, first, of few firms in most markets, second, of large corporations and unions which cannot be dissolved without the most serious consequences for the economy, and, third, of the demands for social justice through government intervention which are bound to arise in any industrial nation which sponsors free, liberal education and permits democratic political elections.

This last concept of competition seems to be the most useful at the present stage of theoretical attainment and actual economic development. Some of the advocates of "useful," "effective," or "workable" competition have worked out positive programs for maintaining those elements of pure competition which work toward greater efficiency, progressiveness, and justice in the economic system without requiring vast and impractical change in the institutional structures of markets.

Several leading contemporary economists, including J. S. Bain, J. M. Clark, and E. S. Mason, have been concerned with the requirements of a workable competitive capitalist economy. One of the best analyses and statements of policy recommendations has come from Corwin Edwards who was chief economist for the Federal Trade Commission. He outlines the structural characteristics of a market system which will serve the essential *purposes* of neoclassical competition without conforming to the limiting neoclassical assumptions. They are as follows: [4]

1. There must be an appreciable number of sources of supply and an appreciable number of potential customers for substantially the same product or service. Suppliers and customers do not need to be so numerous that each trader is entirely without individual influence, but their number must be great enough that persons on the other side of the market may readily turn away from any particular trader and may find a variety of other alternatives.

2. No trader must be so powerful as to be able to coerce his rivals, nor so large that the remaining traders lack the capacity to take over at least a substantial portion of his trade.

3. Traders must be responsive to incentives of profit and loss; that is, they must not be so large, so diversified, so

devoted to political rather than commercial purposes, so subsidized, or otherwise so unconcerned with results in a particular market that their policies are not affected by ordinary commercial incentives arising out of that market.

4. Matters of commercial policy must be decided by each trader separately without agreement with his rivals.

5. New traders must have opportunity to enter the market without handicap other than that which is automatically created by the fact that others are already well established there.

6. Access by traders on one side of the market to those on the other side of the market must be unimpaired except by obstacles not deliberately introduced, such as distance or ignorance of the available alternatives.

7. There must be no substantial preferential status within the market for any important trader or group of traders on the basis of law, politics, or commercial alliances.

Edwards goes on to analyze most carefully the forms of competition which exist in American industrial markets and proposes the kind of vigorous antitrust program which will have to be pursued if present day "mixed economies" are to be reasonably competitive. Although his program includes extensive patent law reforms and a general tightening of antimonopoly laws and their enforcement in the United States, there is no suggestion of atomizing markets or attempting to return to a system of small-scale enterprises. Edwards' analysis, like that of most other students of American industrial economy, uses neoclassical methodology applied to specific markets and industries but avoids making a general case for neoclassical capitalism.

There are many advantages to the traditional, abstract, static analysis over all other kinds of theory. For one thing it has provided the most scientific method of studying the operation of individual firms and industries within an economic system. It has also been able to explain the internal operation of capitalist enterprises with a fair degree of accuracy. Its methodology lends itself to the exploration of many new and important problems in the study of economic systems. Economic growth and development, for example, can be investigated using classical tools. If knowledge, time, and cultural heritage can be added to the traditional productive factors of land, labor, capital, and entrepreneurship, a whole new approach to the understanding of modern, evolving economic systems is opened up. Likewise, the supply and demand for the most dynamic elements of growth, entrepreneurship, and capital can be explored using basically classical methods of analysis. In addition, the classical analysis has provided a method for studying the structural interrelationships which exist in any economic system. Problems of the mobility of labor and other resources, shortages of particular goods and services, efficiency of production and satisfaction of consumers' desires have all yielded to the neoclassical analysis.

Unfortunately classical economic theory still remains essentially static, being more conducive to the study of structures and their interrelationships. It has not been able to change its original bias toward the physical sciences. Based initially on mechanics, which is only a small part of physics today, it has been limited to a highly abstract, though precise, fragment of the scientific world which can be explained without reference to historical perspective or any dynamic theories of development. This overemphasis on mechanics has limited the classical theory's effectiveness in dealing with a science which is perhaps more biological than physical.

Another objection to classical analysis is that, to many, it seems to be a defense of the status quo. Its greatest men have been, by heritage or sympathy, in the dominant class of industrialists. It has implicitly assumed that there is an industrial culture in which all economic activity is immersed. It has concluded that there is a direct relation between marginal productivity and income received, the implication being that everyone is paid just what he is worth. It has optimistically magnified the harmony between self-interest and public welfare while, at the same time, emphasizing the gloomy Malthusian population theory, the scarcity of resources, the law of diminishing returns, and other pessimistic principles which seem, to some people, to obstruct the unfolding of an abundant economic life. Furthermore, classical theory has remained rigidly neutral as between the goals of society although the ends are partly determined by the means. Hence, the development of the market place and the price system as institutions in themselves has been ignored. In spite of these objections, however, the classical theory is still the accepted, standard theory of studying internal economic relationships even though it is not adequate, by itself, to explain the over-all economic system.

CONTRIBUTIONS OF THE DISSENTERS

THE HISTORICAL SCHOOL. The German historical economists added the dimension of time to the static classical analysis and purged the orthodox theory of some of its more unrealistic assumptions. By analyzing the economic history of capitalism, the more recent historical economists have exposed a fallacy which has been a major stumbling block to understanding contemporary economic systems. Because America, Great Britain, and parts of Europe have experienced industrialization and a growth of capitalism and political democracy, all at the same time, there has long been a tendency to identify these three as being the same thing. Economists who have taken the trouble to study the history of capitalism have been able to show that technology is quite independent of both property institutions and political arrangements although there are significant interrelationships. Any of the three may exist simultaneously, in which case they may reinforce each other, or they may develop independently.

Historical economists, both past and present, have also shown that ethics, sociology, and politics are not easily separable from economics. They have fruitfully investigated the relationships among religious, ethical, and economic behavior. They have shown how capitalism can reduce religion to a kind of personal conduct which is quite distinct from the more important social, political, and economic beliefs and behavior patterns. They have explained, for example, how a man can be required by his religion to be scrupulously honest in dealing with his friends yet will sanction the most outrageous frauds when they are directed against the general public, the government, or even specific competitors. Capitalism may permit life to be viewed steadily and complacently but seldom consistently or as a whole.

Nevertheless, the English classicists were moving toward what the historical economist Tawney considered to be a truly Christian way of life. Carlyle's cries for hard work as an end in itself and Ruskin's and Morris' concept of work-pleasure show that the idea of something spiritual was beginning to reappear by the late nineteenth century. History since the rise of modern capitalism has shown that individualism not guided by some kind of religion is likely to become ruthless and dictatorial. The Nazis proved this. The current problem is to control individualism without sacrificing the dignity of the individual. Economic systems which destroy individual dignity and attempt to substitute worship of the state or some leader for religion and God inevitably become totalitarian. Or at least they have so far.

Thus one of the basic problems today is a spiritual or religious one. Somehow men must be taught to subordinate and control their acquisitive instincts, to live for others, to work for more than themselves. We can no more return to an imaginary medieval period than we can ignore modern science and technology. A system of values must be created in which material advantages are made to minister to higher needs. This may be capitalism's greatest failure so far. The historical economics has contributed to the solution of this perplexing dilemma by exposing the origins of contemporary economic theory and stressing their relationships to the present. So far, historical economists have been forced to rely on inadequate data to supplement theories which have too many variables. Their results have been highly suggestive, enriching, and sobering since no contemporary economic, social, or political problem can be appreciated apart from its historical context. But the conclusions, unfortunately, have been too vague and generalized to be useful for basing any systematic theory of contemporary economic systems.

INSTITUTIONALISM. The most original departure in economic theory in the last century was institutionalism. The institutionalists provided an extremely valuable insight into contemporary economic systems. Veblen's emphasis on the social and cultural framework of capitalism has sustained the case method which has proved so useful in some areas of applied economic study such as labor relations, industrial organization, and, to some extent, pricing and production decision in monopoly and oligopoly. Veblen's "leisure class" and "conspicuous consumption" concepts, though now somewhat obsolete, have been useful in reorienting neoclassical demand theory toward more realistic situations. Since many people seem to prefer or aspire to leisure class status, with its consequent luxuries and wastefulness, an avenue is opened by institutionalism for explaining the omnipresent nonprice competition. Although modern consumer behavior may be explainable more as a result of the commercial environment, with its predominance of advertising, rather than as anything instinctual, it still yields to institutionalist analysis. Gadgets, advertised reputations, or even positive uselessness from articles are frequently demanded by consumers for prestige reasons alone. Nor have producers been reluctant to exploit these potential markets. As George Herbert wrote over three hundred years ago, "The buyer needs a hundred eyes; the seller needs not one."

Veblen's theory of capitalism has also been a useful model for more recent economists although some current trends seem to indicate conclusions far different from those foreseen by the early institutionalists. Veblen conceived of industrial capitalism as a whirlpool with centripetal forces drawing the more competitive industries at the edge toward the monopolistic core. It is possible that the framework of this model might be more appropriately used today with the forces in reverse. In the central core are still the "natural" monopolies of power, transportation, and communication and the other "public interest" industries like banking and insurance. But most of the great, dynamic economic activity and growth is no longer here. Interest and importance has shifted to the rim where innovation, diversification, "spinoffs" of unprofitable lines, and rapid expansion from profits have captured the imagination. Of course, it can be argued that corporate giantism has emerged here also and that competition has declined. To offset this, however, it can be shown that in the so-called monopolistic core, inter-industry competition has grown and intensified as product substitution has become effective. Coal, oil, and electricity are all striving for a larger share of the total power market, and railroads have fought a losing battle with airlines, trucks, and automobiles.

The Australian economist, Colin Clark, has proposed a theory of economic development in which a nation is thought to go through three successive stages of growth similar to the three rings of Veblen's whirlpool of economic activity. This theory is also reminiscent of Sombart's theory of capitalist growth. As in Veblen's monopolistic core, Clark says the first stage of a nation's industrialization is in the construction and development of its utilities, transportation system, and financial networks. With these established, heavy industry will be developed next. Finally, after the basic mining, metal, and fabrication industries are developed, consumer goods industries will arise. Thus, what appeared to Veblen to be three types of economic activity (monopolistic, semimonopolistic, and competitive) existing simultaneously were held by Clark to be the major characteristics of capitalism at three different stages of its development. To Veblen and the institutionalists, some kind of social control by government would seem to be required to protect the public from the inevitable growth of monopolies. Following Clark's logic, competition could be relied on to an ever-larger degree since the competitive area would be growing and the monopolistic area declining in relative importance.

Contemporary American experience seems to bear out Clark's thesis to a considerable extent and suggests, possibly, a fourth stage of growth in which services of all kinds may emerge to dominate. Although manufacturing may still be in the ascendency, since total production employment recently surpassed that of service trades, service employment is now half of all U.S. employment compared with a fifth in 1870.[5] And it is apparently growing proportionally. Even the gigantic automobile industry may be yielding its dominance to the new service stage as America's large middle class begins to command enough income to afford the trimmings as well as the cake.

If capitalism enters a stage in which consumers' goods and services play the major role, the institutional economics could acquire a new significance. One of the most serious indictments against the classical economics has been that the theory of demand requires consumers to be rational and have full knowledge of alternatives. In spite of a strong trend toward greater rationalism and knowledge in business, labor, and government, consumers seem farther from attaining these than ever. The enormous variety of goods and services facing the consumer, and the ever-greater emphasis on nonprice competition, such as product differentiation, advertising, guarantees, fancy packaging, and so on—not to mention the fabulous growth of credit terms which often obscure the real price altogether—makes rational purchasing by consumers extremely difficult. Here the institutionalists, with their emphasis on habits, customs, "prestige" motives, and imitation of others, may have pointed to the greatest factor preventing the capitalistic system from attaining its classical objectives of maximum consumers' welfare and rational resource allocation.

The institutionalists conceived of man as being dominated in large measure by his society and, hence, not responsible for a considerable portion of his actions. They tended to think of the human mind not as a machine for calculating utilities and costs, or disutilities, but as an experimental de-

[5] G. J. Stigler, "Trends in Employment in the Service Industries," National Bureau of Economic Research (1956).

vice which made adjustments to ever-changing economic data. "Rationality" was relative to the social environment.

Certainly there is a basis for the belief that human behavior is, at least in part, culturally determined in the modern world of mass propaganda where radio, television, moving pictures, newspapers, and magazines do much of our thinking for us. These media predigest not only the events of the world but the opinions which might otherwise follow from an observation of these events. In this kind of world, where a fad may break out like an epidemic of measles, it becomes increasingly difficult to think independently. Mass media of information, like narcotics, create a tolerance so that increased dosages can be taken. Among the basic principles of advertising, apparently, are repetition (however obnoxious) and association (however far-fetched). Through application of these two principles the desired idea may be either drummed into the reluctant brain by force or sneaked in through association with pleasant experiences. Thus, ideas infiltrate the mind unconsciously, and we tend to hold opinions the source of which could never be traced.

Several distinguished institutionalists proposed remedies to meet the apparent inadequacy of classical competition. John R. Commons, probably the most constructive of the earlier institutionalists, advocated the establishment of administrative commissions to regulate economic activity. One form of government participation was in solving industrial disputes, and Commons favored the establishment of state and federal industrial commissions having industry, labor, and government advisory councils. These commissions would be executive, not policy-making. Their principal functions would be administering labor laws and mediating industrial disputes.

Commons based these arguments on what he called a "public utility theory of labor." Labor was not an impersonal commodity to be sold in the market but was a "public utility" in which the entire community had a vital interest. If the general public developed a feeling of responsibility for good working conditions and labor security, particularly if employers would treat labor as an overhead cost to the firm and the community, then industrial conflict would tend to disappear and government intervention would no longer be necessary. He further felt that laborers acquire rights in their jobs. These grow out of custom since this is the way in which property rights have normally evolved.

Believing that one of man's prime motivating forces was a quest for security, Commons observed that workers are often deprived of the security enjoyed by some other groups because of price fluctuations. He advocated state-encouraged pension and unemployment plans to mitigate the disastrous effects of business cycles on wage earners. Eventually he extended his interests into the field of monetary policy and business cycles because of the effect which they have on the welfare of labor. In Wisconsin, Commons anticipated, and actively promoted, the growth of administrative law and procedure. The widespread use of the administrative commission today is a tribute to much of Commons' early research and analysis. To Commons, the traditional separation of executive, legislative, and judicial powers was inadequate for governing an economy dominated by giant corporate enterprises and powerful unions. Commissions combining all three functions were necessary because of the multiplicity of conflicts between groups that require settlement on the basis of facts. A regulatory agency must have jurisdiction and competence equal to the situation which it is to control. Without destroying the safeguards of legal process, commissions composed of experts and having the authority to make rules (legislative), enforce them (executive), and penalize offenders (judiciary) must be substituted for the lower court. Appeals to the regular judicial process are always retained, and ultimate legislative and executive control over the commissions remain, but within the area of the technical problems of the industry the commission should prevail, according to Commons.

Another institutionalist, Gardner Means, saw the possibilities of social control through many devices depending on the individual need. For example, public ownership of industry could be utilized in some cases where high fixed costs or great public need existed—such as electric power production or low-cost housing—although he recognized that public ownership would not avoid the inflexibilities of private monopolies. The government might control without ownership in some cases, or control over-all prices through commissions, although Means recognized some of the drawbacks of direct price and allocation controls. His principal solution looked toward a broad program of economic planning to be executed through financial controls applied at certain strategic points to insure the proper functioning of the economic system. Particularly he favored government direction of new capital into desired industries and localities.

How to achieve a proper social control of the economy is one of the most burning issues today, and the ideas of the institutionalists will probably form the basis of most new government control programs, even though these origins may not be recognized. The time lag between the inception of an idea and its final fruition is sometimes measured in centuries. Certainly governments, and organized private groups, seeking economic controls in the last half of the twentieth century, will have to rely heavily on the ideas of the institutionalists some of which were advanced decades ahead of their time.

MARXISM. The Marxian theory of capitalism is so hopelessly obsolete that it is finally being openly criticized by professed Marxists in the satellite countries and even in the Soviet Union itself. Marx based his theory of capitalism on the Hegelian dialectic, the economic interpretation of history, and the theory of surplus value. He condemned the private-property basis for capitalism because it was the means of extracting surplus value from labor. The inherent contradictions of capitalism produced an inevitable conflict which culminated in a revolution out of which socialism would automatically result. This historical necessity of socialism was based on a tacit definition of capitalism as a system of absolute private-property rights. The Marxian logic asserted the inevitability of the destruction of these rights. Socialism was then assumed to be a system in which these rights no longer existed. Thus, the inevitability of socialism could be easily demonstrated. Obviously such a definition of socialism as the Marxists implied was inadequate. It is of no use to think of socialism as the negative of absolute property rights or as the negative, opposite, absence, or even the modification of pure capitalism. It requires a positive definition which Marxists have never given it.

Any reasonable comparison of the contemporary economies professing to be based on Marxist theory with those which are not only proves with facts what can be deduced by theory. This is that even though Marxism might have been relevant to nineteenth-century European capitalism, it is surely not relevant to anything today. Unfortunately for the Marxists, they created a political environment in which free discussion could not occur and, hence, economic theory could not develop. The result has been that their theory is nearly one hundred years behind the times. All the major conclusions—the increasing misery of the working class in capitalist countries, recurring and increasingly severe crises, imperialism, and ultimate revolution—have proven to be wrong.

But, discredited as it is in scholarly circles, one underlying principle of Marxism has survived and may be of increasing significance in the future. This is the theory that economic forces determine the course of historical development. In spite of the bankruptcy of modern Marxist thought, the idea that the means of making a living underlies other current events is becoming more pertinent as industrialization and rationalism spread throughout the world. Although technology and the "means of production" do not control history to the exclusion of social, cultural, religious, and other forces, the events of recent years strongly suggest that economics is the dominating force making for social and cultural changes. It is still the source of income which molds the individual's character more than any other single thing. For example, the changing political and cultural patterns in the South of the United States indicates that the consequences of industrialization can overcome long-established customs and traditions in a relatively short time. Industrialization may be a major force leading to an integration of economic systems all over the world. Of course other forces may interfere for a time, but the economic force continues relentlessly in the background.

The real tragedy of Marxism lies in its ossification into an extremely rigid theoretical system. Its main elements, such as the labor theory of value, the theory of surplus value, the economic theory of history, the doctrine of the class struggle, and the theory of imperialism, should have developed into highly refined analytical tools. Instead they grew into a fixed and dogmatic system which now only describes, with continually declining accuracy, the ever-changing world. This theoretical system has degenerated even further into a social myth which, because it transcends economics and embraces all social phenomena, has stirred millions of people to blind, passionate allegiance. Its tremendous emotional appeal is not due to the remnants of logic which cling to it but is due, precisely, to its irrationality, its dogmatism, and its incomprehensibility.

The only way to combat the cancerous growth of this philosophy is to transcend it with a more realistic and flexible science of society which accounts for all major economic, social, political, and historical interconnections. Capitalism's superior efficiency and higher living standards will win it many new subjects but not many new converts. Capitalism's main deficiency has been its inability to justify itself philosophically and culturally in terms of basic human values. Economically and statistically it has proved itself, but man does not live by bread alone. Marxism has done no better (in fact it has done much worse) in terms of material accomplishments in those places where portions of it have been tried out. But the irrational hope which it holds out to its believers has not been matched by any capitalist theory.

KEYNESIAN ORTHODOXY—
THE NEW VIEW OF THE NATIONAL DEBT

Probably the greatest contribution of the Keynesian theory has been that it shifted the center of interest in economics from prices and resource allocation to the problems of full employment, prosperity, and depression. The theory demonstrated that policies that would have one effect under full employment could have precisely the opposite effect in depression. The point (now considered a fairly broad area or range) of full employment is like the looking glass which Alice stepped through. All the rules of logic and order are different on the other side. Thus, reducing taxes or increasing government spending which results in a fiscal deficit causes an inflation in prices under full employment (since production cannot increase to offset the increase in spending) while the same policies in depression have little effect on prices but rather tend to increase output and employment.

While the modern world has not swallowed all the conclusions of the implied Keynesian theory of capitalism, it has clearly accepted the Keynesian framework for looking at economic problems and the Keynesian methodology for attacking them. The positive theory of employment, which is best classified as being both an underinvestment and an underconsumption theory, has become a new orthodoxy in itself. It both explains and justifies the considerable income redistribution which has taken place since the 1930's. In the United States the top 5 per cent of the population now receives after taxes only about 18 per cent of the income compared with 34 per cent in 1929. The top 1 per cent receives after taxes about 8 per cent of the income compared with almost 20 per cent in 1929. The redistribution has been much more marked in Great Britain.

Most of the Keynesian reorientation of economic thinking has centered about the federal budget and, in general, the role of the government in the area of fiscal policy. This change of thinking has exposed several fallacies in traditional attitudes toward the national debt.

The first fallacy is the idea that the government is just like a private business or household and, thus, the national debt is no different from a business or personal debt. Practically all professional economists today would agree that the national debt cannot be thought of in terms of private debt. Without minimizing the great importance of the debt it should be remembered that it is not owed to "outsiders" but is owed by the nation to some of its own citizens who are bondholders. This debt is both a safe and useful investment and a required basis for our monetary and credit system. Since the debt, both interest and principal, must be paid by taxpayers, higher income groups make most of the payment. However, these same groups also own most of the bonds so they are, in part, paying themselves. Nevertheless, a national debt should never be repudiated even if constitutionally possible because this would destroy all confidence in the monetary system and make further credit transactions impossible. Repudiation of the debt would not affect everyone equally. Like nearly every economic policy or legislative act it would benefit some people (in this case, taxpayers who own no bonds) and injure others (in this case, bondholders).

A second fallacy is that the debt cannot go much higher without national bankruptcy. This was a popular notion in the 1930's when reputable bankers predicted that if the U.S. debt ever reached $60 billion the country would be bankrupt. The debt is now nearly five times that much and most economists agree that the nation is in healthier condition than in the 1930's. For one thing there is no danger that the government will "go bankrupt" in the usual sense of the term. The United States government has never defaulted on any of its obligations and, of course, never will since it can always sell new bonds to the banks to get funds with which to pay the interest and principle on the debt. Failing here, it could raise taxes or even print money to pay the debt. Printing money or selling bonds in excess of tax receipts could lead to a disastrous inflation if output did not increase accordingly, but this is still not bankruptcy in the ordinary sense of the term.

Furthermore, it is not the amount of the debt but the relative difficulty of paying the interest which is important. In 1939, the total interest payments amounted to less than 1½ per cent of the national income. Today, with the debt approximately equal to one year's income, the interest is a little less than 3 per cent of the national income. But because living standards are so much higher now than in 1939, Americans can actually afford to pay 3 per cent of the national income in interest more easily than 1½ per cent in 1939 when living standards were lower. Furthermore, interest and principle payments on the national debt are paid to citizens and domestic corporations who hold the bonds and are thus benefited.

Of course, the debt could go so high that there would be a substantial portion of the population living on the interest from their bonds and who would have little incentive to work. Modern democratic governments, by attempting to destroy the old "unproductive" class of private lenders and bondholders could end up substituting a new class of government securityholders in its place. At the same time tax rates would have to be so high to pay this interest that taxpayers would get discouraged and also lose incentive to work and invest.

So far, the evidence of the effects of taxation on incentive are inconclusive. Extremely high progressive income taxes in Great Britain have caused some workers to shun Saturday shifts, even with overtime pay. On the other hand, the high marginal rates have not stopped some of the high-income producers but may have stimulated them to produce more to keep their incomes up. For example, Alec Guinness, the famous British movie star, makes more pictures than most Hollywood actors and acts on the stage simultaneously.

Personal income taxes are higher in Canada than in the United States, yet Canada is surging ahead industrially. But corporate income taxes in Canada are lower. Income tax laws in the United States discriminate against professional people, like writers, whose income (if any) comes in lumps, being very low in some years and high in others. On the other hand, there are many loopholes for these and other independent businessmen for making income look like capital gains, which are taxed at a lower rate in the United States and not at all in Great Britain. Thus, the score is nothing to nothing as far as any positive proof of the over-all effects of high taxes on incentives is concerned.

Considering the gigantic corporate expansion programs of recent years and the ever-rising rates of production and productivity, it is hard to believe that investment has been stifled as yet by the near-record heights of current tax rates. A recent Harvard Business School study shows that rich people are able to keep their tax rate down to about 50 per cent on the average and that since tax rates on capital gains are so much lower than income tax rates, many wealthier investors are stimulated to support promising new ventures.[6] It is suggested that high income taxes thus actually *increase* the risk capital available.

Of course, high taxes will destroy, by degrees, the incentive to work, but there is no single point when taxes or government expenditures get so high that private production stops. There are some people who like to work and probably would continue to work if all their additional income were taxed away. There are others who would not work if they had to pay any direct taxes at all. These probably would like some excuse for idleness anyhow. Most people fall somewhere between these two extremes, and no single level of debt or tax rates will affect them all alike. Nevertheless, there is a real danger that high tax rates could affect a large enough portion of the population to cause productivity and expansion to decline. Then tax cuts could

[6] J. K. Butters, L. E. Thompson, and L. L. Bollinger, *Effects of Taxation* (Cambridge: Harvard University Press, 1953).

well be used to provide the incentive to stimulate production.

A third fallacy is that the national debt shifts the burden to our grandchildren. Our grandchildren will have to pay the debt if it is to be paid at all, but the payment will be *to* our grandchildren as well since those who inherit the bonds will be paid by taxpayers in general, including themselves. The national debt does not permit anyone to consume more than his income temporarily like a private debt does. The goods which are consumed, or used for defense or other purposes, must first be produced by the same nation which has borrowed from its citizens to pay for them. The people who "did without" during the war (due to scarcities) were producing more than they consumed so that the armed forces could use these goods to conduct the war. In total, we did not have the use of more goods than we produced. Likewise, paying off the debt will not force the nation to consume less than it produces, as a private debtor would have to do, since the payments would force some taxpayers to consume less than their regular incomes. Interest and principal payments on the debt are not losses to the economy since they stay inside as someone else's income.

Although the debt is undoubtedly too high, there is some question as to how far and fast it should be reduced. Most of the debt is in the form of bonds which are owned by banks, insurance companies, large business corporations, and federal agencies for investment purposes, such as corporate building funds or the social security reserve. These creditors are not anxious to give up "riskless" securities which now pay about 3 per cent interest in the United States. Once when the French government borrowed funds, the banks refused to lend until the government promised never to repay the debt. Likewise, the British government is still paying interest on debts incurred during the Napoleonic Wars. In the U.S., the national debt forms the basis for the money and credit system since government bonds make up most of the legal reserves of commercial banks.

A fourth fallacy is the idea that it is dangerous for the government to borrow in order to pay interest. This fallacy lies in a misunderstanding of accounting. There is no real difference between using tax revenues to pay interest while borrowing to meet other expenses and using tax revenues for other expenses and borrowing to pay interest. The important thing is whether total expenses exceed total tax revenues or not.

The Keynesian system showed that there is a direct relationship between the government surplus or deficit and the level of prices and production. Increases in the national debt (deficits) are inflationary, and decreases (surpluses) are deflationary. The government borrows by selling bonds to banks or individuals. If the new bonds are sold to banks, the banks make new checking accounts for the government, in payment, and these accounts, since they can be used like money, increase the total amount of purchasing power in use without increasing the amount of goods produced. Thus the government, using this "new" money, competes with individuals for the purchase of existing goods, and the prices of these goods tend to rise. This causes pressure for wage increases, and the deflationary spiral has begun.

Conversely a budgetary surplus means that the government revenues have exceeded expenditures, and consequently more government bonds have been retired than issued. Thus, the amount of purchasing power in the country has declined, and there will tend to be a fall in prices in the more competitive industries and a fall in production and employment in the more monopolistic industries.

Clearly the budget should be balanced over the long run, though not necessarily annually, and the debt should be reduced by government surpluses in times of prosperity such as most of the world has enjoyed since 1945. Canada and England have had budget surpluses since the war, and these have helped to combat inflation by reducing purchasing power. Furthermore, it is much easier to pay off the debt in prosperity when incomes and profits, and hence tax revenues, are high and taxes are more easily collected. But the debt can be reduced in only two ways—less government spending or higher taxes. In 1956, about 20 per cent of all production was sold to the U.S. government. This is in contrast with 5 per cent in 1939 and 1 per cent in 1929. About 84 per cent of government spending now goes for either defense purposes or to pay for past wars (interest, veterans' benefits, etc.). Thus, any substantial reduction of the national debt must involve cutting the defense program or raising taxes. If we cannot bring ourselves to accept either of these unhappy alternatives, then we should be prepared for the consequences of a continually rising national debt. From a practical point of view, modern war and defense conditions have made any substantial reduction of the national debt extremely unlikely. The new view of the national debt, which Keynesian economics has encouraged, merely permits an easier rationalization of doing what we would be forced to do anyhow.

All this government spending, assuming that it will be required permanently for defense or full employment purposes, leads to three serious consequences. First, a slow, long-term inflation can be expected if the budget remains unbalanced. To Keynes this was at least better than deflation because it strengthened the "productive" classes (capitalists and workers) at the expense of "unproductive" old people (who were to be provided for by extensive social security) and idle lending and landowning classes who were assumed to be of no particular benefit to the economy anyhow. In any event, a gradual inflation has accompanied every prosperous period in history, and prices have been rising almost without interruption since the beginning of the Industrial Revolution.

Second, the expanding role of government in the investment field could lead to excessive centralization of governmental functions and growing opportunities for corruption. Keynes felt, however, that decentralization could be secured through government investment in local and regional semiautonomous authorities and corruption could be guarded against if the public was sufficiently enlightened.

Third, Keynesian fiscal policy tools in the hands of a nationalistic government could lead to expenditures on armaments rather than public works and social services. Furthermore, a nationalistic government could, with perfect justification, use Keynesian fiscal policy measures for imperialistic ends. Hjalmar Schacht, the famous German finance minister under Hitler, attempted this kind of policy. This is a serious deficiency for the Keynesian fiscal policy for there is no safeguard against excessive nationalism even after the experience of World War II. But if full employment could once be obtained throughout the world, there would be less nationalistic pressure to "export" unemployment to other nations by tariffs on imports and by dumping goods abroad at low prices. The neoclassical economics was international and as such was at variance with many of the conditions which lead to wars while Keynesian economics makes possible some justification of nationalism. Yet Keynesian economics attacks one of the principal causes of violence, revolution, and war—unemployment. The minor nationalistic implications of Keynesian economics can easily be overstated and unnecessary fears engendered. After all, the most internationalistic of all economic doctrines, *in theory*, was Marxism.

BIG BUSINESS THEORY

The experience of recent years with big business monopolies and oligopolies indicates that the traditional classical assumptions regarding typical and predictable behavior of entrepreneurs and firms does not fit the most important of modern capitalist enterprises. Equilibrium prices and outputs have not emerged, and noneconomic variables seem to be playing an ever-increasing role. Today, relevant economic analysis must be concerned with the adjustment by a few giant firms to changing market conditions, and this involves much more than simple supply and demand analysis. It must include such factors as cost and demand structures of individual firms, market shares, sales outlay, long-run growth, security of capital investment, and many others. The large firm is able to manipulate the very factors which are either held constant or used to determine and predict firm behavior by traditional theory. Thus classical competitive assumptions offer few guideposts for predicting big business behavior. What is needed is a big business theory which is as firmly rooted in twentieth-century life as classical economics was rooted in the nineteenth-century world.

The failure of traditional theory, when applied to oligopoly, is due in part to the retaliatory powers of large firms. By changing any or all market variables themselves, in response to similar actions by rivals, large firms may engage in a wide variety of types of behavior. Prediction of what they may do next is impossible with present techniques. Even the entrepreneurs' motives may change from short- to long-run profit maximization and his attitude, from defensiveness to aggressiveness or from optimism to pessimism. His pattern of action may vary from rational to irrational, and he may seek solutions to his economic problems through political influence.

The inability of traditional price theory to handle these problems so far does not mean that all future attempts will be futile. Nor does it mean that a general theory of capitalism is forever impossible or that, if possible, it cannot rest on a theory of big business pricing and production. But it does mean that a much broader approach to price theory will have to be undertaken and perhaps some new avenues explored.

Several factors which had been reduced to simple dogmatism or assumed away by the classical economists need further study if a realistic price theory for modern capitalism is to be developed. Businessmen's motivations are more complex than was once thought. They may be based on some combination of short-run and long-run profit maximization, security of status, protection of the firm's investment, revenge, power, political advantage, prestige, and so on. The ability to predict a firm's economic behavior depends on the accuracy of the relative weights given to the factors of managerial motivation.

An institutional analysis of sorts is almost imperative in the study of big firms. Price, wage, and production patterns are often determined, in final practice, largely by tradition and custom even though the top management may not be aware of it. Supply, demand, or costs may play little or no role at all in determining the division of the market among firms. Sometimes a defensive philosophy of "live and let live" precludes almost any competition at all.

Maximization of profits may be more complete in a large, departmentalized firm than in a small or one-man firm. Many lower-level executives with moderate discretion could maximize small increments of the firm's income over its expenses in order to win prestige or promotion even where they do not share directly in the firm's profits. Competition within the firm (among salesmen, for example) could result in total profit maximization although the resulting allocation of resources would not necessarily follow the rational pattern which it would under neoclassical competition.

On the other hand, recent expert analysis casts doubt on profit maximizing in large firms. Corporate executives, it is claimed, are supposed to avoid maximizing profits but to attain some "satisfactory" profit level. Charging what the traffic will bear or letting the buyer beware are said to be obsolete practices.[7]

The managers, who get salaries, are now separate from the corporation, which gets the profits (but which has no motives or desires), and from the stockholders, who are not even supposed to know what is going on. Management itself is frequently extremely public spirited and/or inefficient. In either case, the highest possible profits are not being pursued or obtained. It is not possible to generalize about profit maximization in large corporations as yet. There

[7] Maurer, *op. cit.*

do not seem to be enough similarities in the behavior of corporate executives to permit basic psychological assumptions to be made. It will require some consistent corporation rationale before any new specific big business theory can be built. Much empirical study is still needed and, perhaps most of all, some new theories which will embrace group decision-making, corporate bureaucracy, economic and non-economic motives of executives, and the long-run profit test. Unfortunately institutional economic theory has not yet provided the specific tools of analysis for this task although there is reason to believe that it is not inherently incapable of doing so. Many economists are turning to institutional techniques although perhaps not consciously so.

Likewise, game and strategy theory and other mathematical approaches to oligopoly have added little to economic theory so far. Probably the development of any precise and quantitative analysis will contribute more to the theories of national income and employment or national economic planning (where large aggregates permit probability analysis to be used effectively) than to price and production theory where oligopoly has congealed the market system into a few large, but relatively disconnected, power structure entities.

The conspicuous failure of Marxist and other socialist theories to analyze American capitalism accurately has been partly due to the mistaken belief that big business, organized labor, and government are homogeneous groups which react similarly to similar stimuli. In fact, the "government" may be a rural sheriff's reign of terror, a state social worker's tireless devotion to the cause of mercy and charity, or the huge, benign but impersonal bureaucracy of a federal agency. "Labor" may be the aggressive auto workers, the highly conservative printers, or unorganized fruit pickers who have no apparent aims at all. "Business" may be a sprawling politico-economic institution such as General Motors, a gossipy corner druggist, a corrupt state road contractor, or an aggressive manufacturer's agent. It is often said that America's greatness lies in its diversity. American capitalism's resistance to theoretical explanation lies in this same diversity and has forced statesmen and business leaders to govern through the application of rules of thumb and pragmatism rather than to consciously rely very much on abstract price and production theories. Nevertheless, the relative success and popularity which have been enjoyed by the Keynesian and other "aggregate" economic theories continue to inspire many hopefuls to work for the same results from theories of market behavior. Perhaps the very complexity of the problems creates a challenge in itself.

DECLINE OF SOCIALIST THEORY

OBSOLESCENCE OF LIBERAL SOCIALISM. In Chapter 1 five goals of any economic system were set forth. These were optimum employment, stability, consumers' welfare, efficiency, and progressiveness. Several theoretical systems of capitalism and socialism have been advanced to accomplish these same objectives. Every theory considered in this study has sought to achieve these goals although there has not been complete agreement as to the relative importance of the goals.

It is now apparent that if capitalism can maintain full employment and stability it can achieve all that liberal socialism seeks. The neoclassical theory provides a method for attaining the goals of maximum efficiency and consumers' welfare. The historical and institutional theories show how economic laws can be modified and humanized by social controls. The Marxian theory suggests an approach to economic development which modern monopoly theories build on to provide methods of achieving the goal of progressiveness. The Keynesian theory of capitalism demonstrates how the goals of full employment and stability can be achieved. Oligopoly theories hold out hopes for leashing the great powers of big business for a fuller public benefit. Thus, most of what traditional socialist theories seek or have sought can be accomplished under capitalism.

This is especially true of the goals of full and stable employment which are now pursued by socialists everywhere. The Keynesian theory effectively bypassed socialism. Keynes' objections to capitalism were more quantitative than qualitative. Capitalism, he inferred, did not necessarily misdirect or waste resources nor were its basic institutions particularly objectionable. It merely did not automatically insure full employment. The Keynesian principles require the abandonment of laissez faire, but the controls which they imply are indirect and do not destroy the market mechanism. Hence, in themselves, they do not lead to central planning or totalitarianism. On the contrary, the Keynesian controls may actually insure that the price system will work effectively because they are designed to maintain aggregate demand and, thus, full employment. Only under these conditions will the price system automatically allocate resources rationally. Without full employment controls, the market mechanism often develops cumulative tendencies toward contraction of output and employment.

There are plenty of reasons for retaining capitalistic institutions in preference to any others. Private property, aside from its psychological advantages, protects the profit motive which is the best incentive for work and saving yet devised. Capitalism also offers the best chance for maintaining decentralized economic decision-making although it is no absolute insurance against totalitarian control as was proved in the case of Nazi Germany.

The economic planning which both liberal and central socialism requires places great power over all phases of business in the hands of government officials. Conceivably, this power could be used to destroy all enterprise and even democracy itself, but in practice economic planning is part of the very texture of the government in all industrialized countries. It is an attitude of people expressed in conscious thought and action. Planning is not a separate activity but, as an egg is to an omelet, it is the very essence of modern government itself. In Britain, Scandinavia, and other traditionally democratic countries which have experimented with liberal socialism, this power of government has been exercised with extreme caution. The rights of opposition, criticism, appeal, and due process of law have, in general, been scrupulously preserved. Citizens in these countries have had little need to fear that such potential power will be used in an antidemocratic way.

Yet, while the welfare state has brought security without sacrificing basic freedoms, there is a real danger that the high rate of taxation which has resulted will act as a brake on incentives. The controversy over the welfare state has shifted from freedom versus security to security versus progress. Liberal socialism and the welfare state can be achieved in democratic countries without loss of freedom, but it is doubtful whether the relative equality of income which results is compatible with an increasing level of total income. As one British economist remarked, "Only a wealthy nation can afford equality." This means that a certain amount of inequality of wealth is necessary so that there will be sources of funds for investment. Also there must be a promise of adequate reward (after taxes), or businessmen will be hesitant about taking risks.

There is some justification in the argument that relative rather than absolute income differentials will provide enough economic incentives. Also noneconomic motives can be relied on to a great extent in some circumstances, such as nationalized industries where the prestige of being on the board of directors may compensate for a relatively low salary. However, there is the danger in both these cases that the allocation of resources, particularly labor, will be distorted by interfering with the wages which would tend to be set in a free market.

A major weakness in all socialist theory is in the probability of diminishing returns on management, or bureaucracy. In theory, the pure competition of neoclassical economics provides for small units and a decentralization of economic decision-making. Liberal socialism does not guarantee decentralized economic units, and central socialism does not even seem to recognize the problem. But in practice, as has been shown, modern capitalism frequently displays marked bureaucratic tendencies itself. While theoretical socialism seems to make bureaucracy an inherent principle, monopolistic capitalism, in practice, may be quite as bureaucratic, and under such circumstances if democratic institutions have been developed it is better to have the economy run by political officials who are directly accountable to the public than by private industrialists and bankers who are not.

Within any individual industrial plant the differences between a capitalist and a socialist system are neither apparent nor very important. Well-established principles of organization, authority, responsibility, and administration must be followed if any large-scale venture is to be efficient. There is no inherent reason why a very large privately owned firm should necessarily be either more or less efficient, internally, than a publicly owned one. Some large private firms, as Montgomery Ward, have violated basic management principles and consequently have been notoriously inefficient, while some large government-owned enterprises, as Renault of France, have recognized and observed them, thus acquiring a reputation for high efficiency and managerial competence.

The principal dissimilarity between capitalism and socialism is in external or interindustry relationships. Under capitalism the firm may be controlled in large degree by market forces. Under socialism the firm is related administratively, and possibly politically, to the economic planning agency. Rationality in resource allocation might survive such an arrangement, but long-run progressiveness might not. Here again, noneconomic factors, like cultural patterns, may be more significant. In America, for example, the private electric power industry has been more alert to long-term needs than the public sector of the industry while in Britain, where all electric power generation and distribution is government owned, a good example of progressiveness has been set.

Most socialists, outside the Marxist-oriented group, seem to recognize that old-style socialism is obsolete. Throughout the world the noncommunist socialist movement has ceased to call for more public ownership. In some cases public ownership is not even mentioned. The Socialist International has recognized that planning for social justice does not require public ownership of industry and has even admitted that "the evils of capitalism are disappearing." Thus socialist political parties are now typically "liberal" or "progressive" parties and little more.

In spite of the fact that workers' control was sacrificed to economic planning in the British nationalization acts, there has been a steady retreat in Britain since 1948 from the physically planned, directly controlled economy. The system of physical planning set up after World War II and containing quantitative production budgets, manpower requirements, and explicit targets for consumers' goods, investment, and exports has since disintegrated into a forecast of economic activity in monetary terms. The price system is once again asserting itself to control major economic decisions. Thus, to resolve the socialist quandaries the British have retreated to the market system. There should have been no surprise at this because many British socialists had long since recognized that much of their basic theoretical apparatus was obsolete.

The election of Hugh Gaitskell in 1956 as leader of the strongest noncommunist socialist movement in the world, the British Labor party, is further evidence of socialism's swing toward the middle of the road. Gaitskell, a competent theoretical and practical economist, is a firm believer in the price system subject only to indirect fiscal controls. Above all, he has a passion for political democracy which is tempered by a hard-headed realism about economic essentials. Socialist parties generally are following this lead.

USES AND ABUSES OF CENTRAL PLANNING THEORY. In a free-market economy, whether capitalist or liberal socialist, everyone is assumed to be the best judge of his own interests. This is, of course, not always true, but taking a country as a whole, deviations from the self-interest rule are likely to be less expensive in a free-market system than in a centrally planned, autocratic system. The adjustable market system permits general incentives for imagination, ingenuity, and enthusiasm to operate. If there is inactivity it is likely to be due to a lack of individual motivation, to inefficiencies in communication, or to inadequate education. All of these are capable of correction and are not inherent weaknesses of the capitalistic system. Bankruptcies and economic dislocations are safety values which let excess pressure out. The hardships caused by the release of these pressures can be mitigated by government and private actions. In a centrally planned economy there may be a tendency for the whole system to boil over for lack of flexibility and either collapse or have its pressure released in enormous upheavals which threaten the system's stability.

In nations where private initiative has traditionally been low, central planning may permit a more rapid increase in living standards than a free market could. This is because the central planners could push the most important keys to economic development while a market economy would have to wait until individual initiative found it profitable to do so. Particularly, where initiative is already low due to heritage, custom, or tradition, central planning might well increase productivity since in a free-market economy people can choose between work and inactivity and many might choose the latter. The same is true of capital, which might not be invested at all in countries or industries where it is most badly needed unless forced to do so. Lethargy or uncertainties could prevent the profit system from working at all in these "underdeveloped" areas. Nevertheless, even in these special cases the costs of direct regulation, such as administration and supervision of forced labor, must be set against the possible economic gains and in general the use of direction rather than incentive is ordinarily a most inefficient method of production.

The central planning theory based on Marxism and developed into authoritarian socialism in the U.S.S.R. is under increasing pressure for liberalization, partly because it has become so cumbersome, inefficient, and bureaucratic. Part of the difficulty, such as the lack of adequate incentives, is due more to economic institutions than to the planning system, but part is, no doubt, due to the awkwardness and oppressiveness of the planning mechanism itself.

However, planning and socialism are not the same things at all. In fact, at the very time when industrial leaders in the most highly capitalist nations are urging more automation, and rightly so because of its many advantages, it is ironic that automatic electronic equipment, and the theory underlying it, may permit, for the first time, a successful experiment with a form of centralized, governmental planning. Recent research by Wassily Leontieff of Harvard, and others, has developed a method for calculating the interdependence of all the sectors of an economic system. Called input-output analysis, the method involves the construction of a matrix which resembles the mileage table of a road map. As the mileage table shows the distances between all combinations of any two cities, the input-output matrix shows the percentage of the production of each sector or industry which is consumed by all sectors. The classification of economic units, including industries, agriculture, government, and consumers, has been variously set from seventy-five to over five hundred classes.

With this method the effect can be calculated which an assumed output change in any industry would have on all segments of the economy. Thus an increase of 10 per cent in aircraft production would have a determinable effect on many other industries, and the necessary output increases in all those industries would be reflected again on many of the same and other industries and so on. Any given production plan can theoretically be worked out for all the changes required in the entire economy. Of course the number of calculations is tremendous. About a million algebraic steps are required for solving one production plan in a one-hundred-industry analysis, and the number of computations increases by the cube of the number of industries added. Thus, the practical solution to the problems of a centrally planned economy would have been impossible without electronic computers.

Even granted that computers could do the arithmetic in relevant time periods, however, there are limitations to the input-output method. Much more research will be necessary before industries can be precisely enough defined and the coefficients of input-output accurately enough determined for the results to be significant. But the control of commercial operations, both as to the productive processes and the clerical administration, are already being undertaken in many private firms and government agencies by the use of electronic computers and other automatic control equipment. These machines work at such unbelievable speeds and handle such enormous volumes of information that it does not seem unreasonable to expect that in the foreseeable future the problems of administrative bureaucracy which corporate giantism and central economic planning both create may well be solved electronically.

It is too early to predict the impact of new theoretical developments and electronic computers on the prospects of central economic planning under capitalism except to suggest that any successful wartime or emergency experience with production planning, using the input-output matrix and electronic computers, might provide a great temptation to employ central production planning in peacetime. Certainly the knowledge of industrial interrelationships is not going to be ignored. It is likely that national policies directed toward specific industries will develop even though direct controls to achieve the goals of national production planning are not invoked.

Barring war, which would certainly lead to government control and planning for all segments of the economy, the impact of automatic, electronic computers combined with the input-output and other new theories promises to be significant. But even if central economic planning is theoretically possible this need not usher in a dictatorship. Totalitarian regimes of the worst sort, such as Nazi Germany, did not employ rational economic planning to nearly the extent that the United States and Britain did during World War II, and this may have been a major decisive factor in turning the tide of battle. Galbraith, in an impressive passage, stated:

Partly because they were less clear than the democracies about what they were producing, how they were dividing it between military and civilian use, how they were allocating resources between immediate use and investment and how the corresponding income was being divided—all information that was displayed by the new [national income] accounts—the Germans mobilized their economic resources with considerably less skill and boldness than did England or the United States. Because they are modest men, economists never advertised the power of the weapon they had placed in the hands of their governments although its bearing on victory was considerably greater than that of atomic energy.[8]

Yet even the simplest lessons are sometimes the hardest learned. In 1954, U.S. government support of input-output research was cut off for the expressed reason that it could lead to economic planning. As a consequence of this head-in-the-sand attitude, other countries have moved ahead in their research in this vital area. An extension of this logic would have an end of atomic research on the grounds that it could lead to war.

The one most centrally planned economy of all, the U.S.S.R., shows signs itself of yielding to the pressures for decentralization, deconcentration of power, and relaxation of direct regulations. This is not to imply that anything like laissez faire can be expected to appear any more than the opposite trends in the United States will lead to the establishment of direct central planning. But there does seem to be a movement in industrial countries toward a disappearance of the more extreme features of laissez faire on the one hand and authoritarian central planning on the other.

[8] Galbraith, *American Capitalism, op. cit.*, pp. 79-80.

TOWARD A SYNTHESIS OF ECONOMIC THEORIES

The chapters on theoretical capitalism (Chapters 2 through 8) lead to the conclusion that none of the models of capitalism so far devised have been able to present a well-rounded explanation of this complex and evolving economic system. Each theory made important, though only partial, contributions toward a comprehensive interpretation. The classical and neoclassical theories (Chapter 2) were logically complete and provided a useful means for studying the internal workings of any economic system at any time. But they were only quantitatively accurate in the abstract. The historical and institutional theories (Chapters 3 and 4) provided many penetrating insights into capitalist systems, but because they tried to embrace all the social sciences at once without adequate analytical tools, they were unable to achieve much theoretical success or scientific respectability. The Marxian theory (Chapter 5) was conceived in frustration, and although it provided the basis for constructing a useful theory of economic development, it later grew into more of a superstitious theology than a theory of capitalism. The Keynesian theory (Chapter 6) has added much to the knowledge of capitalism's over-all behavior although it neglected the structural relationships which were emphasized almost exclusively by the neoclassical theory. The theories of monopoly and oligopoly (Chapters 7 and 8) have so far failed to come to grips with the dynamics of modern capitalism although they show great promise for the future.

The traditional theories of socialism (Chapter 9) laid the basis for modern social welfare schemes, but their principal arguments for cooperative or government controls have either long since been accepted and incorporated into capitalist system or are no longer relevant. Liberal socialism attempted little more in theory than the Keynesian system has been able to attain in fact so there would seem to be no good reason for changing basic institutions to achieve goals by an untried theory when as much can be accomplished while retaining most of capitalism's unique advantages. Central planning theory has contributed to an understanding of the collectivist features of any industrial economy and to some of the forces underlying economic change, but the dangers it raises of dictatorship are too obvious to make adopting such a system very attractive to the Western democracies. Like liberal socialism, the main objectives of central planning can be attained under capitalism if they are required by war or other national emergencies and with much less trouble or risk that the controls become permanent.

Yet out of all these theories there have gradually emerged three types of methodology for explaining the operation of economic systems. One, commonly called microeconomics, traces its ancestry mainly to the classical and neoclassical theories but not without considerable modification as a result of exposure to other theories. This system of thought has been firmly established for over a century although it is constantly undergoing refinement and improvement. The second, called macroeconomics, is derived from the Keynesian theory and has become generally validated in the last two decades. The third body of economic doctrine, which might be called economic growth theory, is only now in its earliest stage of formation. Although based in part on classical, historical, institutional, Marxian, and Schumpeterian theories, it is still years away from the stage of becoming a general theory.

In spite of some tendency to disparage microeconomics for being essentially static, for being concerned with the economics of firms and households rather than national economic welfare, and for being old fashioned at best, this system of thought still provides the most complete methodology for studying economic problems. There continues to be a vast and growing literature in this field which, after all, is the most directly related to individuals, both as producers and consumers, who are concerned with trying to enhance their economic welfare by increasing their incomes and reducing their efforts and costs. Microeconomic methodology still provides the most satisfactory explanation of the inner workings of any economic system. If modern capitalism is ever to be explained by a total theory, such a theory cannot afford to ignore the essential problems of making an individual living. This is the concern of microeconomics.

But the essential policies which should follow microeconomic analysis concerning the government's role with respect to the market system in modern capitalism are by no means clear. Outright public ownership of industry has been rejected by most economists although regional development projects like the TVA may continue to have great significance in the future. At the other extreme, the atomizing of industry by antitrust action, so that the economy will conform more closely to the classical model, has not found much favor among economists. Nor is any significant body of public opinion behind either solution. Vigorous antitrust actions may be brought against certain industrial giants to remedy specific abuses, but dissolutions, to any significant extent, appear most unlikely. Likewise commission regulation, although firmly established for the public utilities of fuel, power, transportation, and communications, is hardly likely to spread to other industries.

A somewhat more promising type of industrial regulation, public competition, has some particular advantages to commend it but virtually no advocates among either economists or public officials. Government-owned plants, operating within clearly defined limits of comparability and fairness of competition with private plants, could provide a useful yardstick for determining workably competitive costs, prices, and levels of output. If private industry should be reluctant to expand in periods of emergency, this type of device might be employed as an expedient to increase production rather than subsidies and protection to private firms. If regulation is necessary, as in public utilities, then by having the regulating and producing functions combined in one government-owned, experimental, producing enterprise, rather than separated as in commission regulation, the relation between

commercial and social goals might be more clearly understood.

It is much more likely that the pragmatic approach will
prevail. Subsidies, loans, tax concessions, rationing, special
legislation, and collective bargaining contracts within the
framework of privately owned, oligopolistic industry will
probably continue to be used to bolster, restrain, encourage, or threaten private business rather than any more doctrinaire, or even more rational, approach. The final pattern
of capitalist industrial organization has not yet crystallized,
and any comprehensive theory of government control will
probably have to await more empirical research. The large
corporation may thus have to endure even more detailed
study by economists, sociologists, and legal and business
historians before enough generalizations can be made to
justify the formulation of a fully consistent economic policy
by the government.

The macroeconomic theory of income and employment
owes its inspiration to Keynes. Chapter 6 concluded that
the Keynesian methodology had received a lasting place
in the development of systematic economic theory. The
"Keynesian Revolution" has finally been incorporated, with
much refinement and modification, into a complex system of
national, or social, accounting. It is not easy to appreciate
just how important the influence of Keynes has been because, although Keynes's name is hardly mentioned any
more, his major principles form the foundation of what
most businessmen, government officials, and ordinary citizens consider to be the main concern of economics. Within
a decade after his untimely death in 1946, Keynes's basic
principles have become the accepted constitution for most
economists and, implicitly, for most national economic policymakers.

Since World War II, while the substance of the Keynesian theory was being forged into a system of national
accounting, the economics profession has attained the greatest prestige in its history. What was once a highly controversial theory of employment for depression times has

become a national institution. Although its statistical head-quarters are in the United States Department of Commerce, many foundations, business corporations, labor organizations, and universities are gathering tons of data to fit into the system of social accounting which is used to predict the gross national product, net national product, national income, capital and consumption expenditures, employment, and a host of other economic aggregates.

Private businessmen everywhere are rapidly becoming aware of the complexity of their economic system and the interdependence of its various components. Few trade associations, civic organizations, or bankers' or businessmen's groups can meet any more without a professional economist being invited to predict over-all economic conditions for the next year. But the concern of businessmen over the state of the economy goes deeper than this. Economics Ph.D.'s are being employed in huge numbers of business corporations as well as the federal government to study not only the problems of demand, costs, or supply of the firm but to investigate and attempt to forecast general economic conditions. Businessmen are growing more conscious of the relationships among taxes, price levels, wages, employment, sales volume, government spending, and general prosperity. In fact, the whole economic interest of management is enlarging to include not only supply, wages, costs, and demand for their firm but also the national aggregates of employment, income, and production. Management now considers national, or even international, economic conditions among the variables which it faces, to which it must adjust, and over which it has some measure of control and hence responsibility.

The most conservative economists today agree that the government can and must maintain full employment and a reasonable degree of economic stability. Economists are nearly all Keynesians to this extent. Furthermore, practically everyone depends on the Keynesian-based national accounting and statistical data, which is published regularly by the United States Department of Commerce, to appraise the state of the economy and forecast economic conditions.

It is understandable that the major concern of economists, businessmen, and statesmen should turn from the traditional microeconomic problems associated with demand, costs, efficiency, supply, and market competition to the macroeconomic problems of employment, income, investment, consumption, and inflation. In an economy committed to full employment, stability, and prosperity, there is a tendency for restrictive market practices to decline, for more efficient production methods to be used, and for workers to accept labor-saving innovations.

However, in a full employment economy there are inflationary pressures due to structural frictions and immobilities. Even in generally prosperous times, there are depressed areas and pockets of unemployment. Since the re-spending of money channeled into these depressed areas cannot be localized, any attempt to reduce unemployment in them will tend to promote inflation in others. Thus if total spending is to be high enough to absorb these problem areas and maintain economic progress, there will be other sections of the economy with labor shortages and rising prices.

Under conditions of inflation, no matter how gradual, there will tend to be a sellers' market for goods, services, and labor. Competition among firms for customers subsides, but competition among firms and industries for labor increases. Hence the traditional problems of monopoly output restriction and efficiency decline in importance, and problems associated with over-all economic conditions increase in both importance and interest.

The role of the government with respect to the national aggregates of income, employment, spending, investment, and consumption is much clearer than in the industrial market sphere. The truth of the popular saying, among economists, that "we are all Keynesians now" should no longer be doubted by anyone in view of the postwar experiences with both Democratic and Republican administrations. Of course, the entire implied theory of capitalism is not as universally accepted as the role of government in fiscal policy is, and certainly the stagnation thesis is at least temporarily laid to rest.

The government now has the power to prevent widespread unemployment and cyclical fluctuations, and there is a general popular feeling that it should. Several reasons for this widespread view can be found. First, the public is well aware that unemployment was effectively abolished by the government in wartime and sees no reason why it cannot be prevented in peacetime as well. Second, the Great Depression has stimulated a general consciousness and apprehension of the economic, social, and moral costs of unemployment. Third, the depression created an awareness that it simply does not make sense that men should be forced into unemployment and poverty, and their skills and energies wasted, while at the same time surpluses of goods pile up for lack of buyers. Fourth, the major political parties have both claimed credit for prosperity and blamed each other for depression. It is not surprising that enough of this talk has soaked into the public's mind that it is now considered an obligation of the party in power to carry out its inexorable promise of maintaining full employment and prosperity.

Of course, the validity of an economic theory is not usually determined by its popularity, but in this case the psychological factors are highly important. Much consumption spending (especially on durable goods) and nearly all investment expenditures are not based on actual needs but are discretionary. Optimism or pessimism influence, if not determine, them. Accordingly, public support of fiscal policies greatly increases their chances of success.

Theories of economic growth and development have become a major concern in the last few years, probably because of the unprecedented, and largely unexpected, worldwide economic expansion since World War II. Modern economic growth theories draw on practically every earlier economic philosophy including, especially, the theory of capital of the "static," classical economics. Even so, economic growth theory is still too much in its infancy to permit even a summary of general principles. There is a growing literature in the area, but undoubtedly the most significant single contribution to the subject has been made by W. Arthur Lewis in his recent book *The Theory of Economic Growth*.[9] If any book can be comprehensive, penetrating, and inspiring all at once, this one is. Its aim is to summarize and analyze all of the major elements affecting economic growth. Yet as the author admits, it is not a general theory of growth itself in the sense that it offers a set of interrelated principles of something like universal validity. But it does isolate and analyze with great clarity the main causes of growth. The first is said to be the willingness and ability of people to make the kind of efforts necessary for growth. This requires the study of why people desire goods, take risks, specialize, move, and try to economize resources. It follows that the institutions of property, economic organization, family, rewards, and so on must be studied since these greatly influence human efforts toward growth. The second major cause of growth is found in the increase and application of knowledge involving such things as research, innovations, and training programs. The third cause of growth is asserted by Lewis to be in the rate of increase of the amount of capital and other resources per worker. Savings, investment, interest, and productivity theories are all useful here.

It is a temptation to predict that when growth theory reaches the stage of a true science the circle will be complete and the threefold classification of economic methods will be sufficient to explain, theoretically at least, all aspects of actual economic systems and problems. Past experience cautions against such conclusive predictions. But it does seem safe to assert that since economic growth is the one common characteristic of nearly all nations today, regardless

[9] Lewis, *The Theory of Economic Growth* (Homewood, Ill.: Richard D. Irwin, Inc., 1955).

of ideology and institutions, the development and refinement of growth theory will provide analytical tools of increasingly universal application.

All of the major economic theories of the past have been influenced by the conditions of the times. The same is true of the theories and even the methodologies of the present. Just as the classical theory tried to explain the problems of early nineteenth-century England, contemporary microeconomic analysis is groping with oligopoly, macroeconomics with inflation, and growth theory with what historians will probably record as the most distinctive characteristic of the last half of the twentieth century—economic development. A synthesis of theories would follow, and reinforce, a synthesis of actual economic systems.

14

Emergence of a
Universal Economic Order

The future belongs to the man of statistics and the master of economics.——Justice Oliver Wendell Holmes

If society is paralyzed today, it is not for lack of means but for lack of purpose.——Lewis Mumford

THEORIES DOMINATED BY FACTS

CAUSES OF ECONOMIC GROWTH. Reality often leads the way while abstract theory follows. Thus theory may sometimes become more of a rationalization of what has occurred, or is occurring, than a blueprint of what is to happen in the future. The theory of the future cannot escape the facts of the past and present. Modern economic systems, both in theory and in fact, are all traceable to the Industrial Revolution, which produced not only the age of technology but both modern capitalism and socialism. In every nation which has experienced economic growth and industrialization, similar patterns of development have occurred. One of the most significant facts of the mid-twentieth century is the emergence of the United States as recognized leader in world affairs. To a large extent, this political and military superiority has been due to economic achievement—to the attainment of the highest standards of production, efficiency, living standards, and technological progressiveness in the world.

The United States has had no monopoly of natural resources, brains, industriousness, or knowledge. It did not achieve its economic superiority through its rich endowment of natural resources alone, although this undoubtedly was a help. The Indians camped on top of the same resources for thousands of years without developing them at all, and many areas in the world today have vast stores of known but untapped natural resources. Europe, and particularly Great Britain, has always produced proportionately more first-rate theoretical minds. Hard work has also been characteristic of many countries, and long working hours and backbreaking drudgery are more common elsewhere than in the United States. Nor is there a monopoly of knowledge. The professional scientific journals go everywhere. Even military security precautions, which embrace (supposedly) only strategic information, are frankly based on the assumption that a short-time lead is all that can ever be attained. There are no permanent secrets.

Two things, probably more than anything else, have been responsible for America's spectacular economic success, and the same two factors can be seen at work in other countries which have experienced rapid economic growth. The first is capital. Both sides of American industry—management and labor—have more machinery and other equipment to work with than is available in any other nation in the world. The second is the ability and willingness to make the kind of effort required for economic growth. American history has been characterized by a value system which encourages a spirit of adventure, a desire for higher living standards, and a will to economize resources. Economic institutions like property, profits, and other individual "rights" have tended to assure that the rewards for productive effort will be received by those who earn them. Some other nations have had one or the other of these factors to a high degree, but in the United States they have been uniquely combined, and together they go far toward explaining our unprecedented industrial achievement.

The emergence of these conditions of economic progress goes back to the Industrial Revolution in England in the seventeenth and early eighteenth centuries. The steam engine, spinning machinery, and other startling inventions of the seventeenth century permitted an enormous output and a great increase in efficiency. But they also required that production be carried out on an ever larger scale. Hence the medieval guild method of production by a few highly skilled, well-rounded craftsmen gave way to a factory system in which both machinery and labor became highly specialized. In order to organize and supervise the many specialized jobs, a separate function, called management, arose. Thus for the first time production became separated into management on the one hand and labor on the other.

The early twentieth century witnessed another economic revolution—this time in mass production and business organizations. The discovery of assembly line techniques had the effect of further increasing the most economical size of business and industrial units. The use of huge amounts of machinery greatly increased productivity, but it also added such heavy fixed costs to firms that a high and almost continuous level of production became necessary. Industrial organizations have grown to enormous size. Since World War II the American economy has been highly dynamic, not static as the classicists assumed. Economic freedom, flexibility, mobility, and individualism have all encouraged experimentation and growth. The most active element forcing change, however, has been the entrepreneur, who promotes new commercial ventures by inventing, improving techniques, and experimenting with new organizational methods. Although meaning, literally, "undertaker," the entrepreneur presides at the birth, not the burial, of his subject. His functions necessarily involve taking great chances. The entrepreneur's reward for introducing innovation is personal economic gain, and America has had plenty of entrepreneurs who later developed into highly competent industrial managers although entrepreneurship is not synonymous with management. Some bureaucratic corporate managements may be anti-entrepreneurial, actually resisting innovations from below. Entrepreneurship has also developed in the professions and even in the workforce itself, being expressed in the curiosity and restlessness which leads to innovation and rising productivity. Appropriate policies and institutions could encourage a continuation and growth of this important quality. Particularly, adequate incentives and job security could elicit valuable suggestions and improvements from production workers who often withhold cost-saving ideas for fear of downgrading, pay-rate reduction, or layoffs.

The increased size of enterprises caused by the growth of capital has led to many new opportunities for entrepreneurs in management. The enormous funds for large scale business concerns have had to be promoted by selling shares of stock to hundreds of thousands of people. Thus the huge size of the managerial organization needed has required a division in management between owners and operators. Furthermore, the growing intricacy and complexity of production processes has required the use of a highly skilled, professional management. More recently this specialized function has tended to become further subdivided into financial, production, sales, personnel, and other kinds of management, and even the top level of management has divided into policy making and policy administration. Highly specialized, professional management and productive labor, when combined with the great capital investment, have developed such high output per person that wages, production, and profits can all be increased simultaneously. This explodes the classical "iron law of wages" and "wages fund" theories and the Marxian doctrines of exploitation and increasing misery of the workers once and for all. Obviously, wages are not paid at the expense of profits, as classical and Marxian economists thought, since those industries and countries where the greatest profits are being made are simultaneously those where wages are highest also.

Nor has society been split into two groups, the exploiters and the exploited, as Marx envisioned. Workers have vastly improved their economic positions and their social status in recent years even though capitalistic institutions such as profits and private property have continued to be strong. There is conflict, to be sure, but among many groups, not just two. Big business often has conflicting interests with small business; industrial unionists oppose craft unionists; urban dwellers oppose rural folk; farmers' interests are sometimes contrary to those of both labor and business. Actually, automation and other recent developments have had the result of enlarging the middle class—especially skilled technicians—and increasing the proportion of independent professional people and employers. This is exactly the opposite of what Marx predicted.

Furthermore, even though there are many conflicting or competing groups, over-all economic conflict is apparently diminishing rather than increasing. As every insurance actuary knows, the more risks you have and the more decentralized they are the greater is the predictability of results, and hence the smaller is the total risk. The same is true of economic conflict. As more interest groups arose, there was less danger that a single great dispute would cause a fatal division in the economy. Partly as a consequence of the growing middle class, more moderate political attitudes are arising. The extremists of both left and right are suffering a decline of influence.

EFFECTS ON CAPITALIST AND SOCIALIST INSTITUTIONS. Only one major nation in the world has succeeded in industrializing under conditions which are not capitalistic. This is the Soviet Union. Here the necessary technological discoveries upon which the industrialization was based were already known, having been made, developed, and refined in capitalist Europe and America. It remained only to apply them to the feudal, agricultural Russia which, by 1918, was already an anachronism in the twentieth century. The Russians borrowed liberally of western technological accomplishments by importing machinery and engaging the services of western scientists, engineers, and technicians on a large scale in the 1920's and '30's.

Russia in 1918 was not entirely agricultural. In fact, some of the largest single-plant, industrial establishments in Europe were built in Czarist Russia under essentially mercantilist-capitalist conditions. The U.S.S.R. is not yet a highly industrialized nation, and although it can never be determined for sure whether industrialization under the Bolsheviks has been more or less rapid than it would have been under some other system, it seems probable that the previous industrial accomplishments of capitalism contributed substantially to Russia's rapid industrialization. Marx himself admitted that capitalism and industrialization went hand in hand. Nor have the Russians been shy about borrowing capitalist inventions, organizations, and even methodology. Moreover, in recent years they have liberally adopted capitalist economic institutions and techniques, such as wage and income differentials, profit and interest calculations, bond financing, some advertising, economic incentives, and even some limited private property ownership. This may be due to a recognition of the fact that the over-all economic problems of their system are not as radically different from those of capitalist nations as was once thought.

The present economic system of the U.S.S.R., while having borrowed extensively from the capitalist storehouse of techniques and even theory, still lacks laissez faire, private enterprise, and a free-market system. Hence it cannot be properly described as capitalist. However, neither is it socialist in either the utopian sense or the modern Fabian or liberal socialist sense as it does not have, or seem even to aspire to, either equality or economic democracy (workers' control). It is collectivist, not only in the sense that all modern industrial economies are collectivist but also in expressed philosophy and conscious economic policy. But it is probably less equalitarian than the United States. Certainly it is less democratic both politically and economically in terms of workers' control over their means of livelihood and conditions of employment.

In all nations, the problems of industrialization have been met with new organizational and governmental techniques. Many of these techniques, such as new taxation devices, import restrictions, credit institutions, health and welfare schemes, and holding companies, are not peculiar to any one economic system but appear, in modified or disguised forms, in all of them. Some, as central banking, are almost identical in structure as well as function in all industrial economic systems, whether capitalist or not. Others, as oligopoly, are such creatures of their culture that the resemblance from system to system is less obvious. Nevertheless, much of modern industrial capitalist theory and practice is as applicable in the Soviet Union as it is in the United States.

On the other hand, modern capitalism has not been immune to the influence of socialist economic theories. Modern trade unionism and social legislation may have developed in capitalist countries in response to specific needs, but the theoretical basis came from socialist writers of an earlier time. Robert Owen pioneered factory legislation, and the Webbs first defined collective bargaining and unionization. Other British socialists developed the theoretical bases for economic planning and public ownership and operation of commercial enterprises. Just as the Russians may owe the success of their industrialization to the genius of capitalism, so part of the success of capitalism in distributing its benefits equitably, providing a respectable status for labor, and insuring a minimum of security for all may be due to the genius of socialists, albeit of the non-Marxian, Fabian type. Industrial giantism, labor specialization, mass production, automation, and other economic developments thus seem to be inherent in the industrialization process itself, not peculiar to capitalism alone. Hence they tend to unify the factual bases of economic theory in different countries. The basic problems which all economic systems must solve are much the same, and now even the means are growing more alike.

The paucity of reliable information about the Soviet Union precludes any definite evaluation here. However, to the extent that developments in the free world are due to economic conditions inherent in industrialization, rather than the strictly institutional aspects of capitalism and political democracy, the Soviet Union should not be immune to some of the same economic consequences which characterize the free world. If the structure and behavior of a giant American enterprise sometimes resembles its British, or even its Russian counterparts, it may be, as a leading American economist recently remarked, that "a brontosaurus is still a brontosaurus no matter what kind of swamp he lives in."

ONE SYSTEM FOR ALL

This book began by assuming that although there are many theories of the economic order, and many working systems in practice based on them, it would be useful to classify theoretical economic systems into two general groups —capitalist and socialist. It has been recognized throughout that there is continuous variation between the extremes of these systems both in theory and practice, and drawing a line between them is merely an analytical convenience. The terms capitalism and socialism were used with full knowledge that they have widely varying meanings in colloquial usage and are so charged with emotion that rational analysis is made more difficult by their use. The reason for making a hard job even harder by the use of such words is that they are in widespread use among theorists and scholars, as well as laymen, and there is a vast professional literature which is based on fairly homogeneous meanings of these terms. Capitalism was defined in Chapter 1 as embracing an economic system characterized by private property in capital plant and equipment, private profits as the motive for economic activity, a market system for pricing and hence allocating resources and final products, and a minimum of government or other intervention in the operation of the system. Socialism was defined as a system characterized by government or other nonprivate ownership of the means of production, relative equality of incomes, wealth, and status, workers' control or at least participation in major economic decisions, and planning by the government for the welfare of all.

These systems, though distinctly different in theory, are not opposites. Hence if some modifications could be made in each, there might be a basis for a compromise system which would still retain the most valuable elements of each. It is entirely possible that actual economic developments will provide the factual basis for such a marriage of theories. The trends of economic and technological change suggest that a common basis for all industrialized economies may be arising. The modern world is dominated more by facts than theories, and the greatest historical economic fact of all is the Industrial Revolution of the eighteenth century. In recent years, it has begun to spread to Russia and portions of the Far East and is now gaining a foothold in most of the remaining areas of the world. Africa, the Middle East, and South America are clamoring to share in the material wealth which comes from industrial technology.

Every country that has experienced industrialization has, at some stage, undergone a metamorphosis toward a greater degree of individualism, equalitarianism, and political democracy. There has frequently followed a growth of education, a decline of traditionalism, and an eventual attempt to eradicate poverty. In every country where industry has taken root, there has been a great expansion in the size of industrial enterprises, an increase in the concentration of both economic and political control, and a functional separation of ownership from management. Regardless of the legal system of property ownership, the customary or traditional basis of behavior, or the ideologies and theories underlying the economic system, these facts have emerged and now domi-

nate the economic scene. In the future, the forms of industrialization will probably continue to mold the economic,
social, and cultural patterns, wherever they may be.

When the developments in actual working economic systems are analyzed in terms of the established principles of
capitalism and socialism, a hybrid seems to be appearing.
This incipient system seems to lean more heavily on capitalism although it must be remembered that these two systems
were not defined as being the opposite of each other by any
means. Depending on the emphasis placed on the principles
underlying each of these pure types of system, it would be
possible to argue that the new system is more like socialism
or does not resemble either type. Clearly the issue of government ownership of industry has gone into eclipse. Most
socialists will admit that private ownership of capital itself
has not proved to be the cause of exploitation, unemployment, or inefficiency. Thus to those who think in terms of
property titles alone, socialism is surely dead, and capitalism
reigns supreme. But most socialists now consider equality
and economic planning by government to be far more important. The facts show that gross inequalities in income,
wealth, and status have been disappearing even in the most
highly capitalist countries, and there is no longer any major
nation in which the central government has not assumed responsibility for planning for continuing full employment, at
least. It is well established that full employment, stability,
and general prosperity can be attained without changing
basic capitalist institutions. All that is required is that central governments be willing to control the level of expenditures and insure a sufficient degree of equality to maintain
total purchasing power and hence support the mass production industries upon which all highly industrialized economies are based.

The modern industrial economic system has retained the
capitalist institutions of private property and profits, in large
part. In Great Britain, Sweden, and other countries which
have undergone extensive changes under socialist governments, public ownership seems to have about run its course,

and in these countries private profits have continued to motivate most economic activity. Even in the Soviet Union, there have been many concessions made toward private incentive and ownership, and there is apparently great pressure for further liberalization. In most industrial countries, the price system has also survived as the means of control over production and allocation of goods and services. However, the market mechanism has undergone substantial modification from the classical model, being typically controlled by private or government action, so that the triumph of this particular capitalist institution is not so pronounced or easily seen. But direct control by government over prices, quantities produced, and product distribution has been in retreat almost everywhere since World War II. The British have abandoned physical planning with quantitative production budgets, manpower requirements, and explicit targets for consumer goods, investment, and exports. Once again the price system controls major economic decisions. Even in the Soviet Union, there is increasing emphasis on monetary rather than physical controls. The new plan for economic decentralization announced in 1957 is a further move toward liberalism and the market system.

Thus three of the four foundations of capitalism, as defined here, seem likely to be carried over from pure capitalism and incorporated into the newly emerging economic system. First, private property in capital plant and equipment may even grow as industry expands into consumer goods and services, although this could be partially offset by further expansion of public power and transportation services.

Second, economic incentives and profit motivation are well established, and future tax policies seem to favor strengthening them.

Third, the market system is everywhere reasserting itself as the principal mechanism for controlling the allocation of goods and services. Even the U.S.S.R., although it has not denationalized its industries, has made substantial concessions toward re-establishing economic incentives and a pricing system. And, since industrial management has become autonomous and professional, the question of who possesses legal title to industrial property has become pretty much of a dead issue. The only one of the four characteristics of pure capitalism which seems definitely abandoned everywhere is laissez faire.

The new economic system is in the process of adopting three of the four foundations of socialism at the same time. First, a greater degree of over-all equalitarianism is probably inevitable if political democracy is to be continued, although this need not be inconsistent with the growth of economic incentives as mentioned above. Incentives require inequalities but mainly within the fairly narrow limits of a factory or office. The differentials between the lowest and highest paid person in any particular work situation affect incentives most. The worker compares himself with his immediate supervisor, not with remote Hollywood actors or Texas oil millionaires. Thus over-all inequalities could, and probably will, decline while pay differentials increase.

Second, workers' or unions' control over production details and working conditions will probably intensify. Of course, workers nowhere make the final management decisions. Insistence on this has long since been either abandoned in theory or discredited in fact. Workers, for the most part, do not want the responsibility that goes with management, and by its nature the modern industrial enterprise cannot be governed from below. But workers have gained considerable control over the things which are closest to them and mean the most to them. Wages and the details of working conditions are frequently controlled by workers through collective bargaining or consultation and participation plans either with or without unions. Oddly enough, the control by workers over their immediate workplace has advanced as rapidly in the United States as anywhere else. In Great Britain, the more formal workers' control devices have either been discarded in practice, such as workers' representatives on the boards of directors, or else have been tried without conspicuous success, such as the workers' and consumers' consultative councils in nationalized industries. In the United States, workers have greater control in private industry than in regulated utilities or government enterprises. In the government services and public utilities, strikes are forbidden or restricted, and collective bargaining is limited. Wherever the public interest is involved, the rights of labor are likely to be limited. Thus workers' control, a major goal of traditional socialism, has been adopted in modified form but with the most conspicuous success in the more purely capitalist industries and in the more highly capitalist countries, as the United States.

Third, economic planning will undoubtedly have to be extended because of the growing interdependence of all segments of society. Of all these six principles of the new economic system—three capitalist and three socialist—economic planning seems to be the one offering the greatest opportunity for constructive application. There are diminishing returns on the extension of equalitarianism, workers' control, and even private property. But in spite of over a quarter of a century of debate of economic planning, the logical and practical limits of this element are still not in sight. Of course, economic planning need not follow the socialist or institutionalist concepts of central government control over everything. Indeed, it may require planning to preserve the semblance of private enterprise and what is left of the free-market system. Admittedly the government must plan for full employment and stability, but, moreover, private economic organizations are driven to planning for maximum efficiency and even social responsibility.

As the scale of enterprise increases and dependence on mass markets expands, there is necessarily a greater dependence on consumers' purchasing power and hence a growing interfirm and interindustry competition for labor and other resources. Above all, there is an intensifying competition for customers. This increasing competitiveness is not in the classical tradition, but it is nevertheless a powerful regulator of economic activity.

To successfully meet this competition, industry will have to plan as never before. As a matter of self-preservation, private enterprise can be forced to plan if for no other reason than to think up new concepts of operation and control before the government does. Since the classical competitive framework has given way to large-scale enterprises and oligopolistic market structure, this planning must necessarily provide for a harmonious juncture of government and private economic activity. In an economy of large, powerful groups, no single interest can be allowed to dominate. The constructive forces of all must be used.

Governments also can be expected to continue to plan for full employment, stability, and the most efficient use of their resources. Like the weather, business cycles are easier to avoid than to fully understand or predict. All democratic capitalist governments already have enormous powers at their disposal for regulating economic activity, and, with regard to maintaining full production and employment, even the most conservative governments have not hesitated to use them. Modern macroeconomic theories are providing more refined and accurate measures of economic conditions and already provide highly useful guideposts for policy.

Guideposts only point the way, however. They do not actually lead anywhere. But contemporary theory is far better than it used to be. The many controls and compensating mechanisms which have been built into most modern industrial economies since the 1930's can be effective in offsetting adverse economic developments. There are some automatic economic stabilizers, such as public and private unemployment compensation plans, which go into operation when employment and incomes fall. Also, progressive income taxes help to stabilize by leaving proportionately more disposable income for individuals when employment or wages fall. These are only partial depression preventatives, however. Maybe it is better to fall six stories than fifteen, but much more could be done to insure stability and full employment without adversely affecting incentives or seriously undermining basic capitalistic institutions. In fact, capitalistic institutions are more likely to remain vigorous if full employment and stability can be sustained.

John Maurice Clark, who is probably America's greatest living economist, distinguishes five degrees of economic planning.[1] The first is totalitarian control, which is clearly inconsistent with democracy. The second is complete economic collectivism, which, he says, need not extinguish personal and political liberties, but would seriously threaten them, especially in countries such as the United States with its large, heterogeneous population and tradition of individualism. Third, mixed systems, either predominantly collective or private, are possible. These offer the greatest hope, Clark thinks. A predominantly collective mixed economy could effectively control business cycles since the public sector would include those industries which are responsible for the greatest fluctuations of capital outlays. This would be particularly true if housing were included in the collective sector. In a predominantly private mixed economy the smaller public sector could regulate the private sector through "yardstick" competition or compensatory expansion and contraction of capital outlays. Fourth, a regimented private economy is possible although this would require a totalitarian government. Fifth, a private economy with a combination of public and private planning of aggregate demand is conceivable. Under this system, Clark says that partial stabilization and partial prevention of depression and inflation is possible although he implies that this is a ship capable of navigating only the calmest of seas.

It is a temptation to assign contemporary economic systems to their places in these categories. Recognizing that any such classification is a vast oversimplification, it would appear that the U.S.S.R. fits well into the first class of totalitarian control. Into the second category of complete economic collectivism would fall the left wing of the British and European labor parties and, in practice, Sweden and Norway, which have gone far toward controlled economies

[1] *Economic Institutions and Human Welfare* (New York: Alfred A. Knopf, Inc., 1957), pp. 254-57.

without, so far, destroying political and personal liberties. Yugoslavia and some of the Russian satellites, as Poland, may be moving out of the first degree of totalitarian economic planning into this more genuine collectivism. The third class, mixed systems, would seem to include Great Britain, a number of other countries among those leaning toward collectivism, and the United States as a mixed economy which relies more on a predominant private sector. The fourth possibility, the regimented private economy, sounds like Nazi Germany and other fascist countries. The fifth category—the private economy with public and private management of total demand—resembles the ideal of the "New Republicanism" in the United States. It is significant that Clark doubts whether the business-government "partnership" can succeed in its task. Even more significant is the failure to consider automatic regulation through laissez faire as even a possibility. Like complete collectivism, such an extreme approach is unthinkable any more.

A LOOK BEYOND

ECONOMIC TRENDS. The future is never more than dimly seen, but, barring some cataclysmic disturbance, several trends can be distinguished which with some modification for different cultures are common to all major economic systems today. First, it can be expected that the stock of capital goods throughout the world will continue to grow. Capital begets itself, and once a nation can rise above subsistence and begin to save and create capital, this accumulation tends to become automatic. Mechanization, mass production, and finally automation are all stages in this process. The Industrial Revolution was the seed from which modern economic systems grew. Mass production was the flower, and automation, when it arrives in full force, promises to be the final fruit. The institutional and cultural frameworks of different societies may be forced to yield to these economic and technological forces, and the social and cultural systems may tend to be molded after the economic systems and hence tend to become more alike.

A second foreseeable trend is that the size of primary economic units will continue to increase. To take full advantage of developing technology, medium-sized firms will have to go on growing, and organizations of labor, farmers, and others will have to do likewise in order to maintain their positions in the economy. It has been shown that many of the largest business firms in the United States are well beyond their most efficient economic size. They seem to be able to maintain their positions fairly permanently through avantages in large-scale purchasing, favorable banking arrangements, established markets attained by advertising, and political connections. Any of these advantages could well be at the expense of someone else, particularly small competitors and consumers. But so far there is little discernible sentiment for doing anything to control mergers or limit corporate growth. The more practical and appealing approach seems to be to assist smaller, disadvantaged producers to grow so that they can share in the same advantages.

One promising way of accomplishing this has been proposed by Senator William Fulbright of Arkansas and Congressman Wright Patman of Texas. This is to tax corporations progressively, just like individuals. Although the corporation income tax is somewhat progressive in principle, the rates reach the maximum of 52 per cent at $25,000 of corporate net incomes so, actually, nearly all firms pay about the same rate of tax regardless of size. Fulbright and Patman have proposed a substantial reduction of corporation income taxes on small corporate earnings and an increase on larger earnings. It is estimated that total tax revenues could be increased at once by over $2 billion in the United States with the new progressive rates, while reducing the tax burden on 98 per cent of American business corporations. Any laws embodying this principle would help small firms to compete more successfully with their giant rivals.

A third trend, and a corollary of the trend toward larger economic units, is that the scope and jurisdiction of political control will have to expand to keep pace with expanding economic organizations. The long established expansion and consolidation of governments and the degree of penetration of their interference into economic affairs seems likely to continue. As economic activity tends to become increasingly national, and even international, in scale, the corresponding political units must necessarily expand. Of course, many types of enterprises will probably always be local in scope and hence local governments will always have many important functions. The larger cities, especially, will probably become more influential because of the ascendance of interdependent industrial centers. The national governments can be expected to remain of greatest significance, however, because of the dominance of international political and military problems as well as the expansion of much industry to a national or international basis.

If economic, technological, military, and social forces have any strong influence in determining political powers and jurisdictions, it would appear that the long run is surely against the county, state, and other provincial governments. These intermediate authorities are already anachronisms. Technological growth has steadily increased the size, vigorousness, and potency of large metropolitan centers. State and county governments have conspicuously failed to meet the growing public needs of these areas. Most of the talk about states' rights is significantly lacking in any recognition of the duties and responsibilities which necessarily accompany these rights. Ironically, the states which complain most loudly about encroachments on their rights are the ones that have failed most utterly in their responsibilities.

Large corporations transcend political boundaries, and so have many of the problems which they raise. State and county governments have been effectively bypassed by the forces of industrialization. To make matters worse, nearly every state in the United States is dominated politically by its rural areas, to the detriment of its cities. State legislatures siphon off funds from the urban areas, leaving them with a mounting burden of education, housing, welfare, and other public functions. Eventually, the cities are forced to ask for help from the national government. Ironically, it is the rural people who complain the loudest about big federal government while it is their own failure to permit democratic representation that has led to the default of state and county governments in providing for the majority of their populations. Without major economic justification any more, these obsolete constituencies may be expected to put up a vigorous but losing struggle before retiring from their former positions as significant economic and political entities.

The states will no doubt continue to administer education, roads, and, to a lesser extent, commerce, all in cooperation with the national government. Also, the traditional legal and civil functions under the courts and police powers will surely remain purely county or provincial matters. It is on the level of *economic* activity that provincial influence seems destined to yield to the national government. County governments in America have long since given up most participation in economic affairs either for lack of jurisdiction or inability to recognize or cope with the new responsibilities imposed by modern conditions.

A fourth, and unmistakable, trend in the economy is toward further rationalism. The way of knowledge and thought is a one-way street. Once it is begun, there is no turning back. The need for reason, and data to support it, is constantly increasing. The reasoning ability will have to be supplied by the broadening of formal educational systems. Students being educated for the kind of leadership which modern economic systems require will have to concentrate on the tools, techniques, and analytical equipment of theory. In this way only can they escape being confined by the extreme specialization which is required for the efficient operation of complex, interdependent modern societies. The problem today is to retain some degree of independent thought in an increasingly interdependent world. To meet this crisis, higher education systems must produce graduates who possess initiative, think analytically and creatively, use judgment and evaluate problems objectively, and see complex situations in terms of equations, graphs, parameters, and classifications. Above all, they must have an insatiable thirst for more knowledge. This challenge is so formidable that it will require little less than a revolution in educational methods to meet it.

Fortunately, further knowledge and experience tends to temper most abstract theoreticians with a growing tolerance and liberalism. This modifies the rigorousness of super-rationalism and in economic thought leads the strong classical traditionalists, super-Keynesians, and other orthodox extremists into the same moderate middle ground which is being invaded from the other side by the liberal socialists and possibly even some converts from Marxism. The expansion of knowledge on the one hand and the advance of rationalism on the other destroys the ignorance and uncontrolled emotionalism that often characterize the extremes of both right and left. What remains could become a moderate, reasonable middle way.

A fifth trend which can be fairly confidently predicted is that of a continued, though probably moderate, secular inflation. Prices have been rising gradually and almost constantly since the Industrial Revolution, and one characteristic of economic growth areas is rising prices. Thus a reasonable hypothesis would seem to be that there is some positive relationship between inflation and the industrialization process itself. Regardless of this, however, there are at least four reasons for expecting prices, in general, to rise in the future.

First, there is an increasing tendency for most prices to be administered by big business and for wages to be strongly influenced by unions. In both of these cases, there is more flexibility upward than downward. Prices and wages rise more readily than they fall.

Second, governments habitually show more willingness to stimulate prices when they are falling than to arrest them when they are rising since falling prices hurt organized producer groups while rising prices hurt only unorganized consumers.

Third, the large defense expenditures required by the international situation, when combined with constant public pressure to reduce taxes, seem bound to result in a tendency for the national budget, in the United States at least, to be unbalanced more often than not. This, of course, results in total spending increasing by approximately the amount of the government's deficit since net government borrowing ordinarily puts into circulation new purchasing power which is not offset by increased production. This new purchasing power will cause higher prices if the economy is already producing at capacity because at full employment a corresponding increase in production is not possible. Of course "capacity" is not a fixed point. The work week could be extended. Youths, women, and retired people could be employed, but the production they would generate would have to be paid for in wages which would add purchasing power to the spending system. In fact, this extra production would likely be highly inflationary since: (1) Higher than usual wages would have to be paid to get it; (2) It would occur under conditions of diminishing returns; and (3) The kind of workers who would have to be employed tend to spend a higher percentage of their incomes (or save less) than the average of the population.

Fourth, a full employment policy itself is somewhat inflationary. In order to keep unemployment at a manageable minimum, it is necessary that there be more jobs than job seekers because of the lack of perfect labor mobility and knowledge of alternative opportunities. Also, total expenditures must be high enough to wipe out depressed areas. Reducing pockets of unemployment also results in labor shortages and rising wages in other areas since it is impossible to confine the re-spending of government-generated incomes to the unemployment areas. There may be some long-run deflationary trends, but they would have to be more obvious than they have been in recent years to offset these powerful inflationary potentials.

SOME CONCLUDING COMMENTS

It has been said that an economist should have a heart of fire and a brain of ice. The heart of fire is necessary, first, because he must have a real sensitivity and compassion for human suffering everywhere. Economic systems are by and for people, and this means as individuals as well as in the aggregate. Although economics is principally a science of collective human activity, the individual personal element must not be lost no matter what the theory of probabilities or the law of averages may prove.

Second, there must be a subjective motivation for the economist, or he will never fully utilize his capabilities. A passion for logical consistency and quantitative accuracy is not enough inducement even for the most rigorous scientists. There is a necessity for what Adam Smith described in his *Theory of the Moral Sentiments* as sympathy for others. More specifically, in order to inspire genuine devotion to a cause, there must be either a passion for justice, an unselfish love for humanity, an acute sensitivity to human suffering, or a strong feeling of affinity with some power beyond human comprehension. It requires no less than one or more of these to induce the best a man can do.

Unfortunately, the best intentions and motivations are not enough to accomplish reforms in the world. The brain of ice is equally necessary. Without rigorous thinking, the roots of human suffering cannot even be found, much less severed, so that a tree of abundant life may grow in its place. Cold logic must also be applied to the most heart-rending situations if help is to be forthcoming.

The liberal socialists, and probably some Marxists as well, have had an overabundance of compassion. They have often allowed sympathy and emotion to lead them into visionary schemes which are based on idealistic assumptions about human nature. Had it not been for the hardheaded Fabians, with their contempt for what the Webbs called "fuzzy thinking," the socialist cause might have either degenerated into an irrational evangelism or else sunk into complete obscurity. As it is, the coldness and precision of Fabian logic has rescued liberal socialism and made it intellectually respectable in some quarters but only at the expense of most of its emotionally appealing aspects. In fact, to achieve realism, Fabian socialism has had to adopt a pragmatic, short-run philosophy which looks to the solution of specific, practical problems rather than to the remolding of society along any preconceived or doctrinaire lines. Hence it is often indistinguishable from orthodox economics, and it is a fair charge that it has yielded to expedience in the sense that expediency represents realism and hence necessity. The application of a rationalistic attitude by some socialists has caused them to relinquish some of their earlier principles. The result is that there is little left to distinguish them from the progressive thinkers of the more orthodox tradition.

On the other hand, the classical defenders of capitalism and free enterprise have all too often tended to place the mind over the things that matter. With almost an obsession for logical, even mathematical, perfection, they have sometimes pursued geometry with a fervor resembling that of the socialist enchantment with utopias. The results of this modern Ricardianism are as farfetched and unreal as the most raptured flights of socialist fancy.

Public opinion, philosophy, custom, and even law all gradually adjust themselves to the conditions dictated by economic necessity. Medieval life in all its aspects was adapted to agriculture, guild craftsmanship production, and the resulting city-state. Mercantilism was related to a rising commercialism with its strong national state. The classical liberalism reflected the colonial empire which followed the Industrial Revolution. Now a new philosophy based on the economic requirements of the national and even world markets which must be found for the contemporary gigantic industrial machines is being developed. International and perhaps, ultimately, even global political organization will probably be required to solve the economic problems caused by the rise of national and worldwide economic organizations. Furthermore, the development of nuclear weapons makes some kind of international organization imperative, and it is apparent that some wider allegiance is necessary to forestall eventual annihilation.

The relentless march of technology has finally broken through the barriers of both space and time which, in the past, always protected civilization from the most destructive consequences of its accelerating progress. There have been great upheavals in the past, but there was always a geographical frontier to act as a safety valve. There was always time for psychological and cultural adjustment to the requirements of the changing world. Now the physical frontiers of the world have been pushed to the inevitable limits of this tiny globe, and major changes of any kind have worldwide consequences. The interdependence of all nations and economic groups has finally been forced into the open.

Likewise the therapy of time, which formerly healed all things, has lost most of its effectiveness. Major innovations and political and social crises are now appearing so rapidly that the time previously available for human adjustment has been telescoped. Instability and uncertainty have increased so that now even minor disturbances can upset the uneasy international balance. As early as World War I, it could be said that an admiral of the British fleet could lose the British Empire in one afternoon. How much more true this is today with automation, atomic energy, and an international power struggle to trigger a host of upheavals on a moment's notice.

However, barring some colossal diplomatic or military blunder which would upset the present precarious world balance and plunge civilization into a suicidal conflict, the fulfillment of a worldwide economic system, or at least a world of politically separate but economically compatible systems, seems likely to emerge. Economic forces may not be the sole, or ultimate, cause of all world events, but the trends shown here—especially a growing rationalism—will likely strengthen the already increasing potency of the economic determinants of historical development. Then if men of good will cannot resolve their differences at the spiritual, social, or political levels, they may well be driven, reluctantly, to mutual survival by the forces of their interdependent and increasingly similar economic systems.

Index